This companion presents fifteen original and engaging essays by leading scholars on one of the most influential genres of Western Literature. Chapters describe the origins of early verse romance in twelfth-century French and Anglo-Norman courts and analyze the evolution of verse and prose romance in France, Germany, England, Italy and Spain throughout the Middle Ages. The volume introduces a rich array of traditions and texts and offers fresh perspectives on the manuscript context of romance, the relationship of romance to other genres, popular romance in urban contexts, romance as mirror of domestic and social tensions, and the representation of courtly love, chivalry, "other" worlds and gender roles. Together the essays demonstrate that European romances not only helped to promulgate the ideals of elite societies in formation, but also held those values up for questioning. An introduction, a chronology and a bibliography of texts and translations complete this informative overview.

CAMBRIDGE COMPANIONS TO CULTURE

The Cambridge Companion to Modern German Culture
edited by Eva Kolinsky and Wilfried van der Will

The Cambridge Companion to Modern Russian Culture
edited by Nicholas Rzhevsky

The Cambridge Companion to Modern Spanish Culture
edited by David T. Gies

CAMBRIDGE COMPANIONS TO LITERATURE

The Cambridge Companion to Greek Tragedy
edited by P. E. Easterling

The Cambridge Companion to Virgil
edited by Charles Martindale

The Cambridge Companion to Old English Literature
edited by Malcolm Godden and Michael Lapidge

The Cambridge Companion to Dante
edited by Rachel Jacoff

The Cambridge Chaucer Companion
edited by Piero Boitani and Jill Mann

The Cambridge Companion to Medieval English Theatre
edited by Richard Beadle

The Cambridge Companion to Shakespeare Studies
edited by Stanley Wells

The Cambridge Companion to English Renaissance Drama
edited by A. R. Braunmuller and Michael Hattaway

The Cambridge Companion to English Poetry, Donne to Marvell
edited by Thomas N. Corns

The Cambridge Companion to Milton
edited by Dennis Danielson

The Cambridge Companion to British Romanticism
edited by Stuart Curran

The Cambridge Companion to James Joyce
edited by Derek Attridge

The Cambridge Companion to Ibsen
edited by James McFarlane

The Cambridge Companion to Brecht
edited by Peter Thomason and Glendyr Sacks

The Cambridge Companion to Beckett
edited by John Pilling

The Cambridge Companion to T. S. Eliot
edited by A. David Moody

The Cambridge Companion to Renaissance Humanism
edited by Jill Kraye

The Cambridge Companion to Joseph Conrad
edited by J. H. Stape

The Cambridge Companion to William Faulkner
edited by Philip M. Weinstein

The Cambridge Companion to Henry David Thoreau
edited by Joel Myerson

The Cambridge Companion to Edith Wharton
edited by Millicent Bell

The Cambridge Companion to American Realism and Naturalism
edited by Donald Pizer

The Cambridge Companion to Mark Twain
edited by Forrest G. Robinson

The Cambridge Companion to Walt Whitman
edited by Ezra Greenspan

The Cambridge Companion to Hemingway
edited by Scott Donaldson

The Cambridge Companion to the Eighteenth-Century Novel
edited by John Richetti

The Cambridge Companion to Jane Austen
edited by Edward Copeland and Juliet McMaster

The Cambridge Companion to Samuel Johnson
edited by Gregory Clingham

The Cambridge Companion to Oscar Wilde
edited by Peter Raby

The Cambridge Companion to Tennessee Williams
edited by Matthew C. Roudané

The Cambridge Companion to Arthur Miller
edited by Christopher Bigsby

The Cambridge Companion to the French Novel: from 1800 to the Present
edited by Timothy Unwin

The Cambridge Companion to the Classic Russian Novel
edited by Malcolm V. Jones and Robin Feuer Miller

The Cambridge Companion to English Literature, 1650–1740
edited by Steven N. Zwicker

The Cambridge Companion to Eugene O'Neill
edited by Michael Manheim

The Cambridge Companion to George Bernard Shaw
edited by Christopher Innes

The Cambridge Companion to Ezra Pound
edited by Ira Nadel

The Cambridge Companion to Modernism
edited by Michael Levenson

The Cambridge Companion to Thomas Hardy
edited by Dale Kramer

The Cambridge Companion to American Women Playwrights
edited by Brenda Murphy

Lancelot crosses the Sword Bridge, as Guenevere and King Bademagu observe from a tower and two lions await him on the other side. From the Old French Prose *Lancelot*.

THE CAMBRIDGE
COMPANION TO
MEDIEVAL ROMANCE

EDITED BY
ROBERTA L. KRUEGER
Hamilton College, New York

CAMBRIDGE
UNIVERSITY PRESS

CAMBRIDGE UNIVERSITY PRESS
Cambridge, New York, Melbourne, Madrid, Cape Town, Singapore, São Paulo

Cambridge University Press
The Edinburgh Building, Cambridge CB2 2RU, UK

Published in the United States of America by Cambridge University Press, New York

www.cambridge.org
Information on this title: www.cambridge.org/9780521553421

First published 2000
Third printing 2004

A catalogue record for this publication is available from the British Library

Library of Congress Cataloguing in Publication data

The Cambridge Companion to medieval romance / edited by
Roberta L. Krueger.
p.   cm. – (Cambridge companions to literature)
Includes index
ISBN 0 521 55342 3 (hardback) – ISBN 0 521 55687 2 (paperback)
1. Romances – History and criticism.   2. Literature, Medieval –
History and criticism.   I. Krueger, Roberta L.   II. Title:
Companion to medieval romance.   III. Series.
PN671.C36   2000
809´.02–dc21   99-34240 CIP

ISBN-13 978-0-521-55342-1 hardback
ISBN-10 0-521-55342-3 hardback

ISBN-13 978-0-521-55687-3 paperback
ISBN-10 0-521-55687-2 paperback

Transferred to digital printing 2006

CONTENTS

Contents

ILLUSTRATIONS

CONTRIBUTORS

CHRISTOPHER BASWELL is Professor and Chair of English at Barnard College. He also teaches in the Graduate School of Columbia University. He is author of *Virgil in medieval England: figuring the "Aeneid" from the twelfth century to Chaucer* (1995) and of numerous articles on classical tradition in the Middle Ages. He is co-editor of *The Longman Anthology of British Literature*, vol. IA, *The Middle Ages* (1998).

MARINA S. BROWNLEE is the Class of 1963 College of Women Professor of Romance Languages at the University of Pennsylvania. She has written on a variety of medieval topics. Her books in this area include *The Status of the Reading Subject in the "Libro de Buen Amor"* (1985) and *The Severed Word: Ovid's "Heroides" and the 'Novela Sentimental'* (1990), as well as several co-edited volumes such as *Romance: Generic Transformation from Chrétien de Troyes to Cervantes* and *The New Medievalism*.

MATILDA TOMARYN BRUCKNER is Professor of French at Boston College. Her publications include *Shaping Romance: Interpretation, Truth and Closure in Twelfth-Century French Fictions* and *Songs of the Women Troubadours* (in collaboration with Laurie Shepard and Sarah White). Her current book project focuses on Chrétien's *Perceval* and its Continuations.

SHEILA FISHER is Associate Professor of English at Trinity College, Hartford, Connecticut. She has published on Chaucer and on feminist issues in *Sir Gawain and the Green Knight* and in earlier literature.

SIMON GAUNT is Professor of French Languages and Literature at King's College London. He is the author of *Troubadours and Irony* (1989) and *Gender and Genre in Medieval French Literature* (1995). He is co-editor of *The Troubadours: an Introduction* (1999) with Sarah Kay, and of *Marcabru: a Critical Edition* (2000) with Ruth Harvey and Linda Paterson.

THOMAS HAHN teaches medieval literature and culture at the University of Rochester. He is the General Editor of the Chaucer Bibliographies. Among his publications are *History, Text, Theory: Reconceiving Chaucer* (*Exemplaria*, 1990); *Sir Gawain: Eleven Romances and Tales* (1995); *Retelling Tales* (with Alan Lupack; 1997);

Robin Hood in Popular Culture (1999); "Early Middle English" in the *Cambridge History of Medieval English Literature* (1999).

SYLVIA HUOT is University Lecturer in French and Fellow of Pembroke College, Cambridge. She is the author of *From Song to Book* (1987), *The "Romance of the Rose" and its medieval readers* (1993) and *Allegorical Play in the Old French Motet* (1997).

RICHARD KAEUPER, Professor of History at the University of Rochester, writes on royal finance, public order, and chivalry. His books include *Bankers to the Crown* (Princeton, 1973); *War, Justice and Public Order* (1988); and, with Elspeth Kennedy, *The Book of Chivalry of Geoffroi de Charny; Chivalry and Violence in Medieval Europe* (1999). He is editor of and contributor to *Violence in Medieval Society* (forthcoming).

SARAH KAY is Reader in French and Occitan Literature at the University of Cambridge. Her published books include *Subjectivity in Troubadour Poetry* (1990) and *The Chansons de geste in the Age of Romance* (1995). Her current book, *Courtly Contradictions*, will be published by Stanford University Press in 2000.

ROBERTA L. KRUEGER, Professor of French at Hamilton College in Clinton, New York, has published *Women Readers and the Ideology of Gender in Old French Verse Romance* (1993) and various articles on courtly romance and medieval French didactic literature. Recently she contributed "Female voices in convents, courts, and households: the French Middle Ages" to *A History of Women's Writing in France* (forthcoming).

NORRIS J. LACY is the Edwin Erle Sparks Professor of French at Pennsylvania State University. He previously taught at Indianna University, the University of Kansas, UCLA, and Washington University in St. Louis. His authored or edited books include *The Craft of Chrétien de Troyes, The New Arthurian Encyclopedia, The Arthurian Handbook, Reading Fabliaux*, and *Early French Tristan Poems*.

F. REGINA PSAKI is Associate Professor of Romance Languages at the University of Oregon. Her research interests include Dante, Boccaccio, courtly romance, authorial subjectivity, discourse analysis, feminist issues, metadisciplinary issues in Medieval Studies, and translation. She has published articles on Dante's *Divine Comedy*, Boccaccio's *Decameron*, medieval Italian and French romance, the Old Norse *Parcevals saga*, medieval misogyny, and text editing.

ANN MARIE RASMUSSEN is Associate Professor in the German department at Duke University and author of *Mothers and Daughters in Medieval German Literature* (1997). Her current research elaborates on her interests in gender studies, manuscript studies, and fifteenth-century German literature and culture.

FELICITY RIDDY is a professor of English attached to the Centre for Medieval Studies at the University of York. U.K. She is the author of a book on Malory, has edited Middle Scots verse, and has written many articles on medieval English and

Scottish literature and culture. She is currently writing a book on domesticity and urban culture in late-medieval England.

JEFF RIDER is Associate Professor of French and Medieval Studies at Wesleyan University. He has published numerous articles on medieval literature and has co-edited, with Peter Allen, *Reflections in the Frame: New Perspectives on the Study of Medieval Literature* as a special issue of *Exemplaria* (1991). He has edited Galbert of Bruges's *De multro, traditione, et occisione gloriosi Karoli, comitis Flandriarum* (1994) and will soon publish *God's Scribe: The Historiographical Art of Galbert of Bruges*.

EUROPEAN ROMANCE: A SELECTIVE CHRONOLOGY

It is often impossible to determine the precise year in which a romance was composed. Most dates below are approximations, and sometimes scholars have proposed a range of dates.

OF   Old French (including Anglo-Norman)
I   Italian
LG   Low German
MD   Medieval Dutch
ME   Middle English
MF   Middle French
MHG   Middle High German
MO   Medieval Occitan
MS   Medieval Spanish

c. 1138	Geoffrey of Monmouth, *Historia regum Britanniae (History of the Kings of Britain)* [Latin]
c. 1147–60	*Floire et Blancheflor* ("aristocratic" version) [OF]
c. 1150–55	Wace, *Roman de Brut* [OF]
c. 1150–55	*Roman de Thèbes* [OF]
c. 1155(?)–87	Béroul, *Tristan* ("common" version) [OF]
c. 1156	*Roman d'Enéas* [OF]
c. 1160	*Sept Sages de Rome* (original version) [OF]
c. 1160–65	Benoît de Sainte-Maure, *Roman de Troie* [OF]
c. 1165–70	Chrétien de Troyes, *Erec et Enide* [OF]
1169–70 (or *c.* 1230)	*Jaufre* [MO]
1170s	*Trierer Floyris* [LG]

c. 1170–75	Thomas d'Angleterre, *Tristan* ("courtly" version) [OF]
c. 1170–77	Chrétien de Troyes, *Cligés* [OF]
c. 1170–80	Marie de France, *Lais* [OF]
1170–84	Gautier d'Arras, *Ille et Galeran* [OF]
1174–1200	Thomas of Kent, *Le Roman de Toute Chevalerie* [OF]
1170s or 1185–90	Eilhart von Oberge, *Tristrant* [MHG]
1170–85	Heinrich von Veldeke, *Eneide* [MHG]
c. 1174–81	Chrétien de Troyes, *Le Chevalier de la Charrette (Lancelot)* [OF]
c. 1175	Robert Biket, *Lai du cor* [OF]
	Lai du cort mantel [OF]
c. 1175–81	Chrétien de Troyes, *Le Chevalier au Lion (Yvain)* [OF]
c. 1179–91	Chrétien de Troyes, *Le Conte du graal (Perceval)* [OF]
post-1180	Alexandre de Paris, *Le Roman d'Alexandre* [OF]
c. 1180–85	Hue de Rotelande, *Ipomedon* [OF]
1180–90	Hartmann von Aue, *Erec* [MHG]
c. 1182–85	*Partonopeu de Blois* [OF]
c. 1185–90	Hue de Rotelande, *Protheselaus* [OF]
c. 1185–95	Renaut de Beaujeu, *Le Bel Inconnu* [OF]
c. 1188	Aimon de Varennes, *Florimont* [OF]
c. 1190	Hartmann von Aue, *Gregorius* [MHG]
c. 1190–1200	First Continuation of *Perceval* (short version) [OF]
c. 1190–1200	Wauchier de Denain, Second Continuation of *Perceval* [OF]
c. 1195	Hartmann von Aue, *Der arme Heinrich* [MHG]
c. 1196	Ulrich von Zatzikhoven, *Lanzelet* [MHG]
c. 1200	Robert de Boron (verse romances) [OF]
c. 1200	Hartmann von Aue, *Iwein* [MHG]
early 1200s	*Gliglois* [OF]
c. 1200–10	Gottfried von Strassburg, *Tristan und Isolde* [MHG]
1200–02	Jean Renart, *L'Escoufle* [OF]
c. 1200–12	Wolfram von Eschenbach, *Titurel* [MHG]
c. 1200–25	Layamon, *Brut* [ME]
c. 1200–20	Konrad Fleck, *Flore und Blanscheflur* [MHG]

c. 1200–50	*Flors inde Blanzeflors* [MHG]
c. 1204–10	Wirnt von Grafenberg, *Wigalois* [MHG]
c. 1205–12	Wolfram von Eschenbach, *Parzival* [MHG]
c. 1209–28	Jean Renart, *Le Roman de la rose ou de Guillaume de Dole* [OF]
before 1210	*Le Chevalier aux Deux Epées* [OF]
before 1210	Raoul de Houdenc (?), *La vengeance Raguidel* [OF]
c. 1210	*Perlesvaus* [OF]
c. 1215	Non-cyclic Prose *Lancelot* [OF]
c. 1220	*Diu Crône* [MHG]
c. 1220	*La Fille du comte de Pontieu* [OF]
1220–40	Ulrich von Türheim, *Cligés* [MHG]
c. 1220–40	*Libro de Apolonio* [MS]
c. 1220–40	*Libro de Alexandre* [MS]
c. 1214–35	Manessier, Third Continuation of *Perceval* [OF]
c. 1215–35	*Lancelot-Grail* cycle (*Prose Lancelot; Queste; Mort le roi Artu*) [OF]
c. 1225	*Didot-Perceval* [OF]
c. 1225	*La Queste del Saint Graal* [OF]
c. 1225	*Seven Sages* in prose (first of several versions) [OF]
c. 1225–28	*Jaufré* [MO]
c. 1225–40	Guillaume de Lorris, *Le Roman de la Rose* [OF]
c. 1230–35	Prose *Tristan* (first version) [OF]
c. 1235	Rudolf von Ems, *Wilhelm von Orlens* [MHG]
c. 1235	Ulrich von Türheim, *Tristran* (continuation of Gottfried's *Tristan*) [MHG]
1235–40	Post-Vulgate Cycle [OF]
c. 1230–50	*Marques de Rome* [OF]
c. 1226–30	Gerbert de Montreuil, Fourth Continuation of *Perceval* [OF]
c. 1227–30	Gerbert de Montreuil, *Roman de la Violette* [OF]
1227–37	First Continuation of *Perceval* (long version) [OF]
mid–late 1200s	*King Horn* [ME]
mid-1200s	*Joufroi de Poitiers* [OF]

before 1250	*Walewein* [MD]
c. 1250	*Le Roi Flore et belle Jehanne* [OF]
c. 1250	Prose *Tristan*, second version [OF]
c. 1250	Konrad von Würzburg, *Das Herzmaere* [MHG]
c. 1250	*Wigamur* [MHG]
c. 1250–70	*Laurin* [OF]
c. 1255	Ulrich von Liechtenstein, *Frauendienst* [MHG]
c. 1260	Diederic van Assende, *Floris* [MD]
c. 1260–72	Albrecht, *Der jüngere Titurel* [MHG]
c. 1270	*Cassidorus* [OF]
after 1250	First Continuation of *Perceval* (mixed version) [OF]
mid–late 1200s	*Floris and Blancheflur* [ME]
1270–80	Heldris de Cornuälle, *Roman de Silence* [OF]
c. 1260–80	*Flamenca* [MO]
c. 1270–80	Jean de Meun, Continuation of Guillaume de Lorris's *Roman de la Rose* [OF]
c. 1270	*Historia troyana polimétrica* [MS]
1272–98	Arthurian compilation of Rusticiano da Pisa
c. 1275	*Havelok the Dane* [ME]
c. 1275	*Lantsloot vander Hagedochte* [MD]
c. 1280?	Prose *Yvain* [OF]
c. 1284–95	*Crónica de Flores y Blancaflor* [S]
c. 1285	Jakemés, *Le castelain de Couci et la dame de Fayel* [OF]
late 1200s	*Amis and Amiloun* [ME]
late 1200s	*Arthur and Merlin* [ME]
late 1200s	*Tristano Riccardiano* [I]
late 1200s	Rusticiano da Pisa, *Meliadus* [I]
c. 1295	*Gran conquista de Ultramar* [MS]
1300–50	*Flos unde Blankeflos* [LG]
c. 1300	*Guy of Warwick* [ME]
c. 1310	*Libro del Caballero Zifar* [MS]
early 1300s	*Horn Childe and the Maiden Rymnild* [ME]
early 1300s	*Lai le Freine* [ME]

early 1300s	*Sir Degaré* [ME]
early 1300s	*Sir Isumbras* [ME]
early 1300s	*Sir Orfeo* [ME]
early 1300s	*Tristano Veneto* [I]
early 1300s	*La Storia di Merlino* [I]
1300s	*Fiorio e Biancifiore* [I]
1300s	*París y Viana* [MS]
1300s	*El conde Partinuplés* [S]
1300s	*Widwilt* or *Kinig Artus Hauf* [Old Yiddish]
1300–50	*Sir Percyvell of Gales* [ME]
c. 1310	*Lancelot-Compilatie* [MD]
1313	Brother Juan Vives, translation of Post-Vulgate Cycle [MS]
1314	Johann von Würzburg, *Wilhelm von Osterreich* [MHG]
1314–40	*Perceforest* [OF]
c. 1330	*La Tavola Ritonda* [I]
1336–38	Boccaccio, *Filocolo* [I]
before 1350	*Ywain and Gawain* [ME]
before 1350	*Libeaus Desconus* [ME]
c. 1350	*Gamelyn* [ME]
c. 1350	*Octavian* [ME]
1350–61	*William of Palerne* [ME]
1350–1400	*Chevelere Assigne* [ME]
c. 1350–1400	*Sir Gawain and the Green Knight* [ME]
c. 1351	Geoffroi de Charny, *Livre de chevalerie* [OF]
c. 1360	*Ysaïe le Triste* [OF]
c. 1360–70	*La Faula* [MS]
1375–1400	*Athelston* [ME]
c. 1375	*Joseph of Arimathie* [ME]
after 1383	Froissart, *Meliador* [MF]
c. 1385–86	Geoffrey Chaucer, *Troilus and Criseyde* [ME]
c. 1387	*The Canterbury Tales* begun [ME]
1387–93	Jean d'Arras, *Mélusine* [MF]
1391	Arthurian compilation of Jehan Vaillant [MF]

late 1300s	*Gamelyn* [ME]
late 1300s	*Sir Amadace* [ME]
late 1300s	*Le Bone Florence of Rome* [ME]
late 1300s	Alliterative *Morte Arthure* [ME]
late 1300s	Stanzaic *Morte Arthur* [ME]
c. 1400	*Emaré* [ME]
c. 1400	*Sir Torrent of Portyngale* [ME]
c. 1400	*Sir Gawain and the Carle of Carlisle* [ME]
early 1400s	*The Tournament of Tottenham* [ME]
1401	Coudrette, *Mélusine* [MF]
1403 (?)	Christine de Pizan, *Le Livre du Duc des Vrais Amants* [MF]
c. 1420	*Die Beichte einer Frau* (minnerede) [MHG]
c. 1420	Henry Lovelich, *History of the Holy Grail* [ME]
c. 1420	Henry Lovelich, *Merlin* [ME]
1440	*Siervo libre de amor* [S]
1443–60	*Curial y Guëlfa* [S]
1450–1500	*King Ponthus and Fair Sidone* [ME]
c. 1454	Prosification of Chrétien's *Cligés* and *Erec* [MF]
before 1456	Antoine de la Sale, *Le Petit Jehan de Saintré* [MF]
1469–70	Sir Thomas Malory, *Morte Darthur* [ME] published 1485
1470	Arthurian compilation of Michot Gonnot [MF]
1470	Ulrich Füetrer, *Lanzelot* (prose and verse versions) [MHG]
1473	Pulci, *Morgante* [I]
c. 1475	*Lancelot of the Laik* [Middle Scots]
1476–94	Boiardo, *Orlando Innamorato* [I]
1485	Ulrich Füetrer, *Buch der Liebe* [MHG]
c. 1500	*The Wedding of Sir Gawain and Dame Ragnelle* [ME]
c. 1500	*The Greene Knight* [ME]
c. 1500	*The Turke and Sir Gawain* [ME]
c. 1500	*Gologras and Gawain* [ME]
1508	*Amadís de Gaula* [S]
1512	*Primaleón* [S]
1514	*Lisuarte de Grecia* [S]

1516–32	Ariosto, *Orlando Furioso* [I]
c. 1520	Pierre Sala, Prose *Yvain* [F]
1554	Jean Maugin, *Le Nouveau Tristan* [F]
c. 1560	*The Jeaste of Sir Gawain* [ME]
1560–75	Tasso, *Gerusalemme Liberata* [I]
after 1600	*The Wedding of Sir Gawain*; ballad [eModE]
after 1600	*The Carle of Carlisle;* [eModE]
after 1600	*King Arthur and King Cornwall*; ballad [eModE]
1605, 1615	Cervantes, *Don Quijote de la Mancha* [S]
1617	Cervantes, *Los trabajos de Persiles y Sigismunda* [S]

ROBERTA L. KRUEGER

Introduction

The essays in this volume analyze critical features of what is arguably the most influential and enduring secular literary genre of the European Middle Ages. The story of medieval romance's evolution is one of translation and transformation, adaptation and refashioning, and fertile intertextual and intercultural exchange among the linguistic and political entities of medieval Europe. Medieval romance narratives astound the modern reader by their broad circulation in France, Germany, England, The Netherlands, Italy, Scandinavia, Portugal, Greece and Spain, and by the many stories, characters, themes, and motifs they hold in common. These fictions continue to intrigue modern audiences – as they undoubtedly did medieval ones – by the diversity of their forms and subject-matter, the complexity of their narrative strategies and perspectives, and the many critical responses they invite.

Romance's history is integrally bound up with the creation of elite lay culture in courts and wealthy households throughout the European Middle Ages. However, romance narratives are rarely simple reflections of courtly ideals. Romances of all national origins are remarkable for their authors' capacity to remake their shared stories anew in different contexts and to reposition their ethical systems as they respond to particular audiences, in distinct geographic locations and social contexts – often with a critical perspective that calls social ideals or practices into question. The *Companion to Medieval Romance* is intended as an introduction to the voyages, transformations, and interrogations of romance as its fictions travel within and between the linguistic, geo-political, and social boundaries of Europe from 1150 to 1600.

The term "romance" used today to refer to the narratives of chivalric adventures that were first encountered in medieval courts derives from the Old French expression "mettre en romanz," which means to translate into the vernacular French. Consequently, many kinds of vernacular narratives were dubbed "romans" (and were also sometimes called "contes" [tales] or "estoires" [stories/histories]). These stories shared characteristics with other genres, whose boundaries were fluid rather than fixed. But gradually there emerged at royal and feudal courts a dynamic network of fictions, written first in verse and then in prose, that recounted the exploits of knights, ladies, and noble families seeking honor, love, and adventure. These narratives did not conform to a single, easily discernible type; rather, they sprang from diverse origins and took a myriad of shapes. Thanks to over one hundred years of scholarship, in which the stories contained within medieval manuscripts have been edited, analyzed, and interpreted – an enterprise that is still ongoing – the genre of medieval romance has come to encompass far more than the celebrated tales of King Arthur. Medieval romances survive in a rich spectrum of narratives whose themes and issues intersect with virtually every aspect of medieval social and cultural life.

The earliest vernacular romances were free translations of Latin epics and chronicles into French, composed in the mid-twelfth century at the Angevin royal court of Henry II and Eleanor of Aquitaine in England, where Anglo-Norman, a form of Old French, was the literary language of the elite. Simultaneously or soon afterwards, romance fictions were created at other francophone courts in England and on the Continent. The *Roman de Thèbes*, the *Roman d'Eneas*, and Benoît de Sainte-Maure's *Roman de Troie* were imaginative retellings of Classical epics with distinctive additions: descriptions of extraordinary objects, deeper analyses of sentimental affairs, as well as narratorial interventions. Wace's *Roman de Brut* (*c.* 1155) adapted Geoffrey of Monmouth's *Historia Regum Britanniae* (*History of the Kings of Britain*) into a popular vernacular history that disseminated not only the myth of Britain's historical link to Troy through Brutus, Aeneas's grandson, but also the legend of King Arthur, whose Round Table is first mentioned in this romance. Most of these tales telling the "matter of Rome" and the "matter of Britain" were written in rhyming pairs of eight-syllable verses. The lively style of the Old French octosyllabic couplet soon became the preferred mode for clerks who would tell tales of love and adventure to aristocratic audiences in the francophone circles of England and France.

At some point after 1160, a clerk on the Continent, who signed his work "Chrétien de Troyes," created a "molt bele conjointure" ("a beautiful conjoining") of fictional elements that was grafted onto a central stock drawn from Arthurian legend. With *Erec et Enide*, the first full-blown Arthurian romance, Chrétien initiated a series of stories about Arthur's knights, including those of Lancelot and Perceval. His tales of noble love and chivalric prowess launched a vogue for Athurian fiction that altered the course of literary history, first, by inspiring a spate of imitations in verse and then by prompting production of the monumental French prose romances, which in turn inspired translations and adaptations throughout Europe. Arthurian romances were not the first vernacular courtly fictions, but their tremendous popularity – in a wide range of linguistic registers, cultural settings, and aesthetic modes – established them as a major force that other romance authors might choose to imitate, adapt, criticize, or even burlesque, but which they did not often ignore.

At the same time, other early verse narratives, unrelated to Arthurian lore, also sowed the seeds for later cultivation. The legend recounting the adulterous affair between Tristan, nephew of King Mark, and Queen Iseut, which circulated orally in Celtic culture, inspired some of the earliest romance fictions. The Tristan romances of Béroul, composed in France perhaps as early as 1155, and of Thomas in England, written *c.* 1173, are extant only in fragments today. However, these and other written and oral tales of Tristan and Iseut's tragic love traveled widely in Europe and Scandinavia throughout the Middle Ages. Their survival in literary and operatic forms in the present makes the Tristan legend one of the founding romantic myths of European culture.[1]

Floire et Blancheflor, a tale of star-crossed lovers and of religious conversion, had a long-lived and multifaceted career in France, Germany, England, Flanders and Holland, Italy, Spain, and Portugal.[2] The Latin legend of Apollonius of Tyre, which recounts a harrowing escape from incest and a series of wondrous travels and discoveries, inspired vernacular narrative retellings throughout Europe,[3] as did the antifeminist frame-story of the Seven Sages of Rome. Some romancers, such as Gautier d'Arras in *Eracle*, drew their inspiration not from the Arthurian past, but from distant Byzantium. In another register, the femino-centric lais *Fresne* and *Eliduc* of Marie de France were recast into longer narratives that heralded a more "realistic" strain of romances. The framework of biographical romance, which recounts the extraordinary history of an individual or a family, served to tell the stories of exemplary national heroes, for example, in the Middle English *Havelok the Dane*. Romance would continue to provide a mold in which patrons could establish impressive genealogies, as did Jean de Berry for the Lusignan family in Jean d'Arras's *Mélusine* (1393), whose serpentine heroine bears marvelous children.

Early verse romances were composed in writing but intended for public reading, and they often display their author's sense of both literary aesthetics and oral performance. Drawing their material from a broad range of sources that included oral folktales, vernacular epics and saints' lives, courtly lyrics, classical Latin literature and contemporary chronicles, romance authors self-consciously blended ancient and contemporary stories into new shapes, created characters who appealed to the sentimental, moral, and political concerns of their audience, and drew attention to their own art as they did so.

The audience for romance in all its guises grew and diversified throughout the Middle Ages. Noble male and female patrons were evidently eager to listen to stories in which their own ideals and anxieties were reflected, often through the clerk's tongue-in-cheek humor, for they commissioned the composition of romances in manuscripts that could be circulated among court and family members and could be passed along to children or to foreign courts. These might later be recopied or re-adapted in fresh surroundings, in other households, in new linguistic or political terrains. As early as the 1170s, the taste for Anglo-Norman and French romances migrated to nearby German-speaking territories in the area of the lower Rhine. The refashioning of matters French soon became a hallmark of elite culture at the great German courts, as evidenced by authors such as Eilhart von Oberge (*Tristrant*), Heinrich von Veldeke (*Eneide*), and Hartmann von Aue (*Erec*). These romances, in turn, set the stage for a remarkable literary production that includes two of the most celebrated masterpieces of world literature, Wolfram von Eschenbach's *Parzival* and Gottfried von Strassburg's *Tristan*. In England, the shift in taste from romances written in French to romances written in Middle English occurred gradually from the mid-thirteenth century onward as the appeal of romance spread to the gentry and to bourgeois readers. In Italy, too, romances first circulated in French (from the 1220s), although, soon after, they were translated into Italian and, then, Italian authors began to compose their own chivalric narratives, with heroes who strongly reflected Italian civic interests.

Spanish romance developed more independently of French courtly models. From the outset, its stories possessed an extra-textual historical dimension that reflected, in part, the Reconquest, the Spanish aristocracy's 700-year struggle against the Moors. The earliest romances, adaptations of the tales of Alexander and Apollonius, were strongly didactic, and Arthurian themes arrived relatively late in Spain (and sometimes through Italian intermediaries). The relative autonomy of Spanish romance from French sources and its tendency to critique courtly conventions may have helped pave the way for the bold initiative of Cervantes, whose sophisticated juxtaposition of romance and realism in *Don Quixote* launched a new literary adventure, that of the European novel.

Despite the precarious conditions of manuscript culture, large numbers of romances have survived. Over 200 romances are extant in French, over 100 in English, over fifty in Spanish, well over fifty in German, and around 100 in Italian, including the *cantari* (short verse narratives composed for singing); each romance is often preserved in multiple manuscripts. Such abundance reflects not only the long-lived appeal of their intriguing stories, but also the protean ability of romance narratives to adapt to the new contexts in which they found themselves transposed. No single social agenda pervades European romance: individual romances had different functions at distinct moments in their countries of origin and adoption, as the essays in this volume will demonstrate.

Medieval secular literature was both a benefactor of and a contributor to the intellectual renaissance that flourished in European courts, schools, and cities, beginning in the twelfth century. Emerging first in royal and ducal circles, the earliest romances espoused the project of *translatio studii*, the translation and transposition of studies from Greece and Rome to France, and they proudly proclaimed the superior culture of their makers and audiences over the *vilains*, the uncourtly or uninstructed. For an elite minority, romances were a vehicle for the construction of a social code – chivalry – and a mode of sentimental refinement – which some have called "courtly love" – by which noble audiences defined their social identities and justified their privileges, thus reinforcing gender and class distinctions. From the beginning, however, the tension between courtly ideals and social realities was often underscored in the very texts that attempted to mask it. To be sure, the genre includes many texts that boldly celebrate the prowess and independence of knights on horseback, record the glorious past of a family's lineage, or soberly examine the ethical and religious responsibilities of noble men and women. But alongside these, we find ironic romances that poke gentle fun at chivalric pretensions and others that raise voices in opposition to purely secular aristocratic ideals, as do some of the romances centred on the Grail quest.

From the thirteenth century onward, there emerged a new strain of "realistic" romances whose heroes or heroines travel to contemporary towns or cities and devise clever solutions to ordinary problems centered on marriage and the family. Indeed, as romance-writing spread to more modest noble courts and households, and eventually to bourgeois venues, and as tensions increased between the different orders of feudal society with the emergence of new commercial and political interests, chivalric fiction presented itself less as a panel for the advertisement of social ideals than as a forum for the construction and contestation of social identities and values.

Toward the end of the Middle Ages, as the resources of noble families were sapped by the Hundred Years War in France and England, after the Black Death had ravaged Europe, and as cultural production moved increasingly from courts to urban centers or bourgeois households, the themes of romance began to outgrow their original, chivalric molds, and their offspring took a variety of new shapes. The advent of print culture, the second Renaissance of Classical learning, the intellectual and political battles of the Reformation, the discovery of a "real" new world, and the busy commerce of merchants, artisans, and other workers whose activities were far removed from courts and tournaments – these changes demanded new forms. What was once the new literature for a young noble society in effervescent transformation was discarded as the vestige of a class whose privileges were perceived, by some, as beginning to outlive their social utility.

Yet if the forms of chivalric romance gradually changed and faded over time, romance as a mode remained alive within European culture. The great questions posed by romance – about personal and social identity, love and honor, good and evil – were neither resolved nor, at some level, supplanted. Whether in Cervantes's satire, in Shakespeare's adoption of romance motifs, in the reframing of courtly love plots in Marguerite de Navarre or Madame de Lafayette, in the nineteenth-century Arthurian revival, or in twentieth-century recasting of medieval romance themes in fiction and film, the ethical questions as well as the idealizing spirit of romance have endured.

Contemporary critics have viewed romance as a mode that attempts to embellish social reality and escape from history, as one that explores the sacred mysteries of birth, death, and the quest for identity with secular optimism, or as one that sets up a binary opposition between good and evil to protect an elite society from the "Other."[4] It is commonplace to set the genre of medieval romance against its literary descendant, the modern novel, whose realism and discursive complexity are contrasted with the fantasy and ideological directness of its fictional forebears. The essays in this volume attest to the marvelous events and idealized landscapes of medieval romance, but they also show that individual romances are rooted in their historic contexts, whose problems they do not shrink from confronting with sophisticated and often self-reflexive narratives.

The *Companion to Medieval Romance* is presented in three parts. The first, The Origins, Forms, and Contexts of Medieval Romance, begins with Matilda Bruckner's description of the interlace of formal and thematic elements in key twelfth- and thirteenth-century French works whose aesthetic patterns and thematic motifs set the parameters for subsequent adaptation and continuations. Christopher Baswell examines the earliest species of romance, the *romans d'antiquité*, and shows how erotic tensions disrupt the political and intellectual enterprise of romance's foundational texts. Simon Gaunt and Sylvia Huot both consider the complex literary context in which romance texts find themselves embedded. Gaunt reminds us of the close intertextual relationship of romances to *chansons de geste*, saints' lives, and fabliaux – genres with which romance has traditionally been contrasted but with which it shares many common features. Huot describes how romances appear to scholars today in their material contexts – the centuries-old, hand-written parchment and paper folios that preserve their extant copies – and she stresses the ways that manuscript culture shaped the genre's transmission and reception. This section concerns itself primarily with Old French, Anglo-Norman and German texts, since these are the earliest works of vernacular romance narrative.

The essays in part two, European Romance and Medieval Society: Issues for Debate, view romances as a forum for reflection and debate about private and public problems that were central to medieval society. For Sarah Kay, what critics have termed "courtly love" is not a single doctrine but rather a complicated set of issues involving passion, spirituality, and family and institutional allegiances contested between clerical and lay members of court society. Richard Kaeuper's essay demonstrates that romances could operate as an "active social force" as they provide a framework for debate about the questions confronting the knights who evolved into a powerful, and often violent, social group in the High Middle Ages. The propensity of romances to project fantastic and marvelous "other worlds" populated by demons, fairies, monsters or other hyperbolic figures or events, whose features are apparently so different from those found in the "real" world, is precisely what allows their authors and audiences to expose and resolve extraordinary tensions in a way that ultimately valorizes central aristocratic society, as Jeff Rider demonstrates. Roberta Krueger and Sheila Fisher present two views of the way romances in different social and national settings constructed and questioned gender roles. The twelfth- and thirteenth-century courtly French romances Krueger examines create a dynamic space in which questions of gender are debated and gender identities can be playfully reversed or contested, even as traditional norms are affirmed. Reading Middle English "high" literary romances written at least a century later in the context of rising English nationalism and considerable social instability, Fisher finds a more restrictive marginalization of women that reflects anxiety about masculinity.

The essays in part three, European Transformations, describe the centrality of the French prose romances about Lancelot, the Grail, and Tristan to the evolution of romance throughout Europe, as Norris Lacy recounts, and tell the particular stories of romance in Germany, Italy, England, and Spain. This section emphasizes how romance features are transformed by the new accents and guises of different national and social settings. Ann Marie Rasmussen shows how German romances, which rose with the flourishing of courtly culture along the Rhine, attempted to reconcile or mask tensions in a way that might have allowed diverse groups of those privileged by birth, wealth, or training to adopt an elite cultural identity despite their social differences. Several romance authors were members of an inherited rank unique to Germany – that of noble bondsman, which bound men in service to a great lord. German romance's idealized notions of honor and cultural aristocracy may have held special appeal for these ambitious, cultivated men of lesser status. In her essay on Italian romances, Regina Psaki rejects the notion that Italian romances of chivalry are derivative of and somehow inferior to French models. She suggests, rather, that we consider individual works in light of the civil strife and social diversification that characterized medieval Italy. Three Tristan romances dating from the late thirteenth to the mid-fourteenth centuries appear to arise from distinct social strata; as each text attempts to reconcile individual ambitions with collective interests, it demonstrates how chivalry can be appropriated by different social classes to promote commonality and stability in a period of dissension.

Two essays on Middle English romance also demonstrate the social and ethical diversity of late medieval narratives. Thomas Hahn's chapter traces the fate in England of one of the most respected and ubiquitous Arthurian heroes, Sir Gawain, nephew of Arthur. Although best known by today's students of English literature as the morally compromised protagonist of a fourteenth-century alliterative masterpiece, *Sir Gawain and the Green Knight* – whose complex style and themes mark it as a product of elite culture – Gawain was probably more famous in medieval England as the highly successful hero of a dozen popular romances. As they blend courtly motifs with realistic surroundings, as they re-enact predictably happy resolutions to crises of incivility, these stories reveal Gawain's continual appeal as active Young Man to diverse audiences composed of nobles, bourgeois and even laborers. The Middle English romances analyzed by Felicity Riddy, whose venue she describes as "bourgeois-gentry" households, focus on themes and problems of families, marriage, lineage, progeny, and inheritance, and reflect concerns arising from the demographic crisis of late medieval England. Echoing a point suggested by both Psaki and Hahn, Riddy reminds us that the audiences for many late medieval romances are located not in courts or manor-houses but in cities. Within urban centers, the knight errant acquired the status of a mythic figure – not unlike our modern-day cowboy – and came to embody "male autonomy and power," "freedom and mobility."

Finally, Marina Brownlee shows how Spanish romances followed their own distinct course on the Iberian Peninsula. Their constant attention to extra-textual history sets early Spanish romances apart from their more self-absorbed courtly European cousins. Beginning with *Zifar*, the first romance with native Spanish roots, many Spanish romances exhibit a tendency to criticize or mock chivalric ideals, to juxtapose chivalric elements with more realistic features, or to subvert romance conventions, as does the fifteenth-century *novela sentimental*. Although this critical mentality did nothing to stem the immense popularity of chivalric romances in the wake of *Amadís de Gaula* throughout the sixteenth century, it may have prepared a path for Cervantes, as he charted a new course for fiction in the gap between romance and realism.

These essays offer a sampling of the rich fare that is European romance and of the diversity of critical perspectives that it has inspired. The volume is not intended as an exhaustive or comprehensive survey. Articles on French romance predominate, because French romances are so often the literal source for their avatars in Middle English, German, Italian, or Spanish. Chapters on these other European traditions attempt to portray both the scope of these traditions and their particular, local interests; they provide suggestions for further reading. A single volume on such a widespread phenomenon must, perforce, contain some gaps. Unfortunately, we could not devote separate chapters to Medieval Dutch, Old Norse, medieval Portuguese, or medieval Greek romances; happily, several recent studies describe the evolution of romance in some of these traditions and explore their fertile exchange with texts and histories featured here.[5] We have only been able to hint at the rich gallery of cultural representations that romance offers to the reader, who is invited to seek out the stories themselves for a closer view of bodies, clothing, gestures, songs and dances; forests, gardens, villages, and cities; fairies and demons; travel and trade; hunger and feasts; piety and deception; boundaries and transgressions – and the list goes on. Finally, in addition to the exemplary romances highlighted within each chapter, which include both well-known texts and romances whose readership is growing, there are scores of other European romances awaiting the critical attention of readers, scholars, or editors. We hope that the *Companion to Medieval Romance* will inspire further study of individual romances in all European traditions from a multiplicity of perspectives.[6]

NOTES

1 See *Tristan and Isolde: a Casebook*, ed. Joan Tasker Grimbert (New York: Garland, 1995).

2 See Patricia Grieve, *"Floire and Blancheflor" and the European Romance* (Cambridge University Press, 1997).

3 See Elizabeth Archibald, *Apollonius of Tyre: Medieval and Renaissance Themes and Variations* (Cambridge: D. S. Brewer, 1991).

4 For further elaboration of these views, see, respectively, Eric Auerbach. "The Knight Sets Forth," in *Mimesis: The Representation of Reality in Western Literature*, trans. Willard Trask (New York: Doubleday, 1953), 107–24; Northrup Frye, *The Secular Scripture: A Study of the Structure of Romance* (Cambridge, MA: Harvard University Press, 1976); Fredric Jameson "Magical Narratives: Romance as Genre," *New Literary History*, 7 (1975), 135–63.

5 See *Medieval Dutch Literature in its European Context*, ed. Eric Kooper (Cambridge University Press, 1994); Marianne Kalinke, "Norse Romance (*Riddarasögur*)," in *Old Norse-Icelandic Literature: A Critical Guide*, ed. Carol J. Clover and John Lindow (Ithaca: Cornell University Press, 1985), 316–63; Roderick Beaton, *The Medieval Greek Romance*, 2nd ed. (Cambridge University Press, 1996).

6 Support of the Leonard C. Ferguson professorship at Hamilton College is gratefully acknowledged for preparation of this book.

I

ORIGINS, FORMS, AND CONTEXTS OF MEDIEVAL ROMANCE

I

MATILDA TOMARYN BRUCKNER

The shape of romance in medieval France

The shape of romance in medieval France compels, even as it escapes, our urge to define it. This fundamental dichotomy contributes in no small measure to the vitality and appeal of medieval romance from its start in the mid-twelfth century, when French verse romances introduce a new literary type and set up models that will be vigorously imitated and reinvented by romancers for centuries thereafter. To follow this development, we need to analyze closely not only specific shapes but the art of shaping that gives romance its characteristic traits. The self-reflexivity of romance form calls our attention to the way stories are put together in writing by authors who enjoin the reader to admire the work's shape, its *conjointure*, as a source of pleasure, but no less as a source of meaning.

If shape is paramount in defining romance, it is in part because romance is the shape-shifter par excellence among medieval genres, a protean form that refuses to settle into neat boundaries prescribed by modern critics. If we line up a spectrum of medieval literary types, we can distinguish romance from saints' lives, epic, lyric, short tales, all contemporary competitors for audience attention. But we also have to account for the way romance interacts with and even co-opts these other forms and materials. Romances may end after 3000 verses like *Floire et Blancheflor* or stretch to 30,000 like the *Roman de Troie* – with a variety of intermediate sizes in between. Eight-syllable rhyming couplets dominate the linear narrative of romance, but occasionally give way to ten- or twelve-syllable lines and epic or lyric stanzas. From the thirteenth century on, verse competes with prose, as the pattern of change itself remains the major constant of the romance genre.

From its inception, romance is an art of reshaping through rewriting. The term designates first an act of linguistic and cultural transposition: the translations of Latin epics into French (*romanz*), made between 1150 and 1165 to give lay audiences access to the matter of Antiquity. But *romanz* soon represents a particular kind of writing in the vernacular, as Chrétien de Troyes and his contemporaries locate their works within a network of shared forms and storymatter. Their romances call for a public of connoisseurs able to recognize the interplay of repetition and transformation. Any given romance appears simultaneously as a whole or a fragment with respect to that larger intertextual dialogue.

This chapter cannot exhaustively survey all the shapes of romance, as they will appear in this volume. It aims rather to highlight certain patterns and potentials, established by the first practitioners of the art and abundantly exploited by subsequent generations of romancers. The main focus thus falls on experiments in French romance in the second half of the twelfth century, with views back to the transition from the antique romances and forward to the continuation of verse romance in the thirteenth century. The geographical and cultural extension of French romance includes works composed in Occitan in the south of France, as well as Anglo-Norman romances circulating in England and on the Continent.

AUTHORS AND THEIR PUBLIC

One of the most striking aspects of romance that differentiates it from contemporary literary types is its characteristic positioning along a triangle that links author, story, and public. Unlike the jongleur whose voice speaks for the collectivity commemorated in the exploits of their shared heroes, the epic deeds of Roland or Charlemagne, the romancer appears as a clerkly figure whose school training enables him to instruct a particular segment of society by telling stories that take place at some distance from both narrator and public, whether chronologically, linguistically, or geographically. This shift emphasizes the role and the specific character of the storyteller, who is simultaneously a writing author and an inscribed narrator speaking directly to an audience of "readers." In the medieval context, these are frequently listeners, as romances are read out loud. Although author and narrator cannot be fully separated, the written character of the romance genre permits it to play with the distinction, even as it situates itself in relation to the literary tradition of Latin letters.

The prologues that typically introduce romances establish right from the opening move an explicit contract between romancer and audience. They valorize the role of the author/narrator and thus offer a useful starting point to explore the characteristics of each member of the triangle connecting romancer, storymatter, and public. The clerk's school-training in rhetoric and the art of topical invention is immediately foregrounded in the use of maxims that demonstrate the author's learned stance and justify his obligation to share what he knows – his *senz* or *sapïence*. Two antique romances, the *Roman de Thèbes* and the *Roman de Troie*, begin with this topos. Both cite the authority of previous authors as guarantors: Homer, Plato, Virgil, Cicero and Solomon are called upon to testify on their behalf. The task of remembrance is served by such knowledgeable authors, whose linguistic and artistic competence makes their stories accessible to a wider public. While the authors of *Thèbes* and *Eneas* (which has no prologue) remain anonymous, the romancer who composed *Troie* identifies himself as Benoît de Sainte-Maure and thus adds his own name to the authors cited. Subsequent romancers may choose to remain anonymous, but Benoît's act of self-naming is characteristic of the romance genre, where authors frequently identify themselves, either in a prologue or epilogue and sometimes in both. Chrétien de Troyes, Gautier d'Arras, Heldris, Gerbert – the list of named romancers could be extended, yet we cannot do much more than attach them to the works in which they appear. In the case of Jean Renart, who hides his name in anagrams at the end of *L'Escoufle* and *Guillaume de Dole*, we may even wonder if that proper name might be a pseudonym, with its allusion to the crafty fox of fables. Given the lack of information about who these authors were in their historical context, I refer by necessity to the authorial projections found in the romances themselves.

Chrétien de Troyes, the most influential among those who follow the antique romances, clearly responds to the example of his predecessors. The opening maxim of *Erec et Enide* establishes both his link to romance tradition and his difference, since it comes not from prestigious Classical or biblical authors but rather from common, indeed vulgar, wisdom. Citing a peasant's proverb, he tells us not to neglect what has value beyond its vile appearance. Chrétien thus adroitly provides a variation on the obligation to share the fruits of his study and at the same time supplies an apology for his radical shift in subject matter from Latin written sources to oral stories based on the matter of Britain and its marvelous adventures. In this prologue, Chrétien foregrounds his art, his ability to form a "molt bele conjointure" (14: "very beautiful joining") from stories that others corrupt and pull to pieces. Punning on *Crestiens*, he boasts that his story will remain in our memories as long as Christianity itself endures. Author and romance are thus mutually defined in this act of self-naming, reiterated in each of his five romances.

If first-person narrator and third-person author are more or less fused in such prologues, the playing out of the romance itself frequently demonstrates that the persona of the storyteller, created by his acts of narration, should not be confused with the person of the author nor with the latter's full orchestration of the whole work. Consider Chrétien's *Chevalier de la Charrette* as a case in point. In the opening lines, he introduces another important figure in the romance arena: the patron, the first and primary member of his courtly and aristocratic public. The naming of Marie de Champagne as commissioning patron for the *Charrette* reminds us that not only counts and kings, but ladies, queens, and countesses, play an important role in the reception of romance. Thus in the prologue to *Ille et Galeron*, Gautier d'Arras names Beatrice of Bourgogne, Empress of Rome, as his patron, while in the epilogue he adds Count Thibaut de Blois as the patron who brought the work to completion. Verbal echoes that appear in the praises offered to Marie and Beatrice suggest that Chrétien and Gautier may be responding to and rivaling each other. Is it possible that doubling may also be part of the intertextual play: to *Ille*'s two patrons correspond the *Charrette*'s two authors? In any case, the relay of responsibilities between Chrétien and Godefroi de Leigni, who tells us in the epilogue that he has completed the romance with the original author's full accord, not only puts into question the identity of the narrator's *je*, it destabilizes the original contract between author and patron. If Marie's patronage deserves praise, the prologue makes it very clear that the roles of author and narrator will remain primary throughout.[1]

FILTERING STORYMATTER THROUGH THE NARRATING VOICE

The storymatter of romance ranges widely, inviting and defying our efforts to classify it into Arthurian and non-Arthurian romances, adventure romances, idyllic, Byzantine, or realistic romances. In general, prologues vary considerably in how much information they reveal about the story to follow. Some include detailed plot summaries (e.g., *Thèbes*); others simply name the main character(s), or specify their lineages (e.g., *Florimont*); some offer nothing at all about the story (e.g., *Roman de Silence*). But in each case, the prologue gives useful signals about the character of the narrating voice that will serve as a guide for understanding and interpreting what follows. By his choice of title as given in the prologue to *Le Chevalier de la Charrette*, Chrétien makes his romance an enigma: what could a knight possibly have to do with a cart? Hue de Rotelande's prologue to *Ipomedon* claims to translate a story from Latin without indicating anything about the contents, but his extended play on folly and wisdom furnishes an appropriate beginning for a romance whose hero – and narrator – will revel in travesty and disguise pushed beyond any appearance of functionality.

Chrétien's narrators, like many others, typically remain uninvolved in the story they tell: their distance from the narration allows the play of irony that clearly distinguishes romance from the modes of epic or saint's life.[2] Where Chrétien's irony remains gentle and occasionally comic, Hue de Rotelande and the anonymous author of *Jaufre* enjoy more parodic and burlesque manipulation. The degree of distance, the play with contrasts and parallels between narrator, author, characters and story, open a wide field for experimentation. Consider the different interpretations of the Tristan and Iseut legend, which exerted such fascination over the medieval public. Béroul's version comes to us in a fragmentary state with neither beginning nor end, but the character of his interventions assures us of his sympathetic stance toward the lovers. His is a narrating voice that recalls the epic jongleur's identification with his material; he repeatedly calls on us to side with the lovers against the traitorous felons who pursue them. While Thomas of England shares Béroul's concerns for establishing the authenticity of his version in the face of competitors, he chooses a different stance *vis-à-vis* love. His point of view as narrator simultaneously separates him from and associates him with the lovers. Narratorial omniscience allows him access to his characters' thoughts. He reports in direct discourse extensive monologues, as the exiled Tristan suffers the doubts and torments that characterize his love for Iseut, married to Mark. His omniscience varies considerably, however, when he presents Iseut aux Blanches Mains, who remains opaque to his capacity for psychological analysis. Because he has not felt what they are feeling, the narrator ultimately refuses to judge which of his four main characters suffers the most. Those who can judge are those who have direct knowledge of love and, not surprisingly, it is to lovers of all sorts that Thomas directs his romance.

That romance speaks to lovers is a staple of the genre and marks the path of its divergence from the Latin and vernacular epic traditions that contributed so much to its beginnings. In the Old French "translation" of the *Æneid*, the combination of Ovidian love topics and Virgilian epic served as one of the distinguishing characteristics of *Eneas*. *Floire et Blancheflor*, among the earliest romances to attain great popularity, begins with the typical opening gesture of contemporary epic songs: "Oëz, seigneur" (1: "Listen, lords"). Vernacular epic frequently furnishes material and models for romance treatment: descriptions of arming, knightly combat, assembled barons in counsel, and so on. Reversing the order of historical appearance, romance may even establish prior claims in the genealogy of epic heroes, as when Floire and Blancheflor are identified as the progenitors of Berte au grand pied, the mother of Charlemagne. Both genres interact in the course of the twelfth and thirteenth centuries, as many romances continue to exploit the materials and traits of oral poetry not only to profit from earlier or alternate modes of discourse but to play on the mixed character of their own transmission and reception as written narratives read out loud in castle hall or manor house chamber (and in later centuries in bourgeois settings as well). In *Floire* the opening epic call is quickly elaborated to address the courtly audience more specifically targeted by romance: knights and maidens, damsels and noble youths are invited to listen, as are all "those suffering from love" (2: "Cil qui d'amors se vont penant").

The anonymous author of *Partonopeu de Blois* takes the romance play with love a step further by alternating and combining in the narrator's voice the stances of lyric lover and didactic clerk. The ample dimensions of *Partonopeu*'s prologue allow the narrator to give himself both the credentials of the learned, school-trained author and the qualifications of the lover. He quotes St. Paul, knows his antique sources (Partonopeu's genealogy goes back to the Trojans by way of the kings of France), and lectures his public on how to use stories that mix good and evil as examples for good and bad conduct. But he also notes the glorious return of springtime and hears the amorous singing of larks, nightingales and orioles. Joy and youth summon him to sing, as they do the lyric poet, but the romancer will respond by putting an adventure into writing. Later interventions allow him to reflect not only on his lack of success in love but on more general themes: the blindness of lovers or the disharmony created when beauty and chastity are allied. The embryonic story of the narrator and his lady gradually builds and insinuates itself alongside that of the characters until we learn in the epilogue, following the celebration of Melior and Partonopeu's marriage, that the narrator has by no means exhausted all the potential of his tale (now over 10,000 verses long): he has only stopped momentarily because his pain in love is so great. At the lady's request, a 4000-verse Continuation follows – with his own love no further advanced.

As these examples demonstrate, the persona of the narrating voice as filter for the tale told, as well as link to the romance public, may vary considerably from work to work and even from one part to another in the same work. Narrators may be distanced, or engaged, or both (depending on the textual moment or level considered); they are, by turns, economic or generous in their commentary, sympathetic or judgmental, gently or broadly ironic, learned and clerical in their teaching role, or amorous and involved as lovers whose own stories compete with and sometimes even interact with those of their characters. Later romances will continue to explore the possibilities. In the epilogue to *Le Bel Inconnu*, Renaut de Beaujeu (or Bâgé), who may be following the lead of *Partonopeu*, makes his hero's future depend on the author/narrator's. Obliged by Arthur to marry the lady he has rescued from an evil enchantment, Guinglain has been forced to abandon the fairy mistress he really loves. But if Renaut's lady will show him a fair countenance, he will continue the tale and bring Guinglain back to his beloved. Jean Renart's insistence on the technical virtuosity and difference of his *Roman de la Rose* (with its lyric insertions), as well as the ironic, even comic, play of his narrator, may be considered one of the many fruits born from Chrétien's models. By contrast, the narrators of the Prose *Lancelot* and the Vulgate Cycle in general will adapt and enormously amplify Chrétien's matter while for the most part abandoning his narrating voice. The witty *je* who mimics the oral storyteller by calling attention to his role gives way to the more impersonal stance of a story that claims to tell itself as transparently as the written text allows: now the story says . . . here the story says . . . The intricate tissue of the interlaced account thus propels its readers through the maze of intersecting storylines.

TOPICS AND TYPES

A further view into the storymatter of romance uncovers the use of recurrent patterns at all levels of the narrative. The frame of Arthur's court typically furnishes the setting for the opening and closing scenes, as well as the celebration of the hero's interim successes. In non-Arthurian romances like *Ipomedon* or *Partonopeu de Blois*, other courts fulfill the same function. The Round Table supplies an abundance of standard characters who recur from romance to romance – Gauvain, Keu, Sagremor, etc. And character types return as well: the dwarf, the lady who needs a champion, the Proud Knight, and so on. Typical scenes like the tournament may become the focus of elaborate concatenations. In the second part of *Cligés*, the eponymous hero arrives incognito at Arthur's court and distinguishes himself at a three-day tournament in which he triumphs each day disguised in armor of a different color. Variations on this outstanding but gratuitous exploit reappear frequently in subsequent romances. Hue de Rotelande orchestrates a complex, comic variation in *Ipomedon*'s version as the doubly disguised hero plays simultaneously two separate roles. At a tournament arranged to determine who will marry La Fière, his disdainful lady (a type borrowed from the first part of *Cligés*), Ipomedon imitates the multi-colored performance of Cligés on three successive days, while spending each morning and evening at a different court in the parodic role of "the Queen's lover," a man apparently without honor who claims to eschew prowess for the pleasures of the hunt. In the three-day tournament for Melior's hand that alone constitutes the entire second part of his romance, Partonopeu too fights incognito, although he keeps the same armor from day to day so that his achievements will all accrue to the same man and earn him the right to marry his beloved Melior. The narrator magnifies his appearance each time by setting it in tandem with his companion Gaudin – and thus anticipates the elaborate tournament that occupies about a third of the narrative in the *Livre de Caradoc*, a complete romance included in the First Continuation of Chrétien's *Perceval*.

Cligés's arrival at the Oxford tournament plays on a conventional pattern that shapes many romances. Indeed, it appears earlier in the same romance with his father Alexandre: a "fair unknown" comes to Arthur's court to be knighted and claims the first challenge to launch his knightly career. Perceval, too, follows this narrative scheme but with significant and comic variations, since he arrives from the forest (where he has grown up with no knowledge of courtly conventions) and finds a court in considerable disarray. *Jaufre*, the only Arthurian romance that has come to us in the Occitan corpus, does a more traditional rendition of the fair unknown pattern in its opening scenes, but later plays with burlesque delight on the comic example of *Perceval*. In the *Conte du Graal* the Blood Drops scene leads to Perceval's reunion with the Arthurian court, which will crown his progress in the first part of the romance and launch a second series of exploits after the crisis caused by the announcement of his failure at the Grail Castle. The three drops of blood contrasted against white snow remind Perceval of the face of his beloved Blancheflor. Lost in contemplation of her *semblance*, Perceval is challenged by Sagremor and Keu, who are both unhorsed when they try to take the unknown knight to Arthur. Each time Perceval resumes his revery, until finally Gauvain's more courtly approach is able to establish friendly contact and mutual introductions. In *Jaufre* a similar series of jousts between the hero and the knights of Brunissen, into whose garden he has inadvertently strayed, redeploy many of the same elements used in the *Conte du Graal*. But they are rearranged to lead into the meeting of the hero and the lady who will become his beloved and finally his wife. Although there is some uncertainty about the dating of *Jaufre*, either contemporary with Chrétien's romances or *c.* 1225–28, it seems clear that a pattern of resemblance and variation goes beyond their mutual participation in romance conventions, which, for a public familiar with both, pulls these two romances into each other's orbit for more specific intertextual play. We are thus expected to recognize how individual romances reinvent common elements and (re)shape their own contours both against the abstraction we call romance tradition and through the more particular allusions that differentiate even as they connect specific romances.

THE ROMANCE ART OF DESCRIPTION

The way Chrétien has taken the description of Blancheflor and moved it into the narrative development of the plot and the psychological development of the hero, recalls the important role played by descriptions in the texture of romance narrative in general. The simple, chronological plots of the early antique romances typically frame and juxtapose a series of amplifications based on topical subjects: portraits of the characters' idealized beauty, elaborate descriptions of objects and monuments (e.g., tombs, tents, automatons), accounts of embassies, debates, combats, and hospitality, as well as the stages of love carefully portrayed in lovers' monologues and meetings. These romances continue the Classical convention of ecphrases, descriptions of art works as elaborate set-pieces, as in the two descriptions of Adraste's tent (*Roman de Thèbes*, 3235–72, 4300–85): both the natural and the human world are extensively represented, with a detailed world map, the twelve seasons of the year, the history and laws of Greece, etc. A golden eagle, embellished with precious stones, crowns the top and sends out a fiery blaze as soon as the sun's rays touch it (3261–72). That commanding eagle will reappear in a whole series of tent descriptions, which continue to play through romance tradition from the abbreviated description of

Eneas's pavilion (7315–22) to a series of tents more closely tied to the individual and amorous adventures of Arthurian heroes.

Chrétien, in particular, uses such descriptions to link *matiere* and *san*. In his last, unfinished romance, Perceval sees a wondrous tent soon after leaving his mother and jumps to the conclusion that it must be a church, since his mother told him in her parting advice that churches (which he has never seen) are beautiful edifices. When he then discovers a maiden sleeping inside, the episode intersects comically with the kind of erotic encounter figured by the tent in Marie de France's *Lanval*, where the fairy's pavilion also sports a golden eagle and provides a mistress and abundant gifts for the needy hero. Perceval continues to misunderstand and misapply his mother's advice on love, as he helps himself to the lady's kisses and pries off her emerald ring. Perceval will later have to correct his foolish, but deadly, mistakes when he encounters the lady and her jealous friend, whose punishment of her "infidelity" has entailed both persecution for her and death for a whole series of knights.

When the First Continuation picks up the thread of Chrétien's romance by continuing Gauvain's adventures, he offers new variations on the tent description as invitation. First, Gauvain comes upon a tent, topped with the characteristic golden eagle and painted with birds and flowers and beasts. Within he finds a maiden who seizes the occasion for love. When combat ensues with her brothers and father, their vengeance is postponed because of Gauvain's previous wounds. When the episode is resumed much later, Gauvain himself recounts what happened earlier, but the second version offers a tale of rape rather than seduction initiated by a willing lady. Multiple views thus highlight the problematic status of the paradigm itself: the tent constitutes a remote space, a special place for love, yet it remains difficult to assign a place to the woman who inhabits it, be she fairy, maiden, or lady.

The themes of female sexuality and fidelity are equally problematic in Jean Renart's *Roman de la Rose* (known as *Guillaume de Dole* to distinguish it from Guillaume de Lorris and Jean de Meun's romance). The heroine Liénor's birthmark becomes the crux of narrative play on the power of description to set conflicting events into motion. Jean Renart's work shows how non-Arthurian romance mirrors the tendency of Arthurian romances, in verse as in prose, to follow Chrétien's models by embedding description in diverse narrative patterns. It demonstrates further how topical descriptions may be oriented in new directions by later romancers, in particular by a technique of "glissement" or sliding.[3] This sideways movement is illustrated first in the way Guillaume, the apparent hero whose accomplishments are highlighted through the tournament in the first part of the romance, becomes a secondary character in the second part, which places his sister at the center of a plot based on the popular wager tale. Jealous of the Emperor's love for Liénor and his interest in Guillaume, the seneschal visits their home and learns about Liénor's birthmark, "the red rose on the white and tender thigh" (3364–65), emblematic of her sexuality. When the seneschal falsely claims to the Emperor that he knows Liénor in all the biblical ramifications of the term, she uses disguise and false tales – in particular, a story of rape in which she is the victim, the seneschal the perpetrator – to prove her innocence and establish his guilt. In this second type of slippage, the beauty of the birthmark becomes problematized, first discredited and finally rehabilitated through Liénor's own ingenuity. Description of the marvel is thus redefined in the process of narrative invention in much the same way that Jean Renart has redefined the character of romance through his use of a wide variety of lyric insertions, all sung by the characters. The combination of narrative and lyric "setpieces" sets a new vogue for romance that can be seen in Gerbert de Montreuil's *Roman de la Violette* and the *Roman du castelain de Couci et de la dame de Fayel*.

Guillaume de Lorris's own *Roman de la Rose* offers yet another approach to mixing lyric and romance, this time through the multiple resources of allegory. The narrator is transformed through dream into a lyric lover engaged in a narrative quest of his beloved, now figured and fragmented as a rose in a garden. Unlike Arthurian romance where chivalric prowess generally leads to the rewards of love, the quest here is related to the art of loving and the *gradus amoris*, the stages of love that begin with the perception of the beloved's beauty and culminate in love's ultimate joy. Allegorical figures and descriptions proliferate as action slows and then stops: Guillaume's lover fails to achieve his quest, which requires the continuation of Jean de Meun to bring it to completion. Before allowing the lover to storm the lady's castle and pluck the rose, however, the second author opens up further possibilities for protean hybridization: his enormous amalgam includes the extended discourses of allegorical and non-allegorical figures, scientific materials, contemporary polemics, and classical stories rewritten. The continuation stretches Guillaume's unfinished romance from 4000 verses to 20,000 plus, a striking contrast to the tidy dimensions of *Guillaume de Dole*'s 5655 verses, or the standard length of Chrétien's romances, between 6000 and 7000 verses.

NARRATIVE STRUCTURES: MULTIPLE SEGMENTS AND INTERLACE

Such contrasts in length, as well as the relation between romance and continuation, raise important questions regarding the nature of romance as narrative structure. What are the basics of romance narrative in the twelfth century? How does the wide range of possibilities explored pick up from the antique romances and lay the groundwork not only for the continued production of verse romances in the thirteenth century but for the new phase marked by prose romance cycles?

This is an enormous field, and I can only begin to sketch some of the most significant patterns of romance construction. A number of key techniques will have wide and varying applications: the segmentation of the narrative into episodes, the use of analogy to build intra- and intertextual patterns, the interlacing of narrative segments or lines. With a corpus of five romances and his genius for crystallizing powerful models that operate directly or indirectly in the developing romance tradition, Chrétien's work provides a valuable starting point to explain and illustrate these techniques, as well as their potential for reinvention.[4] In *Erec* and the *Chevalier au lion* (*Yvain*), the adventures of the knightly heroes follow a similar path briefly summarized. An initial problem or lack launches the hero on a quest, which is realized in a series of episodes. The hero's success is celebrated by marriage with his beloved, discovered and won as a result of his prowess. But a crisis soon disrupts their happiness. The hero's reputation cast in doubt, he must once again set out on a series of adventures to redefine his identity. His success in these further trials sets a new level of extraordinary achievement and culminates in the celebration of the hero's triumph. This is figured by the coronation of Erec and Enide in the final scene of *Erec*; *Yvain*'s ending, with the reconciliation of Laudine and the Knight of the Lion, is rather more problematic.[5] The pleasure of romance is usually to be found in the play of resemblance spiced with difference.

There have been many critical disagreements about how exactly to characterize the overall design of this complex plot. Arguments for bipartition and tripartition generally hinge on the role attributed to the moment of crisis that brings together and sets into dynamic motion what comes before and after the turning point. Two crucial aspects remain clear. Romance puts together multiple stories; these multiple segments echo each other through analogies and the interplay of repetition and variation. The *sans* that will emerge from romance depends on our recognition and interpretation of such patterns, since romances do not make explicit what meaning(s) they offer, even though authors and narrators assure us that they do indeed produce meaning.

While Chrétien himself explored different narrative structures in his other romances, the pattern that can be clearly discerned in *Erec* and *Yvain* provides a model that helps make sense of many romance plots by contemporary and successive romancers, witness *Ipomedon*, *Florimont*, *Gliglois*, and *Meraugis de Portlesguez*. Other romances offer adaptations of the model through omission and duplication. The idyllic romance *Floire et Blancheflor* omits the initial series of adventures, since the lovers are already united at the beginning, but subsequent events follow the same pattern as that of the model. Other romances amplify the model with two storylines generated by two ladies, as in the interlaced adventures of Guinglain with Blonde Esmeree and the Pucele de l'Ile d'Or. In *Ille et Galeron* the two lines run parallel and concurrently, starting from the moment of crisis that interrupts Ille's marriage to Galeron, the first culmination of his knightly career. When he loses an eye, he despairs of her love and goes off to Rome, where he falls in love with Ganor. The second storyline is added and pursued, as each plot's crisis corresponds to the other's momentary union. The conflict is resolved when the first wife retires to a convent and makes way for the second lady to become Ille's wife. Gautier d'Arras thus amplifies in romance form the same story that appears in Marie de France's lai *Eliduc*.

EPISODIC ORGANIZATION

The basic module of this narrative structure is the self-contained episode, marked by its narrative function (hospitality, combat, etc.) and typically following a standard sequence of motifs.[6] While the narrative function thus remains constant, its realization in any given instance is subject to amplification and abbreviation. The demonstrations of the hero's prowess repeatedly take the form of combat, for example, but the adversaries and beneficiaries constantly change. The juxtaposition of episodes within the overarching quests of romance narrative does not require but may occasionally use the logic of causation. In general, episodic construction in romance is disjunctive, reiterative not organic. It follows the non-mimetic logic of design, which builds the narrative structure through echoes and conventions constantly reinvented. In the Tristan romances, for example, once the love potion connects Tristan, Iseut, and King Mark in an unresolvable triangle with no solution but death, the intervening episodes will all follow the same pattern that moves from separation of the lovers to reunion and back to separation again, as the final act is anticipated and deferred.

Other patterns may invite comparison of recurrent elements while at the same time moving the plot forward more vigorously. Gradualism frequently builds in tension and progress. In the series of adventures that constitute the second half of *Erec et Enide*, during which both husband and wife must dispel accusations of fault, echoes among the episodes act as an implicit commentary on the couple's actions, but they also trace a linear trajectory, as the adventures become increasingly difficult and move from private defense to public weal. Interlace is another important technique for linking episodes. All five of Chrétien's romances show how he takes full advantage of the potential suspense generated by interweaving. In *Le Chevalier au Lion*, when Yvain agrees to defend Lunete in a judicial combat against her three accusers, he must first seek hospitality for the night. There the knight of the lion agrees to defend his host's family against a giant before leaving the next morning for Laudine's castle, where he will arrive just in time to save Lunete from being burned at the stake. Interlacing not only achieves narrative goals of creating suspense or handling multiple lines of plot;

it offers a potential commentary on the characters, episodes, or narrative segments juxtaposed and woven together.

INTERLACE AND ROMANCE EXPANSION

Interlacing as a narrative technique operating at many different levels catches some of the most fundamental – and contradictory – impulses of romance construction. It expresses both the impetus to segment the narrative into separate units and the equally powerful compulsion to associate and continue romance across such divisions. The chronological development of the genre from the mid-twelfth to the mid-thirteenth century charts the shifting and combined force of these two tendencies, as the cyclical impetus of the antique romances follows a detour through the works of Chrétien de Troyes, and then emerges redefined in the prose cycles that continue to reshape the history of romance.

Just as Virgil's *Æneid* appropriated the tradition of Greek literature, its history and legends, by rewriting Homer's *Odyssey* and *Iliad* as part of Rome's own legendary history, so the romances of *Thèbes*, *Eneas* and *Troie*, taken together, translate and rewrite the account of Classical civilization and its encounter with the east, as empire moves inexorably westward. As Eneas goes to Italy to found Rome, so the Trojan Brutus in Wace's *Roman de Brut* becomes the eponymous founder of Britain. Amplification and the continuity of history remain the constitutive modes underlying the antique romances.

Geoffrey of Monmouth's history of the kings of Britain as translated by Wace furnishes a framework, the *pax arthuriana*, within which Arthurian romances proliferate. In *Erec* and subsequent romances, Chrétien's founding gesture operates by stepping outside that history and replacing its linear march forward with the spiralling designs of romance. The discontinuities and patterns of each individual romance thus play with and against the possibility for continuity and continuation. A new beginning for a genre itself in the process of beginning thus appears, as each of Chrétien's five romances forms a distinct and separate whole. The energy released by such fragmentation opens the door to new and multiple departures: situations, materials, themes, and characters, may now be explored and reinvented from a variety of angles that may resist synthesis or resolution in any overarching frame. To capitalize on that freedom, many Arthurian and non-Arthurian romances will follow Chrétien's powerful example in setting the outward dimensions and the individual status of their own romances. In size and comprehensive scope, this format may initially seem a regression from the point of view of the antique romances, but Chrétien's substantial corpus also includes significant models for linking romances and rediscovering the impetus toward totalization implied in romance cycles. It is worth noting that at least one medieval editor-scribe carried through on that impulse by recording in a single manuscript (Paris, Bibliothèque Nationale, fonds français, 1450) the three antique romances and the *Roman de Brut*, with Chrétien's five romances and the First *Perceval* Continuation sandwiched into the account of Arthur's reign. Similarly, Hue de Rotelande presents his two romances as continuations of *Thèbes*, where the heroes of *Ipomedon* and *Protheselaus* first appear, and as continuations of each other, since one brother's tale follows the other's.

Chrétien himself seems to experiment constantly with ways of associating romances, as well as distinguishing them. If, in general, the story of Tristan and Iseut remains a constant subtext in Chrétien's romances, in *Cligés* he follows explicitly the model of the two-generational legend in his own bipartite narrative, telling first the story of Alexandre and Soredamor, then the story of their son and Fénice. Inter- and intratextual echoes proliferate and overlap, as Chrétien's constantly displaced variations on the famous lovers ironically interact to destabilize the place for judgment: anti-Tristan, neo-Tristan, super-Tristan? In his next two romances, Chrétien not only seems to work at the same time or alternately on both works, he invites his public to do likewise. A number of specific allusions included in the *Chevalier au Lion* refer to the events of the *Chevalier de la Charrette* and create a pattern of interlace that weaves together their two plots. This concatenation combined with the parallel construction of their titles, the lack of an official prologue at the begining of *Yvain*, and thematic echoes of all sorts, invite readers to consider these two romances in tandem and interpret the patterns of repetition and variation that play across their gaps and points of convergence. I have already referred to the problematic continuation of the *Charrette* by Godefroi de Leigni, but the most radical step toward continuation and interlace in Chrétien's corpus is his last and most enigmatic romance.

The *Conte du Graal* realizes the potential for interlacing separate plot lines with multiple heroes, unexpectedly making Gauvain a second hero in a story that originally seemed to belong to Perceval alone. At the traditional moment of crisis, which requires the hero to undertake a second series of adventures, Chrétien doubles the accusers who arrive at Arthur's court and sends both Perceval and Gauvain out on quests. Perceval will try to return to the castle of the Fisher King to ask the questions about lance and grail that he failed to ask in his previous visit, but first the narrator will follow the adventures of Gauvain, as the king's nephew sets off for Escavalon to fight a judicial combat. In the midst of Gauvain's adventures, the narrator recounts Perceval's visit to his hermit uncle, which takes place after five years of fruitless adventures. A strange time warp into the future opens, but just as this single episode promises to reorient Perceval's quest, the narrator loops back to Gauvain's story, whose adventures continue to accumulate. When Chrétien's narrative stops abruptly mid-sentence, both quests remain unfinished, despite the uncharacteristic accumulation of over 9000 verses.

The manuscript tradition testifies to the fascination exercised by this incomplete story and demonstrates the power of romance narrative to generate continuations and retellings that continually postpone endings. Four continuations and repeated reworkings follow in the wake of Chrétien's romance. They pick up the unfinished threads of his plot and constantly reinvent the materials of his originating masterpiece. The first continues only Gauvain's tale and leads him several times to the Grail castle, where new marvels and tests rewrite Chrétien's episode and keep open the narrative impulse. A second continuator returns to Perceval, whose adventures now follow the pattern set by Gauvain, mixing amorous quest and grail adventure. It ends in mid-episode at the Grail castle, at which point two more romancers take up the narrative. Manessier and Gerbert apparently worked independently of each other, but in two manuscripts an editor has collated all four continuations and inserted Gerbert's before Manessier's more standard ending (some 65,000 verses in all).

The puzzles of the *Conte du Graal* operate on many different levels, including of course the mysterious grail, but no less so the enigmatic association of two heroes linked across an unexpected and asymmetrical pattern of interlace left suspended in an uncustomarily lengthy romance by Chrétien's standards. Equally problematic are the allusions to Arthurian history included in the *Conte du Graal* through the characters' comments. References to events told by Wace in the *Roman de Brut* point back in time to the difficult transition between Utherpendragon's and Arthur's reigns and forward to the moment of destruction that will mark the end of Arthur's kingdom. Given these hints, as well as the connections suggested among Chrétien's own romances, the groundwork for the prose romance cycles of the thirteenth century, with their interlaced episodes and multiple heroes, has clearly been laid. The five parts of the Vulgate Cycle will weave together the stories of Arthur's kingdom, the love of Lancelot and the Queen, and the quest for the holy Grail (entrusted to a new virginal hero, Galahad the son of Lancelot), all arranged in the chronological history of Arthur's rise and fall. Interlacing and continuation, amplification and cycle-building, along with the continued production of individual verse romances, will continue to characterize romance writing in the thirteenth century and beyond, thanks to the powerful models set into motion by the antique romances and Chrétien de Troyes's corpus.

As later chapters will demonstrate more fully, the protean shapes of romance respond to the multiplicity and complexity of problems the genre engages for contemporary audiences, whether medieval or modern. The strategies and techniques of romance, its displacements and designs appear to create a world of evasion and play, mesmerizing in its intricacies and flourishes. Yet the apparent frivolity of romance may not be incompatible with the seriousness of its invitations to recognize and reflect on important contemporary issues played out through its many facets. Consider, in this respect, the themes already evoked in this discussion of romance shaping: problems of identity linking the individual and society; the role of love within competing value systems; power relationships and relations of affection; the effects of language and representation, as well as the interplay of history and romance. The philosophical and socio-historical questions that romance confronts by indirection and formal patterning remind us finally of the inseparability of form and content. We cannot begin to consider the genre's themes and issues without fully engaging the playful shapes of romance.

NOTES

1 For further analysis of these issues in the *Charrette*, see my *Shaping Romance: Interpretation, Truth, and Closure in Twelfth-Century French Fictions* (Philadelphia: University of Pennsylvania Press, 1993), 84–90; and David Hult, "Author/Narrator/Speaker: The Voice of Authority in Chrétien's *Charrete*," in *Discourses of Authority in Medieval and Renaissance Literature*, ed. Kevin Brownlee and Walter Stevens (Hanover and London: University Press of New England, 1989), 76–96.

2 See Peter Haidu, *Aesthetic Distance in Chrétien de Troyes: Irony and Comedy in "Cligès" and "Perceval"* (Geneva: Droz, 1968).

3 Douglas Kelly, "The Art of Description," in *The Legacy of Chrétien de Troyes*, ed. Norris J. Lacy, Douglas Kelly, and Keith Busby (Amsterdam: Rodopi, 1987), vol. 1, 216–20.

4 Cf. Norris Lacy, *The Craft of Chrétien de Troyes: An Essay in Narrative Art* (Leiden: Brill, 1980).

5 Roberta Krueger, *Women Readers and the Ideology of Gender in Old French Verse Romance* (Cambridge University Press, 1993).

6 See Peter Haidu, "The Episode as Semiotic Module in Twelfth-Century Romance," *Poetics Today*, 4/4 (1983), 655–81.

SUGGESTIONS FOR FURTHER READING

Hanning, Robert. *The Individual in Twelfth-Century Romance*. New Haven: Yale University Press, 1997

Kelly, Douglas. *Medieval French Romance*. New York: Twayne Publishers, 1993.

Maddox, Donald. *The Arthurian Romances of Chrétien de Troyes: Once and Future Fictions*. Cambridge University Press, 1991.

Vinaver, Eugène. *The Rise of Romance*. Oxford University Press, 1971.

2

CHRISTOPHER BASWELL

Marvels of translation and crises of transition in the romances of Antiquity

Alexander the Great approaches the beautiful and rich Queen Candace. He is disguised as his own messenger, and travels under the protection of Candace's son. Long ago she had sent Alexander letters offering both her realm and her love, but only if he would take her as his equal ("si a pier la volt avoir").[1] Since then he has heard a prophecy of his approaching death and has defeated his last great enemy, the emperor Porrus of India, but now he puts aside both militancy and impending mortality. Candace awaits, gorgeously dressed, attended by minstrels,

> E se fist vieler e harper un nouvel son
> Coment danz Eneas ama dame Didon,
> E coment s'en ala par mer od son dromon,
> Cum ele s'en pleint sus as estres en son,
> E cum au de roin se art en sa meson.
> Pensive en est Candace del torn de la chançon.
> Es vous donc son fiz! Candeules ot non,
> E tient par le poing destre son noble compaignon.

> And she had them playing on viol and harp a new tune
> How lord Eneas loved lady Dido,
> And how he went off to sea in his swift galley,
> How she cried her lament up to the rooftop,
> And how at last she burned herself in her palace.
> Candace was pensive at the close of that song,
> When behold! Here's her son, Candeules was his name,
> Holding his noble companion by the right hand.

> (*Roman de Toute Chevalerie*, 7650–57)

Candace's choice of music and her thoughtful reaction seem prescient: Alexander too will dally with her briefly then return to imperial conquest in frank relief. Yet the implication is not just one of erotic analogy. Some readers at least would recognize here a version of earlier history and lineage, in that Alexander's Macedonian ancestors were, it was thought, also survivors of Troy.[2]

This passage in Thomas of Kent's *Roman de Toute Chevalerie* conflates dynastic history, courtly eroticism, and a self-conscious reworking of Latin models; in all these ways it exemplifies the group of French and Anglo-Norman texts that have been called the *romans d'antiquité*. Thomas's late twelfth-century Alexander romance, and the roughly contemporary *Roman d'Alexandre* of Alexandre de Paris, come at the end of the first blossoming of the "romances of Antiquity," well after the anonymous *Roman de Thèbes* (1152 or a little before) and *Roman d'Eneas* (c.1155), and the *Roman de Troie* by Benoît de Sainte-Maure (1160 or soon after). Thomas claims connection to these predecessors by this overt reference as well as by a series of geographical overlaps and historical summaries of Alexander's classical forebears at Thebes and Troy. At the same time, the *Roman de Toute Chevalerie* often encounters its predecessors in ways that contest, or at least re-examine, their preoccupations. Although she does soon lose her lover as did Dido, for instance, Candace first solicits Alexander as a feudal equal ("a pier"), controls the terms of their affair, sees Alexander off without explicit regret, and appears firmly in power as she leaves the narrative. By such complex echoes and inversions of literary models, the romances of Antiquity group themselves into a recognizable cluster, if not quite an independent genre.[3]

The clerkly poet is almost explicitly figured in the scene. Alexander and Candace meet not just in the presence of Candeules, but also the performers of the "nouvel son." This group, performers of one erotic story and audience of another, nicely reflects the anomalous position of educated clerks (most of them in some level of holy orders) at the secular court in the twelfth century. It is a persistent habit in the romances of Antiquity to interpolate versions or icons of their own learned makers within their texts: poets, inscriptions and epitaphs, buildings and fabrics decorated with scientific and cosmological learning.

The learned, clerkly poet brought ancient narrative to his aristocratic audience. The very scene of Queen Candace listening to a new version ("un nouvel son," 7650) of an already ancient tale provides a mirror within the text for the key role played by the romances of Antiquity in twelfth-century aristocratic culture. They made available to an aristocratic audience with little command of Latin the stories of what it often considered its own genealogical past. This past was at once distant by chronology, yet connected by genealogy, and through it the clerical redactors created a discursive space in which to regard the political conflicts and erotic negotiations of their own time, as well as the unstable family lines resulting from both. This was especially relevant to the Anglo-Norman court with which most of these texts are to some degree connected; that court embraced a mythical, double Trojan genealogy as descendants of the Norseman Rollo and through the Britons (descendants of the Trojan Brutus) whose island they occupied.

History lessons notwithstanding, the scene is also doubly an erotic interlude, in which Dido's tragic love and Candace's incipient affair mirror one another in a way that lifts both, to a degree, out of time. This function of similitude and repetition, especially around moments of heightened eroticism, tends to resist, even subvert, the linear narration of history. Alexander's military triumph over the emperor of India is bracketed, and to some degree conditioned, by his earlier receipt of Candace's letters and later the "amur fine" (7755) of their actual encounter. Much of the interplay of history and erotics, here and elsewhere in the romances of Antiquity, occurs around the actions and subjectivity of powerful women, women sometimes able like Candace to invite their men to accept them as equals, and willing to exploit their riches as much as their beauty for purposes of seduction.

This moment in the *Roman de Toute Chevalerie*, then, makes a series of deft gestures to three central aspects of the romances of Antiquity. First, the clerk's vernacular retelling of stories from learned Latin sources serves an aristocratic society's sense of its heroic past and its current political destiny, even shaping the former to underwrite the latter. These texts involve a translation of empire as well as learning; they both record and extend the widespread historiographical notions of *translatio studii* and *translatio imperii*, the inexorable westward movement of learning and power, from ancient Troy to Greece to Rome to Europe. Second, the romances of Antiquity offer a way of looking through the mirror of the past at a range of ways, some of them unstable and unnerving, in which social order was translating itself into a new form: new modes of power, possessions and their transmission across generations, and the articulation of women's power in this world. Third, these and other romances enact a new and heightened sense of how the most intimate experience of love and eroticism interacts with the experience and shape of the public world. The sections that follow will focus on these three aspects in turn.

ANCIENT STORY AND "NOUVEL SON": *TRANSLATIO STUDII*

Study of the great classics of the Roman imperial period was virtually uninterrupted during the Middle Ages. It was considerably advanced and widened, though, during a florescence of monastic and other ecclesiastical schools that has been called the "renaissance of the twelfth century." The quality of readings in ancient Latin poetry was enriched by the era's interest in science, cosmology, and history; and its impact was broadened by the increasing role of Latin writing and documents as governance slowly became more centralized, especially in northwestern Europe. The stories recounted in the romances of Antiquity derive from this reinvigorated study of poetic epics such as Virgil's *Aeneid* and Statius' *Thebaid*, and of quasi-historical sources in Latin prose such as the late antique

"Dares and Dictys" (fictive witnesses of the Trojan war), and the many narratives of Alexander the Great.[4]

The Roman poet Ovid also enjoyed a popularity in the schools that was virtually unaffected by his preoccupations with pagan mythology and eroticism. Ovidian love casuistry and its armature of rhetorical strategies were studied in poems like the *Amores*, *Ars Amatoria*, and *Heroides*. His stories and witty style were widely imitated in twelfth-century Latin poetry, and contributed to the vernacular romances' long internal dialogues on love, depiction of interior states, and scenes of erotic pedagogy. These elements of Ovidian love psychology (and its darker terrors) account for sometimes massive expansion from the romances' narrative sources, especially in the *Roman d'Eneas* and *Roman de Troie*.

Together, these readings and learned exercises in ancient stories were enough of a fashion to invite the parody of Walter Map, a writer connected to the court of Henry II. "A notable wonder! the dead live, and the living are buried in their stead!" he complains in *Courtiers' Trifles* (1183–93); "the excellences of our modern heroes lie neglected and the cast-off fringes of Antiquity are raised to honour."[5] Walter Map's strictures reflect the degree to which such clerkly learning made itself felt at court; and this in turn implies the role of learned clerks as mediators between abstruse Latin texts and the vernacular culture of secular aristocrats.

The clerks who turned antique story into French and Anglo-Norman poems were also working within, and helping mold, the contemporary vernacular modes of *chanson de geste* and romance. The *chanson de geste* was long thought to be the earlier genre. Usually it was simpler in narrative form and style, loosely structured in irregular "laisses" of ten-syllable lines linked by end-line assonance. Certainly its themes of national heroes (like Charlemagne and Roland) and military exploits reflect a heroic ethos, and its convention of public performance points back to early oral epics. Whatever its still-debated origins, though, *chanson de geste* was being produced in the same time and place that witnessed early romance, and the *romans d'antiquité* exploit resources of both forms. While their central narratives concern heroic battle and territorial conquest, the romances of Antiquity also explore themes of romance: private quest, the role of women, eroticism, marvels and prodigies. Their heroes must often choose or negotiate between the claims of public heroism and private experience. These ancient tales use the romance form of eight-syllable lines in rhymed couplets; and like later romances they are self-consciously bookish works, intended for a more meditative and private reading even if, as in the scene with which this chapter opened, they were performed out loud.[6]

The clerkly redactors of Latin texts into the vernacular were highly active and imaginative agents in this moment of cultural appropriation. They engage in a self-conscious revision of Latin models, and have an often playful and willfully anachronistic habit of comparing, contrasting, or directly inserting contemporary places, times, and institutions within that past. They thereby generate a comparatively safe imaginative space within ancient story to register aspects of their own time. This has a triple impact. First, it normalizes or domesticates Classical story; second, it validates contemporary modes of power by writing them into a mythic past and distant place; and yet, third, it provides a securely ancient mirror in which to investigate the anxieties of the present.

The scene of Candace and Alexander for instance, a wealthy queen inviting the erotic attentions (yet respect) of a great conqueror, might suggest analogies to the courtship of Eleanor of Aquitaine and Henry II; and the episode of Candace trying to manipulate and pacify her fractious and rebellious sons, soon after that scene, could seem particularly piquant in view of the rebellion of Henry's son in 1173–74 and his ongoing squabbling with his brothers. Or in the *Roman de Thèbes*, Edyppus encounters his father Laÿus at religious games that suggest tournament – a defining form of aristocratic militancy in the mid-twelfth century, but still officially discouraged. This turns into "une mellee" (*Thèbes* 231) as tournaments often did, and Laÿus' head is cut off by his own son, radically emblematizing just the challenge to central power that tournament (a frequent disguise for vendetta conflict or the training of private armies) could engender. It is this provocatively modern "mellee," as much as the antique myth of destiny, that becomes the source for incest, that ultimate disruption of orderly genealogy, and for civil war in the *Roman de Thèbes*.

As governance and justice were slowly but persistently centralized, especially in the Anglo-Angevin realms of Henry II, the clerk himself – capable of producing charters, edicts, and judicial records – had a growing if always marginal power in the secular world of the court.[7] The defining crisis of Henry's reign was with a clerk, Thomas Becket, who had risen to the highest ecclesiastic office through the court bureaucracy. Learning thus was both a component and a reflection of civil power, and elements of arcane knowledge feature repeatedly in the romances of Antiquity, repeating not just the substance of the clerk's learning but equally his sense of his presence in the venues of power.

As the Greek king Adrastus prepares for a major battle in the *Roman de Thèbes*, the narrative pauses for a long description of his tent. The panel over the entry to the tent holds a world map ("mappamonde") that depicts all five zones of the planet, and includes both the inhabited northwest and the east as far as the four rivers of Paradise (4223–68). Other panels in the tent depict the months and seasons, the laws of the ancient Greeks, and the stories of their kings (4269–84). Such decoration pulls clerkly learning and cosmology into the literal narrative of romance, reconfiguring the way that classroom methods, especially allegory, folded much of the same material into commentary on Latin texts like the *Thebaid* or *Aeneid*.

This sense of the clerk's place is explicit in the prologues of several *romans d'antiquité*, especially that of Benoît to the *Roman de Troie*. Those who have "sciënce" (19, 23), he says, must share it or mankind will be left like beasts, and learning die with them. So Benoît will put the Latin story into "romanz" for those who don't read Latin letters ("n'entendent la letre," 37–38). This is not just a mundane activity, though; Benoît draws upon men he calls "wondrous clerks" ("clers merveillos," 45, 80, 99), and implicitly includes himself among those whose learning partakes of marvel. Indeed the tent of Adrastus, like many other vehicles of learning within the romances, is itself presented as a marvel, gorgeously worked in gold and surrounded by a gleaming border of precious stones. It is explicitly called "merveilleux" and is painted with "meinte merveille" (4217, 4222).

This wondrous tent, that bears almost a textual, learned narrative within the broader story of battle, emblematizes the way the clerkly redactors encode their roles in the romances of Antiquity. They do so as well, though, in other marvels of artifice and action that explore more unnerving, even darker implications in their new power of the word and the book. Tombs become stages for marvelous artifice and astounding feats of technology, increasingly as the romances develop and respond to one another. They are supplied with elaborate machinery like the eternal flame in the tomb of Eneas' companion Pallas, and the bodies they hold, like Pallas', are often elaborately preserved against corruption (*Eneas*, 6408–518). Often supplied with epitaphs, they suggest both the permanence and the eerie stasis of the book within a culture of texts performed.

The critical place of writing in at once recording and transmitting heroic achievement is most explicit in the tomb of Alexander in the *Roman d'Alexandre*, probably the last of these romances to be completed. It is built from solid gold and silver, its hundred windows are made from the skin of a wondrous serpent, and it is surmounted by a golden statue of Alexander himself, holding an apple. The statue has "grant senefiance," "great meaning," which the author now offers to tell "en romans," just as he found it in the history (IV, 1539–42). That history, though, is not in a book, but explicitly engraved on the tomb's stone. Here, the wonder tomb and the wonder of the clerkly translator into romance enter a complete circularity.

ANCIENT STORY AND NEW SOCIETY: *TRANSLATIO IMPERII*

Two emergent forces, both unstable and highly contested, were especially important in the political and social development of northern Europe in the twelfth century. First, the conceptual organization of the aristocratic clan had begun hesitantly to shift toward a narrower, "agnatic" notion of the family unit based on the male line, that often included (though it did not consistently practice) patrilineage; this began also to aid the family's control of stable units of power, land, and feudal rights across generations.[8]

At the same time, in the intellectual realm, there arose a related apparatus of largely secular narratives – histories and genealogies – that underwrote the origins and continuity of such lineage. A series of secular dynastic histories resulted, tending to pull away from the religious model (derived from Augustine and Orosius) that had viewed human history largely within the scheme of salvation.[9] By far the most influential of these secularized histories was Geoffrey of Monmouth's *History of the Kings of Britain* (*c.* 1138), which reinforced the myth of the Britons' Trojan ancestry, connected their later kings to the Roman imperial line, and recounted an alliance between King Arthur and some early Normans, among other points of convergence between Britons and Normans.

Like Geoffrey's *History*, the earlier romances of Antiquity – *Thèbes*, *Troie*, and *Eneas* – help provide a mythic prehistory and genealogical source for imperial formation in northwest Europe, especially by recounting episodes in the westward movement of power, or *translatio imperii*, from Troy to Rome and thence to France and England. Together they narrate a patrilineal genealogy especially relevant to the Anglo-Normans, in which primogeniture and the rule of the father, as well as armed militancy, ultimately support the accumulation of land and power in a single family line. The romances of Antiquity seem, I will claim, at once to mirror the emergent concept of agnatic lineage in the society for which they were produced, and yet provide imaginative spaces in which to view the dangers, even terrors, the dark inverses of their intellectually and socially dynamic culture.

Translatio imperii and the rule of fathers are most overtly coded into the *Roman d'Eneas*, in the persons of those good first sons Eneas and Ascanius, and in Latinus' engagement of his heiress Lavine to Eneas, despite protests (and accusations of sexual deviance) by her mother.[10] Along with this genealogical source and model, the romances of Antiquity also fold into themselves many elements that their audience would recognize as supports or results of this system of transmission: law, written codes, baronial councils, the rise of a more centralized royal government, and the shift from vendetta conflict and private war to judicial action.[11]

Why then do we also encounter, deeply embedded within the same texts, so many elements that seem to challenge these very models of lineage, imperial transmission, and male power? Eneas drifts from claims of male ancestry to call Italy a grandmother, for instance, though only as a passing rhetorical trope (9366). The romances of Antiquity may attempt to enact a tidy succession of power from east to west, from father to son, yet they are rife with elements that complicate the smooth notion of a patriarchal line. These complicating elements reflect, in part, the tensions surrounding inheritance, patrilineage, gender, and the sources of wealth that characterize twelfth-century society.

Some of these destabilizing elements, I would suggest, bespeak the continuing social model of clan organization and the realities of women's power in the society that produced the romances of Antiquity. The narrower, "agnatic" family descending through a male line was only a concept in the twelfth century, whatever the influence it had in the development of chronicles and genealogies. The Angevin empire of Henry II and Eleanor of Aquitaine in fact emerged from civil strife in England between King Stephen and the empress Matilda, which had arisen when the Anglo-Norman throne descended through two women (Matilda and Stephen's mother Adela of Blois) in the absence of a controlling father or direct male heir; and Eleanor herself was heir to an enormous territory. Further, the many national and dynastic heirs to Troy in the romances and their audiences (Britons, Macedonians, Franks, Danes and hence Normans) together imply the structure of clan. Indeed, as the number of written genealogies increased after 1100, and as the social range of their users also grew, they came to comprise a repetitive and overlapping "clan" of what are, taken individually, patrilineal lines.

Certain textual products of a culture can of course encode that culture exactly by exploring its boundaries or limits, and the fears aroused by archaic (but still powerful) or emergent (but still unstable) structures of social order. They can be both normative and cautionary. This is particularly true of texts like the *romans d'antiquité*, which consciously occupy a meeting place of history and the imagination. A culture can thereby explore under the restraint of artifice exactly those taboo pressures which it imagines as capable of destroying it. By conflating a normalized past and mythicized present, the authors of these romances can examine complicated, often anxious transitions in contemporary society and politics.

The grand claim of patrilineal rights propounded by the hero of the *Eneas* is not unchallenged – Latium descends through marriage to Lavine – though it does finally triumph. The dynastic theme of the *Eneas* is typical of the romances of Antiquity, but its relative lack of anxiety about that theme is idiosyncratic. In other texts of this group, anxieties about paternity, agnatic genealogy, and the place of women are far more obtrusive. In the *Roman de Thèbes*, the young Edyppus is mocked by his knightly peers because he doesn't know his father or family (157–64). His quest to identify that father leads tragically to a dense implosion of lineage, with all the relationships of clan (mother, father, sister, brother, uncle, aunt) forced onto too few bodies within the agnatic family Edyppus thought he was engendering.

In the ensuing civil war between Edyppus' two sons, the episode of Darius the Red (Daire) explores a still more complex crisis of law, feudal loyalty, and genealogy. Daire is a minor baron of Ethïoclés, but controls a key tower in the walls of Thebes. Late in the war, his son is captured by Greek forces supporting Pollinicés, who will only free him if Daire allows the Greeks to occupy his tower. The existence of a daughter is no comfort to his wife; property and wealth mean nothing to her without "our heir" ("nostre oir," 7394). Daire's loyalties are thus divided between his lineage and his weak and untrustworthy king Ethïoclés. Rather then defy the king outright (which would constitute treason), the crafty Darius manages to so enrage Ethïoclés at court that he strikes him on the head in fury, thus providing an "acheison," a legal occasion for Daire to withdraw his feudal homage and make his tower available to Pollinicés.[12]

Still another crisis of rights and legal procedure ensues, between the king and his barons, in a sequence of scenes that echo debates about strong-arm kingship and baronial counsel in the Angevin realm. The Thebans drive the Greeks from the tower and Daire is taken prisoner. Ethïoclés wants to burn Daire immediately, without trial, but his barons insist he delay and consider their own debate about royal privilege, customary law, and feudal obligation. The legal wrangling and the king's wrath are at this impasse when another system of courtly influence intrudes, to which my discussion will return below.

Further challenges to the stability and self-regard of militant aristocratic culture, and its extension through male lineage, make frequent appearances in the romances of Antiquity. Mercantile wealth, not armed might, underwrites the power of Dido's Carthage (and her seductiveness) in the *Roman d'Eneas*; and connected to that is an emphasis on Carthaginian industrial and defensive technology. Women who hold power, especially prominent in the Alexander romances, pose implicit challenges to patrilineage. Commoners in power, clerks or serfs who administer rights or property for a king, equally point toward an unnerving alternate path to social consequence. In the *Roman de Toute Chevalerie*, the emperor of the Medes is killed by two serfs he had raised from the dust, who hope thereby to gain advancement from his conqueror Alexander: "Si quident a honur et hautesce venir" (3665). In the *Roman d'Alexandre*, the dying emperor explicitly warns Alexander against trusting serfs ("Ne creés vos cuivers," III.280), and the men who later poison Alexander are themselves serfs he had raised (IV.132–35).

Both the Alexander romances, written toward the end of the twelfth century, interrogate patrilineage in an exposed, particularly anxious fashion. Alexander's is an empire that was known, historically, to have fragmented almost instantly upon his death. While a wife and son appear, belatedly and ineffectually, to witness the king's death in the *Roman d'Alexandre*, no heir is even mentioned at the close of the *Roman de Toute Chevalerie*, where Alexander divides his realm "A ses bons compaignons e a ses chers amis" ("Among his good retainers and dear friends," 7956).

In fact, the *Roman de Toute Chevalerie* can be seen as a romance of uncertain, multiple, and absent fathers, almost an anatomy of the weak points in patrilineage. This Alexander is at once heir to the talents and lands of a sequence of fathers, yet merely the symbolic son of several, the certain son of none, and (despite approaches by Candace) never a father. The text elaborates the widespread legend that Alexander was sired not by the conqueror Philip of Macedon, but adulterously, by the exiled magician-king of Libya, Nectanabus (135–408, a story the Roman d'Alexandre vehemently denies, 1.145–94). Yet Nectanabus gets into Olympias' bedroom by claiming to be only a messenger for her real suitor, the god Ammon, and Alexander will later claim (with disastrous excess) to be the son of a god. Before that, however, Alexander encounters a whole sequence of dying fathers. He kills Nectanabus (476–99); he weeps at the death of his enemy Darius the Mede (to be distinguished from the Theban Darius the Red), whose last acts both render feudal homage – kneeling and offering his hands – and make Alexander his heir (3677–709); he even mourns his stallion Bucifal as a good man does a close relative: "Pleint le e regrete cum bon hom son parent" (4144). At once the sum of all their qualities, Alexander yet dies without father or heir; killer of his own father, he drinks poison when he fails to heed his mother's warning about an inverse linguistic "father," Antipater (7890–C181). Only the erotically resourceful queens – Alexander's mother Olympias and Candace – seem to survive unscathed. There scatter throughout this text all the uncertainties about male lineage that are overcome or skirted by Eneas or Darius the Red in the Thèbes.

TRANSLATIONS OF EROS: PRIVATE DESIRE AND PUBLIC POWER

The fate of Darius the Red, discussed above, had come to a double impasse in the unresolved legal debate of the Theban barons and their common resistance to extra-legal royal violence. It is eroticism, and the gender discounted within patrilineage, paradoxically, that resolve the crisis of Darius' male line and thereby shift the text back into the main narrative of the Theban conflict. The episode of Darius the Red pulls oddly away from Theban "history." Even by articulating so elaborately the unresolved, destabilizing pressures among family feeling, feudal loyalty, baronial law, and royal will, the long episode (almost 900 of the Thèbes' some 10,500 lines) brings the narrative to a halt, drawing it instead into almost a thematic stalemate, with nowhere to go except the anxious repetition of the extended baronial debates. This digressive loop into self-regard repeats, at the social level, the urge away from history and into doublings, analogy, analysis, and hyperarticulated subjectivity that is characteristic of the erotic elements which burgeon in the later romances of Antiquity, and are further elaborated in romances like those of Chrétien de Troyes.

As debate continues in the baronial council, King Ethïoclés is struck suddenly by love for Darius' beautiful daughter, and this leads him to accept the barons' advice and pardon Darius. Love, "cortoisie," and female agency thus return the king to clemency and a proper legal bearing toward his knights. The scene employs a characteristic linguistic play of these romances, doubling chivalric and legal behavior upon eroticism by way of metaphor. When Darius approaches the king, Creon says to him, with a certain snide contempt, "Autre se combatra por vous!" ("Another will do battle for you!" 8134), placing the girl as a metaphorical champion in a trial by combat. Womanhood and eros are deeply problematic here. They help return the king to a stable relation with his barons, and they help shift the narrative from this hyperextended digression back to the original history of civil war. Yet in doing these things, women and erotics intervene in the work of law, they supersede the ineffective baronial council, and they double the system of chivalry by enacting it in the play of metaphor. The harmonizing of feudal relations thereby achieved is merely an accident in a new causal chain of the king acting among desired women.

The psychology and casuistry of desire, and the power it can give women, are most openly a major structural strategy in the two texts at the chronological center of the first florescence of romances of Antiquity, the *Roman d'Eneas* and *Roman de Troie*. Despite its substantial role in both, love is for the most part effectively subordinated to dominant structures of public order, militant male power, and patrilineage.[13] The *Eneas* explores the social action of women largely in terms of wifehood and motherhood, or the failure to achieve those roles. By contrast, the *Troie* includes a sequence of passionate affairs, almost all broken by the forces of history itself, or by the more powerful agencies of family and its motives.

Dido may be the most famous tragic lover in the classical tradition, and her presence in the *Eneas* is even more important than in the *Aeneid*. Dido's initial passion for Eneas involves all the tropes for private and especially transgressive love that the medieval school tradition was crafting out of its reading of Ovid: fire, poison, intoxication, madness, and repeated wordplay between *l'amor* and *la mort* ("s'amor a mort la trait," her love is dragging her toward death, 1972). Yet the practical motivations for love, and its public impact, constantly surround Dido's emotions. In an early dialogue, her sister Anna reminds Dido that a man like Eneas can provide safety and protection: "A land or realm cannot well be long maintained by a woman" (1349–50). Yet, once the affair begins, Dido leaves her public world behind. The city goes unprotected, its defensive walls unfinished. In the fire of her passion she leaves her public duty unheeded ("an nonchaloir," 1411, literally "unwarm"), and her epitaph emphasizes a death resulting from love radically private and unshared, "amor soltaine" (2142). The epitaph is forgiving in tone, though, once the destabilizing intrusion of female erotics into public order has been contained by death and the little urn ("une asez petite chane," 2131) that holds her ashes.

If Dido's love (in the eyes of her barons) has transgressed her oath to her late husband and her obligations to the state, Lavine's love for Eneas is carefully sited so as merely to reinforce a decision her father has already made for her, and a military outcome already leaning toward Eneas. Lavine's discovery and pursuit of her love for Eneas are narrated within dense, self-consciously learned play among Ovidian imagery and metaphorized chivalric practice. Love is presented as a harsh schoolmaster, yet Lavine is a good enough student to signal her desire by means of a letter in Latin (8776–8844). Love's arrow has wounded her, but she wraps her love letter around an actual arrow and has it shot near Eneas. This endangers a truce, as her bowman had feared, but Eneas and then his men understand its purport and peace continues; the circle of metonymy is completed when Lavine's letter on the arrow causes Eneas a wound from Amor's golden dart. This moment, among many others, nicely suggests how feminine erotic agency and its destabilizing potential are acknowledged, but then either contained or neatly aligned with male will, in the *Eneas*.

Eroticism is similarly normative, if more persistently tragic, in Benoît's *Roman de Troie*, a narrative prehistory of the *Eneas* that was however written after it. Here, the story of Troy's civic disaster is matched by a series of passionate but disastrous love affairs, each leading to a hero's death. Andromacha is the good wife of Ector, appropriate both in birth and the way her love operates literally within chivalric terms. Yet her prophetic dream of Ector's death in battle is tragically ineffectual, and he angrily refuses to allow erotic or familial emotion to restrain his militant role. Earlier, the narrative of war had slowed into an account of the affair of Troïlus and Briseïda. When Briseïda is traded to her father in the Greek camp, she is soon located within another male mode, that of misogyny: the narrator knows that she will turn her love elsewhere and find comfort among the Greeks, while Troïlus will be pressed by passion for her to his death in battle with Achillés. Achillés' love for Polixenain arises when he sees her at a memorial for Ector's death; and his assassination, plotted by Ecuba, exploits that love to avenge his killing of Troïlus. The chivalric excellence of Achillés is extravagantly metonymized as a losing battle with "fine amor" (17547). For Achillés, his love is explicitly his death, like that of Narcissus: "Jo aim ma mort" (17696). So fully does love replace Achillés' chivalric instinct that he offers to stop the war in exchange for Polixenain; and it is in pretended negotiations that Hecuba arranges for Paris to kill him.

These erotic passions are not the only ones at once to underwrite and undermine the progress of political history and chivalric values in the romances of Antiquity. Homoeroticism is also registered in hints, assumptions, and openly hostile assertions. If its presence is sporadic, this may reflect how paradoxically powerful is the homosocial bond in romance, both to spur on chivalric valor in the battle cohort and potentially to block the lineage that chivalry serves. Achilles and Patroclus ("Patroclon" in *Troie*) are the most famous male lovers of Greek heroic narrative, and Benoît's portrayal of them heightens homoeroticism at the moment of Patroclon's death. As Achillés repeatedly faints over his lover's corpse, he calls him "handsome sweet love" ("beaus douz amis," 10335), exactly the phrase Briseïda will later use to Troïlus, and the whole scene is tinged with the language of erotic possession that typically describes heterosexual couples. In the *Eneas*, the devotion and death in arms of the warrior couple Nisus and Eurialus (4906–5302) is very closely based on the story in the *Aeneid*, but the entire romance is so restructured that their story occupies its exact center. Sexuality among men becomes explicit and threatening, moreover, when Amata tries to disenchant her daughter with the stranger hero by calling Eneas a traitor and sodomite (8581–95), an accusation that Lavine will later briefly revive, when she fears Eneas is unresponsive to her explicit desire.

The role of eroticism, in any form, is more openly troubled, complex, almost queasy at the beginning and end of the first flowering of the romances of Antiquity, in the *Roman de Thèbes* and the *Roman de Toute Chevalerie*. Heterosexual desires, even certain gestures of courtly love play, pepper the *Thèbes* here and there, but they are more primitive than in the later romances, and often more explicitly uncomfortable, literal in their physicality, even violent. Ysmaine (Ismene), a sister of the warring sons of Edyppus, is moved to love of Athes by his military skill; she uses the tropes of love-madness, but then just says to herself that she thinks she'll go to bed with him, whether that's smart or foolish: "coucherai moi o lui, ce croi" (l. 2692). Athes has been wearing one of her sleeves on his lance; his lord Ethïoclés also carries a sort of love token, but with violent connotations. As a nasty joke ("gaberie," 6273) he has his lady's legs painted on his shield, next to a deep cut. His every encounter with lance or sword, then, is an implicit sexual violation of her image.

In the Alexander romances, the last of this group to take on their final form, attitudes toward courtly sexuality and the powerful roles women could play therein are considerably more sophisticated and nuanced, and generally more positive. These texts contain several prominent women who comfortably engage their own sexuality and play effective if always contained roles in statecraft and lineage. In the *Roman de Toute Chevalerie*, Alexander's mother Olympias seems almost to connive in the staged prophecies and divine visitations by which Nectanabus seduces her. This initiates a pattern in the text, of women able to use love as a political move, or merely a brief dalliance, and who survive their affairs with their influence largely intact. Candace, whose affair with Alexander we examined above, is a key instance. Her exchange with the conqueror is full of courtly language and gesture, yet part of the effect of her letters and later affair is diplomatic. Alexander never bothers with explicit conquest of her land; his erotic triumph (which she herself prompted) seems sufficient, and she is left in power, not only over her land but equally over her fractious sons.

Because these women practice such modes of power in an ongoing though highly self-conscious and successful negotiation with superior male power in the person of Alexander, they seem to be folded into his ambitions, autonomous but dependent. In each of these instances women's influence through eroticism and matrilinear descent, while real, is circumscribed. The social terror of patrilineage fully abandoned is registered, though, in one of Alexander's many journeys to exotic lands. In Ethiopia, the audience learns, only women know their offspring, men neither their father nor child; they are like beasts in the field ("cum bestes en pasture," *RTC*, 6708). This sense of human identity itself undone in so wholly matriarchal a system is reinforced by a series of value-laden terms: "There is no race in the world of so ugly a practice, / For they neither love reason nor live by measure" ("Ne gent n'ad al siecle de si laide faiture, / Car il n'aiment reson ne vivent en mesure," *RTC*, 6712–13). Throughout the romances of Antiquity, reason and measure are the social habits most persistently subverted or exceeded by eroticism in all its forms, never more threateningly than here.

The romancing of Antiquity by no means ends with its first florescence in the middle and later twelfth century.[14] The texts discussed above were actively copied and read at least through the close of the fourteenth century. Their stories are drawn into romances about far different subjects. Antique stories in romance vernaculars continue to be told, sometimes with explicit reference to these earlier texts. They are brought into other languages, including the still authoritative Latin, as when Guido delle Colonne redacts the *Roman de Troie* as *Historia Destructionis Troiae*, which has its own enormous vernacular progeny in all the European languages. These romance narratives, though, tend to split along two paths. On the one hand, the romances of Antiquity become source materials for the enormous production of encyclopedic prose histories in the thirteenth century and after. The *Histoire ancienne jusqu'à César*, produced in the 1230s and repeatedly copied and revised, for instance, explicitly cites the *Roman d'Eneas*.[15] On the other hand, individual erotic episodes from the romances expand into free-standing works, none more famously than the story of Troïlus and Briseïda, who move through Latin and Italian to emerge into English literature in Chaucer's *Troilus and Criseyde*. Yet when Chaucer's successor John Lydgate comes to retell Guido in Middle English for King Henry V in *Troy Book*, his translation of "history" constantly finds itself crossing with and echoing Chaucer, pulled almost to a standstill by Lydgate's emotional attachment to Criseyde. The energy of our continued engagement with these stories is fueled, in large part, by the unresolvable tensions of eroticism and history reflected in this divide.

NOTES

1 Thomas of Kent, *Roman de Toute Chevalerie*, 6952. Unless otherwise indicated, translations are mine.

2 In an intriguingly similar moment, Chaucer's Criseyde is listening to an episode from the Theban legend as Pandarus, another messenger with (at the least) disguised motives, approaches her. *Troilus and Criseyde* II.100–08.

3 The *Thèbes*, *Troie*, and *Eneas* are grouped together in some manuscripts, sometimes in company with Wace's *Roman de Brut*, though never all together. None of the vernacular Alexander manuscripts includes these texts.

4 Alexander was historically documented, unlike the legends of Thebes, Troy, and the foundation of Rome. Stories of his life entered Western Europe through a dizzying range of texts that passed through Greek and Hebrew as well as Latin.

5 *De nugis curialium*, ed. C. N. L. Brooke and R. A. B. Mynors (Oxford: Clarendon Press, 1983), 405.

6 The Alexander romances have a somewhat different relation to these two modes. Despite their "romance" fascination with geographical marvel and scenes of erotic encounter, they are formally closer to *chanson de geste*, written in laisses of twelve-syllable lines (the "Alexandrine," also used by some *chansons de geste*) with a flexible and expandable structure of combat episodes. Also like many *chansons de geste*, the *Roman d'Alexandre* of Alexander de Paris is an assembled piece, cobbled together from a number of prior poems that stretch back to the beginning of the twelfth century.

7 See Michael Clanchy, *From Memory to Written Record: England 1066–1307* (Oxford: Blackwell, 1993), esp. chs. 1 and 2.

8 Howard R. Bloch, *Etymologies and Genealogies: A Literary Anthropology of the French Middle Ages* (Chicago and London: University of Chicago Press, 1983), 66–79.

9 Frances Ingledew, "The Book of Troy and the Genealogical Construction of History: The Case of Geoffrey of Monmouth's *Historia regum Britanniae*," *Speculum*, 69 (1994), 665–704.

10 For a fuller discussion, see Baswell, *Virgil in Medieval England*, ch. 5, "The Romance *Aeneid*."

11 See Christopher Baswell, "Men in the *Roman d'Eneas*: The Construction of Empire," in *Medieval Masculinities: Regarding Men in the Middle Ages*, ed. Clare Lees (Minneapolis: University of Minnesota Press, 1994), 149–68.

12 The episode is further interwoven with details of chivalric practice, as when the son is allowed to be his own messenger to Daire; he must return the next day because he has left his honor hostage with Pollinicés ("ma foi y ai lessi, en gages," 7244). See also Nolan, *Chaucer and the Tradition of the "Roman Antique"*, 48–74.

13 For a range of perspectives emphasizing romance eroticism, from Ovidian to post-Freudian, see Simon Gaunt, "From Epic to Romance: Gender and Sexuality in the *Roman d'Eneas*," *Romanic Review*, 83 (1992), 1–27; Huchet, *Le Roman médiéval*; Jones, *The Theme of Love*; Nolan, *Chaucer and the Tradition of the "Roman Antique"*, ch. 3; and David Shirt, "The Dido Episode in the *Enéas*: The Reshaping of Tragedy and its Stylistic Consequences," *Medium Aevum*, 51 (1982), 3–17.

14 For the continuing life of antique narrative in medieval literature, see Nolan, *Chaucer and the Tradition of the "Roman Antique"*, chs. 4–6.

15 The *Histoire* is unedited. For discussion and references, see Baswell, *Virgil*, 20–28, 271–72.

SUGGESTIONS FOR FURTHER READING

Baswell, Christopher. *Virgil in Medieval England: Figuring the "Aeneid" from the Twelfth Century to Chaucer.* Cambridge University Press, 1995.

Cary, George. *The Medieval Alexander.* Cambridge University Press, 1956.

Cormier, Raymond J. *One Heart One Mind: The Rebirth of Virgil's Hero in Medieval French Romance.* University, Mississippi: Romance Monographs, 1973.

Desmond, Marilyn. *Reading Dido: Textuality and the Medieval "Aeneid."* Minneapolis: University of Minnesota Press, 1994.

Huchet, Jean-Charles. *Le Roman médiéval.* Paris: Presses universitaires de France, 1984.

Jones, Rosemarie. *The Theme of Love in the "Romans d'Antiquité."* London: Modern Humanities Research Association, 1972.

Nolan, Barbara. *Chaucer and the Tradition of the "Roman Antique".* Cambridge University Press, 1992.

Patterson, Lee W. *Negotiating the Past: The Historical Understanding of Medieval Literature.* Madison: University of Wisconsin Press, 1987.

Poirion, Daniel. *Résurgences: Mythe et littérature à l'âge du symbole (XIIe siècle).* Paris: Presses universitaires de France, 1986.

3

SIMON GAUNT

Romance and other genres

In the opening lines of *Guillaume de Dole* (*c.* 1209–1228), Jean Renart claims that his text is both a *romans* (lines 1 and 11) and "une novele chose" ("a new thing") because he interpolates lyric stanzas into his narrative (13–14).[1] He thereby simultaneously signals continuity and change. He writes a romance, but self-consciously produces something different from previous romances. He plays on the parameters of two textual traditions (romance and lyric), but in incorporating one type of text into another he troubles these parameters as he evokes them: he gives the stasis with which lyric frames desire a forwards (narrative) movement and he injects a startling formal and temporal rupture into his romance since the lyrics necessarily halt the action temporarily. *Guillaume de Dole* is thus a romance that contests the generic framework to which it belongs. Furthermore, even the term Jean uses to designate the genre he seeks to change – *romans* – is problematic. *Roman* derives from the expression *metre en roman*, "to translate into the vernacular," and initially means simply a narrative translated from Latin. If some writers use the term in a manner that suggests a distinct category of text that we call romance,[2] *roman* is not infrequently used to describe texts that we think of as belonging to other genres, while some 'romances' are called *contes* by authors or rubricators.[3] Thus if the genre is unstable, so is the terminology used to designate it.

Precise generic terminology usually derives from critical discourse and it is therefore hardly surprising that generic labels are not used with any consistency in Old French. But the opening of *Guillaume de Dole* does make it clear that Jean expected his audience to have a sense of what a romance was and therefore to be attuned to what modern critics would call genre, that is the categorization of texts into types: otherwise how could it appreciate the extent to which the interpolated lyrics made his romance a "novele chose"? The purpose of this chapter is to examine the interaction of romance with other genres and to suggest thereby that dialogue with other genres was a major factor in the evolution of romance and in the formation of its own generic specificity. However, as my brief examination of the opening of *Guillaume de Dole* demonstrates, such an inquiry raises a number of complex theoretical and literary-historical questions. What are literary genres and how are they defined? What is romance? And what has led critics to assume so unanimously a generic coherence in a corpus of texts that is also clearly so disparate?

One of the most influential theorists of genre in recent years is Fredric Jameson.[4] Seeking to move beyond a simple typology of texts, he argues that our sense of genre derives from a particular association of form and content: thus neither form nor content is adequate in itself to define a genre. This leads to two important points. Firstly, the distinction between form and content is not a clear one in that the association of content and form in a genre means that form in itself signals content; we can talk therefore of the *content of form*.[5] Secondly, genres are inherently ideological constructs; the formal and structural features of a text do not produce aesthetic effects that can be divorced from content and thereby from ideology, but on the contrary they signal participation in a discursive framework that implies a world-view with a heavy ideological investment.[6]

However, as Jean Renart's use of interpolated lyrics in a romance suggests, a genre is never an immutable, static object and the boundaries between genres are neither fixed nor impenetrable. If, when we read, we often have recourse to what Hans-Robert Jauss calls a *horizon of expectations* for the type of text we think we are reading – a horizon of expectation that would encompass a particular ideologically charged configuration of form and content – these expectations may be confirmed, but they may also be toyed with or foiled.[7] Readers and writers may value continuity in a genre, resist change and demand that a winning formula be repeated; alternatively they may value variation, experimentation, and innovation. A genre is thus constantly transformed through textual production as new texts add new features and thereby new expectations; similarly a text can play on more than one horizon of expectations, sometimes to bring two sets of generic paradigms into conflict, sometimes to produce a new genre. This perpetual dialogism means that a genre is always in the process of becoming something different Thus, as far as medieval romance is concerned, any attempt to identify an archetypal romance to which critics can turn to discover what romance *is* will inevitably fail to account for the richness and diversity of the genre.

What then is romance? Cesare Segre remarks that "the link between love and chivalric exploits involves a true 'constitutive model' for most medieval romances."[8] This brief formulation is an apposite starting point for an analysis of early Old French romance: written in octosyllabic rhyming couplets, the earliest surviving texts date from around 1150 and tell stories set in a distant, often Classical or Arthurian past. Segre further argues for the centrality to romance of what he calls "the author – character dialectic" (p. 29): an author-narrator may seek to identify with his characters, but he may also mark a critical distance from them. In other words, there is often a plurality of perspectives in romance which explains why so many critics see irony as an important feature of the genre. The ubiquitous irony of romance is undoubtedly informed by the opposition between *chevalerie* and *clergie* that underscores many texts: a clerical narrator offers an ironic perspective on his chivalric hero. This points to two more important features of romance. Firstly, the plurality of perspectives, enabled by an oscillation between narration and direct or indirect discourse, leads to an interest in individual psychology and identity: thus romances frequently narrate an individual's quest for his "true" identity through love and chivalric exploits.[9] Secondly, the chivalric hero's negotiation of his position in society – whether through marriage, conquest, or inheritance – are dominant themes of early romance, albeit viewed from the ironic perspective of clerical narrators.

The interplay of form and content helps to explain why, in the thirteenth century, romance can change so radically and yet retain a sense of generic cohesion. Thus the ideological resonance of Arthurian subject matter is so strong that thirteenth-century prose narratives remain romances, despite the abandonment of the octosyllabic rhyming couplet. Similarly, the setting of some thirteenth-century romances in the historical present, rather than in the distant past, is an innovation that romance absorbs easily because the link between love and chivalry persists. And yet, as we shall see, such innovations inevitably entail dissonance as well as continuity: the interplay between form and content means that if either changes, the rereading and transformation of older generic paradigms leads to ideological reorientation.

What then are the prevalent ideologies of early romance? I have already drawn attention to the centrality of the chivalric hero and clerical narrator: the ideological investments of these two figures need, however, to be seen in the context of the milieu they inhabited, which is also the milieu for which romances were produced: the secular court.

The characters of romance are the characters of the secular court: the king or lord, his wife, their sons and daughters, knights in his service, his seneschal, constable and retainers, his clerks, and more lowly servants. The court – a legal, financial, and social center – was the forum in which temporal power was exercised and established through rituals designed to demonstrate the lord's superiority. An intensely political environment, the court was also a place where individuals from a variety of cultural and social backgrounds met.[10] As far as we can tell texts (including romances) were usually read aloud to a group by a physically embodied narrator.[11] Who would have been present at such readings? We can only assume that any one of sufficient rank to participate in a court's leisure activities would have had the opportunity to listen to romances in a court where they were available, to wit high-ranking noblemen, possibly an occasional king, knights, court officials and noblewomen. The array of perspectives in romance no doubt mirrors the array of perspectives of its public. Thus, for example, as Roberta Krueger has argued,[12] early romances anticipate and engage with the responses of women readers, even if the knight remains the central protagonist and the dominant perspective that of the clerical narrator.

Romances are ideologically complex because they engage with the interests and fantasies of a group of people who were heterogeneous despite their being bound together by belonging to, or being in the orbit of, the courts of the French, Anglo-Norman and Occitan aristocracy. If the reading of a romance could create what some scholars call a *textual community* (a group of people whose group-identity derives from a shared reading experience),[13] this textual community had schisms within it. Furthermore, courts differed depending on where they were, their size, and importance. This variation clearly has an impact on literary reception and production. For example, Susan Crane has argued for the specificity of Anglo-Norman romance, suggesting that it was more questioning of courtly convention than Old French romance: the courts depicted in romance, she maintains, are fictional projections of French courts, and bear little relation to the more stable and peaceful courts of Anglo-Norman England, hence the difference in outlook.[14]

Romances, therefore, are truly 'courtly' in that they stem from and belong in the court. But they were by no means the only type of literary text that courtly audiences read and enjoyed. The modern canon of Old French literature – as reflected in criticism and in university curricula – is dominated by romance, possibly because it is the most accessible type of medieval text for modern readers. But in privileging romance critics create a skewed, even erroneous view of medieval literary culture. If quantities of surviving manuscripts are an index of popularity, then *chansons de geste* (tales of heroic deeds from the age of Charlemagne, usually composed in decasyllabic stanzas of unequal length that were either rhymed or, more often, assonanced) and hagiography (tales of the lives, and often lengthy deaths, of saints, usually written in octosyllabic rhyming couplets) were at least as popular as romances in the thirteenth century. Traditional literary history depicts the second half of the twelfth century as a period when *chansons de geste* were in decline and romance in the ascendant, but in fact over 100 *chansons de geste* survive in over 300 manuscripts and most of these poems were composed after 1150. Sarah Kay's recent work shows the extent to which the *chanson de geste* is a dynamic genre flourishing concurrently with romance in the later twelfth and early thirteenth centuries; she also illustrates how the two genres engage in a dialectic with each other, thereby requiring us to rethink received views about the specificity and ascendance of romance.[15] Although it is likely that some early *chansons de geste* were transmitted orally and addressed to a broad non-courtly audience, many surviving texts are preserved in luxurious compilations that were clearly commissioned for a wealthy lay audience. In other words, their likely public was the same courtly audience that listened to romances and indeed sometimes *chansons de geste* and romances are preserved in the same compilations. The same is true of hagiography, where form, style, and transmission suggest a courtly audience for many texts. But it would again be wrong to assume that romance is the dominant genre: it is salutary to compare the survival of Chrétien's *Charrette*, a seminal text for modern readers, in just eight manuscripts, to that of only one version of the nowadays largely ignored *Vie de Sainte Marguerite* in over 100.

If romance was not necessarily the prevalent genre for courtly readers, manuscript compilations often confirm not only that transmitters of medieval texts and contemporary readers had a sense of genre, but also that they read a variety of genres concurrently and that these genres interacted in fruitful and meaningful ways. Thus if for many manuscripts genre is the organizing principle in that they contain only texts belonging to one genre arranged for sequential reading, many others contain a variety of genres. Romances are found in compilations with *chansons de geste*, with hagiography, with didactic texts, with lais (short narratives supposedly of Breton origin), with fabliaux (short comic texts, often bawdy), with *branches* of the *Roman de Renart* (parodic beast fables and epics), and with lyrics. The compilation of romances with texts from other genres surely encourages the dialectical reading of the romances in question against the horizon of expectations of the genre(s) alongside which they are placed; multi-genre compilations surely therefore call into question the boundaries between genres that single-genre manuscripts would seem to establish. For example, Sandra Hindman has recently demonstrated how reading Chrétien's *Erec* in the context of Paris, Bibliothèque Nationale, fonds français 24403 (*c.* 1300), which sandwiches it between two *chansons de geste* (*Garin de Monglane* and the *Ogier le Danois*), suggests an interpretation centered on the value of chivalric exploits rather than on love:[16] in the context of this manuscript, romance ideology by no means holds sway, on the contrary it is contained, colonized and, redirected by epic ideology. Similarly, reading the romances compiled in the thirteenth-century Chantilly 472 in the context of this manuscript casts light on how they might have been read dialectically against the other genre in the compilation, in this case beast epic: this important collection of Gauvain romances and of romances in which Gauvain is an important figure concludes with an extract from the *Perlesvaus* concerning Gauvain followed by nine *branches* of the *Roman de Renart*. The repetitive antics of the animals in the *Renart* mimic, echo and subvert those of Gauvain. The compilation as a whole therefore suggests an essentially comic vision of romance. An alternative, more high-minded, model of romance is offered by manuscripts that interweave romances with didactic texts: thus, in a manuscript like Paris, Bibliothèque Nationale, fonds français 24301, which contains didactic texts and romances by Robert de Blois and which may well represent an authorial compilation, romances become *exempla* within a didactic frame.[17] Significantly, even manuscript compilations that contain only romances can play on competing horizons of expectations. To give a famous example, Paris, Bibliothèque Nationale, fonds français 1450 arranges a series of romances into a continuous narrative sequence, interpolating Chrétien's five Arthurian romances into Wace's *Brut,* so as to suggest a history and genealogy of the kings of England:[18] romance here veers markedly towards vernacular history, showing that if, as Gabrielle Spiegel has argued, courtly romance influenced the writing of history in the twelfth and thirteenth centuries, historical writing also influenced romance.[19]

However, evidence from manuscript compilations concerning romance's relations with other genres tells us how texts were transmitted and read in the thirteenth and fourteenth centuries and not necessarily about how twelfth- and early thirteenth-century romances related to other genres in their production, or in the context of their original reception by contemporaries of their authors. There is, nonetheless, ample evidence in the texts themselves to confirm that early romances engage dialectically with texts in other genres and that the process of intertextual transformation I outlined earlier operates across as well as within genres.

Intertextuality between genres can be thought about in terms of influence. Thus the influence of romance on hagiographic texts (particularly in relation to descriptions of women saints) or on *chansons de geste* that have love stories, such as the *Prise d'Orange* or *Girart de Roussillon,* has drawn sustained critical comment.[20] However, the notion of influence, stressing as it does imitation and similarity, posits the priority of one genre over the other, a relation in other words of cause and effect. The notion of influence can blind us therefore to difference, dissonance, and contestation. For example, the majority of women saints, unlike romance heroines, acquire status through their refusal of marriage. Similarly, the love plots of the *Prise* and *Girart* have a relation with, but are ultimately subordinate to, the dominant themes of conquest and conflict, while the premise that the presence of a love plot in a *chanson de geste* is in itself a mark of romance "influence" is questionable since love is an integral part of several *chansons de geste* that either predate the earliest surviving romances, or at the very least are contemporary to them. Romance horizons of expectations may be evoked in these texts, but they are also contested. I prefer to consider the relation between romance and other genres in terms of contestation, rather than influence, because we can thereby see what contemporary readers found problematic in romance, rather than simply what they liked (which is all too apparent in any case). Furthermore, if texts in other genres contest the values of romance and if the contestation of the values of other genres is also clearly a feature of romance, it is equally apparent, as I will argue, that romance ideologies are questioned from within romance through play on the horizons of expectation of other genres.

Conflict between genres can be particularly important when a new genre is emerging. As Jauss argues new genres necessarily evolve from old genres.[21] For a new genre to emerge, new conditions of production, new needs and drives leading to new ideologies, must exist. For a new genre to be recognized as such, readers must be able to distinguish it from dominant contemporary genres. The process whereby a new mode of writing emerges from previous modes can be the result of a deliberate strategy on the part of authors. The formative years for Anglo-Norman and French romance were – as far as we can tell – the decades following 1150. The dominant vernacular genres at this time – again as far as we can tell – were the *chansons de geste* and hagiography, although it is likely that the production of written texts was limited and that dissemination was largely oral. There was also, at this time, an emergent lyric tradition in Occitan, though it was restricted to just a few courts. Several texts from this early formative period of romance appear to engage with the ideology of other genres deliberately to produce something different.

One of the earliest surviving texts that modern critics think of as romance is *Floire et Blancheflor* (*c.* 1150). It is the story of two children who resemble each other strikingly although they are not related: Floire is the son of a pagan king and Blancheflor the daughter of a captive Christian woman. After trials and tribulations, they marry and Floire converts to Christianity. In the prologue the couple are placed in an epic genealogy: they are Charlemagne's grandparents (6–12). The text is thus situated in relation to the *chansons de geste*, but from the outset its parameters are different: we are told that the story will be edifying for lovers (1–5), no mention is made of heroic deeds and the text is composed in octosyllabic rhyming couplets rather than the decasyllabic laisses (stanzas of unequal length with assonanced ten-syllable lines) that characterize *chansons de geste*. Now to call *Floire* a romance begs a number of questions, for it is by no means certain that a concept of "romance" existed as early as the 1150s, while the Byzantine setting distinguishes the tale from near-contemporary *romans antiques* and early Arthurian romances. And yet the text is implicitly recognized as a romance by later transmitters. For example, it is included in an important late thirteenth-century compilation of romances (Paris, Bibliothèque Nationale, fonds français 375), whereas at least one later version of the twelfth-century text is rubricated as a *roman* (Paris, Bibliothèque Nationale, fonds français 19152, fol. 193a). Significantly, *Floire* has what seems to be a second prologue in which a narrator claims to have heard the tale while dallying with two noble maidens in a luxurious bedchamber; they heard it from a clerk, who got it from a book (33–56).[22] In shifting the source of the tale from Carolingian legends to learned clerks telling women tales from books, the poet shifts the generic parameters of the tale away from those of the *chansons de geste*. Since *Floire* goes on to relate how a male individual's identity is formed through a love affair, rather than heroic deeds, with hindsight we can see that the text has entered the world of romance, a world it perhaps has a hand in creating. But in order for this to happen, it would seem that the world of the *chansons de geste* needs to be evoked only to be discarded.[23]

The period *c.* 1150–*c.* 1170 seems to have been crucial to the development of a horizon of expectations for romance. Chrétien de Troyes, writing in the decade immediately after this, did not so much invent romance as guide it firmly in a direction that it had already taken. The link between love and chivalry, the "author – character dialectic", and the play on a plurality of perspectives are already present, for example, in a text like the *Eneas*. However, Chrétien does innovate in that love becomes not only the source of the hero's new social identity (as it is for example in *Floire*, in which love makes Floire convert to Christianity, or in the *Eneas*, where Eneas becomes a king through his marriage), but also an experience that leads to spiritual progress. These elements, crucial to the success of the new genre, may derive from romance's interaction with two other genres: the troubadour *canso* and hagiography.

The ennobling and improving qualities of love are frequently evoked in the work of troubadours like Bernart de Ventadorn which Chrétien probably knew and drew upon in his analysis of the psychology of love.[24] However, if Chrétien presents love as a source of spiritual improvement, he simultaneously undercuts this idealization of love with irony and humor, rather like many of the troubadours he imitates.[25] He therefore follows in the footsteps of the troubadours, even if his ironic gaze is a little more piercing.

Chrétien's play on the horizon of expectations of vernacular hagiography is perhaps more complex. For example, many features of Lancelot's career in the *Charrette* are redolent with religious symbolism: when he climbs onto the cart, Lancelot shows that he understands the value of humility when in pursuit of a higher goal; he then becomes a messiah figure to the captives in the land of Gorre; and during the course of his deliverance of them his body is wounded in a manner that is tinged with Christological imagery (see 3112).[26] Lancelot is a secular saint, offering an image of asceticism that is in some ways similar to that of the heroes or heroines of hagiographic texts; when he steps into the cart, like many saints in contemporary texts, he rejects the path expected of him and instead makes himself into an outcast who derives strength from an inner faith in the value of an abject course of action, reviled by those around him, but implicitly valued by the text's readership. The eroticism of the *Charrette* further marks a link with hagiography since in many saints lives the union of the saint with Christ is figured through erotic metaphors. And yet this eroticism also marks the conflict between romance ideology and hagiography for Lancelot is a saint in the religion of love rather than in the true religion. When he steps into the cart it is Love (for a woman), rather than love of God, that pushes him into this act of humility (375–77); similarly, when he crosses the sword bridge, it is Love, not God, that "drives and leads him" (3114). If Chrétien invites us to think of Lancelot as a secular saint, he also implicitly invites us to think about how problematic this notion is: he worships the queen, we are told, with more ardor than he does any holy relic (4650–53). The horizon of expectations of another genre is evoked and absorbed here to contest the values of romance from within rather than the values of the other genre.

Play on other genres in romance generates debate about the values of past as well as contemporary literary traditions. A striking example of this is the delightful Occitan romance *Flamenca* (*c.* 1272), which narrates the adulterous love of Flamenca and Guilhem de Nevers, who conduct their liaison in a manner that conforms perfectly to blue-prints deriving from twelfth-century courtly *cansos*.[27] Thus, Guilhem falls in love with Flamenca without seeing her and needs to adopt elaborate strategies to talk to her since she is guarded closely by her jealous husband. Hilariously, he disguises himself as a clerk, bribes the local priest and thereby manages to talk to Flamenca for a few seconds at the altar rail each week. Syllable by syllable they slowly build up a dialogue that bears a striking resemblance to a *canso* by Peire Rogier, a troubadour whose poetic activity predates *Flamenca* by some 100 years, and they thereby contrive to meet to consummate their passion. Flamenca and Guilhem's behavior is portrayed as verging on the blasphemous: the narrator comments that as a clerk Guilhem serves God only because of his lady and when re-enacting one element in the exchange at the altar Flamenca and her ladies-in-waiting substitute a romance for Guilhem's Psalter (that of *Floire*, see *Flamenca*, 3817–18, 4477–86). The implication is again that courtly literature, in elevating love to a religion, treads on questionable moral ground. And yet the author of *Flamenca* clearly revels in the courtly antics he describes and his critique of the lost world of the twelfth-century troubadour *canso* is tinged with nostalgia. As with so many authors of romance, the clerk who wrote *Flamenca* was torn between disapproval and enjoyment of courtly culture, a conflict that reflects the position clerks occupied in courts, to which they belonged, but as outsiders.

Interaction with other genres contributes to romance's dynamism. It fuels romance's proclivity for debate and dialogue not just about the values of other genres, but also about the ideological parameters of romance itself. As I have already noted, attention to this intertextual engagement between genres offers modern students of romance an insight into contemporary reception and above all into what medieval readers of romance found problematic. Furthermore, when romances absorb elements from other genres to operate a critique from within, this often mirrors a critique that is already taking place in the genres from which they borrow. I should like to conclude with two examples of this phenomenon: the Anglo-Norman *Ipomedon* (*c.* 1180) by Hue de Rotelande and fabliaux, then *La Queste del Saint Graal* (*c.* 1225) and hagiography.

Ipomedon is an overtly comic romance in which the hero repeatedly disguises himself, alternately feigning worthlessness and proving his prowess, as a response to a vow made by the appropriately nick-named La Fiere ("the proud one") to love only the most worthy knight in the world.[28] The three main women characters (La Fiere, her lady-in-waiting Ismene, and the Queen of Sicily) fall in love with Ipomedon as a foppish courtier and even as a repulsive fool; La Fiere also falls in love with him in a series of heroic guises, fearing she will never again see the effete young man with whom she originally, much to her consternation and shame, became infatuated. The motif of disguise or incognito is by no means unusual in romance, witness the Tristan romances. But the relentless repetition of Ipomedon's adoption of a sequence of disguises is gratuitous (despite the humor), unless of course the intention is to show La Fiere in the worst possible light by satirizing her fickleness. Thus in the concluding episode, having already abandoned La Fiere twice and having proved his worth fighting incognito in tournaments and elsewhere many times over, Ipomedon, again incognito, defeats Leonin, a hideous Indian prince who is attempting to take La Fiere by force, only then inexplicably to disguise himself as Leonin and claim victory, which has the effect of putting La Fiere to flight (9909–76). Significantly, Ipomedon's antics are brought to an end not by La Fiere recognizing him, but by his being recognized by a long-lost brother who comes to her aid (10231–88). When subsequently reunited with La Fiere, Ipomedon claims to have always acted for her sake ("pur vus", see 10386–91), but his purpose seems to have been to teach her a lesson rather than to undertake acts of chivalric prowess for her sake. Since the text is punctuated with obscene and misogynous asides,[29] *Ipomedon* offers an extensive critique of the way some romances seem to elevate haughty women to a position of power over men. The subordination of a man to a woman is of course problematized elsewhere in romance, for example in Chrétien's *Charrette*, but *Ipomedon* is nonetheless remarkable because of its overt humor and obscenity, its repetition, and its use of the disguise motif as a means to deceive, all of which strongly recall the fabliaux.

As Kathryn Gravdal has argued, *Ipomedon*, a parodic romance in itself, has structural similarities to *Trubert*, a thirteenth-century fabliau which clearly parodies romance.[30] In *Trubert*, as in *Ipomedon*, the hero disguises himself over and over again to humiliate repeatedly and gratuitously a hapless local aristocrat. If the victim in *Trubert* is a man rather than a woman, the misogyny of *Ipomedon* resonates strongly with other fabliaux that parody romance such as *Le Chevalier qui fist parler les cons*,[31] in which a questing knight is given the power to make a woman's vagina and anus answer questions and thereby reveal her duplicity, desire, or fickleness. *Le Chevalier*'s hero uses his gift ruthlessly, though to comic effect, at court. If the tone of *Le Chevalier* is different from that of *Ipomedon* the willingness to expose women's ostensible fickleness makes Ipomedon comparable to the fabliau knight. The implications of the fabliau are that women are unworthy objects of veneration, enslaved as they are to their sexuality, and since the text flags itself as a parody of romance, *Le Chevalier* is a critique of the elevation of women in romance and of romance's mystification of women's nature (as the *fableor* sees it). But comparison with *Ipomedon* reveals that this critique is already undertaken within romance itself and romance thus shows itself to be adept at accommodating debate and dissent. The treatment of women in romance is controversial even for writers and readers of romance, and the "link between love and chivalric exploits," although it may be a "constitutive model" for the genre, is hotly debated and contested. Ipomedon's chivalric exploits are hardly inspired by a woman, while the value of the link between love and chivalry is undermined by his actions. But if *Ipomedon*'s fabliaux-like qualities contribute to its questioning of romance ideology, as with all parodies it also reproduces what it subverts. The text's very engagement with the problematics of romance signals a commitment to the genre.

A similar process of simultaneous subversion and reproduction takes place in *La Queste del Saint Graal*.[32] In the *Queste*, the traditional heroes of Arthurian romance – Arthur himself, Gauvain, but particularly Lancelot – are gradually marginalized as the chosen knight, Galahad, moves towards the Grail and union with God. It is obvious that the *Queste* attempts to reorientate romance away from secular towards spiritual concerns. Riddled as it is with allusion to the Scriptures and with exegetical allegory, its most important intertext outside romance is the Bible rather than any vernacular genre, while Galahad himself is explicitly compared to Christ.[33] However, the *Queste* was composed to be read as part of the cyclical prose *Lancelot* and only four out of forty-three manuscripts transmit it independently of the cycle. If it contests the values of romance, the *Queste* does so from within the framework of romance. This may – as we will see – compromise the force of its attack, but it is striking that the horizon of expectations of another vernacular genre – hagiography – is called into play to enhance the critique of romance. I am thinking here less of the portrayal of Galaad, who like many saints obviously imitates Christ, than of the portrayal of Lancelot as anti-hero and of how he represents precisely the opposite of a medieval saint.

Lancelot's position in the *Queste* is equivocal. If the romance is read in isolation, Galahad is undoubtedly the hero. However, if the *Queste* is read in the context of the prose cycle to which it belongs, it becomes part of a longer narrative, the hero of which is Lancelot, in many respects the incarnation of the romance ideal because of the link in his career between love and chivalric exploits. Thus the *Queste*'s marginalization of Lancelot in favor of Galahad is an assault on romance ideology, but what is the reason for the opprobrium with which Lancelot is liberally and consistently treated in the *Queste*? The answer is simple: his steamy affair with Guenevere. As Lancelot himself confesses: "il est einsi que je sui morz de pechié d'une moie dame que je ai amee toute ma vie, et ce est Guenievre, la fame le roi Artus" ("it is the case that I have committed a mortal sin with a lady of mine, whom I have loved all my life, I mean Guenevere, King Arthur's wife," p. 66). This renders explicit the criticism of Lancelot that some critics have thought implicit in Chrétien's *Charrette*. But whereas Chrétien draws our attention to Lancelot's betrayal of Arthur[34] and to his devotion to Guenevere rather than to God, the *Queste* dwells repeatedly on the fact that Lancelot is tainted by sins of the flesh. Critics have expressed surprise that in enumerating the virtues that Lancelot once possessed, virginity comes first, ranked above humility, patient endurance, rectitude and charity (pp. 123–25).[35] And yet the *Queste* is so obsessively insistent on the importance of virginity that the strange hierarchy of virtues it proposes has to be accepted at face value and assumed to be deliberate. The value of virginity is repeatedly extolled. Thus Perceval laments: "Las! Chetif! tant ai esté vilx et mauvés, qui ai si tost esté menez au point de perdre ce ou nus ne puet recouvrer, ce est virginitez, qui ne puet estre recovrée que ele est perdue une foiz" ("Alas! Miserable wretch that I am. I have been so vile and wicked that I have been quickly led to the verge of losing that which no man can ever recover, his virginity, which can never be recovered once it has been lost," p. 111). The text makes a distinction between *pucelages* and *virginitez* (p. 213), the former being a mere physical state, the latter a spiritual virtue depending on the virgin having never had a corrupt thought, and in this the *Queste* echoes patristic thinking on virginity.[36] Finally, the first reason cited for Galahad's election as Grail-knight is his virginity (for example p. 263) while all those who are unchaste are excluded from the quest altogether.

The obsession with sexuality in the *Queste* evokes the horizon of expectations of vernacular hagiography, where the value of virginity is obsessively reiterated.[37] Indeed, Lancelot's flawed chivalric heroism in the *Queste* is in some ways analogous to that of Saint Gregory in Old French versions of his life. As I have argued elsewhere *La Vie de Saint Grégoire* presents Gregory as quite deliberately choosing to model himself on a romance hero.[38] The child of brother/sister incest, he rejects the life of a monk to be a knight and, like the Bel Inconnu, embarks on a quest to discover the identity of his father, as a result of which marries his mother. Gregory's sin (like Lancelot's) is sexual and it is explicitly attributed to his pursuit of *chevalerie* rather than *clergie*, the former being portrayed as inherently sinful (version A1, 1206–10). *La Vie de Saint Grégoire* therefore mounts a devastating attack on romance in that a romance hero can never be anything other than a sinner, unless of course he repents of chivalric ambitions and atones for them. Reading Lancelot against Gregory shows the extent to which the qualities that make him the archetypal romance hero oppose him to all that is saintly and exclude him from the Grail quest.

It is striking, however, that with the *Queste* we once again see that a critique of romance redolent of another genre is present in romance. Critics have recently argued that the religious valence of the *Queste* has been overstressed and that it should be read first and foremost as romance: thus the religious symbolism could be read as a valorization rather than a negation of romance values since the Round Table is overtly interpreted as the successor to the table of the last supper and the table of the Holy Grail (pp. 74–78), while the allegorical interpretations of knightly exploits merely pit one mode of storytelling against another.[39] Above all it should be borne in mind that the *Queste* always was and remains part of a secular romance cycle and that as such it is not the end of the story. It is quite literally contained by other romances and if its author sought to appropriate romance for a religious agenda, his text was subsequently reappropriated for the genre he sought to hijack, by the author of *La Mort le roi Artu*, its sequel, and by the compilers of the cyclical manuscripts of the prose *Lancelot*. Lancelot is reinstated as the hero of the Arthurian world once the *Queste* is over. If there is an invasion of romance in the *Queste*, romance is versatile enough to accommodate the intruder and to be enriched by the intrusion.

If romance is not the dominant narrative form of the twelfth and thirteenth centuries, it is perhaps its proclivity for absorbing paradigms from other genres to enable ideological debate within its own highly flexible generic parameters that leads to its undoubted triumph over rival genres such as the *chansons de geste* in the later Middle Ages, although the growing hegemony of prose probably also served to elide differences between longer narrative texts and therefore to reduce the specificity of romance.[40] But romance in the earlier period is all the richer for its contact with other genres. Indeed, I would argue that it owes much of its success to this contact.

NOTES

1 See Jean Renart, *Le Roman de la Rose ou de Guillaume de Dole*, ed. F. Lecoy, CFMA 91 (Paris: Champion, 1979).
2 See, for example, Chrétien de Troyes, *Le Chevalier de la Charrette*, 1–2 and 7101 and Renaud de Beaujeu, *Le Bel Inconnu*, 6247.
3 For example the *chanson de geste Daurel et Beton* is rubricated as "lo romans de Daurel et Beto," while *Floire et Blancheflor* is called a *conte*; see *Daurel et Beton*, ed. Charmaine Lee (Parma: Pratiche Editrice, 1991), 41, and *Floire et Blancheflor*, 3341.
4 See *The Political Unconscious: Narrative as Socially Symbolic Act* (London: Methuen, 1981), 103–50.
5 *Ibid.*, 99.
6 See also Tzvetan Todorov, "The Origin of Genre," *New Literary History*, 8 (1976), 159–70 and for a more detailed elaboration my *Gender and Genre*, 3–10.

7 *Toward an Aesthetic of Reception,* trans. Timothy Bahti (Minneapolis and Brighton: Harvester, 1982), 88.

8 "What Bakhtin Left Unsaid", 36.

9 See Hanning, *Individual in Twelfth-Century Romance.*

10 On secular courts see Linda M. Paterson, *The World of the Troubadours: Medieval Occitan Society c.1100–1300* (Cambridge University Press, 1993), 90–119.

11 Several texts depict romances being read aloud to a group; a famous example is Chrétien de Troyes: *Yvain,* 5362–72. Sandra Hindman argues that the material state of Chrétien manuscripts suggests they were used frequently; see *Sealed in Parchment,* 3–9.

12 See *Women Readers.*

13 See Brian Stock, *The Implications of Literacy: Written Language and Models of Interpretation in the Eleventh and Twelfth Centuries* (Princeton University Press, 1983), 88–240.

14 *Insular Romance,* particularly pp. 134–45. The cultural specificity of Occitan, northern French, and continental Plantagenet courts also merits attention.

15 See *Chansons de Geste in the Age of Romance.*

16 *Sealed in Parchment,* 129–62.

17 See Krueger, *Women Readers,* 156–82 on this compilation.

18 On this manuscript, see Huot, *From Song to Book,* 27–34.

19 See *Romancing the Past: The Rise of Vernacular Prose Historiography in Thirteenth-Century France* (Berkeley, Los Angeles and London: University of California Press, 1993).

20 On hagiography and romance see Brigitte Cazelles, *The Lady as Saint: A Collection of French Hagiographic Romances of the Thirteenth Century* (Philadelphia: University of Pennsylvania Press, 1991), 16–18; on the *Prise* and romance see Claude Lachet, *La Prise d'Orange ou la parodie courtoise d'une épopée* (Paris: Champion, 1986); on *Girart* and romance see *Girart de Roussillon,* ed. and trans. Gérard Gouiran and Micheline de Combarieu du Grés (Paris: Livre de Poche, 1993), 15–18.

21 *Toward an Aesthetic,* 23.

22 On the prologue(s) to *Floire,* see Krueger, *Women Readers,* 7–9 and Gaunt, *Gender,* 85–87.

23 *Floire*'s most recent editor, Leclanche, believes that the two prologues are thirteenth-century additions. But both prologues are in all surviving manuscripts that contain this portion of the text and it is not clear why he believes them to be later additions. I have argued elsewhere that epic values are similarly evoked and marginalized in the *Eneas* (c. 1156), see *Gender and Genre,* 75–85.

24 See Leslie T. Topsfield, *Chrétien de Troyes: A Study of the Arthurian Romances* (Cambridge University Press, 1981), particularly 50–52 and 165–71.

25 See Tony Hunt, *Chrétien de Troyes: Yvain* (London: Grant and Cutler, 1986), 52–66, and Lucie Polak, *Chrétien de Troyes: Cligés* (London: Grant and Cutler, 1982), 36–49.

26 See Topsfield, *Chrétien,* 143. See also Sarah Kay's essay in this volume.

27 See *Flamenca: Roman Occitan du XIIIᵉ siècle,* ed. Jean-Charles Huchet (Paris: 10/18, 1988). On *Flamenca* and the *canso* see Kay, *Subjectivity in Troubadour Poetry,* 198–211.

28 See *Ipomedon,* ed. Holden. See Crane, *Insular Romance,* 158–73, on *Ipomedon*'s humor; Hanning, *Individual in Twelfth-Century Romance,* 123–35 on identity.

29 On which see Krueger, *Women Readers,* 73–82.

30 *Vilain and Courtois,* 121–30. For the text of *Trubert,* see *Fabliaux érotiques,* ed. Luciano Rossi and Richard Straub (Paris: Livre de Poche, 1992), 345–529.

31 Rossi and Straub, eds., *Fabliaux érotiques*, 197–39; on the generic signals of the text see pp. 36–41.

32 See *La Queste del Saint Graal*, ed. Pauphilet.

33 See particularly Matarasso, *Redemption of Chivalry*.

34 See Gaunt, *Gender and Genre*, 97–99.

35 See Matarasso, *Redemption of Chivalry*, 145 and 153.

36 On which see R. Howard Bloch, *Medieval Misogyny and the Invention of Western Romantic Love* (Chicago University Press, 1991), 106–09.

37 See Gaunt, *Gender and Genre*, 185–97.

38 See *Ibid.*, 200–12; for parallel editions of all the Old French versions see *La Vie du Pape Saint Grégoire*, ed. Hendrik B. Sol (Amsterdam: Rodopi, 1977).

39 See Nancy Freeman-Regalado, "*La Chevalerie celestiel*: Spiritual Transformations of Secular Romance in *La Queste del Saint Graal*," in *Romance: Generic Transformation from Chrétien de Troyes to Cervantes*, ed. Kevin Brownlee and Marina Scordilis Brownlee (Hanover and London: University Press of New England, 1985), 91–113, and E. Jane Burns, *Arthurian Fictions: Rereading the Vulgate Cycle* (Columbus: Ohio State Press, 1985), 55–77.

40 See Michel Zink, "Le Roman," in *La Littérature française aux XIVe et XVe siècles*, ed. Daniel Poirion (Heidelberg: Winter, 1988), Grundriss der romanischen Literaturen des Mittelalters, VIII/1, pp. 197–218 (esp. pp. 203–5).

SUGGESTIONS FOR FURTHER READING

Crane, Susan. *Insular Romance: Politics, Faith and Culture in Anglo-Norman and Middle English Romance*. Berkeley, Los Angeles and London: University of California Press, 1986.

Gaunt, Simon. *Gender and Genre in Medieval French Literature*. Cambridge University Press, 1995.

Gravdal, Kathryn. *Vilain and Courtois: Transgressive Parody in French Literature of the Twelfth and Thirteenth Centuries*. Lincoln Nebr, and London: University of Nebraska Press, 1989.

Hanning, Robert. *The Individual in Twelfth-Century Romance*. New Haven and London: Yale University Press, 1977.

Hindman, Sandra. *Sealed in Parchment: Rereadings of Knighthood in the Illuminated Manuscripts of Chrétien de Troyes*. Chicago University Press, 1994.

Huot, Sylvia. *From Song to Book: The Poetics of Writing in Old French Lyric and Lyrical Narrative Poetry*. Ithaca and London: Cornell University Press, 1987.

Kay, Sarah. *Subjectivity in Troubadour Poetry*. Cambridge University Press, 1990.
  The Chansons de Geste in the Age of Romance: Political Fictions. Oxford University Press, 1995.

Krueger, Roberta. *Women Readers and the Ideology of Gender in Old French Verse Romance*. Cambridge University Press, 1993.

Matarasso, Pauline. *The Redemption of Chivalry: A Study of the Queste del Saint Graal*. Geneva: Droz, 1979.

Segre, Cesare. "What Bakhtin Left Unsaid: the Case of Medieval Romance," in *Romance: Generic Transformation from Chrétien de Troyes to Cervantes*, ed. Kevin Brownlee and Marina Scordilis Brownlee (Hanover and London: University Press of New England, 1985), 23–46.

4

SYLVIA HUOT

The manuscript context of medieval romance

This essay examines aspects of the manuscript transmission of Old French and Middle High German romance. Though space does not permit a comprehensive pan-European survey, the comparative examination of two literary traditions allows for a broader consideration of the medieval literary manuscript in its varied forms. Anyone who has studied romances in their original manuscripts knows that the experience is markedly different from that of reading them in modern printed editions. On the one hand, there are no line numbers, no glossary or index of proper names, no explanatory introduction or critical apparatus; there may be no indication of the author's name, and possibly not even a title. Punctuation is sparse, and not always consistent. On the other hand, there may be features that enhance the reading experience, such as illustrations – sometimes quite prolific – and explanatory rubrics that chart the narrative or thematic subdivisions of the text. A scribe might embellish the text with flourishes and doodles that call attention to key words, passages, or motifs; scribes and readers alike often marked lines that they considered important with the marginal indication "Nota." The medieval manuscript shapes our encounter with the text in a way quite different from that of a modern edition; and it often bears the personal reactions of generations of past readers, a material reminder of the communal nature of literary reception (Fig. 4.1).

In strictest terms, one cannot speak of a romance manuscript tradition wholly distinct from other genres, since there are many examples of generically diverse manuscript anthologies. However, the compilation of manuscripts devoted largely or entirely to romance was a common practice. Despite the diversity of the manuscript tradition, a general survey of the surviving corpus allows for the identification of certain overall patterns and tendencies. And the examination of individual manuscripts is an invaluable guide to the medieval reception of particular texts.

Overall, a consideration of manuscript traditions alerts us to the diversity of medieval reception both of individual romances, and of romance as a genre. Depending on the manuscript presentation of a given text, the presence or

4.1 The end of the *Roman d'Eneas* and the beginning of the *Roman de Brut* in a thirteenth-century manuscript. A slightly later medieval hand has added an explanatory title in the upper margin ("This is the romance of the kings of England and of their deeds"), repeated below in a modern hand, which also inserted a title at the opening line of the *Brut*. The marginal glosses date from the fifteenth century.

absence of illustrations, and the other texts, if any, with which it was transmitted, medieval readers might perceive it as part of a larger narrative sweep; they might see it as one of many self-contained tales of chivalric adventure, while still seeking to compare its treatment of crucial issues with that of other texts; or they might receive it entirely on its own. As such they might be encouraged to read it in various ways: as a good story, providing excitement and sentimental pleasures; as an illustration of social or political values, and of the trouble that results when these are abandoned; as part of a grand exposition of the historical continuity in which Greco-Roman, Judaeo-Christian, and indigenous European cultures were fused; and so on. The different manuscript formats that survive hint at the quite different contexts in which romances were read, and the different priorities that medieval readers brought to them.

As with all medieval texts, when a romance appears in more than one manuscript, there will be at least some minor variants among them, and sometimes quite significant divergences. A given text may be abridged, amplified, or otherwise reworked: sometimes modestly, but other times so extensively that the result is virtually a new text.[1] This proliferation of variants and multiple versions is often the result of scribal emendations, executed sometimes for greater clarity or simplicity, sometimes to make a text more edifying or more entertaining as the case may be, or to highlight or suppress particular themes, motifs, or characters. It can also, of course, be the result of scribal error, ranging from the obfuscation of a single word to the inadvertent omission of whole passages. Errors in a scribe's model, in turn, could necessitate the composition of new lines or the rearrangement of words to restore lost rhymes or to impose meaning on a passage that had become nonsensical. The editorial and literary interventions of scribes are often so considerable as to blur the distinction between "author" and "copyist." The fluidity of the text, always potentially open to revision or continuation, and the resulting lack of authorial control over textual transmission, are important areas of difference between medieval manuscript culture and that of the modern printed book.

The analysis of textual emendation and adaptation is indispensable to the study of literary reception. The changes undergone by a given text can tell us much about ways that it was read and understood by individual readers, in response to changing social or political circumstances, and in different milieux. It is particularly important, when studying the influence of an earlier text on a later writer or artist, to consider what version(s) of that text he or she might have known. Yet for those wishing to study the original author, or the social and intellectual milieu in which the text was composed, manuscript variants may pose a problem. This problem is particularly acute for the editor of a medieval text, who must work through its different versions and determine what form of the text is appropriate for modern publication.

The great variety found in manuscript traditions, and the different purposes to which editions may be put, have given rise to different editorial approaches.[2] An editor may seek to reconstruct the original text insofar as possible, through an evaluation of the evidence of the surviving manuscripts; this is the "Lachmannian" approach, named for the nineteenth-century German philologist Karl Lachmann whose work exemplifies this approach. Alternatively, an editor may choose to present the transcription of a single manuscript, preferring an actual medieval text – albeit somewhat altered from the original – to a hypothetical reconstruction: an approach known as "Bédierist," for the French philologist Joseph Bédier who pioneered this type of edition. In the latter case, an editor might select a manuscript on the basis of its presumed proximity to the original text; or one that presents a clearly altered version, deemed important for its influence on later writers, or simply for its literary merits. In practice, an editor is likely to combine aspects of both approaches.

When manuscript variants are particularly divergent, it is often necessary for a text to be edited more than once, according to different principles. Only in this way can the modern reader be given access to the text and its history, from the projected early version(s) that gave rise to the surviving manuscripts, through the different forms that it assumed at the hands of scribal editors and adaptors. Through scrutiny of the manuscript tradition – both its overall patterns and the characteristics of individual manuscripts – we can examine the ways in which a text was subject to processes of reading, interpretation, and transformation throughout the medieval period.

PATTERNS OF COMPILATION

Organizational principles of manuscripts containing romances include the construction of author corpora, of continuous narrative sequences, and of more mixed compilations, some of which exhibit thematic unity, while others are more varied.[3] Most commonly, verse and prose romances are transmitted separately. And romances in both prose and verse are most likely to be found in the company of other courtly or feudal narratives. The resulting anthologies may be focused on a particular type of text, such as Arthurian romance; or they may include a mix of romance and epic, and combine tales variously set in Antiquity, in the Carolingian era, in the Arthurian world, or in contemporary medieval times. Other anthologies, finally, are true miscellanies in which romances are transmitted with a wide range of other texts, including courtly and religious lyric, fabliaux, didactic allegory, and moral and devotional treatises. These patterns of transmission can be illustrated through a few examples.

One recurring pattern in French romance manuscripts is a chronological progression, generally beginning with the matter of Troy and Antiquity and moving into Arthurian material. Such compilations illustrate the topos of *translatio imperii* – the transfer of imperial power and culture from Greece or Troy to Rome and thence to medieval Europe – that is perhaps most famously articulated in the prologue to Chrétien's *Cligés*. A classic example is Paris, Bibliothèque Nationale, fonds français 1450, which dates from the mid-thirteenth century.[4] This manuscript opens with the *Roman de Troie*, narrating the Trojan War; the story is then continued with the flight of the surviving Trojans and their journey to Italy, in the *Roman d'Eneas*; Wace's *Roman de Brut*, which attributes the founding of Britain to a descendant of Eneas and carries the narrative into Arthurian times, links this ancient history to the medieval world. The account of Arthur's reign in the *Brut* is expanded through the insertion into the romance of Chrétien's five romances, a striking scribal intervention that will be discussed below. The final text in the collection is the prose *Dolopathos*, a version of the *Sept Sages de Rome*, and is set in imperial Rome. A similar progression of *romans antiques* and Arthurian romance occurs in the famous early thirteenth-century manuscript signed by the scribe Guiot (Paris, Bibliothèque Nationale, fonds français 794), which originally began with a series of texts treating of Classical Antiquity – *Athis et Prophilias*, *Troie*, *Brut*, and the *Empereurs de Rome* – before moving on to the Arthurian romances of Chrétien de Troyes.[5]

This pattern of chronological compilation, repeatedly found in French manuscripts, takes a different form in the German tradition, where it is less frequent. Unlike its French model, for example, Heinrich von Veldeke's *Eneide* is never coupled with Arthurian material, but is generally transmitted along with other romances set in Classical Antiquity – such as the romance of *Mai und Beaflor*, that of Troy, or that of Alexander – or with chronicles.[6] Manuscripts of the *Eneide* are thus similarly governed by a historical framework, but lack the specific preoccupation of using romance compilations to create a narrative continuity linking the ancient, Arthurian, and medieval worlds. A chronological progression can also be discerned in the mid-thirteenth-century manuscript St. Gall, Stiftsbibliothek, 857, which contains Wolfram's *Parzival*, the *Nibelungenlied* and *Klage*; Stricker's *Karl der Große*; Wolfram's *Willehalm*; and, added at the end, a hymn to the Virgin.[7] Here, the reader is led from the legendary Arthurian past and early heroic era, to the somewhat more historically grounded legends of the Carolingian world.

Author compilations are not common in the romance tradition; many romances are anonymous, and many known romance authors can be identified with only a single text. Nonetheless, there are a few instances – all the more striking for their rarity – in which several works by a single author are grouped together, creating an explicit or implicit author corpus. But even in these examples, it is not always clear to what extent authorship was a guiding factor in the compilation. Among German romance poets, only two – Wolfram von

Eschenbach and Hartmann von Aue – seem to have inspired author compilations, and both of these examples are problematical. Several works by Hartmann – his *Iwein*, first and second *Büchlein* (a treatise on love), and *Erec* – appear in the *Ambraser Heldenbuch* (Vienna, Österreichische Nationalbibliothek, Ser. n. 2663), a large anthology of twenty-five texts including both courtly romance and heroic epic as well as the humorous *mären*.[8] The late date of this compilation (1504–17) sets it somewhat apart from the main body of medieval manuscripts, although it is of course possible that its textual groupings reflect those found in earlier sources. In any case, the extent to which authorship influenced the compiler is far from clear. Hartmann's works do not form an unbroken series: the first three are separated from *Erec* by Heinrich von dem Türlin's *Mantel*, in which Erec and Arthur also figure, and which also addresses issues of love. One can only speculate whether the manuscript's compiler, or its original readers, would have considered *Erec* more closely bound to texts with which it shared an author, or those with which it shared narrative and thematic motifs. Moreover, neither Hartmann's lyric corpus nor his non-Arthurian works, *Der arme Heinrich* and *Gregorius*, are included. In a large anthology such as this, the presence of *Erec* and *Ywein* might well be due more to their common treatment of Arthurian material, or to their respective approaches to the conflict of love and chivalric exploits, than to their common authorship.

Assorted works by Wolfram von Eschenbach appear in the mid-thirteenth-century manuscript Munich, Bayerische Staatsbibliothek, Cgm 19, which originally contained Wolfram's *Parzival*, his *Titurel*, and his dawn songs.[9] At first sight one might well assume that these generically diverse texts were compiled as an author corpus. Yet it is notable that the volume does not contain all of Wolfram's works: his epic *Willehalm* is omitted. Thus while authorship was surely a factor, it is likely that the primary purpose of the compilation was to assemble two romances pertaining to the story of the Grail. Wolfram's lyrics could have been included not only on the basis of authorship, but also because their treatment of aristocratic love made them appropriate to a volume of amorous and chivalric adventures.

Among French romance authors, Chrétien de Troyes and – some hundred years later – Adenet le Roi are the only ones whose corpus can be found transmitted as a group. The poetic corpus of Adenet le Roi includes the romance *Cleomadés* and three *chansons de geste*. Normally these are transmitted individually or in the company of texts by different authors, but the late thirteenth-century manuscript Paris, Bibliothèque de l'Arsenal, 3142 – a large anthology of narrative and didactic verse evidently made for Marie de Brabant, wife of King Philip III of France – opens with the collected works of Adenet.[10] Adenet's authorial persona is stressed, furthermore, by an opening page miniature and two historiated initials presenting author portraits.

But as in the previous examples, here too a seemingly straightforward author compilation becomes more complicated upon closer examination. While it is surely no accident that Adenet's works are grouped together, and while Adenet's strong presence in prologues and epilogues does create a powerful authorial persona that carries over from one text to another, one must also consider that the anthology as a whole consists of texts compiled for the entertainment and edification of Marie de Brabant. Adenet began his career as minstrel at the court of Brabant, and maintained close ties with Marie. Common patronage may thus have been as much a factor in the Arsenal compilation as common authorship.

In the case of Chrétien de Troyes the situation is different, since no manuscripts survive that are contemporary with either the poet or his immediate patrons. Common patronage thus cannot explain the manuscript association of Chrétien's romances; but, as in the case of the Hartmann and Wolfram compilations, it is possible that narrative or thematic concerns influenced the assemblage of his romances. Two thirteenth-century manuscripts present all five of the romances now attributed with certainty to Chrétien: the Guiot manuscript (Paris, Bibliothèque Nationale, fonds français 794) and Paris, Bibliothèque Nationale, fonds français 1450.[11] Both are large anthologies containing works by other poets as well, and again it is difficult to assess the extent to which each can be considered to present an author corpus, preserved as such. Although Chrétien's romances did appear as a continuous series in the Guiot manuscript, there are no rubrics or miniatures identifying authorship. Only in Bibl. Nat. f. fr. 1450, where Chrétien's romances are inserted into Wace's *Brut*, are they identified as emanating from a single author. Thus while one cannot deny the significance of the various compilations of the works of Hartmann, Wolfram, Adenet, and Chrétien, Bibl. Nat. f. fr. 1450 is unique among surviving romance anthologies in explicitly heralding a series of romances as an author corpus. Ironically, it is also a copy in which most of Chrétien's prologues – those passages in which he names himself and discourses upon his authorial practices – have been omitted, and in which Chrétien's poetic œuvre is used to augment that of another author. The primary purpose of the sole surviving instance of an explicit presentation of a romance author corpus is apparently not that of highlighting the accomplishments of a particular author, but rather that of producing an authoritative account of the exploits of Arthur's knights.

The existence of these compilations is a tribute to Chrétien's powerful reputation as a poet. Nonetheless it is instructive that neither *Guillaume d'Angleterre* nor the songs attributed to Chrétien are included in any of the complete collections of the romances signed "Crestiens." The case of Chrétien is very much like that of Hartmann and Wolfram: the works of a famous romance author might be gathered together when they also shared a narrative frame or common courtly register, but authorship alone was not a sufficient basis for the compilation of generically or thematically diverse texts. And conversely, the mere presence of more than one text by the same author does not necessarily reflect any particular interest in authorship. Many romance anthologies simply present tales of love and chivalric adventure, undoubtedly chosen entirely on the basis of narrative interest. In this respect, romance manuscripts differ notably from lyric manuscripts in both French and German, the vast majority of which are arranged in author corpora. The organizational principles of romance manuscripts can, however, be compared to those of the *Heldenepik* and *chanson de geste* manuscripts compiled in the thirteenth and fourteenth centuries, which similarly tend to be grouped in narrative cycles with little or no concern for authorship.

The phenomenon of narrative compilation can be compared to that of poetic continuation, in which a romance perceived as incomplete is continued by a different poet. Chrétien's *Chevalier de la Charrette*, for example, is never found without the conclusion signed by Godefroi de Leigni. More spectacularly, his *Conte du Graal* inspired four lengthy continuations, at least one of which is included in all surviving manuscripts of that romance; indeed its accumulated continuations, written by various poets and pieced together by scribes, are many times longer than the original fragment left by Chrétien. Nor was the phenomenon of continuation unique to the French tradition. The *Tristan* of Gottfried von Straßburg is nearly always transmitted with one or more continuations.[12] In one manuscript of Wolfram's *Parzival*, material from the French continuations of Chrétien's *Conte du Graal* has been interpolated into the romance, while in another, *Parzival* is accompanied by *Titurel* as a means of expanding upon the Grail story. Both phenomena – the creation of narrative sequences and the production of continuations – reflect a view of the text as open, and of the manuscript volume as a space within which texts by different authors can interact and merge.

Perhaps the most impressive example of literary collaboration and compilation is the prose *Lancelot-Graal* cycle, which forms a more or less continuous story moving from the origins of the Grail through the rise and fall of Arthur's kingdom. The grand narrative constructed by these compilations focuses not on the transmission of the culture and imperial might of Classical Antiquity, but on the spread of Christianity and the sources of continuity – both genealogical and material – linking European Christendom to the immediate context of Christ's Passion. Although sheer length precludes the existence of manuscripts containing the entire *Lancelot-Graal* cycle, the composition of this series of closely associated texts by various anonymous authors, and their assemblage and emendation by scribal editors and compilers, is a process analogous to that of the compilation and continuation of verse romances.

The *Lancelot-Graal* was adapted into Middle High German prose in the *Prosa-Lancelot*, which comprises translations of the Old French *Lancelot*,

Queste dou saint graal, and *Mort le roi Artu*. Moreover, the vast verse romance *Der Jüngere Titurel* reflects a similar impulse to compile all of the stories relevant to the Grail. And just as the prose *Lancelot-Graal* cycle draws on earlier verse romances, so the *Jüngerer Titurel* is a continuation of Wolfram's unfinished *Titurel*, itself a supplementary text to his *Parzival*. Thus what French writers and scribes accomplished through the compilation of texts and continuations on the one hand, and the construction of a comprehensive prose cycle on the other, German poets accomplished through the creation of a large, composite text.

Finally, although romances are most commonly transmitted in the company of other courtly, feudal, and chivalric narratives, they also appear in more diverse compilations, some of which exhibit thematic unity. In the manuscript Prague, Státni knihovna CSSR, R VI Fc 26, dated 1464–67, the last eleven texts – which originally formed a separate codex – exhibit considerable generic diversity, including treatises on the art of love, love letters, *Minnereden*, and a single romance, Hartmann's *Ywein*.[13] The majority of these texts address the topic of love in one way or another, and it is most likely on that basis that *Ywein* was included. A late thirteenth-century manuscript of Chrétien's *Conte du Graal*, in turn (Paris, Bibliothèque Nationale, fonds français 12576) follows that romance with two devotional poems by the Reclus de Molliens, the *Miserere* and *Roman de Charité*, suggesting a view of the *Conte du Graal* as an exposition of the moral and spiritual aspects of knighthood.[14] Some manuscripts, finally, are true miscellanies, combining texts in different genres and sometimes even in different languages, and were surely conceived more as one-volume libraries conveniently bound into a single volume, than as unified books. It would be difficult to ascribe any particular rationale to the arrangement of texts in collections such as these. Instructive though it may be to identify the underlying principles of manuscript compilation, one must always bear in mind that not all medieval anthologies reflect a master plan.

THE ILLUSTRATION OF MEDIEVAL ROMANCE

Manuscripts of medieval romance range from low-budget productions with no decorations at all to lavishly illuminated luxury manuscripts. Among French manuscripts, a developed romance iconography does not appear before the mid-thirteenth century, while more extensive illustrative programs occur in German manuscripts even from the early thirteenth century. The format of romance illustration, moreover, is markedly different in French and German manuscript traditions. In French romance manuscripts, full-page or even three-quarter-page miniatures are rare. Instead, romances are typically illustrated with historiated initials or with framed miniatures set into one column of text or, less frequently, extending across the entire page (Fig. 4.2). Illustrated manuscripts of German romance, however, typically feature full-page illuminations arranged in two or three vertical registers, occupying both sides of the folio (Fig. 4.3). The French style is thus based on the illustration of individual narrative moments, with miniatures occurring at the point to which they refer; the illustrations, sometimes in conjunction with rubrics, both visualize the narrative and also mark its divisions. When multi-compartment miniatures do occur, they are usually at the beginning of a work, and provide visual introduction by illustrating its opening episodes. The German style, on the other hand, results in an alternation between textual and visual narrative, with the illustrations often placed at some remove from the episodes they depict.[15]

The iconography of medieval romance – and of vernacular literature in general – is far less fully studied and catalogued than that of sacred manuscripts, such as Bibles and Books of Hours. As a result, it is difficult to generalize about the nature of romance illustration as a genre. Here, I will approach the subject through the consideration of two key questions, both of which have been central to recent scholarly work. First, to what extent does the choice of episodes selected for illustration in a given manuscript, and the narrative or descriptive details included in the miniatures, offer a guide as to how the texts were understood by medieval audiences? And second, to what extent do the illustration and overall format of manuscripts allow us to gauge the relative importance of oral delivery and written transmission in the medieval reception of romance?

Certain aspects of romance illustration confirm conclusions about literary reception already suggested by the general survey of manuscripts. As one might expect from the relatively low importance of authorship in romance collections, for example, author portraits are extremely rare and, when they do occur, are commonly associated with the illustration of aristocratic patronage. Even when romance authors are depicted, in other words, this may be motivated less by an interest in authorial identity for its own sake than by a concern with the framework of patronage, and the relationship of the individual patron to the social and cultural values explored in the texts. In this respect it is noteworthy that no author portrait survives for Chrétien de Troyes, despite the striking instances of author corpora and the prominent presence of his name in prologues and epilogues. There is, however, an illustration of a noblewoman presumably to be identified with Marie de Champagne at the head of the *Chevalier de la Charrette* in the Guiot manuscript (see p. 136). Even though Chrétien's romances occupy an important place in this anthology, collectively providing an account of the Arthurian kingdom within a larger historical framework, the sole motif chosen for visual representation is the evocation of the local countess.

Much of the current work on romance illustration focuses on the examination of which episodes and descriptive details are selected for illustration, and on the comparison of illustrative cycles in different manuscripts of the same text. The

4.2 The illustration of the "eaten heart" episode in a fourteenth-century manuscript of the *Roman du castelain de Couci et de la dame de Fayel.*

4.3 An illustration of Lavinia and her mother in an early thirteenth-century manuscript of Heinrich von Veldeke's *Eneide*.

underlying assumption is that the artists – or the patron or manuscript planner who instructed them – would have chosen to illustrate those episodes deemed most important for his or her reading of the text. Thus Sandra Hindman, for example, has noted the omission of any representation of the marriage of Yvain and Laudine in the otherwise heavily illustrated copy of *Yvain* in Paris, Bibliothèque Nationale, fonds français 1433.[16] Yvain and Laudine are not depicted as a married couple until the very end, where a double miniature shows Yvain on his knees begging Laudine's forgiveness as well as a representation of the couple in bed. Hindman sees this omission as deliberate, serving to impose on Yvain's story the model of the young unmarried knight who wins his lady through a long process of chivalric exploits, and for whom marriage comes at the end, not in the middle, of the story. And Michael Curschmann, in a brief discussion of the illustrations of Gottfried's *Tristan* in the mid-thirteenth-century manuscript Munich, Staatsbibliothek, Cgm 51, points out that the artist deploys his images in such a way that the two sides of Tristan's character – invincible warrior and saviour of his people, and devoted lover, dependent on the good graces of Isolde – are juxtaposed in parallel sequences.[17] In this way Gottfried's romance becomes the vehicle for an exposition of the relationship between the public and private dimensions of knighthood.

In all, a complex assortment of factors would have governed the nature and distribution of miniatures in any given manuscript. Illustrative programs might be designed through careful reading of the text, but manuscript planners might also be influenced by other concerns, such as a desire to place miniatures at more or less regular intervals, or financial constraints requiring sparse illustration or the cessation of illustration beyond a certain point in the text. A reluctance or inability to conceive new images, in turn, might limit an artist to the illustration of stock scenes such as battles and banquets – or to the appropriation, for entirely pragmatic reasons, of visual models from other literary genres. But while such considerations certainly recommend prudence in our interpretation of romance iconography, the study of illustrative cycles and of iconographic patterns remains no less important; for a series of illustrations might still play a role in shaping reception of the text in question, even if it was not originally intended as an interpretive statement.

Among French manuscripts, prose romances are overall more heavily illustrated than verse ones. This phenomenon has led many scholars to the conclusion that prose romances can be linked to the advent of a different kind of reading, a reception more visual and more linked to the book; whereas verse romances, at least initially, were more likely to be received through oral reading or recitation. Not only illustration but also rubrication varies considerably among manuscripts. Verse romances often lack internal rubrication entirely, especially in copies dating from before the end of the thirteenth century, again suggesting that such manuscripts may have been intended primarily for oral reading. According to this view, illustration and rubrication alike would have developed as an aid to the private reading of romance and as a visual enhancement of books intended to be seen, and not merely heard, by their owners.

There is no question that oral reading and recitation were common means by which medieval audiences received romances.[18] Numerous texts include descriptions of such scenes. The narrator of *Floire et Blancheflor* claims to have first heard the story he is about to present as it was told by an aristocratic lady to her sister; she in turn learned it from a *clerc*, who had found it in a book. This scenario – whatever its degree of fiction or truth as regards the origins of *Floire et Blancheflor* – points to a mixed practice in aristocratic society of oral and written transmission, in which stories might be read aloud from books; then recounted and probably elaborated upon without the benefit of the book; then proposed, possibly in altered form, to a poet who would commit the story once again to writing, probably with further elaborations of his own. The famous prologue of Chrétien's *Charrete*, in which he claims to have received the substance of the story from Marie de Champagne, suggests a similar practice.

That romances were read aloud is further indicated in the frequent use of formulaic expressions such as "Listen, lords" and "Now you will hear," as well as in narrative passages that describe the oral consumption of romance. An oft-cited passage in the "Pesme aventure" episode of Chrétien's *Yvain* describes an aristocratic maiden reading a romance to her parents. And in the early thirteenth-century *Galeran de Bretagne*, the heroine distinguishes between oral and visual reception of different kinds of literary material in describing her own pastimes, including literary consumption: "Que je ne face aultre mestier / Le jour fors lire mon saultier / Et faire euvre d'or ou de soie, / Oÿr de Thebes ou de Troie" ("that I pursue no other occupation every day but to read my psalter, and do needlework in gold or silk [and] hear about Thebes and Troy" (3879–82)). This enumeration of a young girl's daily activities suggests the different ways in which different literary material was experienced: sacred scripture through private reading, romances through oral reading or recitation. A predominantly oral reception of romance could explain the relative lack of rubrication and illumination in romance manuscripts copied before the late thirteenth century.

The oral reading of romances, however, was not limited to the early period of verse romance composition. In his *Dit dou florin*, written in 1389, Jean Froissart states that he entertained Gaston Phebus, Count of Foix, for an entire winter with an oral reading of his voluminous romance *Meliador*, presented in brief nightly installments. And in his *Espinette amoureuse*, written about 1369, Froissart's persona falls in love with a lady whom he finds engaged in a reading of *Cleomadés*, and who agrees to meetings in which the two take turns reading aloud to one another.

These passages and others like them show that various patterns of reading – oral and silent, private and public – coexisted in the reception of romance from the twelfth through the fourteenth centuries at least. The mere fact that an aristocratic patron hired a poet to read aloud did not necessarily mean that the former was not perfectly capable of reading books and admiring their visual qualities. Gaston Phebus, for example, was himself the author of a treatise on hunting, preserved in lavishly illuminated manuscripts. The passage in *Yvain*, like that in the *Espinette amoureuse* two centuries later, suggests that the aristocratic owners of manuscripts might themselves have been the ones to read them aloud; in this case, they could certainly have benefited from miniatures and rubrics, and illustrations could easily have been shown to the small groups described in these passages.

In what ways, then, might prose romances be linked to a movement toward a more visual mode of romance reception, one more centered on the book and less dependent on oral presentation? And how might such a process be reflected in changing practices of manuscript illustration and rubrication? Many prose romances themselves date from before the middle of the thirteenth century, and are thus contemporary with the earliest surviving manuscripts of verse romance. The rise of literary prose, and the gradual process by which it virtually replaced verse romance, coincides with the production of vernacular manuscripts of all kinds in increasing numbers. The distribution of surviving manuscripts reflects both the huge popularity of the great prose romances, and the extent to which a vogue for verse romance in the twelfth and earlier thirteenth centuries was replaced, during the later thirteenth and fourteenth centuries, by one for prose. Of the twelfth-century verse romances of Tristan, for example – those of Béroul and Thomas d'Angleterre – there remain only fragments, while the thirteenth-century prose *Tristan* survives in over eighty copies. The romances of Chrétien seem to have enjoyed a wider distribution, to judge from the considerable number of thirteenth-century copies, but even they do not survive in manuscripts dating from later than the early fourteenth century; while copies of the prose *Lancelot-Graal* cycle survive in far greater numbers, and date from the thirteenth through the fifteenth centuries.

Paradoxically, the increased production throughout the thirteenth century of illuminated copies of verse romances, and of large verse compilations, may be a reflection of the same social and cultural forces that also fostered the rise and eventual dominance of prose romance. In fact, it is likely that the reception of verse romance in the later thirteenth and fourteenth centuries was influenced by familiarity with the prose romances. In Chrétien's *Conte du Graal*, for example, the representation of the Grail as a liturgical vessel reflects a sacramental reading of this mysterious object that is more fully developed in the *Lancelot-Graal* cycle than in Chrétien's text and its continuations.[19] Moreover, the scenes selected for illustration in the *Conte du Graal* are quite frequently those corresponding to episodes in the prose cycle, suggesting again that the verse rendition of the Grail quest was increasingly read through the lens of the prose version.[20] That the prose cycle in some way helped to shape the illustration of the *Conte du Graal* further supports the contention that the impulse to produce illuminated copies of Chrétien's romance was itself linked to the more visually oriented culture of reading associated with the rise of prose romance.

Evidence concerning medieval lay literacy is scant and difficult to interpret, but overall it does appear that while some twelfth-century aristocrats may have been capable of reading romances, their numbers would have been small; and that lay literacy, at least in the vernacular, increased markedly over the thirteenth and fourteenth centuries. While both verse and prose romances can obviously be read either silently or aloud, and while both are transmitted in manuscripts both with and without decoration, prose romances may well have arisen in response to a growing demand among the laity for reading material. The development of more elaborate programs of illustration and rubrication in vernacular manuscripts – including but by no means limited to romance – would be a further result of the growing market for vernacular books, and of the increased expectation that the lay owners of such books would not merely hear them read aloud by a court minstrel or *clerc*, but would also read the books themselves in both private and group settings.

As the foregoing discussion has indicated, the study of romance manuscripts sheds light primarily on questions of literary reception. Although manuscripts provide our only means of access to medieval texts, the study of manuscripts themselves, as cultural artefacts, generally tells us more about subsequent readers of those texts than about the circumstances of their composition or the meaning that they held for their original audiences. It is not until the late thirteenth century that one finds romance manuscripts more or less contemporary with the texts that they contain, and most surviving manuscripts postdate the composition of the texts by anywhere from a few decades to two or three centuries. This gap is an important aspect of the study of medieval literature, since it means that for the twelfth and much of the thirteenth centuries, we have no means of accessing texts exactly as they were formed by their authors or received by their first audiences. Through careful analysis of their contents, however, manuscripts can allow us to approach, at least, the earlier textual versions that lie behind the surviving copies. And the evidence that they provide for literary reception can, in turn, help us to establish a literary and cultural context for the work of contemporary poets, even if those works themselves are preserved only in later copies.

NOTES

1 See Elspeth Kennedy, "The Scribe as Editor," in *Mélanges Jean Frappier*, vol. 1, Textes Littéraires Français (Geneva: Droz, 1970), 523–31; Mary B. Speer, "Wrestling with Change: Old French Textual Criticism and *Mouvance*," *Olifant*, 7 (1980), 317–23.

2 For discussions of editorial practice and how it has evolved, see Bergmann and Gärtner, eds., *Methoden und Probleme*; Foulet and Speer, *On Editing Old French Texts*.

3 For descriptions of the contents of selected romance manuscripts, see Becker, *Handschriften und Frühdrucke*; Busby, *et al.*, eds., *Manuscripts of Chrétien de Troyes*.

4 Sylvia Huot, *From Song to Book*, 27–32; Lori Walters, "Le Rôle du scribe dans l'organisation des manuscrits des romans de Chrétien de Troyes," *Romania*, 106 (1985), 303–25.

5 See Mario Roques, "Le Manuscrit fr. 794 de la Bibliothèque Nationale et le scribe Guyot," *Romania*, 73 (1952), 177–99.

6 On the *Eneide*, see Becker, *Handschriften und Frühdrucke*, 19–29, 168–69.

7 See *ibid.*, 78–79.

8 See *ibid.*, 52 and 153–55.

9 See *ibid.*, 82–85.

10 See Huot, *From Song to Book*, 39–45.

11 For descriptions and discussion of these and other Chrétien manuscripts, see Busby, *et al.*, eds., *Manuscripts of Chrétien de Troyes*. The so-called Annonay manuscript, dating from the late twelfth or early thirteenth century and surviving only in fragments, also contained at least four of Chrétien's romances.

12 See Becker, *Handschriften und Frühdrucke*, 35–51 and 170–71.

13 See *ibid.*, 73–75.

14 See Hindman, *Sealed in Parchment*, 38–39.

15 On the differences between the French and German styles of romance illustration, see Michael Curschmann, "Images of Tristan," in *Gottfried von Straßburg and the Medieval Tristan Legend*, ed. A. Stevens and R. Wisbey (Cambridge: Brewer, 1990), 1–17.

16 Hindman, *Sealed in Parchment*, 52.

17 Curschmann, "Images of Tristan."

18 See Green, *Medieval Listening and Reading*.

19 Emmanuèle Baumgartner, "Les Scènes du Graal et leur illustration dans les manuscrits du *Conte du Graal* et des *Continuations*," in Busby, *et al.*, eds., *Manuscripts of Chrétien de Troyes*, vol. 1, 497–98.

20 Busby, "Illustrated Manuscripts of Chrétien's *Perceval*," 360.

SUGGESTIONS FOR FURTHER READING

Becker, Peter Jörg. *Handschriften und Frühdrucke mittelhochdeutscher Epen*. Wiesbaden: Ludwig Reicher, 1977.

Busby, Keith, Terry Nixon, M. Alison Stones, and Lori Walters, eds. *The Manuscripts of Chrétien de Troyes*, 2 vols. Amsterdam: Rodopi, 1994.

Foulet, Alfred, and Mary Speer. *On Editing Old French Texts*, Edward C. Armstrong Monographs on Medieval Literature, 1. Lawrence: Regents Press of Kansas, 1979.

Gärtner, Kurt, ed. *Methoden und Probleme der Edition mittelalterlicher deutscher Texte*. Tübingen: Max Niemeyer, 1993.

Green, Dennis H. *Medieval Listening and Reading: The Primary Reception of German Literature 800–1300*. Cambridge University Press, 1994.

Hindman, Sandra. *Sealed in Parchment: Readings of Knighthood in the Illuminated Manuscripts of Chrétien de Troyes*. University of Chicago Press, 1994.

Honemann, Volker, and Nigel F. Palmer, eds. *Deutsche Handschriften 1100–1400: Oxforder Kolloquium 1985*. Tübingen: Max Niemeyer, 1988.

Huot, Sylvia. *From Song to Book: The Poetics of Writing in Old French Lyric and Lyrical Narrative Poetry*. Ithaca: Cornell University Press, 1987.

II

EUROPEAN ROMANCE AND MEDIEVAL SOCIETY: ISSUES FOR DEBATE

5

SARAH KAY

Courts, clerks, and courtly love

The term "courtly love" was coined in 1883 by Gaston Paris with reference to *Le Chevalier de la Charrete* (also known as the *Lancelot*) by Chrétien de Troyes, the earliest surviving narrative of the adulterous love between Arthur's knight Lancelot and his Queen Guenevere.[1] This romance, with its disquieting combination of illicit sex and quasi-mystical love, has remained ever since in the forefront of discussions of what "courtly love" might be. The resulting drawback of these discussions, in my view, has been their assumption that such love was susceptible of codification as a system of rules or doctrines. This essay will seek to locate "courtly love" more broadly as a series of questions which are debated across large numbers of texts, and which can be traced back to the tensions within medieval court life. These tensions are responded to very differently by Chrétien's immediate precursors, the *Eneas* seeking to contain them within safe limits while the *Tristan* romances give rein to their potential disruptiveness. Within the two poles represented by these two influential stories, Chrétien himself explores various ways of negotiating the pressures of medieval court life. His *Lancelot* is the most famous, but by no means definitive, outcome of these explorations.

In this romance, Lancelot follows on the tracks of Guenevere who has been abducted from Arthur's court by Meleagant and taken to his remote kingdom, Gorre. Lancelot secures the Queen's release, and the liberation of the many other prisoners from Arthur's lands who are also held there, by fighting Meleagant; he appears in the role of a saviour, a Redeemer even. However, Lancelot's motive for these deeds is not some altruistic desire to free the oppressed but his adulterous love for the Queen. Just thinking of her makes him unconscious of the world around him; when he finds a comb with some of her hairs in it, he swoons in adoration. If he is a Redeemer, it is (at least in part) because he would be willing to suffer death for the sake of Love. Thus on his way to Gorre Lancelot must cross a river by a bridge formed from the blade of a sword; he cuts his palms and the soles of his feet in a way reminiscent of the wounding of Christ's hands and feet on the cross (3102–09). Once in Gorre, he consummates his passion for the Queen in a night of love which is described in explicitly religious language:

> et puis vint au lit la reïne,
> si l'aore et se li ancline,
> car an nul cors saint ne croit tant.
>
> . . .
>
> Au lever fu il droiz martirs,
> tant li fu gries li departirs
> car il i suefre grant martire.   (4651–53, 4689–91)

[and then he came to the queen's bed, and worships and bows down before her, for there is no holy relic in which he has greater faith . . . When he rose he was just like a martyr, so sorry was he to leave since it makes him suffer such great martyrdom.]

Lancelot escapes undetected but the following day Kay, who had also followed Guenevere to Gorre, is falsely charged with having slept with her. This alleged adultery is roundly condemned by Kay and Meleagant; we are left to surmise whether Lancelot should be thought guilty of the same charge. Quasi-mystical love and adulterous sex are provocatively compounded, the text apparently meting out to Lancelot both condemnation and acclaim.

The *Lancelot* was composed, so the prologue asserts, on the instruction of Marie de Champagne, wife of Henry the Liberal, Count of Champagne (*r.* 1152–81), and regent for her son during her widowhood (1181–97). Although the dates of Chrétien's romances are uncertain, the *Lancelot* is thought to date from the late 1170s, when Henry was still alive. By the time Marie is a widow, Chrétien is addressing the prologue of his final romance, *Le Conte du Graal* (*Perceval*), to Philip, Count of Flanders (*r.* 1157–91). Here, the love interest is vastly reduced as compared with all Chrétien's other romances; what predominates is a quest oriented towards what appear to be spiritual goals. Perceval must find the grail castle, and ask the questions that will restore its wounded king to health and its devastated lands to fertility. Like Lancelot, his role is to be a rescuer, and even a Redeemer, but in the "safer" sphere of kingship and, indeed, of religion. The controversial metaphors of the *Lancelot* have, it would seem, returned to relatively unproblematic literal usage.

In 1175, at about the time Chrétien is thought to have been composing the *Lancelot*, Philip discovered that his own wife, Isabelle of Vermandois, was involved in an adulterous liaison with one of his knights. He set a trap for the couple, caught them together, and had the knight shamefully killed by having his head held down a sewer; the Countess he confined to her apartments.[2] When Isabelle died in 1182, Philip for a while courted Marie de Champagne; but in 1184 he instead married Mathilda of Portugal. The composition of the *Perceval* has been thought to coincide with the relationship between Marie and Philip, during which time they acted as political allies against the strengthening powers of the French king, Philip Augustus.

This brief history poses a number of conundrums about the relationship between courtly literature and courtly society, and between court poets and their patrons. Marie de Champagne was the widow of a count, and Philip of Flanders was a count likewise. Such people belonged to the aristocracy, which in the twelfth century regarded itself as an hereditary caste, distinguished by inherited "blood" as well as by inherited estates.[3] Both the Count of Champagne and the Count of Flanders directly controlled more wealth and human resources than did the King of France at the same period. (The French king did not become more powerful than his vassals until the expansionist policies of Philip Augustus, who ruled 1180–1223, had borne fruit.) Clearly the male members of the aristocracy allowed themselves more sexual freedom than was compatible with the teaching of the Church, which frowned on all sexual activity outside marriage, and set strict limits even on marital sex. Clearly, also, these same men would be adamantly opposed to adultery by their wives, since on the wife's fidelity depended the assurance that the family's "blood" and estates passed to the lord's own children. Yet a married female patron can, apparently, commission a romance that paints adultery in terms of mystical adoration at roughly the same time as a neighboring aristocrat is basely executing an adulterous rival. And the self-same aristocrat serves as dedicatee of a far more "proper" romance even though he, at about the same time, aspires to a liaison with that same female patron. The fictions of romance, then, certainly are not a direct reflection of the social practices of their audience, although they may of course reflect their fantasies.

A further turn to the complexity of these relationships is provided by the fact that Chrétien probably did not finish either romance. The epilogue of the *Lancelot* claims that Chrétien entrusted its completion to a clerk who names himself Godfrey de Lagny. It has been suggested that this is merely a feint, and that Chrétien himself completed the romance under an assumed name;[4] if true, this would represent an even more striking disavowal of its contents than his merely failing to finish it. The *Perceval* likewise lacks an ending, a subsequent continuator attributing its incomplete state to Chrétien's having died. It is a bizarre coincidence that Chrétien should have failed to complete in his own name either of the romances whose composition was undertaken for a named patron, whereas he had no difficulty in finishing three others, none of which names a dedicatee. We witness here an uneasy collaboration between people of different social standing (high-ranking patrons and a commissioned writer), as also a somewhat awkward negotiation between different kinds of discourse (those of secular love and knighthood, and of religious experience). The unfinished state of the *Lancelot* and the *Perceval* suggests that these relations of collaboration and negotiation may actually have broken down, or at least been suspended. To probe these relations, we need to look more closely at the role of the court in the formation of ideas of courtliness and courtly love.

COURTLINESS AND COURTLY LOVE

There have been many attempts to define what one might mean by courtly love.[5] For Gaston Paris,[6] it entails furtiveness because of the risk of discovery, especially for the woman; a consequent raising of her prestige *vis-à-vis* her lover, whom she may treat capriciously; the responding willingness of the man to demonstrate his devotion by deeds of prowess; and adherence to a code of manners or rules. The next most influential definition of courtly love was probably that of C. S. Lewis,[7] for whom it consists in submission to the precepts of Humility, Courtesy, Adultery and the Religion of Love. The 1960s saw a lively controversy about the term "courtly love." Was it "an impediment to the understanding of medieval texts," as claimed in the title of a provocative essay by D. W. Robertson, Jr., who held that medieval society could never have licensed a literature praising adultery?[8] The traditional view, defending and refining the term "courtly love" against Robertson's onslaught, was maintained by Jean Frappier.[9] Since then, the influence of the German Marxist critic Erich Köhler has led to more sociological (including feminist) approaches to the nature of medieval love. Köhler's own view was that "courtly love" served as a means of uniting upper and lower nobility in a common ideology;[10] R. Howard Bloch countered that, through "courtly love," the individual accepts subjection to an impersonal authority ("Love") which anticipates that of the modern citizen to the "state."[11] Similarly concerned with courtly love as a fundamentally political problematic are feminist medievalists who denounce its misogyny and masculine bias.[12] Bloch responded to this by exposing the ecclesiastical bases of this misogyny.[13] In a different tradition, psychoanalytic critics have sought to identify courtly love with psychic expressions of desire.[14] The *Lancelot* is important or even central in most of the above discussions.

The term "courtly love" itself reflects modern critical assumptions more than medieval practice. The expression *amour courtois* is rarely attested in medieval texts, which speak instead of *fin' amor* (in Occitan) or *amour fine* (in French); of *bone amour*, or simply *amour* (as in *aimer par amour*). Of these medieval terms, only *fin' amor* is widely used today. Prior to the success of the term "courtly love," medievalists of the late eighteenth and nineteenth centuries experimented with other designations, such as "chivalrous love."[15] This range and hesitancy in nomenclature between medieval and modern usage reflects potential differences of emphasis. "Chivalrous love" centers attention on the male lover-hero, who alone can embody chivalry. "Courtly love" emphasizes a link between love, its social setting (the court), and its ways (courtliness): the set of social qualities and skills required for distinction at court, and which include refined speech, elegance of manner and dress, cheerfulness and deference – a polished exterior which, to the skeptical, could be equated with hypocrisy. *Fin' amor*, by contrast, draws attention away from either social rank or social setting to concentrate on the intensity and purity of inner feeling (the word *fin* suggests the refining of metal, and images of love as refining, in this sense, are not uncommon in courtly texts). It may be quite asocial or even antisocial; the lovers in Beroul's *Tristan* describe their love as *fine* (2722), and live at odds with their community, to the point of being expelled from it.

While I shall continue to use the term "courtly love," I wish not to lose sight of this tension between inner intensity and outward decorum which the dichotomy *fin' amor* – "courtly love" suggests. Indeed, the combining of spiritual and sexual elements, which is characteristic of so many "courtly love" texts, vividly invokes this tension between desire and regulation. In my view, the reason why courtly love is so elusive of definition is precisely that courtly representations of love are built upon internal tensions, while also seeking to mask them. Courtly texts do not so much propound precepts as raise alternatives, permitting contradictions to surface, but within a restricted agenda of shared preoccupations. Is love foolish or moderate? Ecstatic or rational? Socially beneficial or antisocial? Spiritual or sensual? The tensions underlying this agenda stem from the environment in which courtly literature was produced. If we want to understand the internal complexities of courtly literature, and the complex interaction between courtly poets, courtly patrons, courtly literature, and courtliness, we must scrutinize what they all have in common: the court.

As Bezzola has shown, courtly literature seems to have arisen from the literary activity of feudal and princely, rather than royal, courts. The period of its development is *c.* 1100–1160, and it apparently originated in Poitou-Aquitaine, and among the counts of Anjou just to the north of Poitou, before spreading to England following the accession of the Angevin family to the throne of England; links with southwestern France were then reaffirmed by the marriage between Henry II and Eleanor Aquitaine in 1154. Its momentum, still according to Bezzola, derived from the interaction between aristocracy and clergy in secular courts.[16] The early twelfth century saw what has been described as a "managerial revolution" whereby the administration of aristocratic households (the basis of the "court") grew enormously more complex.[17] It became standard practice for courts to adopt the imperial model of two departments: a lay department whose principal officers were the chamberlain, seneschal, constable, butler, household knights and other minor functionaries; and a clerical one, headed by one or more chaplains, with a team of subordinate clerks.[18] By "clerks" is meant individuals in holy orders; these were exclusively men who had attained some level of education, but were not necessarily "clergy" in the modern sense. Clerks admitted to the three degrees of major orders – priests, deacons, and sub-deacons – were committed in principle to celibacy. Then there were clerks in minor orders, who were educated men fitted to administrative or diplomatic tasks: writing letters, reading aloud, or keeping records.

These two groups, lay and clerical, that made up the household staff, were united by their common aim of servicing the political, economic, and administrative needs of the court, and of staging the increasingly showy lifestyle of the twelfth-century aristocracy. Often, senior clerical and lay staff would stem from the same family background, and close ranks against anyone perceived as outsiders.[19] Court clerks promoted literacy and learning in lay princes, whilst themselves serving as courtiers of their masters. Under the influence of such clerks, the aristocracy became progressively more "clericalized," whilst the clerks, conversely, became increasingly engaged in lay interest. Yet there were also ample reasons for tension between the two groups, who belonged, in medieval social thinking, to two separate "orders," each with its characteristic training, dress, and expectations, and dependent legally on separate jurisdictions. Clerks were dependent on canon law, and were tried in church courts, whereas justice was administered to the laity in secular courts. There is plenty of evidence both of lay anticlericalism, and of clerical condemnation of the lay courtly world.[20]

The convergence of clerical and lay interest which gives rise to "courtliness" was therefore not a smooth nor an uncontested process. The earliest vernacular literature to explore the emergent notion of courtly love was that of the troubadours, originating apparently in the entourage of William, ninth Duke of Aquitaine and seventh Count of Poitou (r. 1086–1126). Some of William's own compositions are fiercely anticlerical, and controversy about the ethics of *amor* raged in the generation of troubadours who succeeded him. By the time of the troubadour Bernart de Ventadorn (fl. 1147–70), the characteristic contradictoriness of *fin' amor* is well in evidence. Love is described as simultaneously social (the source of all worth, a model for human relations) and antisocial (bringing folly and isolation to the lover); as both sensual and erotic in its desire for physical union, yet also as deeply spiritual. This view of love, then, effects a balancing act between lay and clerical discourses, but one that is precarious, and whose immediate past is full of controversy.[21]

Bernart de Ventadorn provides one context in which to read the *Lancelot* – and with it, modern discussions of courtly love – since he and Chrétien appear to have known one another: they exchanged lyric poems in which they debate the passionate versus the rational aspects of love.[22] Marie de Champagne, whom Chrétien credits with the "substance and meaning" of the *Lancelot*, was doubly connected with the Aquitanian–Angevin axis of courtly writing. Marie's mother Eleanor was grand-daughter of William IX (the first troubadour), daughter of William X (a significant troubadour patron) and, by the 1170s, wife of Henry II

Plantagenet (for a time apparently a patron of Bernart de Ventadorn). And Marie's husband, Henry the Liberal, was a cousin (though not a close one) of Henry II: they had the same great grandfather, William the Conqueror. There is, therefore, both a personal and what we might call an institutional basis for Chrétien's responsiveness to the "courtly" ideas in contemporary Occitan poetry.

The strength of Chrétien's link with the court of Champagne has been questioned, since his name does not appear in court documents.[23] However, recent work on the troubadours suggests that they may have been court retainers, often but not always clerks, who composed and performed under a stage name, thus providing a service additional to their administrative duties.[24] "Chrétien" has all the appearance of an assumed name, upon which the author likes to pun, and which, together with the surname "Troie"/Troy, allows him to play on the conjunction (or disjunction) of Christian and Classical (hence pagan) elements in courtly literature.[25] Maybe, then, the author we know as "Chrétien" was an administrator whose intervention in the clerical–lay dialectic of contemporary court life is signaled by his very *nom de plume*: both laity and clergy would see themselves as "Christian," and the adoption of this name may mark a desire to smooth over potential rifts within a court audience. In the two romances which he left unfinished he may have felt that this involvement tipped uncomfortably towards one extreme or other of the dialectic: towards profane interest in the *Lancelot* (when he is bidden to depict adulterous love in quasi-religious terms), and towards clerical interest in the *Perceval* (when he is commissioned to write about spiritualized knighthood). It is noteworthy that when both stories are recast as part of the vast early thirteenth-century prose *Lancelot-Grail*, the tension between secular and religious preoccupation is mitigated, with religion coming off best: Lancelot's love for Guenevere is "sinful" and prevents him achieving the (now more emphatically Christian) adventure of the Holy Grail.

I turn now to the relatively safer ground in the middle, which Chrétien occupies in his other romances, and which many other "courtly love" writers also explored.

CLERKS, LOVE, AND THE SCHOOLS

Clerks were above all men of education, who need not have identified strongly with the Church and its teachings. Education meant, in the first instance, a knowledge of Latin, and thus the ability to read and imitate the literature of Classical Antiquity. The twelfth century has been described as an "age of Ovid" because of the predominant influence of writings by the Classical Latin poet Ovid particularly on the literature of love. Ovidian motifs – love as a fever, a sweet pain or a welcome wound, the beloved as a medicine or an enemy to be overcome – are scattered throughout the lyric poetry of the troubadours. An even more important element of the Ovidian inheritance is writerly self-awareness about love as an art of literary composition as much as of emotion. Medieval courtiers composing for performances at court were obviously alert to this self-consciously performative dimension of their texts, which from the 1150s onwards included works we categorize as romances. A work in this tradition, although not a romance, is Andreas Capellanus's *De Arte honeste amandi* (*Art of Courtly Love*). This clever and ironic text humorously applies medieval techniques of intellectual codification and argument to the Ovidian erotic tradition, with such success that for a long time scholars accepted it as a serious treatise on love. [26]

Ovid's influence is particularly strong on courtly texts dating from the period *c.* 1150–1170, which saw the composition of the Old French *Piramus et Thisbe*, *Philomena*, and *Narcissus* (all based on Ovid's *Metamorphoses*). During this same period, the *romans antiques* (adaptations into the vernacular of Latin epic poems) were also composed. This is the peak, as far as literature is concerned, of what is referred to as twelfth-century humanism. The most influential, as also the most "Ovidian," of the *romans antiques* was the *Roman d'Eneas*. This translation/adaptation of Virgil's *Aeneid* was probably undertaken for Plantagenet patrons, and contains an enormously expanded treatment, in the Ovidian manner, of the love between Eneas (Aeneas) and Lavinia and their eventual marriage. Its favorable reception appears to have determined the success of romance as a genre. By saving Aeneas from the clutches of an unworthy Dido, but instead marrying him to a suitable heiress, and declaring him the founder of Rome, the *Eneas* shrewdly combines the theme of love with those of marriage, dynasty, and empire. Here is a safe outcome for a love which is still clearly in some senses "courtly": cultivating inner intensity and outward elegance of expression, phrased in a complex Ovidian rhetoric, composed for a court, by a court poet, and calculated not to alienate male aristocratic interest.[27] Like Lancelot, Eneas is symbolically wounded in the cause of love; Lavinia fires an arrow at him with a love letter around it, and though the arrow misses him, the letter "wounds" him with reciprocal desire. This "wound" prepares the way for marriage and empire, a far cry from the disturbing stigmata of martyrdom later endured by Lancelot.[28]

Chrétien's debt to the *Eneas* is manifest in explicit borrowings from it, most notably in *Erec* and *Cligés*.[29] The enormous importance of the Troy legend in his day (Aeneas came originally from Troy, and twelfth-century kings of both France and England laid claim to Trojan ancestry) may have motivated the surname "de Troie," which appears in *Erec*, and which seems to draw attention to the Classical, humanist preoccupations of court poetry at the time of its composition. The *Eneas* may also have influenced the way Chrétien combines love with marriage (though less obviously with dynasty and empire) in his romances of *Erec* and *Yvain*, and also (though more problematically) *Cligés*. The celebration of a refined but passionate love which culminates in marriage is also found in numerous other romances: for example, *Floire et Blancheflor* and *Ille et Galeron* (both appearing in the wake of the *Eneas*), or *Jaufre*, a later (*c.* 1225–28?) Occitan romance indebted both to the northern French model of Arthurian romance and to the courtly love poetry of the troubadours. I shall look here more closely at the example of *Cligés*.

The first part of this romance tells how a young knight, Alexander,[30] son of the emperor of Byzantium, goes to Arthur's court, where he falls in love with Guenevere's attendant, Soredamors. After much Ovidian love-rhetoric, clearly imitated from the *Eneas*, the couple marry, but die shortly after the birth of their child, Cligés. Like Alexander, Cligés also goes to Arthur's court, but he has already fallen in love and, unluckily for him, with the bride (Fenice) of his uncle Alis, his father's younger brother. As a result of an earlier agreement with Alexander, Alis is nominally Emperor of Byzantium (though Alexander retained effective power); Alis swore an oath not to marry so that he would have no heirs to contest Cligés's succession. There is, therefore, poetic justice in Cligés's falling in love with Alis's bride, and she with him. However, the couple do not consummate their love until, by a series of clever devices, they have (1) prevented Alis from consummating his marriage, (2) convinced him that Fenice is dead and (3) concealed her in an ingeniously contrived hideaway where Cligés can visit her. Eventually they are discovered, but Alis dies of rage on learning he has been deceived, and Cligés and Fenice take the throne.

All these maneuvers are highly questionable from a moral and even a legal standpoint, but they are a humorous development of the thematics of the *Eneas*: how can one combine love, marriage, dynasty, and empire, when "real life" seems determined to make them incompatible? In a scene modeled on Lavinia's dialogue with her mother in *Eneas*, Fenice consults with her governess Thessala, and realizes that she loves Cligés. Since she is on the point of marrying Alis, her consternation is understandable. How is she going to remain true to the man she loves? This "courtly" aspiration to an ideal love is comically twinned with a far more practical concern. How is she to avoid bearing Alis a child who might deprive Cligés of his inheritance? Thessala's solution – a potion which will render Alis impotent – incongruously combines symbolic invocation of the magic of true love with the pragmatic value of a contraceptive device. This plot acknowledges the anxiety of male aristocrats regarding adultery – on the part of their wives, that is – and humorously directs it to an outcome which has a specious air of legitimacy and reassurance. As the only son of an eldest son, Cligés has a right to the empire; the young couple, tormented by love, have their hearts set on its healing union; and therefore (the spurious argument runs), they have a double right to drug and deceive Fenice's husband. That this conclusion does not really satisfy anyone is betrayed by the romance's closing lines, recording how all future empresses of Byzantium were kept under guard and attended only by eunuchs. The harmony between love, marriage, dynasty, and empire is not easily, or convincingly, achieved. The unproblematic assurances of the *Eneas* are humorously undermined. They may have obtained in the remote past, but *Cligés*, with its host of references to contemporary life,[31] is unable to endorse them.

RELIGIOUS AND SACRILEGIOUS LOVE

Another important element in *Cligés* is its explicit relationship with the story of Tristan and Iseut. If the *Eneas* provides a model for a domesticated passion reconcilable with patriarchal interest, the *Tristan* is its antithesis, a constant threat of adultery and social breakdown. The two poles of the *Eneas* and the *Tristan* structure Chrétien's thinking throughout his *oeuvre*. In wanting to remain true to Cligés, Fenice seeks to avoid Iseut's predicament of sleeping with two men (3099–114); in deciding to pretend to "die" and then go into hiding rather than run away with Cligés, she is likewise seeking to avoid the *Tristan* lovers' public outlawry (5195–59). In the *Lancelot*, the scene of Kay's trial for allegedly sleeping with Guenevere is also imitated from the *Tristan*, inviting us to compare the lovers in the two stories.

The *Tristan* legend stems from a quite different cultural background from the *Eneas* – Celtic rather than Classical – and its magical and fatalistic elements give it a quite different appeal from the relatively rational and optimistic outlook of the *Eneas*. Tristan was adopted as the prototype of the courtly lover from very early in the troubadour tradition, so we suppose that one of the earliest surviving romances, signed by Thomas – like the *Eneas*, it is a product of Anglo-Norman courtly society, but survives only in fragments probably dating from the 1160s – is certainly not the first. Thomas's text demonstrates to what extent the *Tristan* story, as treated by court writers for court audiences, elevates love into an experience analogous to religion, and thus raises the question of whether a love which poses as "spiritual" is not thereby sacrilegious. In Thomas's *Tristan*, so far as it can be reconstructed from better-preserved versions, Tristan disguises himself as a pilgrim, thus realizing in narrative terms the image of the lover-as-pilgrim found in early troubadour lyrics; and like a saint, Tristan is simultaneously sublime and degraded[32] (as indeed is Lancelot in Chrétien's romance). The quasi-religious character of the love between Tristan and Iseut is especially prominent in the German version of the romance by Gottfried von Strassburg.[33] Gottfried has the exiled lovers live not in a bleak forest, as Beroul does, but in an exquisite cave where they require no material subsistence but feed instead on the delights of love, surrounded by a decor overflowing with religious symbols and moral allegories.[34]

Just as the *Eneas* inspired imitators of its careful harmonization of love and marriage, the more challenging approach to "courtly love" pioneered by the *Tristan* was to prove highly successful. Not only does the legend survive in the *Prose Tristan*, and undergo translation into several languages, it was also, as we have seen, adapted (and disputed) by Chrétien, and went on to provide the basis for many later medieval narratives, such as *La Chastelaine de Vergi* or the opening episode of *Joufroi de Poitiers* (in which the Count of Poitiers seduces a married woman by disguising himself as a hermit). On a larger scale, it informs the whole of the magnificent Occitan romance of *Flamenca*. Like *Joufroi*, *Flamenca* concerns the seduction of a married woman by a man posing as a cleric. He really *is* a cleric, however; and this is no vulgar seduction, but a full-blown *mise-en œuvre* of the tradition of troubadour poetry, distant love, nightingales and all.

Flamenca is married by her parents to Count Archambaut of Bourbon, but his delight in his new wife's beauty quickly turns to obsessive jealousy and he confines her in a tower, letting her out only to bathe at the healing spa baths, or to attend church; and then she must be swathed in clothing from head to foot, so that she is virtually invisible. Hearing of her plight, young Guilhem de Nevers resolves to "liberate" her. He is a knight, but has also been educated at Paris University (that is, he has been a clerk). It is this latter training which proves invaluable. He gets retonsured and admitted to assist at the office, thus enabling him to speak to Flamenca whenever she comes to church; and his well-schooled tongue is skillful in contriving courtship while putting other people off the scent. The whole of the middle section of the romance depicts his slow wooing of Flamenca in the very course of Mass; success is achieved when they consummate their love in the bath house. The text thus disquietingly literalizes its principal metaphors: courting (*pregar*, literally "to pray") takes place when the couple should be praying, and the "healing" of love's "sickness" or "wound" takes place in the house of healing! Here is not just exploitation of a religious register to describe profane love (as we have seen in other texts), but, as Sankovitch points out, a thorough narrative interlocking of religious and erotic events.[35]

The position of the narrator of *Flamenca vis-à-vis* his protagonists is hard to assess. Composed in late thirteenth-century Occitania, the romance records the demise of southern French courts as much as it reviews their past glories, and seems to hesitate between nostalgia and irony towards them. Indeed, an ironic attitude towards the courtly representation of love, which is discernible in romances from Chrétien onwards, becomes more pronounced in the late twelfth and early thirteenth centuries with such works as *Aucassin et Nicolete* (which is not itself a romance, but pastiches romance motifs) and Jean Renart's *Roman de Guillaume de Dole* (a kind of comic opera of a romance with inset sung lyrics). The "religion of sex" in particular came progressively to be viewed in more overtly skeptical terms. Continuing the *Roman de la Rose* which had apparently been begun in the 1230s by Guillaume de Lorris, Jean de Meun (c. 1276–77) openly burlesques the interference between religious and erotic discourses.

Guillaume de Lorris's first-person protagonist dreams that he is entering a paradisal garden where he meets with the personifications of various courtly virtues, some of whom look like angels. The God of Love – Amor – presides there and initiates the dreamer to his rule by imposing ten commandments upon him. Guillaume's poem, dedicated to his love for the mysterious "rose," bathes in the quasi-mystical absorption so characteristic of the poetry of the early troubadours. Jean de Meun's tone, by contrast, is stridently satirical. He takes pleasure in prising apart the delicate fusion of the sensual with the spiritual effected by his predecessor. The culmination of this effort is an outrageous sermon exhorting its listeners to sexual activity so that they may be assured of a place in heaven. The name of the preacher, Genius, may invoke the descent of the heavenly soul to mortal man, but it can also signify the power of generation lodged in genitalia; in his own nature, Genius thus combines the tensions between spiritual and sensual forces. His sermon is intended to rouse the dreamer to a last effort to win the rose, but its principal content is an attack on the *Rose* of Guillaume de Lorris for failing adequately to describe paradise. The garden of Love – the courtly garden – does not satisfy Jean de Meun. He is bent on rewriting its sensuality as explicit heterosexual intercourse and its spirituality as "real" heaven. His very literalism entails the collapse of the whole, elegant, courtly agenda: for who in thirteenth-century Christian Europe is ever going to admit to believing that sex *really* makes you go to heaven?

CONCLUSIONS: COURTS, COURTLINESS, COURTLY LOVE

I have argued that representations of love in courtly texts do not constitute a doctrine, but rather an agenda which reflects the preoccupations of medieval courts: their concern with decorum, elegance, display, and affluence, but above all with limiting the potential for schism, and trying to negotiate the lay and clerical interests of the various courtiers and their masters.

In romance, the limits of this agenda seem to be set by the *Eneas* on the one hand and the *Tristan* on the other. In the romances attributed to Chrétien, the limits are set rather more narrowly, the *Tristan* and the *Eneas* forming constant points of reference, but Chrétien himself apparently drawing the line at the *Lancelot* (on the *Tristan* side, as it were) and the *Perceval* (which, in its concerns with kingdom and dynasty, more closely resembles the *Eneas* though it is more explicitly Christian). In historical reality, the limits were set more narrowly again. The self-definition of aristocracy as a hereditary caste set strict rules on the sexual behavior of married women, and the sanctions for breaking these rules were severe. Putting an adulterer's head down a sewer scarcely suggests a recognition that his activities have mystical value. Nevertheless aristocratic women (and men too) commissioned works of courtly love, and no doubt they and other members of aristocratic households found gratification in fantasies of passion.

Fantasy is always motivated; and that of courtly love is so public, so self-promoting, and so conventionalized, that it must correspond to institutional as well as to individual needs. It is easy to see how the tradition of courtly love in the manner of the *Eneas* could command general assent since it accords both with secular values of family and inheritance, and with church teaching confining sex to marriage. It would possess some appeal for each of the different constituencies, lay and clerical, that made up a court, flattering patriarchal ambition whilst simultaneously satisfying ecclesiastical prescription. The *Tristan* tradition, however, while it effects a *rapprochement* between love and religious experience, also flouts, through its theme of adulterous passion, exactly those principles of dynastic continuity and church authority which the *Eneas* upholds. The success of this kind of narrative is less easy to account for – unless, as has been argued in Thomas's case, the narrator's position is one of active disapproval.[36]

Jaeger has suggested that the way Gottfried represents love as in conflict with the demands of the outside world, but in accord with the dictates of a higher, more mysterious power, may be a means whereby the courtier poet defends a private space of inner sensitivity for himself against the constant public requirements of court life.[37] In a world dominated by competition for advancement, material interest, and superficial display, such love offers the promise of spiritual depths and secret virtues. But it also offers, I think, a way of combining the discourses of the lay and clerical constituents of the court in a way that is more risky, more uneasy, and perhaps for medieval audiences more exciting, than the manner pioneered by the *Eneas*. On one hand, an attempt is made to unite both groups in a common ideology. Members of the clergy would acknowledge the appeal of a mystical vocabulary, so different either from ecclesiastical prescription or the self-conscious playfulness of neo-Ovidianism; while the laity were also susceptible to the discourse of religious commitment, summoning them to crusade or cloister.[38] To the extent that human love can be described in such a language, it is, indeed, "religious." But on the other hand, such an ideology also admits the incompatibility of the two groups, since the discourse of one (the clergy) is used metaphorically to endorse the sexual proclivities of the other (the laity) which, in reality, the clergy (and especially those in major orders) were exhorted to condemn. To this extent, there is an uneasy acknowledgment that the "religion of love" is also sacrilegious; although it took someone apparently unconnected with a court – the university scholar and cleric Jean de Meun – to point this out. Thus whilst (in Jaeger's terms) adultery may be a defense erected by the individual against the group, it may also be an attempt to address the group by negotiating the differences between its members.

Crucial to the framing of the agenda of courtly love, and probably responsible for composing the romances considered here, are the courtier-clerks whose skills range from the humanist learning necessary for neo-Ovidian poetry to the familiarity with biblical, liturgical, and devotional language displayed in the more mystically inclined romances. Depending on whether they acknowledged allegiance more to their secular masters, to the world of learning, or to ecclesiastical authority, such clerks would no doubt react differently to the issues on the courtly agenda; while the very fact of having more than one allegiance would enable them to distance themselves ironically from any. Thus they have composed a literature that contributes to the elegance of court society, through its polish, rhetorical proficiency, and refinement; that hints at unspoken and unspeakable depths, even though these may be a delusion created by the glitter of the surface; and that promotes a sense of consensus and cohesion whilst simultaneously retreating from it. Courtly love fictions encode the divisions and contradictions of court life, and the problematic status of the clerks who made their careers there. As a result, they are both resistant to definition and also powerful transmitters of their struggle with social tension. The traditions inaugurated in the twelfth century are embraced by subsequent masters of European literature such as Dante and Chaucer, and critiqued by some of its mistresses, like Christine de Pizan and Marguerite de Navarre. Through their splendors and evasions, their idealism and disavowal, the romances of the Middle Ages have left their mark on Western sensibility.

NOTES

1 Gaston Paris, "Etudes sur les romans de la Table ronde," *Romania*, 12 (1883), 459–534. Gaston Paris was an influential French medievalist for whom (p. 519) the *Lancelot* is the first literary example of courtly love.
2 See Reto R. Bezzola, *Les Origines et la formation de la littérature courtoise en occident* (500–1200) (Paris, 1966–8), Part III, vol. 1, 118–19, and vol. 2, 429–30.
3 See Georges Duby, *Medieval Marriage: Two Models from Twelfth-century France* (Baltimore: The Johns Hopkins Press, 1978), 7–11.
4 David Hult, "Author/Narrator/Speaker: The Voice of Authority in Chrétien's Charrette," in *Discourses of Authority in Medieval and Renaissance Literature*, ed. Kevin Brownlee and Walter Stephens (Hanover and London: University Press of New England), 76–96.
5 For more detail see Roger Boase, *The Origin and Meaning of Courtly Love* (Manchester University Press, 1977).
6 See note 1.
7 C. S. Lewis, *The Allegory of Love: A Study in Medieval Tradition* (Oxford: Clarendon Press, 1936).
8 D. W. Robertson, Jr., "The Concept of Courtly Love as an Impediment to the Understanding of Medieval Texts," in *The Meaning of Courtly Love*, ed. F. X. Newman (Albany: State University of New York Press, 1968), 1–18.

9 Reprinted in Jean Frappier, *Amour courtois et Table Ronde* (Geneva: Droz, 1973).

10 Köhler's works on courtly literature have been translated into Italian as *Sociologia della fin'amor: Saggi trobadorici*, ed. Mario Mancini (Padua: Liviana Editrice, 1976).

11 *Medieval French Literature and Law*, 215–48.

12 See for instance Roberta L. Krueger, *Women Readers*.

13 R. Howard Bloch, *Medieval Misogyny*.

14 See Jacques Lacan, *Le Séminaire, VII. L'Ethique de la psychanalyse*, ed. Jacques-Alain Miller (Paris: Seuil, 1978), 167–84. Lacanian-influenced studies of courtly love include Charles Méla, *La Reine et le graal* (Paris: Seuil, 1984) and Jean-Charles Huchet, *Littérature médiévale*.

15 See Jean Frappier, *Amour Courtois*, 33–41.

16 Bezzola, Origines, Parts II and III; Aldo Scaglione, *Knights at Court*.

17 Ruth Harvey, "*Joglars* and the Professional Status of the Early Troubadours," *Medium Aevum*, 72 (1993), 221–41, p. 229 and n. 71.

18 See Maurice Keen, Chivalry (New Haven and London: Yale University Press, 1984), 23; C. Stephen Jaeger, *The Origins of Courtliness: Civilising Trends and the Formation of Courtly Ideals 939–1210* (Philadelphia: University of Pennsylvania Press, 1985), 19–48; Kate Mertes, *The English Noble Household 1250–1600: Good Governance and Politic Rule* (London: Blackwell, 1988); David Crouch, *William Marshal: Court, Career and Chivalry in the Angevin Empire 1147–1219* (London and New York: Longman, 1990), 41–42, 134–48, 150; idem, *The Image of Aristocracy in Britain, 1000–1300* (London and New York: Routledge, 1992); Linda Paterson, *The World of the Troubadours* (Cambridge University Press, 1994), 107–10.

19 On aristocratic and Christian elements in chivalry, see Keen, *Chivalry*, 16; on the common background of aristocrats and clergy see Keen, *ibid.*, 32, Bezzola, *Origines*, Part II, vol. 1, 19, 130, and vol. 2, 456.

20 See Crouch, *William Marshal*, 42–45, 150; Jaeger, *Origins of Courtliness*, 54–66 and 176–94.

21 See also my "The Contradictions of the Courtly Lyric and the Origins of Courtly Love: The Evidence of the *Lauzengiers*," *Journal of Medieval and Early Modern Studies*, 26 (1996), 209–53.

22 Chrétien's lyric, "D'Amors qui m'a tolu a moi," is printed in Méla's edition of *Cligés*.

23 John F. Benton, "The Court of Champagne as a Literary Center," *Speculum*, 36 (1960), 551–91, p. 562.

24 Harvey, "*Joglars* and the Professional Status of the Early Troubadours."

25 Roger Dragonetti, *La Vie de la lettre au moyen âge. (Le conte du Graal)* (Paris: Seuil, 1980), 20–22; Sarah Kay, "Who Was Chrétien de Troyes?" *Arthurian Literature*, 15 (1996), 1–35.

26 See Peter L. Allen, *The Art of Love: Amatory Fiction from Ovid to the Romance of the Rose* (Philadelphia: University of Pennsylvania Press, 1992).

27 See Helen C. Laurie, "*Eneas* and the Doctrine of Courtly Love," *Modern Language Review*, 64 (1969), 283–94.

28 See Helen C. Laurie, "*Eneas* and the *Lancelot* of Chrétien de Troyes," *Medium Aevum,* 37 (1968), 142–56; Michel Zink, "Héritage rhétorique et nouveauté littéraire dans le "roman antique" en France au moyen âge: remarques sur l'expression de l'amour dans le *Roman d'Enéas*," *Romania*, 105 (1984), 248–69.

29 E.g. *Erec et Enide*, 5329–40, 5880–85; and *Cligés*, 5233–35. See Michelle A. Freeman, "Structural Transpositions and Intertextuality: Chrétien's *Cligés*," *Medievalia et*

Humanistica, 11 (1982), 149–63, p. 155, and *The Poetics of Translatio studii and Conjointure. Chretien de Troyes's "Cligés"* (Kentucky: French Forum, 1979), especially ch. 2.

30 Allusion to the legend of Alexander the Great, hero of another group of *romans antiques*.

31 On contemporary reference in *Cligés*, see Lucie Polak, *Chrétien de Troyes: "Cligés"* (London: Grant and Cutler, 1982), ch. 1, and Anthime Fourrier, *Le Courant réaliste dans le roman courtois en France au moyen âge* (Paris: Nizet, 1960).

32 See Brigitte Cazelles, "*Alexis* et *Tristan*: les effets de l'enlaidissement," *Stanford French Review*, 5 (1981), 85–95; Denyse Delcourt, *L'Éthique du changement dans le roman français du xiie siècle* (Geneva: Droz, 1990), ch. 2.

33. See James F. Poag, "The Onset of Love: The Problem of the Religious dimension in Gottfried von Strassburg's *Tristan*," in *Semper Idem et Novus (Festschrift for Frank Banta)*, ed. Francis G. Gentry (Göppingen: Kummerle, 1988), 285–305.

34 See Neil Thomas, "The Minnegrotte," *Trivium*, 23 (1988), 89–106.

35 Tilde Sankovitch, "Religious and Erotic Elements in Flamenca: The Uneasy Alliance," *Romance Philology*, 35 (1981–82), 217–23, 218.

36 As does Tony Hunt, "The Significance of Thomas's Tristan," *Reading Medieval Studies*, 7 (1981), 41–61.

37 *The Origins of Courtliness*, ch. 12.

38 This is not, of course, to exclude psychological motivations. A psychoanalytic account of the courtly love phenomenon is advanced in Julia Kristeva, *Histoires d'amour* (Paris: Denoël, 1983) and see the critics cited in note 14.

SUGGESTIONS FOR FURTHER READING

(a) Historical/sociological:

Scaglione, Aldo. *Knights at Court: Courtliness, Chivalry and Courtesy from Ottonian Germany to the Italian Renaissance*. Berkeley: University of California Press, 1991.

(b) Psychoanalytical:

Huchet, Jean-Charles. *Littérature médiévale et psychanalyse: pour une clinique littéraire*. Paris: Presses universitaires de France, 1990.

(c) Literary:

Bloch, R. H. *Medieval French Literature and Law*. Berkeley: University of California Press, 1977. Esp. 215–48.

  Medieval Misogyny and the Invention of Western Romantic Love. University of Chicago Press, 1991.

Gaunt, Simon. *Gender and Genre in Medieval French Literature*. Cambridge University Press, 1995. Ch. 2.

Krueger, Roberta L. *Women Readers and the Ideology of Gender in Old French Verse Romance*. Cambridge University Press, 1993. Esp. ch. 2.

6

RICHARD KAEUPER

The societal role of chivalry in romance: northwestern Europe

What did medieval people mean when they used the word "chivalry" (Latin, *militia*, French, *chevalerie*)? The simplest sense was hardy deeds in a fight with edged weapons. A second meaning was social, the body of knights in one place or even all knights, thought of as a distinct group. The third meaning, more abstract, referred to their ideas and ideals, to chivalry as the ethos of the knights. All three senses of the word appear (often intertwined) in romance literature, one of our best (if least used) sources on medieval society.

Yet the historian reading romance in order to understand chivalry faces diffi-cult questions. Historians still believe that by careful use of evidence a "real" medieval world can be partially recovered; yet how can romance, which seems so totally "unreal," form a part of this evidence? Some scholars have thought that since it is imaginative literature, romance must be discounted as merely escapist storytelling. Some have considered the chivalry portrayed in its pages dreamlike, a thin veil pulled over the realities of a harsh world,[1] and completely divorced from grinding social tensions or violence. An audience limited by gender would further reduce the importance of romance as historical evidence by cutting read-ership in half – picturing men reading (or listening in hall to) *chansons de geste* with their endless war and tenurial disputes; women in chamber reading the more psychological romances with love interest.

This chapter takes a different view on all these points. As Elspeth Kennedy has shown, knights in the very real world referred frequently and familiarly to these works of literature. A "two-way traffic" connected these men of war, law, and politics with Arthurian romance no less than *chanson de geste*.[2] Many owned copies of these texts. Some, such as the father of the famous legist Philippe de Beaumanoir, even wrote romance themselves.[3] Geoffroi de Charny, the leading French knight of the mid-fourteenth century and author of a didac-tic manual called *The Book of Chivalry*,[4] apparently knew romances like the *Lancelot do Lac*[5] and wrote of men who might love Queen Guenevere.[6] In addi-tion to borrowing from the imagery of the *Ordene de chevalerie*[7] (another ver-nacular didactic manual), Ramon Llull, who wrote the most popular book on chivalry in the Middle Ages, likewise drew heavily on thirteenth-century prose romances.[8]

Moreover, the romances include enough of combat and war, of the detailed effects of sword strokes on armor and the human body beneath, of the particulars of feudal relationships, and of the tactical maneuvers that lead to victory, to lead us to conclude that these texts were meant for knights as well as ladies.

Their conduct also shows that the literature is reaching knights, as students of chivalry have shown in case after case. Larry D. Benson's examination of the tournament in the romances of Chrétien de Troyes and in the biography of William Marshal, for example, concluded that we have on the tournament field an excellent case of the interplay of life and art impossible if knights were not deeply steeped in chivalric romance as well as *chanson*.[9]

Authors of historical accounts of the knights' actions sense no gap between what they describe and accounts in imaginative literature; often they stress the links between the two. John Barbour (*d.* 1395) terms his chronicle of Robert Bruce a "romanys."[10] Both Barbour and Sir Thomas Gray assure us that if all the deeds of Edward Bruce in Ireland were set down they would make a fine romance.[11] Other active knights shared the sentiment. Robert Bruce often told "auld storys" to his men in trying times, to buck them up. According to his biographer, during a tedious passage over Loch Lomond he merrily read out passages from the romance of Fierabras.[12]

Knights, in sum, say that they have read this literature, they show that they have read it by using it in their own writings, and they show by their actions that they have read it and are bringing it into their lives.

To understand how the chivalry discussed in romance was an active social force, not merely a gossamer veil of escapism, we need to recall what basic forces were stirring in the age in which chivalry emerged. By the twelfth century (some historians would insist a good deal before) Europe had entered the era of intense activity and accomplishment we often call the High or Central Middle Ages – Marc Bloch's Second Feudal Age, Charles Homer Haskins's Renaissance of the Twelfth Century, R. W. Southern's era of Medieval Humanism.[13] Among much else the era saw socio-economic and demographic growth, a surge in the piety of laypeople, the reform in the Church, and the early formation of the Western state. If full of vigor and constructive energy, this society certainly faced all the problems associated with rapid growth, new wealth, new social groupings and structures. Can any measure of distributive justice be found? What violence is licit, what illicit? Who decides and exercises violence? Does God bless any violence? How should gendered relationships be structured? What is piety and who governs its exercise? The list could be considerably extended.

Chivalry (in one of its meanings or another) deals with all these matters. Its expression in romance literature is no simple "mirror to society" but an active social force. To read chivalry in romance simply as a set of personal qualities in a knight risks reducing chivalry to a "micro" force; it was, in fact, a "macro" force doing major social work. As the practice and ideal code of the dominant strata of lay society for roughly half a millennium (say, from the late eleventh to the sixteenth centuries), it became the framework for debate about how the dominant laypeople should live, love, govern, fight, and practice piety – real issues with real consequences. Romance literature, one of the major purveyors of chivalric ideals, thus becomes the locus of debate about such basic social issues. The tension crackles. Romance is not simply a literature of celebration or agreement; it is a literature of debate, criticism, reform. We can at least sense the force and importance of these debates in romance by following three lines of investigation, recognizing how much these interlock and that others are possible and fruitful.[14]

CHIVALRY, ROMANCE AND VIOLENCE

The violence of the medieval world would astound a modern time-traveler. There is good evidence that many medieval people, too – however small the minority of pacifists among them – saw this violence as a problem distorting the more ordered society they were creating: they say so repeatedly in their writings; they instituted a peace movement in the late tenth century; during the following centuries they strengthened judicial institutions in the search for peace.[15]

Textbook-level surveys often portray chivalry as an uncomplicated species of solution to this problem: the knights internalized a code of restraint and matters got better. The actual situation was considerably less straightforward. Some scholars have recently advanced convincing arguments that the advent of chivalry did, indeed, bring changes in warfare. In contrast to an earlier era, the taking of prisoners (and ransoms) usually replaced mass slaughters; a clearer set of conventions regulated the fate of those besieged.[16] Yet war as conducted by the chivalrous still meant raiding and ravaging more than set-piece battle. Given the looting and widespread destruction (especially by fire), the general population may not have especially noticed much improvement as towns and villages were torched, bridges were broken, populations were forced to migrate, vines were cut, shipping was sunk or burned.

Even if romances miss tactical and organizational changes in the method of conducting war, the fierce side of the ideology of chivalry seems important in thinking about the problem of public order in general. For in one of its most significant dimensions, chivalry meant the worship of prowess, and prowess (whatever gentler qualities idealists wanted to associate with it) meant beating an opponent with really good hacking and thrusting. Chivalry was a code of violence in defense of a prickly sense of honor (and the honorable acquisition of loot to be distributed in open-handed largess) just as thoroughly as it was a code of restraint. The term "deeds of chivalry" (often literally *chevaleries*) is tirelessly used in romance to describe heroic work with lance and sword.

In his *Book of Chivalry*, the practicing knight Geoffroi de Charny establishes a scale of merit based on knightly prowess: individual jousting in tournament is good, free-form fighting in the *melée* of tournament teams is better, but real war (involving both previous types) is best. "Qui plus fait, miex vault" ("He who does more is of greater worth"), is Charny's *leitmotif*. The "doing" is, of course, done with edged weaponry.

Characters in romance deliver fawning praise for this sort of "doing." A knight who has seen Lancelot perform in a tournament (in the *Lancelot*) can scarcely find words sufficient to praise his prowess:

> vos am puis je dire plus de .M., car je l'aloie touz jorz sivant por veoir les merveilles qu'il faisoit; si li vi occirre a .V. cox .V. chevaliers et .V. sergenz si vistement quiil fandoit pres que par mi les chevax et les chevaliers et de moi meesmes vos di je quiil fandi mon escu en .II.moitiez et trancha ma sele et coupa mon cheval par mi les espaules, et tot a .I. sol cop . . . je li vi abatre a .I. retrous de lance .III. chevaliers . . . se la force en estoit moie, il ne se partiroit ja de moi, ainz le tandroie avec moi, car plus riche tresor ne porroie je mie tenir.

> [I could recount more than a thousand fine blows, for I followed that knight every step to witness the marvelous deeds he did; I saw him kill five knights and five men-at-arms with five blows so swift that he nearly cut horses and knights in two. As for my own experience, I can tell you he split my shield in two, cleaved my saddle and cut my horse in half at the shoulders, all with a single blow . . . I saw him kill four knights with one thrust of his lance . . .if it were up to me, he'd never leave me. I'd keep him with me always, because I couldn't hold a richer treasure.][17]

What is at issue here is not a set of idealized abstractions but the bloody, sweaty, muscular work Sir Thomas Malory called "dedys [deeds] full actuall."[18] Such deeds leave combatants "waggyng, staggerynge, pantyng, blowyng, and bledyng."[19]

We need to remember that all of this violence was effected by a knight's own skilled hands; chivalry was not simply a species of officership distanced from the bloody work with swords and spears. Summing up hundreds of years of this tradition, Sir Thomas Malory, writing his *Morte Darthur* in the late fifteenth century, refers time and again to the wondrous work done by his knights' hands, firmly gripping their weapons. We are assured that Lancelot has won Joyeuse Garde, his refuge, "with his owne hondis," that Arthur "was emperor himself through dignity of his hands," that Arthur awaits a tournament where "[the knights] shall . . . preve whoo shall be beste of his hondis."[20] We hear Outelake of Wentelonde proudly stating his claim to a lady: "thys lady I gate be my prouesse of hondis and armys thys day at Arthurs court."[21] Such hands wield a lance or sword well. Seeing King Pellinore cut Outelake of Wentelonde down to the chin with a single swordstroke, Meliot de Logurs declines to fight "with such a knyght of proues . . ."[22]

Chronicle and biography – traditional "historical" sources – speak the same language as romance: all show the same emphasis on the knights' bloody hands-on work. In a characteristic romance passage from *The Story of Merlin*, the young Arthurian heroes (Sagremor, Galescalin, Agravain, Gaheret, Guerrehet) have fought so well in a battle against the Saxons that "lor bras et lor pies et les crins et les testes de lor cheuaus degoutoient tout del sanc et des cheueles" ("their arms and legs and the heads and manes of their horses were dripping with blood and gore"). They are described as having "fait mainte bele cheualerie et de biaus cops tant que prisier et loer les en droit on et vous tenir pour tels comme vous estes" ("done many a beautiful deed of knighthood and struck many a handsome blow, for which everyone should hold them in high esteem").[23] In his biographical chronicle John Barbour praises Edward Bruce, the brother of the Scottish king, as "off [of] his hand a nobill knycht," and assures us Robert Bruce slew fourteen Englishmen at a ford "vif [with] his hand."[24] Barbour's praise could come from the pages of romance:

> A der God quha had yen bene by
> & sene hove he sa hardyly
> Adressyt hym agane yaim all
> I wate weile yat yai suld him call
> Ye best yat levyt in his day.[25]

[Dear God! Whoever had been there and seen how he stoutly set himself against them all, I know well he would call him the best alive in his day.]

Barbour similarly stresses the bloody character of such fighting, writing of grass red with blood, of swords bloody to the hilt, of heraldic devices on armor so smeared with blood they cannot be read.[26] Gerald of Wales unforgettably characterized Richard I of England as not only "fierce in his encounters in arms," but "only happy when he marked his steps with blood."[27] The historian of Lion-Heart's crusade more than once records Richard hewing off enemy heads and displaying them as trophies in camp, or riding into camp after a night of skirmishing with more Muslim heads hanging from his saddle.[28] Such trophies were not limited to crusading; after the bloody battle of Evesham (1265) during an English civil war, the head and testicles of the defeated Simon de Montfort were sent as a gift to Lady Wigmore.[29]

The biography of the greatest knight at the turn of the thirteenth century, the *Histoire de Guilliame le Maréchal*,[30] is a veritable hymn to prowess as the defining quality of chivalry. The author heaps praise on William for his great deeds of arms and records encomiums to his prowess from leaders of lay and clerical society alike. Chivalry becomes prowess pure and simple time and again in his pages. At the siege of Winchester, for example, he tells us that groups of knights sallied forth each day "to *do* chivalry" ("por *faire* chevalerie").[31] The knight can *do* chivalry just as he can *make* love: it has this dimension as a physical process. At the battle of Lincoln, says the biographer, the French did not have to look far to "find chivalry," the quality here again clearly equated with prowess on the battlefield. Knighting the Young King, the eldest son of Henry II, William asks God to grant him prowess and to keep him in honor and high dignity. The author also tells us it was right for William to be the "master" of the young king while he prepared for this day because William increased his pupil's prowess.[32]

Nearly two centuries later Froissart, the ardent chronicler of chivalry at work in the Hundred Years War, asserted that "Si comme la busce ne poet ardoir sans feu, ne poet le gentilz homs venir a parfait honneur ne a la glore dou monde sans proece" ("as firewood cannot burn without flame, neither can a gentleman achieve perfect honor nor worldly renown without prowess").[33]

If all of this valorization of chivalric violence tells us something important about how knights liked to conceptualize their role, so do the calls for restraint, the dark fears about the effects of war and violence.[34] A writer sometimes creates a specific image of unusual power and vividness, conveying across the centuries the elemental fear created by knightly violence. The author of the *Perlesvaus* (written in the early years of the thirteenth century) produces just such an image in the huge, knights in black armor who appear more than once in the pages of his romance.[35] We first see these dread figures through the eyes of Perceval's sister when she comes to the Perilous Cemetery:

> La damoisele esgarde tout environ le cimetire la ou ele estoit entre les sarques, si le voit avironé de chevaliers toz noirs; et avoient glaives ardanz et enblambez, et venoient li un vers les autres, et fesoient tel esfrois et tel noise que ce sembloit que toute la forest acraventast. Li plusor tenoient espees toutes rouges autresi comme de feu, et s'entrecoroient seure et s'entrecoupoient et poinz et piez et nés et testes et viaires, et estoit le fereiz molt granz . . .

> [As the maiden peered around the graveyard from where she stood among the tombs, she saw that it was surrounded by knights, all black, with burning, flaming lances, and they came at each other with such a din and tumult that it seemed as though the whole forest were crumbling. Many wielded swords as red as flame, and were attacking one another and hewing off hands and feet and noses and heads and faces; the sound of their blows was great indeed . . .]

Bertran de Born, an active southern French knight and poet of the later twelfth century, declared that "War is no noble word when it's waged without fire and blood."[36] We can be sure that the English king Henry V agreed; speaking two centuries later he declared that "War without fire is like sausages without mustard."[37] This sentiment was far from theoretical, as shown by accounts of repeated fourteenth-century English raids in the French countryside.

Campaigning of this sort is reflected in another haunting literary image, the *terre gaste*, the land laid waste. In his *Perceval*, Chrétien de Troyes pictures entire regions desolated by knightly warfare. The beautiful Blancheflor tells Perceval, who seeks lodging in her castle, that she has been besieged by a knightly enemy through winter and summer; her garrison of knights has been cut down by violent death and capture. The siege has produced a veritable wasteland in this region: streets stand deserted, houses and even churches lie in ruins.[38]

Even more significantly, when Chrétien presents a world cursed by the hero's failure to ask the right questions of the Fisher King, questions which would have cured the king and restored his pacific rule, he reveals a cursed land that seems to be afflicted by war: ladies will be widowed, lands will be laid waste, girls will be left in distress and orphaned, and many knights will die.[39] The Chandos Herald, writing the life of the Black Prince late in the fourteenth century, tells his readers how his master's host behaved between the Seine and the Somme during their invasion: "Mais les Englois poier iaux esbatre / Misent tout en feu et a flame. La firent mainte veve dame / Et maint povre enfant orfayn ("the English to disport themselves / put everything to fire and flame. / There they made many a widowed lady / and many a poor child orphan").[40]

Orderic Vitalis (the twelfth-century Norman chronicler) tells an even more striking story in Book XII of his *Ecclesiastical History*. On a raiding expedition which yielded an important prisoner and much booty, Richer of Laigle "did something that deserves to be remembered for ever":

> While country people from Grace and the villages around were following the raiders and were planning to buy back their stock or recover it somehow, the spirited knights [*animosi milites*] wheeled round and charged them, and when they turned tail and fled continued in pursuit. The peasants had no means of defending themselves against a mailed squadron and were not near any stronghold where they could fly for refuge, but they saw a wooden crucifix by the side of the road and all flung themselves down together on the ground in front of it. At the sight Richer was moved by the fear of God, and for sweet love of his Saviour dutifully respected his cross. He commanded his men to spare all the terrified peasants and to turn back . . . for fear of being hindered in some way. So the honourable man, in awe of his Creator, spared about a hundred villagers, from whom he might have extorted a great price if he had been so irreverent as to capture them.[41]

Not seizing the bodies of the peasants whose homes he has already looted (out of respect for the potent symbol of the cross) earns him eternal remembrance and the adjective "honorable" or "noble" (*nobilis*); indirectly, Orderic speaks volumes about ordinary practice and the fears it generated.

ROMANCE, CHIVALRY, AND PIETY

Their lives may have featured showy acts of violence, but knights were thoroughly pious. As the chivalric example *par excellence* in the late twelfth century, William Marshal went on pilgrimage to Cologne, fought as a crusader, founded a religious house, and died in the robe of a Templar, having made provision to be received into the order years before. His biographer records William's belief that all his knightly achievement was the personal gift of God.[42]

Geoffroi de Charny (more than a century later) similarly went on crusade, and founded a religious house. Through a sheaf of requested papal licenses we can sense his piety no less than his influence: he had the right to a portable altar, the right to receive full remission of temporal punishment for sin from his confessor when facing death, the right to hear a first Mass of the day before sunrise, the right to have a family cemetery alongside the church he founded. He was more famously the first documented owner of the Shroud of Turin.[43] As readers of his *Book of Chivalry*, we know in detail how thoroughly he agreed with William Marshal's belief in God as the fountainhead of all chivalric honor. Charny sets out this formula time and again. A healthy mixture of fear and gratitude can be the only proper response on the part of knights.

Romance reinforced this orthodoxy. It reminded knights of the undeniable function of priests in the sacramental system of which the knights were willing, prudent participants. They knew that they needed priests as conduits for divine grace, especially at critical, liminal points in life. Knights in this literature regularly state their fear of dying without confession.[44] In the *Lancelot*, Arthur himself, thinking that he is about to die, cries out, "'diex vraie confession quar iou me muir'" ("'Oh, God! Confession! The time has come!'").[45] In Chrétien's *Perceval* one key injunction the hero hears from his mother as he starts out into the world is to go to church or chapel to hear Mass regularly.[46] When Galahad passed a chapel, as readers of the *Quest of the Holy Grail* learned, "il tourna cele part pour oir messe car li anuioit moult quant il ne looit cascun ior" ("he turned towards it for he was really troubled if a day passed without hearing Mass").[47] Lancelot in the *Mort Artu* regularly hears Mass, says the proper prayers "einsi comme chevaliers crestiens doit fere" ("as a Christian knight should"), and confesses to an archbishop before his single combat with Gawain.[48] Balain and his brother, dying tragically from their mutually inflicted wounds, take the sacrament and beg Christ for forgiveness of their sins "tele que chevalier crestiie doivent" ("as any Christian knights should").[49]

In fact, in our literary evidence knights seem to swim in a sea of piety, using religious language even in situations that strike modern sensibilities as purely secular. "En non Deu, vos lo verroiz ja comme lo plus bel et lo miauz taillié que vos onques veissiez au mien espooir" ("In God's name, I think you will find him the most comely and well-made youth you have ever seen"), Sir Yvain says to the Queen, speaking of Lancelot in the *Lancelot do Lac*.[50] All knights in romance seem to swear constantly by some favorite saint, or by the relics in some church near at hand.

The Marshal, Charny, and their cousins in romance were model knights, however, and not simply model Christians. In company with all knights, they lived by the sword, and the founder of their religion had said some troubling words about such lives. We might well expect that the opposition of piety and violence is the nub of tension. Yet if it is often a nagging worry, it is not the focus of tension, for in their ethos the knights combined their violence and their piety rather handily. Prowess, as knights like Geoffroi de Charny knew, is a gift of God and like all divine gifts must be used well. God, as the greatest chivalric lord, grants worthy men a chance to earn honor, the reward for their strenuous effort. In return, the knight had ideally to follow common standards for a good, religious, layman. Powerfully present even if seldom stated explicitly is the corollary that God will understand and forgive the slips that mar the moral scorecards of his good knights, especially since the very toughness of their lives functions as a form of penance. Malory tells us that on the Grail quest Gawain heard more about his sins (especially his heedless killings) from a hermit-confessor than he wanted, and so hurried off, using the excuse that his companion, Sir Ector, was waiting for him. He had already explained to the hermit that he could accept no penance: "I may do no penaunce, for we knyghtes adventures many tymes suffir grete woo and payne."[51]

The real tension emerges rather from the mixture of lay piety and lay independence within chivalric ideology, that is, between the eagerness of the knights to be, and to be recognized as, good Christians and their distinct unwillingness to be dominated by clerics (necessary sacramental specialists though clerics might be). Knights did not simply and obediently bow before clerical authority and, bereft of any ideas of their own, absorb the lessons and patterns for their lives urged on them by their brothers, sisters, and cousins wearing tonsures and veils. They absorbed such ideas as were broadly compatible with the virtual worship of prowess and with the high sense of their own divinely approved status and mission; they likewise downplayed or simply ignored most strictures that were not compatible with their sense of honor and entitlement. If sometimes the yawning gap separating the two systems of belief stimulated inspired writing (as in the *Quest of the Holy Grail*, or *Sir Gawain and the Green Knight*), more often the gap was simply, willfully, not seen.

At its most vigorous, knightly independence can take the form of blistering blasts of anti-clericism. Romance can even picture physical assaults on the clergy.

Gamelyn, the son of a knight in a fourteenth-century English romance, spends an enjoyable afternoon cracking the tonsured pates and clerical bones of a host of heartless churchmen come to feast with his wicked brother who has shamefully defrauded him; he cheerfully specializes in robbing clerics while outlawed for this deed.[52]

The themes of piety and independence may appear most clearly in the sacred mythology chivalry constructed for itself. Since it is pictured as originating in the age and circle of Christ himself, before any clerical hierarchy had even come into being, the element of independence is obvious; yet this knightly mythology also drew on the associative piety and valorization produced by correlations and allusions, by similarities in typologies with the priestly mythology.

Some of the most interesting stories written into this mythology concerned Perceval, Galahad and the Grail. In the body of romance which establishes their careers both Perceval and Galahad live up to the expectations raised by their high lineage, a blood line going back to the great knight Joseph of Arimathea, who cared for the entombment of that most precious relic in the world, the body of Christ, and who cared as well for that most famous sacerdotal object, the Holy Grail. In fact, in the loose and allusive way in which these romances so often suggest parallels with sacred mythology, Perceval and Galahad recall the functions of Christ himself, or at least those of his functions which would appeal most readily to knights. In the *Quest of the Holy Grail*, Galahad enters Arthur's hall in a scene filled with signs of Pentecost and the coming of the Holy Spirit; he wears Christ's colors; his greeting to the knights is, "Peace be with you," the words Christ spoke to his disciples when he met them in the upper room after the resurrection. Religious valorization of this intensity comes from authors who walk the border – only as thick as a penstroke – between the pious and the unthinkable.

These, after all, are knights for whom God performs miracles. Galahad brings healing to a man lame for ten years near the end of the *Quest*.[53] Even Lancelot's blood performs if not quite a miracle, a marvelous cure when it restores Agravain in the *Lancelot do Lac*.[54] In Malory's *Morte Darthur* Lancelot heals the grievously wounded Sir Urré simply by a laying on of hands.[55]

Less dramatic, yet equally illustrative, is the creation of the famous nine worthies (using three sets of the sacred threes so prevalent in Christian thought). These great heroes across the centuries extended chivalric roots back not only into the Classical past but into the soil of Ancient Israel: the most recent set was, of course, medieval European (Arthur, Charlemagne, and the crusader Godfrey of Bouillon); behind them stood three "knights" from Classical history (Hector, Alexander, Julius Caesar); the earliest set came from Jewish history (Joshua, David, Judas Maccabeus). This fusion of Judaeo-Christian and Classical history gave chivalry the most ancient and most venerable lineage possible.

Sometimes the same effect was achieved not by anchoring accounts of origins in historical time and personage, as with the nine worthies, but by presenting them as standing essentially outside of time, as mythical "events" which could explain and justify chivalry, even though they could not be placed on any chronological line that began with Adam and Eve in the earthly paradise.

In his vastly influential book on chivalry (which in this instance as others seems to draw on the *Lancelot do Lac*), Ramon Llull presented a human Fall from virtue redeemed by the creation of chivalry in just such a distant, misty and unspecified past. To ensure order and virtue the human race was divided into thousands and the knight was chosen as literally one out of a thousand as the most noble and most fit to rule and fight.[56] Christine de Pisan, writing in the early fifteenth century, similarly posited the creation of chivalry as one antidote to a world gone wrong. Knighthood is, in fact, to "keep and defend the prince, the country and the common good."[57]

ROMANCE, CHIVALRY, AND THE GOVERNANCE OF KINGS

Kings and knights had much in common. By the High Middle Ages kings (joined by all lay lords) considered themselves knights; the knights had long thought themselves quasi-independent kinglets. If the king led in war, settled sticky disputes among his chivalrous followers (when they voluntarily brought them to him), and troubled them as little as possible in their own estates, all could go smoothly. This is the ideal pattern usually projected in romance and in didactic manuals. In one of his books, Ramon Llull described chivalry as "the disposition with which the knight helps the prince maintain justice"; his *Book of the Ordre of Chyvalry* announces that all knights should truly rule territories, the obvious shortage of such territories alone preventing this world order.[58] In his own *Book of Chivalry* (written for the French king's new Order of the Star) Geoffroi de Charny included a long list of questions and answers illustrating ideal royal rule.[59]

One romance after another shows this accepted link between kings and their knights. A wise man-at-arms in the *Lancelot do Lac* defends Arthur's kingship to a doubting Claudas: "car ce cist seus hom estoit morz, ge ne voi que ja mais meist chevalerie ne tenist gentillece lo ou ele est" ("for if that man were to die, I do not know who could ever preserve knighthood and uphold noble conduct").[60] The *Story of Merlin* takes the same line, asserting that able kings secure order; rebellions against Arthur's father, Uther Pendragon, had increased with the king's age and weakness.[61] The *Lancelot* makes a similar point: the land was sorely troubled by disorders while Arthur was imprisoned by the False Guenevere:

quant le baron de bertaigne se virent sans seignous si commenchierent a guerroier
li vm econtre lautre mez li haut homme du pais ne le porent souffrir.

[Now seeing their land without a master, the barons began to war with one
another, though this was unbearable to the worthy and noble among them who
sought only the general good.][62]

As so often, the position is summed up by Malory, who admires "stabylité" in
the political order no less than in love. The link between Arthur and Lancelot,
the great king and the great knight, is crucial. In the *Morte Darthur* when that
link has snapped, all the knights worry:

> "For we all undirstonde, in thys realme woll be no quyett, but ever debate and
> stryff, now the felyshyp of the Rounde Table ys brokyn. For by the noble felyshyp
> of the Rounde Table was kynge Arthur upborne, and by their nobeles the kynge
> and all the realme was ever in quyet and reste. And a grete parte," they sayde all,
> "was because of youre moste nobeles, sir Launcelot.[63]"

Of course, since it was the imminent shattering of the Round Table that occa-
sioned this credo, we are led to look again for basic tensions at work in chivalry.
If the illicit love of Lancelot and Guenevere usually captures most of our attention in Arthurian romance, we can recognize that kin rivalry and knightly com-
petitiveness contribute powerfully to the destructiveness at work throughout the
later romances in the Vulgate or Lancelot-Grail cycle and in Malory's great
book.

Guenevere's father, King Leodagan, "who was a good ruler and lawgiver,"
condemns the knight Bertelay for slaying another knight even though he had followed the proper forms by breaking faith with the man and openly threatening
him with death.[64] Asked about the killing, Bertelay insisted on his right to kill
any man who called him a criminal, once he had broken faith with that man. The
defense is, of course, that of Ganelon in the *Chanson de Roland* of perhaps a
century earlier: taking revenge against an enemy openly is no crime against a
king. What have kings to do with this anyway? Charlemagne's answer in the great
epic, validated by a trial by combat which reveals the will of God, emphasizes
public good over private revenge and leads to Ganelon's terrible death as
a traitor.[65] King Leodagan's position, though milder, would have pleased
Charlemagne; the king told Bertelay that he was mistaken; he should have sought
justice in the royal court, where he would have been treated fairly.

Bertelay's reply assures personal loyalty but asserts private right: "'Sire fait il
vous dites uostre uolente mais encontre vous ne mesfis ie onques riens ne ia ne
ferai se dieu plaist.'" ("'Sir,' he said, 'say what you will, but I have never done
you any wrong, nor will I ever, God willing'"). But King Leodagan's court, composed for this case of King Arthur, King Ban, King Bors, and seven distinguished

knights, orders Bertelay disinherited and exiled. King Ban, speaking for the court, explains the decision:

> por ce quil prist la iustice sor lui del cheualier quil ochist et par nuit car la iustice nestoit mie sieue.

> [The reason is that he took it upon himself to judge the knight he killed, and at night, but justice was not his to mete out.]

Bertelay goes off into exile, accompanied by a handsome following of knights who had benefited from his largess, "car moult avoit este boins cheualiers et uiguereus" ("for he had been a good and strong knight").

Early in the *Merlin Continuation* (much concerned with "firsts," with the origins of chivalric customs) a squire asks Arthur to take vengeance for his lord, killed in what the king calls the first of "these trials of one knight against another." The squire tells Arthur that as king by God's grace he has sworn to right "tous les mesfais que on feroit en ta terre, fust chevaliers ou autres" ("the misdeeds that anyone – a knight or any other person – did in the land"). Arthur goes in person to confront the killer, who turns out to be Pellinor. Before the inevitable joust, Arthur and Pellinor assert contradictory views about individual right to violence and royal responsibility: Arthur raises the fundamental issue of licit violence, asking the knight by what right he insists on fighting all who would use the forest passage.

Pellinor, addressing Arthur as a knight, asserts a knight's right: "Sire chevaliers," fait il, "jou meesmes em pris le congié sur moi sans auctorité et sans grasce d'autrui" ("Sir knight . . . I gave myself leave to do this, without authority or grace from anyone else.") Arthur will not accept such a sense of private right, tells the knight he is wrong, and orders him never again be so bold as to undertake such a thing.[66]

Such royalism is praised in the Middle English *Havelok the Dane*, which states specifically that a model king enforced order even against knights:

> Of kniht ne havede ne never drede
> That he ne sprong forth so sparke of glede,
> And lete him knawe of hise hand-dede,
> Hu he couthe with wepne spede;
> And other he refte him hors or wede,
> Or made him sone handes sprede,
> And "louerd, merci!" loude grede.   (90–96)[67]

[He had no fear of any knight that prevented him from shooting out like a spark from a coal to let him know the deeds of his hands, how he could use weapons. He either confiscated the man's horse and gear or made him cower, hands outspread, loudly crying out, "Mercy, Lord."]

All such cases in literature reinforce the debate over licit violence and royal sovereignty that appears so prominent in these centuries. Kings and their administrators often show that they considered knightly violence in the form of feud and private war the core of the problem of public order in their realms. Even Ramon Llull, traditionally the voice of chivalric idealism, agreed. In a work now seldom read he refers to knights as "Devil's ministers," and asks pointedly "Who is there in the world who does as much harm as knights?"[68]

Many flesh and blood people in this era could have enthusiastically seconded such a question. The chronicler Orderic Vitalis, as we have seen, worried over knightly violence, as did the royal advisor and biographer Abbot Suger of St. Denis; so did the notary who compulsively penned the famous account of the anarchy following the murder of Charles, Count of Flanders in 1127.[69] The villagers of Cagnocles whose homes were burnt out by Giles de Busigny in a private war in 1298 could add their voices,[70] as could all the French villagers looted, abused, left homeless by the raids of English armies sweeping across the countryside in the next century. No doubt we would hear vigorous phrases from John of Massingham who, in 1316, claimed to have been sitting at dinner with his mother in a little English village, "in the peace of God and in the peace of our lord the King," when the door was suddenly smashed by a gang led by "Sir Thomas de Ingaldesthorp, knight, constable and keeper of the peace . . . and other unknown evildoers." [71]

If the ironic implications for knighthood are interesting, so are the phrases about peace being guaranteed by God and the king. Despite their active leadership in war beyond the borders, kings were regarded within their realms as the guarantors of the peace on earth desired by God. Increasingly their involvement took specific legal form as they worked to extend their peace, to provide mechanisms for the resolution of disputes, to control castle-building and – most significant for our themes – to limit private war. Inevitably, the sense of royal sovereignty taking on legal form clashed with the chivalric ethos, so clearly expressed in romance.[72] In the very long run, the autonomy and proud prowess of the chivalrous would be mastered by the emergent state. In the short run, the tensions again crackled.

NOTES

1 Johan Huizinga, *Autumn of the Middle Ages*, tr. Rodney J. Peyton and Ulrich Mammitzsch (University of Chicago Press, 1996).

2 Elspeth Kennedy, "The Knight as Reader of Arthurian Romance," in *Culture and the King: The Social Implications of the Arthurian Legend*, ed. M. B. Shichtman and J. P. Carley (Binghamton: State University of New York Press, 1994).

3 Bernard Gicquel, "*Le Jehan le Blond* de Philippe de Rémi peut-il être une source du *Willehalm von Orlens?*" *Romania*, 102 (1981), 306–23.

4 Printed in Richard W. Kaeuper and Elspeth Kennedy, *The Book of Chivalry of Geoffroi de Charny: Text, Context and Translation* (Philadelphia: University of Pennsylvania Press, 1996).

5 Elspeth Kennedy, ed., *Lancelot do Lac* (Oxford: Clarendon Press, 1980); Corin Corley, tr., *Lancelot of the Lake* (Oxford University Press, 1989).

6 Kaeuper and Kennedy, *The Book of Chivalry*, 118–19.

7 Keith Busby, ed., *Raoul de Hodenc, Le roman des eles. The Anonymous Ordene de chevalerie* (Amsterdam: J. Benjamins, 1983).

8 Alfred T. P. Byles, tr., *The Book of the Ordre of Chyvalry* (London, 1926).

9 "The Tournament in the Romances of Chrétien de Troyes and L'Histoire de Guillaume Le Maréchal," in Larry D. Benson, John Leyerle, eds., *Chivalric Literature* (University of Toronto Press, 1989), 1–24. Cf. Richard Barber and Juliet Barker, *Tournaments, Jousts, Chivalry and Pageants in the Middle Ages* (New York: Wiedenfield, 1989).

10 McDiarmid and Stevenson, eds., *Barbour's Bruce*, 3 vols. STS (Edinburgh, 1980–85), I. 446.

11 Sir Herbert Maxwell, tr., *Scalacronica: The Reigns of Edward I, Edward II, and Edward III as recorded by Sir Thomas Gray* (Glasgow, Madehose, 1907), 57.

12 McDiarmid and Stevenson, eds., *Barbour's Bruce*, I. 267–70.

13 Marc Bloch, *Feudal Society*, tr. L. A. Manyon (University of Chicago Press, 1961), 59–72; Charles Homer Haskins, *The Renaissance of the Twelfth Century* (New York: Meridian, 1957); R. W. Southern, *Medieval Humanism and Other Essays* (Oxford: Blackwell, 1970), 29–61.

14 Issues of gender would make a fourth topic; see the essays in this volume by Roberta Krueger and Sarah Kay.

15 *The Peace of God: Social Violence and Religious Response in France around the Year 1000*, ed. Thomas Head and Richard Landes (Ithaca: Cornell University Press, 1992); Richard W. Kaeuper, *War, Justice and Social Order: England and France in the Later Middle Ages* (Oxford University Press, 1988).

16 John Gillingham, "1066 and the Introduction of Chivalry into England," in *Law and Government in Medieval England and Normandy*, ed. George Garnet and John Hudson (Cambridge University Press, 1994), 31–56; Matthew Strickland, *War and Chivalry: The Conduct and Perception of War in England and Normandy, 1066–1217* (Cambridge University Press, 1996).

17 William W. Kibler, tr., *Lancelot Part V*, 161–62, in Norris Lacy, gen. ed., *Lancelot-Grail* 5 vols. (New York, 1993–96); Alexandre Micha, ed., *Lancelot*, 9 vols. (Geneva: Droz, 1979), vol. 4, 198–99.

18 Eugene Vinaver, ed., *Malory, Works* (Oxford University Press, 1971), 23.

19 *Ibid.*, 198.

20 *Ibid.*, 415–16, 111.

21 *Ibid.*, 72.

22 *Ibid.*, 72–73. Malory draws on a long-held belief. See, e.g. Roberta Krueger, tr., *Lancelot Part IV*, 71; Micha, ed., *Lancelot*, vol. 1, 260.

23 Rupert T. Pickens, tr., *The Story of Merlin* (Vol. 1 of *Lancelot-Grail*, gen. ed. Norris Lacy), 268; Sommer, ed., *Vulgate Version*, vol 2, 185.

24 McDiarmid and Stevenson, eds., *Barbour's Bruce*, IX.486; VI.313.

25 *Ibid.*, VI.67–180; l. 315 notes that fourteen were slain "with his hand."

26 *Ibid.*, II.366–70; X.687; XIII.183–85.

27 Thomas Wright, ed., *The Historical Works of Giraldus Cambrensis* (London: Bell, 1887), 160.

28 James Morton Hubert and John L. La Monte, tr., *Crusade of Richard Lion-Heart by Ambroise* (New York: Columbia University Press, 1941), 7439–40; Gaston Paris, *L'Histoire de la guerre sainte par Ambroise* (Paris, 1897).

29 John Maddicott, *Simon de Montfort* (Cambridge University Press, 1994), 344.

30 Meyer, ed., *L'histoire de Guillaume le Maréshal*, 2 vols. (Paris: Renouard, 1891, 1894). No English translation is available, but see Sidney Painter, *William Marshal: Knight-Errant, Baron, and Regent of England* (Baltimore: The Johns Hopkins University Press, 1933), and Georges Duby, *William Marshal; the Flower of Chivalry*, tr. Richard Howard (New York: Pantheon, 1985).

31 Meyer, ed., *Histoire*, 176. My italics.

32 *Ibid.*, 16830–33 (battle at Lincoln), 2088–89 (knighting), 2635–36 (increase of prowess).

33 Quoted in Siméon Luce, *Chroniques de J. Froissart* (Paris: Renouard, 1879), vol. 1, 2.

34 R. Howard Bloch, *Medieval French Literature and Law* (Berkeley: University of California Press, 1977), 63–107.

35 The several quotations that follow come from Nigel Bryant, tr., *The High Book of the Grail* (Cambridge: D. S. Brewer, 1971), 144, 176–78, 221; W. A. Nitze and T. A. Jenkins, *Le Haut livre du Graal; Perlesvaus*, 2 vols. (University of Chicago Press, 1932), 222–23, 274–78, 344.

36 Paden, Stankovitch, Staeblein, eds., *The Poems of the Troubadour Bertran de Born* (Berkeley: University of Chicago Press, 1986), 358–9.

37 Quoted in John Gillingham, "Richard I and the Science of War in the Middle Ages," in J. Gillingham and J. C. Holt, eds. *War and Government in the Middle Ages* (Cambridge University Press, 1984), 85.

38 Nigel Bryant, tr., *Perceval, the Story of the Grail* (Woodbridge: D. S. Brewer, 1982), 20; William Roach, ed., *Le Roman de Perceval* (Paris: Droz, 1959), 1749–70.

39 Bryant, tr. *Perceval*, 50; Roach, ed., *Perceval*, 4675–83.

40 Pope and C. Lodge, eds. and trs., *Life of the Black Prince* (Oxford University Press, 1910), 236–39.

41 Marjorie Chibnal, ed., tr., *The Ecclesiastical History of Orderic Vitalis*, 6 vols. (Oxford University Press, 1969–80), vol. 6, 250–51.

42 Meyer, ed., *Histoire*, 6171–92, 7274–87, 9285–90, 18216–406.

43 Kaeuper and Kennedy, *The Book of Chivalry*, 5–48.

44 E.g., Carroll, tr., *Lancelot Part II* (vol. 2 of *Lancelot-Grail*, gen. ed. Norris Lacy), 219; Sommer, ed., *Vulgate Version*, vol. 3, 396.

45 Rosenberg, tr., *Lancelot Part III* (vol. 2 of *Lancelot-Grail*, gen. ed. Norris Lacy), 276. Sommer, ed., *Vulgate Version*, vol. 4, 76.

46 Roach, ed., *Perceval*, 567–94.

47 Sommer, *Vulgate Version*, vol. 6, 34.

48 Jean Frappier, ed., *La Mort le Roi Artu*, 3rd ed. (Geneva: Droz, 1964), 11–12; 169.

49 Gaston Paris and Jacob Ulrich, eds. *Merlin*, vol. 2, 56.

50 Kennedy, ed., *Lancelot do Lac*, 156; Corley, tr., *Lancelot of the Lake*, 70.

51 Vinaver, ed., *Malory, Works*, 535, 563.

52 Sands, ed., *Middle English Verse Romances* (New York: Holt, Rinehard, Winston, 1966), 169–71, 177, discussed in Kaeuper, "An Historian's Reading of the *Tale of Gamelyn*," *Medium Aevum*, 52 (1983), 51–62.

53 Pauphilet, ed., *Queste del Saint Graal* (Paris: Champion, 1923), 275–76.

54 Kennedy, ed., *Lancelot do Lac*, 539.

55 Vinaver, ed., *Malory, Works*, 663–71.

56 Alfred T. P. Byles, ed., *The Book of the Ordre of Chyvalry* (London: EETS, 1926), 14–18. Kennedy, ed., *Lancelot do Lac*, 142–43; Corley, tr., *Lancelot of the Lake*, 52.

57 S. Solente, ed., *Le livre des fais et bonnes meurs du sage roy Charles V par Christine de Pisan*, 2 vols.(Paris: Champion, 1936), vol. 1, 111–16.

58 *Ars Brevis* in Anthony Bonner, tr., *Selected Works of Ramon Llull*, 2 vols. (Princeton University Press, 1985), 624. Byles. tr., *Book of the Ordre of Chyvalry*, 27.

59 Kaeuper and Kennedy, *The Book of Chivalry*, 138–47.

60 Kennedy, ed., *Lancelot do Lac*, 35.

61 Sommer, ed., *Vulgate Version*, vol. 2, 77.

62 Rosenberg, tr., *Lancelot Part III*, 265: Sommer, ed., *Vulgate Version*, vol. 4, 51.

63 Vinaver, ed., *Malory, Works*, 698–99.

64 The following is drawn from Pickens, tr., *The Story of Merlin*, 339–41; Sommer, ed., *Vulgate Version*, vol. 2, 310–13.

65 See laisses 270–91.

66 Asher, tr., *Merlin Continuation* (vol. 4 of *Lancelot-Grail*, gen. ed. Norris Lacy), 175, 179; Gaston Paris and Jacob Ulrich, eds., *Merlin, roman en prose du XIIIe siècle* (Paris: Firman Didot, 1986), 174, 188.

67 Donald B. Sands, *Middle English Verse Romance* (New York, 1966).

68 Quoted in Jocelin Hillgarth, *The Spanish Kingdoms, 1250–1516* (Oxford University Press, 1976), 60, from the *Book of Contemplation*. The Catalan, kindly supplied by Prof. Hillgarth in correspondence, reads: "E doncs, Sènyer, qui és lo mon qui tant de mal faça com cavallers?"

69 Chibnall, ed. and tr., *Ecclesiastical History*; Henri Waquet, ed. and tr., *La Vie de Louis VI le Gros* (Paris: Champion, 1929); James Bruce Ross, tr., *The Murder of Charles the Good* (New York: Harper, 1967).

70 Robert Fossier, "Fortunes et infortunes paysannes au Cambrésis," in *Economies et sociétés au moyen âge* (Paris, 1973), 171–82.

71 From an unpublished "ancient petition" (SC 8) in the Public Record Office, London.

72 Kaeuper, *War, Justice and Public Order*, 134–269.

SUGGESTIONS FOR FURTHER READING

Barron, W. R. J. *English Medieval Romance*. London: Longman, 1987.

Bloch, R. Howard. *Medieval French Literature and Law*. Berkeley: University of California Press, 1977.

Crane, Susan. *Insular Romance: Politics, Faith, and Culture in Anglo-Norman and Middle English Literature*. Berkeley: University of California Press, 1986.

Crouch, David. *William Marshal: Court, Career and Chivalry in the Angevin Empire, 1147–1219*. London: Longman. 1990.

Duby, Georges. *The Chivalrous Society*, tr. Cynthia Postan. Berkeley: University of California Press, 1977.

Gravdal, Kathryn. *Ravishing Maidens: Writing Rape in Medieval French Literature and Law*. Philadelphia: University of Pennsylvania Press, 1991.

Kaeuper, Richard W. *War, Justice and Public Order: England and France in the Later Middle Ages*. Oxford: Clarendon Press, 1988.

Kaeuper, Richard W., and Elspeth Kennedy, *The Book of Chivalry of Geoffroi de Charny: Text, Context and Translation*. Philadelphia: University of Pennsylvania Press, 1996.

Keen, Maurice. *Chivalry*. New Haven: Yale University Press, 1984.

7

JEFF RIDER

The other worlds of romance

An aristocratic society lies at the center of the fictive worlds proposed by most medieval romances. The life of this literary aristocracy may have borne relatively little material resemblance to the lives of its medieval audiences, but it is nonetheless linked in recognizable ways to their interests, longings, ambitions, concerns, and values. And thanks to the significant continuity between medieval literary practices and modern ones, something of this implicit identification between the audience and the aristocratic society at the heart of romance survives for the modern reader. Even we modern readers, that is, sense that the members of the central aristocratic society we encounter in a romance are the protagonists with whom it is assumed we will identify, that the central aristocratic society is in some sense "our" society.

Opposite this central aristocratic society, most medieval romances establish, or assume the existence of, other social "worlds" of various kinds. The members of these other worlds may resemble the members of the central society – they may be as sophisticated, rich, elegant, well-mannered as members of "our" society – but their worlds are nonetheless recognizably different from "ours." Their motives and customs may be enigmatic or at least strange, and they themselves may be monstrous.

The study of these romance other worlds over the last one hundred years has been largely preoccupied with a search for the sources on which their authors drew in creating them. It has shown that these sources were both popular and learned, and included Classical, Germanic and Celtic traditions concerning "real" other worlds that were thought to surround the everyday world of common experience.[1] It has demonstrated the romances' fertile cultural eclecticism and has helped modern readers better understand them insofar as it has given us a more precise idea of the resonances their authors were seeking to create when they incorporated this motif or that element in their fictive other worlds. When, for example, one reads in Chrétien de Troyes' *Chevalier de la Charrette* of *c.* 1177 that Lancelot entered the land of Gorre by a bare-footed, bare-handed crossing of a bridge made out of an immense sword (*Charrette*, ed.

Méla, 3003–35; trans. Staines, 207–08), it is useful to know that some medieval people sometimes imagined the soul's passage to or through a "real" other world in terms of a bridge-crossing.[2] It is even more interesting to learn that nail-studded bridges were part of the furniture of the Christian other world in the recorded visions of an Irish knight in 1149, and an Essex peasant in 1206, and that in the vision of a German peasant in 1189 the souls of the dead had to cross a field of thorns, in some instances bare-foot, in order to reach the "real" other world.[3] These visions show us that twelfth- and thirteenth-century audiences who heard or read Chrétien's romance may well have interpreted Lancelot's crossing as a passage to an other world, and that Chrétien may well have intended them to do so.

Even though an author drew on ambient cultural traditions in creating it, a romance's other world was a fictive world created to stand over and against the equally fictive world of its central aristocratic society. The purpose of the above-mentioned visions of the "real" other world, whose audiences are invited to compare them to their existing notions about that world, is vastly different from that of Chrétien's description of the world of Gorre, whose audiences are invited to compare it, not to any "real" other world, but to Logres, the fictive world of the romance's central Arthurian society. Chrétien did not borrow a motif from traditions concerning the "real" other world in order to say anything about that world, but in order to designate Gorre as an other fictive world, an other world than Logres.

An encounter between the central world and an other one is one of the most common ways of beginning a romance, but the nature and consequences of this encounter differ according to the status of the central aristocratic society at that moment. When, as is often the case, the central society is in a state of peace and plenitude, a state often represented by a joyous court gathering, the otherworldly intervention comes as a threat to this aristocratic well-being that must be dealt with and resolved. In Geoffrey of Monmouth's *Historia regum Britanniae*, for example, Arthur decides to hold a plenary court in Caerleon to celebrate his conquest of Gaul. To this gathering he summons the lords of all the lands he has conquered. They come from Scotland, Wales, England, Ireland, Iceland, Gotland, Norway, Denmark, the Low Countries, Brittany, Normandy, Anjou, Poitou, and Gaul. "Preter hos," writes Geoffrey, "non remansit princeps alicuius precii citra hyspaniam quin ad istud edictum ueniret" ("Once they are listed, there remained no prince of any distinction this side of Spain who did not come when he received his invitation"). Into this gathering of the entire Arthurian aristocracy "duodecim uiri mature etatis. reuerendi uultus. ramos oliue in signum legationis dextris ferentes. moderatis passibus ingrediuntur. & salutato rege. litteras ei ex parte lucii hiberii" ("twelve men of mature years and respectable appearance came marching . . . at a slow pace. In their right hands they carried olive branches, to show that they were envoys. They saluted Arthur and handed to him a communication from Lucius Hiberius"), the "procurator" of Rome. This letter threatens war unless Arthur returns Gaul to Rome, and thus provokes Arthur's last great foreign campaign, during which he is betrayed by Modred and Guinevere (*Historia regum Britanniae*, ed. Griscom, IX.xii–xx, 451–67; trans. Thorpe, 225–36). Respectable and ceremonious as they are, these men nonetheless represent a hostile and alien world, the empire of Rome, and their entry into "our" world threatens its peace and survival.

This narrative-launching irruption of another world in the central social world may be rather more striking and mysterious than the Roman ambassadors, and the menace it poses may be rather more frightening. At the beginning of *Sir Orfeo*, for example, Queen Heurodis and two of her ladies take a walk in an orchard at noon one day in May. The queen falls asleep under a tree and awakes screaming, writhing and tearing at her face and clothes. When she can talk, she relates that a fairy-like king accompanied by a vast train came to her in a dream, took her away with him, showed her his realm, and promised to return for her at the same time and place the next day and take her away with him forever. If she resists or tries to hide, he told her, she will be found, torn limb from limb, and taken with them all the same. King Orfeo, her husband, surrounds her with knights the following day in an effort to protect her, but she is snatched away nonetheless (*Sir Orfeo*, ed. Bliss, 77–82, 162–74, 193–94; trans. Tolkien, 124–27). Orfeo leaves his kingdom as a result of this abduction, and the story is set in motion.

As this appearance of the King of Faërie in a dream shows, the border between the central and other worlds may be psychic as well as physical. Another, even more troubling narrative-launching psychic irruption of an other world is to be found in Hartmann von Aue's *Gregorius*. This romance begins with the birth of twins, a boy and a girl, to the duke and duchess of Aquitaine, and their mother's death in childbirth. The duke dies ten years later, at which point the devil, taking advantage of the siblings' natural affection for one another, lures them into incest. The hero of the poem is born from their union and set adrift in a boat.

The celestial other world may also launch the narrative by irrupting within, and disrupting, a stable and harmonious central world. *Guillaume d'Angleterre*, which is perhaps the work of Chrétien de Troyes, relates that the pious King William woke up one night at the normal hour for Matins but heard a thunderclap instead of the bell he expected. He opened his eyes

> Et vit une si grant clarté
> Que dou veoir touz esbloÿ.
> Avec ce une voiz oï
> Qui li dist: "Rois, va an essil,
> De par Deu et de par son fil
> Lou te di je qu'il lou te mande.
> Fei tost ce que il te comande!"

[and beheld such a brilliant brightness that he was dazzled. At the same instant he heard a voice speak to him: "King, go into exile. From God and His Son, I tell you this, that He so commands you and through me so orders you."] (*Guillaume d'Angleterre*, ed. Holden, 80–86; trans. Staines, 451.)

A similar sort of divine intervention occurs at the beginning of Hartmann von Aue's *Der arme Heinrich* (*The Unfortunate Lord Henry*) when the prosperous hero, who enjoys "êren unde guotes / und vroelîches muotes / und wertlîcher wünne" ("honor, possessions, a happy heart, and earthly joy"), is suddenly struck with leprosy "von sînem [God's] gebote" ("through God's command") (*Der arme Heinrich*, ed. Paul, 75–83, 116–19; trans. Tobin, 2–3). Thus afflicted, he sets out to find a cure.

The other worlds evoked in these various romances are of different kinds and belong to different traditions – the realistic, even historical world of imperial Rome in the *Historia regum Britanniae*, the underworld of *Sir Orfeo*, the fiendish world of *Gregorius*, the celestial one of *Guillaume d'Angleterre* and *Der arme Heinrich* – but they all function in a similar way. They disrupt the order of a peaceful, stable aristocratic world, bring about the hero's departure from that world, and launch the narrative. Narrative-launching otherworldly interventions may also occur, however, in response to pre-existing problems or tensions within the central aristocratic society which it cannot resolve on its own, or in order to bring to light faults in that society which might otherwise go unnoticed and uncorrected. In this case, the otherworldly intervention is not a threat to be countered but a catalyst that helps the central aristocratic society attain a new order by provoking a process through which a problem in that world is resolved or a fault in it is exposed.

Sir Gawain and the Green Knight provides a good example of this sort of intervention. When we first encounter the Green Knight who rides into Arthur's Christmas court at Camelot, he seems an otherworldly apparition come to disrupt a joyous aristocratic world. He is green, "Half etayn" ("half a troll"), "an aghlich mayster" ("a perilous horseman"), carries "a hoge and vnmete" (an "ugly and monstrous") axe in one hand, proposes a bizarre, gory and seemingly fatal contest, and his appearance results in the hero's departure from Arthur's court and launches the narrative. We later learn, moreover, that he was sent to the court by Morgan La Faye in the hope that his appearance would frighten Guinevere to death. The Green Knight is an ambivalent figure, however – he is also described as "þe myriest in his muckel þat my3t ride" ("the seemliest for his size that could sit on a horse"), speaks in courtly fashion, is richly dressed, holds "a holyn bobbe" ("a holly-bundle") in his other hand, and calls his strange contest "a Crystemas gomen" ("a Christmas pastime") – and his intervention exposes an unlooked-for fault in Gawain and in Arthur's other knights who, at the end of the poem, adopt Gawain's green "syngne of . . . surfet" ("token of . . .

trespass") or "token of vntrawþe" ("token of . . . troth-breach") as the emblem of their belonging to Arthur's household (*Sir Gawain and the Green Knight*, ed. Tolkien and Gordon, 130–466, 2433, 2459–62, 2509; trans. Tolkien, 28–36, 85–87). Arthurian society seems harmonious when the Green Knight appears in its midst, but this harmony is hollow, masking the knights' underlying failure to live up to the ideals they profess, or, more charitably, their ignorance of just how demanding those ideals can be. By exposing both this fault and its universality, the Green Knight's intervention simultaneously gives Gawain and the other knights the opportunity to correct it, reduces the shame attached to it, and increases their solidarity both through this reduction of shame and because they all share the fault.

The function of the fairy-made mantle of the *Lai du cort mantel* (*Lai of the Mantle*) and horn of Robert Biket's *Lai du cor* (*Lai of the Horn*) (a lai is a brief tale, a mini-romance, devoted to a single episode) is similar to that of the Green Knight's Christmas pastime, and they are similarly ambiguous.[4] Both arrive in the midst of a joyous court gathering and both at first appear to threaten the peace and stability of the central aristocratic world. Both, however, are beautiful, richly-made courtly accessories and both initiate a process of discovery that exposes hidden, but almost universally shared faults in the Arthurian society, thus rendering them less shameful, giving the members of that society the opportunity to address them, and ultimately increasing their solidarity.[5] Unlike the Green Knight's test, however, which shows that none of Arthur's knights can live up to their ideals of courage and honor, the mantle and horn tests do accomplish their ostensible goal of singling out the absolutely faithful couple or lady. They thus simultaneously preserve an – otherworldly? – ideal of fidelity and provide models of its attainment, while removing or reducing substantially the shame attached to not living up to it.

One of the most intriguing examples of this kind of otherworldly intervention in response to a fault in the central aristocratic world is to be found in Marie de France's lai of *Lanval*. Here, Lanval, a foreign knight in Arthur's service, does not leave the central aristocratic society in response to an otherworldly provocation but as a result of Arthur's failure to reward him for his service and give him the means to maintain himself as a member of his household. Impoverished and troubled, Lanval rode out of the town until he came to a stream in a meadow before which his horse "tremble forment" ("trembled violently"). He dismounted, turned his horse loose to graze, "Le pan de sun mantel plia / Desuz sun chief, puis se culcha. / Mult est pensis pur sa mesaise, / Il ne veit chose ki li plaise" ("folded his cloak to place beneath his head, then lay down, very disconsolate because of his troubles, and nothing could please him") (*Lanval*, ed. Rychner, 41–52; trans. Burgess and Busby, 73; trans. modified). Two ladies came to him as he was lying there (in the stream and in Lanval's introspective state when he first sees these ladies, half-way between waking and sleeping, we find the suggestion of both a physical border between "our" world and an other world, like the river separating Logres from Gorre, and a psychic one, like the one Heurodis crosses in her sleep) and conducted him to their beautiful, rich mistress, who told him that she had come from her distant homeland to find him. If he proved himself worthy, she told him, she would be his lover and make him inexhaustibly rich. Lanval promised to do whatever she wished and wanted to stay with her, but, after an afternoon in her tent, she sent him back to Arthur's court, giving him the means to support himself there and promising to come to him, albeit secretly, whenever he desired.

As a result of Lanval's return and strange new wealth and the Queen's misconduct and lies, Arthur is eventually made to bring an accusation of treason against Lanval. The accusation is proved false when Lanval's mysterious lady appears and subsequently, and finally, takes him away with her to her country. Arthur is not himself condemned, and there is no mention here of his failure in his duty *vis-à-vis* his household knight, Lanval, but his public humiliation feels like a kind of punishment for this failure, and the end result is the same: Lanval leaves his household and court. Ultimately, that is, the otherworldly lady's intervention is intended to punish Arthur for his lapse, to correct a fault in the central aristocratic society which it is itself unwilling or unable to correct, and this is why she, rather curiously, forces Lanval to return to the court rather than leaving with him immediately.

In contrast to the other examples I have cited above, the otherworldly intervention in *Lanval* does not launch the story, which is set in motion by Arthur's lapse. It serves rather to keep the story going by transforming the initial problem into a more narratively attractive and tractable one, and thus to bring about its resolution. Two other well-known examples of this kind of "intermediate" intervention are to be found in Merlin's helping Uther Pendragon to satisfy his desire for Ygerna in the *Historia regum Britanniae* – without his help neither the story nor history could go on (*Historia regum Britanniae*, VIII.xix, ed. Griscom, 422–26; trans. Thorpe, 204–7)[6] – and in Perceval's night at the castle of the Fisher King in *Le Conte du Graal*, an episode that turns a facile *Bildungsroman* into a most complex one by transforming a sin – of which Perceval, as his cousin and uncle tell him, is not aware – into a silence before the grail (*Le Roman de Perceval, ou, Le Conte du Graal*, ed. Busby, 2976– 3625, 6390–412; trans. Staines, 376–84, 416–17).

Other worlds have a complementary function in medieval romances in addition to their narrative one of setting the story going, keeping it going, or changing its direction. These worlds, that is, also define the central aristocratic world by valorizing certain of its elements or aspects and offering visions of what it is not, and provide representations of its materially or morally unrealizable aspirations.

The Green Knight's "Crystemas gomen," the fairy mantle and the fairy horn are three examples of otherworldly characterizations and valorizations of protagonists and the ideals they represent. Other examples abound. In *Lanzelet*, one encounters "der Eren steine . . . / . . . / daz . . . den man niht vertruoc, / an dem was falsch oder haz" ("the Stone of Honor . . . [which] did not endure a man in whom was falseness or malice"). When Lanzelet approached the Stone, therefore, the members of the court "dûhtes alle guot genuoc, / daz in der stein sô wol vertruoc" ("were all pleased to see how well the stone suffered him") since this indicated his moral nobility (*Lanzelet*, ed. Hahn, 5178–81, 5193–94; trans. Webster, 96). In order to survive the test of the Bed of Marvels in the *Conte du Graal*, similarly, a knight cannot "'de covoitise soit plains / Ne . . . ait en lui nul mal vice / De losenge ne d'avarisse. / Coars ne traïtres n'i dure, / Ne foimentie ne parjure . . . '" (have "'any trace of the evil vices of slander or greed. No coward or traitor survives there, nor any man forsworn or perjured'"); he must, rather, be "'Sage et large, sanz covoitise, / Bel et hardi, franc et loial, / Sanz vilonie et sanz tot mal'" ("'perfectly wise and generous, noble and handsome, loyal and bold, free of villainy and vice, and without a trace of covetousness'"; *Le Conte du Graal*, ed. Busby, 7556–60, 7594–96; trans. Staines, 430). Reserved for "li mieldres chevaliers del monde" ("the world's best knight"), the Siege Perilous of the Round Table and the sword in the floating stone that washes up at Arthur's Pentecostal court gathering at the beginning of *La Queste del Saint Graal* function similarly to single out Galahad (*La Queste del Saint Graal*, ed. Pauphilet, 4–12; trans. Burns, 4: 4–6).

These devices for providing material, visible signs of spiritual, invisible qualities, all fulfill the common wish to have tangible proof of another person's affection, fidelity, honesty, etc.: to be able to see into another person's heart and mind. They are also all marvels: things which, according to Hugh of Saint Victor, we apprehend without comprehending; effects, according to Thomas Aquinas, whose causes we cannot discern.[7] The "marvels" that one finds in the fictive worlds of the romances – actions or occurrences which one cannot comprehend or whose causes remain obscure – are indeed "marvelous" to the fictive characters who inhabit those worlds, just as they would be to the audiences of the romances if they encountered them in their everyday world, but they are not truly marvelous to the members of these audiences – whether medieval or modern – because they know that these fictive marvels are "caused" by the author of the romance. One cannot, that is, really marvel at fictive marvels, even though one recognizes that one would marvel at them if one really encountered them in life. A fictive marvel is, rather, a kind of enigma that makes a reader ask, not "what is its cause?" but "what does it mean?"

The links between marvels, wish fulfillment, and other worlds are not fortuitous. Because it is not "our" world, an other world is not bound by the material limits of our world or the mechanical limits of our ignorance. Other worlds, as travel narratives and modern science fiction likewise teach us, are full of wonderful objects, mysterious motivations, and advanced, incomprehensible technologies. In them, we can imagine the means of fulfilling all our desires (hence the link between the exotic and the erotic) without having to worry about exactly how it is done: the causes may remain obscure; the effects are all that count. The other worlds of romance are thus dream worlds in which the materially or morally frustrated aspirations of their authors and audiences may find at least veiled representation and imaginary satisfaction through, when necessary, devices whose workings are obscure and ultimately unimportant (like the "machinationes" ["gear"] and "medicaminibus" ["drugs"], the "nouis artibus. & . . . inauditis" ["methods which are quite new and until now unheard-of"] through which Merlin dismantles the stones of Mount Killaraus and changes Uther's appearance so that he may sleep with Ygerna [*Historia regum Britanniae*, VIII.xii, VIII.xix, ed. Griscom, 413, 425; trans. Thorpe, 198, 206]).

Because romance other worlds are, or at least may be, dream worlds, wish worlds, they are the place where the acquisitive and utopian longings of their audiences found expression. The author of *Sir Orfeo*, for example, describes Faërie as

> . . . a fair cuntray,
> As briȝt so sonne on somers day,
> Smoþe & plain & al grene
> – Hille no dale nas þer non y sene.
> Amidde þe lond a castel he siȝe,
> Riche & real & wonder heiȝe:
> Al þe vt-mast wal
> Was clere & schine as cristal;
> An hundred tours þer were about,
> Degiselich & bataild stout;
> þe butras com out of þe diche
> Of rede gold y-arched riche;
> þe vousour was auowed al
> Of ich maner diuers aumal.
> Wiþ-in þer wer wide wones,
> Al of precious stones;
> þe werst piler on to biholde
> Was al of burnist gold.
> Al þat lond was euer liȝt,
> For when it schuld be þerk & niȝt
> þe riche stones liȝt gonne
> As briȝt as doþ at none þe sonne.
> No man may telle, no þenche in þouȝt,

þe riche werk þat þer was wrouȝt:
Bi al þing him þink þat it is
þe proude court of Paradis.

... a country fair
as bright as sun in summer air.
Level and smooth it was and green
and hill nor valley there was seen.
A castle he saw amid the land
princely and proud and lofty stand;
the outer wall around it laid
of shining crystal clear was made.
A hundred towers were raised about
with cunning wrought, embattled stout;
and from the moat each buttress bold
in arches sprang of rich red gold.
The vault was carven and adorned
with beasts and birds and figures horned;
within were halls and chambers wide
all made of jewels and gems of pride;
the poorest pillar to behold
was builded all of burnished gold.
All that land was ever light,
for when it came to dusk of night
from precious stones there issued soon
a light as bright as sun at noon.
No man may tell nor think in thought
how rich the works that there were wrought;
indeed it seemed he gazed with eyes
on the proud court of Paradise.
(*Sir Orfeo*, ed. Bliss, 351–76; trans. Tolkien, 131– 32.)

One of the most remarkable of these utopian visions is found in Ulrich von Zatzikhoven's description of the land to which the infant Lanzelet is taken by his fairy abductress. It is an extraordinarily brilliant, happy, magic kingdom inhabited by 10,000 ladies dressed in brocade and silk. Their diamond-gated castle is built on a crystal mountain in the middle of the sea:

dâ wârens âne vorhte.
swer die burc worhte,
der zierte si mit sinnen.
siu was ûzen und innen
von golde als ein gestirne.
dehein dinc wart dâ virne
innerthalp dem burcgraben,

der ez hundert jâr solte haben,
ez waere ie ebenschoene.
da enwart ouch nieman hoene
von zorne noch von nîde.
die vrowen wâren blîde,
die dâ beliben wonhaft.
die steine heten sölhe kraft,
die an daz hûs wârn geleit,
daz man uns dervon seit,
swer dâ wonet einen tac,
daz er niemer riuwe pflac
und imer vroelîche warp
unz an die stunt daz er erstarp.

[those within were quite without fear. Whoever wrought the castle adorned it with great art. Outside and in, it was of gold like a star cluster. Nothing inside that castle moat aged; though a hundred years old, it stayed always as beautiful as ever. There also no one was disgraced by anger or envy. The ladies who dwelt there were blithe. The stones whereof the place was built had such virtue, so we are informed, that whoever dwelt there a day would never feel sorrow but would live always in joy till the hour of his death.]

While Lanzelet lived among these ladies,

dâ sach er manigen gelimpf,
wan si alle hübsch wâren.
si lêrten in gebâren
und wider die vrouwen spechen.
. . .
ze mâze muos er swigen.
harpfen und gîgen
und allerhande seiten spil,
des kund er mê danne vil,
wand ez was dâ lantsite.
die vrouwen lêrten in dâ mite
baltlîche singen.

[he had a chance to see much courtesy, for they all had beautiful manners. They taught him how to behave and how to make answer to ladies . . . He learned to keep silence at the proper time. About harping and fiddling and playing all sorts of stringed instruments he knew more than a little, for it was the custom of the country. The ladies likewise taught him to sing confidently.]

When the boy was older, the sea fairy who ruled the land sent for mermen to teach him to use a sword and shield as a form of exercise and he also had to learn there how to play athletic games, to jump, wrestle, run, toss stones, throw darts and hunt with hawk, pack, and bow.

This description of the sea fairy's realm is more, however, than an expression of utopian aspirations. Like "Tahiti," "South America," or "Persia" in eighteenth-century French literature (or the Middle Ages or the post-apocalyptic future in modern cinema), her otherworldly realm is an imaginary place beyond "our" world into which we may project and rearrange aspects of "our" world and from which we may view it critically. Ulrich's emphasis on the use of a sword and shield as a form of exercise and the express absence from this land of knights, of "ritterschaft" ("knightly horsemanship"), "harnasch" ("armor"), "turnieren unde rîten" ("tourneying and riding"), and of anyone to teach Lanzelet to "strîten" ("fight") amount to a critique of the notions of courtesy and chivalry (*Lanzelet*, ed. Hahn, 189–306; trans. Webster, 27–29). The distinction between courtliness and knighthood that underlies Ulrich's description of this realm is not also a distinction between "womanly" and "manly": he does not equate courtly with womanly and knightly with manly. Hunting, fencing, stone-tossing are both manly and courtly. The distinction he makes between courtly and knightly is founded, rather, on a distinction between grace – which may be both physical and social, feminine and masculine – and violence. Mermen, at least, are not excluded from courtliness nor are specifically mermasculine activities. Violence is.

The other worlds of romance are invested with the erotic desires of their audiences as well as their acquisitive and utopian ones, and Jacques de Caluwé even suggests that the Other World may above all be "la concrétisation d'un éternel désir: celui de déculpabiliser l'amour parce qu'il est naturel . . . . Désir de s'abandonner et de trouver chez l'autre le plaisir sans péché et la transcendance sans ennui" ("the concretization of an eternal desire: the desire to render love innocent because it is natural . . . The desire to let oneself go and find sinless pleasure with another and transcendence without tedium").[8] When the frustrated, somnolent Lanval looked down the river, for instance, he saw coming towards him "dous dameiseles: / Unc n'en ot veües plus beles! / Vestues furent richement / E laciees estreitement / En dous blialz de purpre bis; / Mult par aveient bels les vis!" ("two damsels . . . more beautiful than any he had ever seen: they were richly dressed in closely fitting tunics of dark purple and their faces were very beautiful"). These ladies conducted him to a magnificent tent, and when he stepped inside, he found a maiden – "Flur de lis e rose nuvele, / Quant ele pert el tens d'esté, / Trespassot ele de bealté" ("who surpassed in beauty the lily and the new rose when it appears in summer") – lying on "un lit mult bel – / Li drap valeient un chastel – / En sa chemise senglement: / Mult ot le cors bien fait e gent!" ("on a very beautiful bed – the coverlets cost as much as a castle – clad only in her shift. Her body was well formed and handsome"). She told him that she loved him passionately, had come from far away to find him, and that if he proved "pruz e curteis, / Emperere ne quens ne reis / N'ot unkes tant joie ne bien" ("worthy and courtly, no emperor, count or king will have felt as much joy or happiness as you"). When Lanval responded that he would do anything she asked and wanted nothing more than to stay with her for ever, she "S'amur et sun cors li otreie" ("granted him her love and her body"). The two spent the rest of the day together on her bed and, although she forced him to return to the city, she promised to come to him whenever he wished "'A faire tut vostre talent'" ("'to do your bidding'") (*Lanval*, ed. Rychner, 55–60, 93–116, 133, 168; trans. Burgess and Busby, 73–75).

Questioned about her son's father in Layamon's *Brut*, Merlin's mother recounts that she, too, has had an otherworldly lover, "þa faeireste þing þat wes iboren, / swulc hit weore a muchel cniht al of golde idiht" ("the fairest creature ever born, in the guise of a tall warrior all arrayed in gold"). As she lay asleep each night "ȝis ich isaeh on sweuene . . .; / þis þing glad me biuoren and glitenede on golde; / ofte hit me custe, ofte hit me clupte, / ofte hit me tobaeh and eode me swiðe neh" ("I saw this in a dream, this creature glittering in gold, gliding towards me; it kissed me repeatedly, it embraced me often, often bent down towards me and pressed very close upon me") (*Brut*, ed. and trans. Barron and Weinberg, 7839–44, 405).

The otherworldliness of Blancheflor's castle of Beaurepaire is highly attenuated in the *Conte du Graal*, but it is a new and other social world for Perceval, and he comes upon it after traversing a forest and, notably, "i. pont . . . / Si feble . . . / Qu'a paines cuit qu'il le sostiegne" ("a bridge so feeble that he thought it could scarcely support him"), which he nonetheless crosses without "que mal ne honte / Ne encombrier ne li avint" ("evil mishap or disgrace"), and Blancheflor's night visit to his bed in this threadbare other world is straight from an adolescent daydream (*Le conte du Graal*, ed. Busby, 1712–17, 1950–2000; trans. Staines, 361, 364–65).

The other world may also be home to more troubling assignations and desires. Chrétien, for example, is careful to situate Lancelot and Guenevere's night of ecstatic, blood-drenched, adulterous and treasonable love-making in Gorre (*Le Chevalier de la Charrette*, ed. Méla, 4546–721; trans. Staines, 225–27), while Hartmann characterizes the incestuous desire that launches *Gregorius* as "fiendish," which is to say both otherworldly and bad. Another sort of troubling eroticism finds expression in the "penetrative" divine punishments meted out in *La Queste del Saint Graal*: an angelic knight thrusts a lance through Bademagus's shoulder in punishment for his having borne away a shield intended for Galahad, while Nascien receives a celestial spear through the shoulder when he leaves a boat that he entered without knowing that he was not supposed to

(*La Queste*, ed. Pauphilet, 29, 208; trans. Burns, 11, 66). Similar, and even more anatomically troubling, wounds are found, notably, in the *Conte du Graal* (435–37, 3507–15; trans., 345, 382) and *Guigemar* (Marie de France, *Les Lais de Marie de France*, ed. Rychner, 89–122; trans. Burgess and Busby, 44).

When Perceval was marooned on an island in *La Queste del Saint Graal*, "une damoisele de trop grant biauté . . . vestue si richement come nule mielz" ("an exceedingly beautiful and richly attired lady") came to the island in a black-sailed boat, set up a tent and invited him into it for a meal. Unaccustomed to wine, Perceval drank so much "qu'il eschaufa outre ce qu'il ne deust. Et lors resgarde la damoisele qui li est si bele, ce li est avis, que onques n'ot veue sa pareille de biauté . . . et tant qu'il la requiert d'amors et la prie qu'ele soit soe" ("that he became flushed. As he looked at the young woman, she seemed so beautiful to him that he felt he had never seen anyone of equal beauty . . . he finally asked for her love"). When he promised to be her faithful knight, she responded that "'ferai quan que vos plaira'" ("'I will do as you wish'"), adding, "'vos ne m'avez mie tant desirree a avoir com je vos desirroie encor plus. Car vos estes un des chevaliers dou monde a qui je ai plus baé'" ("'Believe me, I have wanted you even more than you have desired me. You are one of the knights that I hoped passionately to have'") (*La Queste del Saint Graal*, ed. Pauphilet, 105, 109; trans. Burns, 34, 36). The lady, of course, was the devil.

The ecclesiastical tendency, so evident in the *Queste*, to diabolize sexual desire in fact produced a constant anxiety about the moral status of the otherworldly lovers called forth to satisfy it. This anxiety is apparent, for example, in *Yonec* and *Desiré* whose otherworldly lovers (a man in the first case, a woman in the second) take communion to demonstrate that they are not diabolical.[9]

The other worlds of romance also provide visions of what the central aristocratic society is not, thus defining its identity. Physical difference is one of the most obvious ways of reinforcing identity and the other worlds of romance abound with dwarves, giants, and other physically outlandish creatures whose aberrations circumscribe the physical normality of the central aristocratic world.[10] In Chaucer's parodic *Tale of Sir Thopas*, for example, the first, and only, being the hero encounters when he enters "sweet Fairy-land" is "a greet geaunt, / His name was sire Olifaunt, / A perilous man of dede" ("a mighty Giant . . . / . . ., Sir Elephant by name, / A perilous man indeed"), who threatens to kill Sir Thopas's horse with a mace unless he leaves (*The Canterbury Tales*, ed. Robinson, VII.807–16, 165; trans. Coghill, 197–98.)

There are, however, subtler and more important differences between the inhabitants of other worlds and those of the central aristocratic society. In *Historia regum Britanniae*, the forces that make up the Roman army against which Arthur fights in Gaul are pagan and come from the southern and eastern Mediterranean lands, from northern Africa and the Middle East (*Historia regum*

Britanniae, x.i, ed. Griscom, 467–68; trans. Thorpe, 236). This society's – and its primary audience's – identity as northwestern-European Christians is thus reaffirmed by the nature of its enemies. As Sir Elephant's mace demonstrates, giants and dwarves are wont to fight with rude weapons like clubs and whips which require only brute force in their manipulation, whereas aristocratic heroes commonly fight with weapons and techniques that require skill, training, and substantial fiscal and technological resources. The predominantly aristocratic identity of the romances' central society and audience is likewise reflected in the bourgeois and commercial element of many other worlds. One might think, in this connection, of the more than three hundred ships moored at the other-worldly city of *Yonec* (*Les Lais de Marie de France*, ed. Rychner, 369–70; trans. Burgess and Busby, 90–91), the medieval sweatshop that Yvain discovers at the "Chastel de Pesme Aventure" ("Castle of Most Ill Adventure") which owes its inception to ".ii. fix de dyable" ("two sons of the devil") (Chrétien de Troyes, *Le Chevalier au Lion*, ed. Hult, 5103–342; trans. Staines, 317–20), the merchants whose marvelous arrival saves Beaurepaire from starvation in *Le Conte du Graal* (ed. Busby, 2524–65; trans. Staines, 371), or the redolently bourgeois other world of Escavalon in that same romance (5703–6087, esp. 5754–87, 5912–49; trans., 408–13, esp. 409, 411). The fact that women are far more likely to rule in other worlds than in that of the central aristocratic society, while fairies, which is to say women who have mastered arcane knowledge and difficult skills, are always otherworldly creatures, also says something about gender expectations in the world of this fictional central aristocracy, and its real-world audience.

As Sir Orfeo discovers when he is admitted to the fairy-king's castle, moreover, the other world can be as dystopian as utopian:

> . . . he gan bihold about al
> & seiȝe liggeand wiþ-*in* þe wal
> Of folk þat were þider y-brouȝt,
> & þouȝt dede, & nare nouȝt.
> Sum stode wiþ-outen hade,
> & sum non armes nade,
> & sum þurth þe bodi hadde wounde,
> & sum lay wode, y-bounde,
> & sum armed on hors sete,
> & sum astrangled as þai ete;
> & sum were in water adreynt,
> & sum wiþ fire al for-schreynt.
> Wiues þer lay on child-bedde,
> Sum ded & sum awedde . . . .
>
> . . . he began to gaze about,
> and saw within the walls a rout
> of folk that were thither drawn below,

and mourned as dead, but were not so.
For some there stood who had no head,
and some no arms, nor feet; some bled
and through their bodies wounds were set,
and some were strangled as they ate,
and some lay raving, chained and bound;
and some in water had been drowned;
and some were withered in the fire,
and some on horse, in war's attire;
and wives there lay in their childbed,
and mad were some, and some were dead . . .

(*Sir Orfeo*, ed. Bliss, 387–400; trans. Tolkien, 132.)

The other worlds of romance thus functioned for their medieval audiences in much the same way the other worlds depicted by narrative literature, films, television shows, and consumption-oriented magazines do for us today. Their eroticism and violence, the glimpses they provided of utopian and dystopian worlds, of the romantic conundrums of wealthy royalty, are the medieval equivalent of the equally idealized and artificial images of life proffered by our media. Like the other worlds of modern cinema, television, and print, the other worlds of medieval romance were the laboratories of fears and longings whose monstrous, elegant and fantasized elaborations medieval audiences enjoyed in the same ways that we do those of our media.

The other worlds, the anti-worlds, whose existence medieval romances explicitly establish or implicitly assume thus play a number of important roles in their workings.[11] They serve as narrative engines whose representatives, messages or gifts intervene to set a story going, keep it going, or change its direction; they valorize the ideals of the central aristocratic world; they permit the representation and imaginative satisfaction of its materially or morally unrealizable desires; they confirm and elaborate its identity through representations of what it is not. And their peculiar complexity comes from their ability to do all of these things simultaneously. The fairy salve which cures Yvain of his madness, for example, is a narrative device which moves the story forward, signals that it is a fiction, tells us that such medicaments and such women do not exist in "our" world, and, simultaneously, represents a desire to have the one and be the other (Chrétien de Troyes, *Le Chevalier au Lion*, ed. Hult, 2946–3041; trans. Staines, 292–93).

Other worlds are thus at one and the same time narrative devices and the repositories of everything "we" lack and are not, and of everything "we" would like to have and to be. If the central aristocratic community is the subject of a medieval romance, the other social worlds it assumes or projects form its predicates. It is through their coming together that a state becomes a story and engenders meaning.

NOTES

1 See, above all, Howard Rollin Patch, *The Other World According to Descriptions in Medieval Literature*, Smith College Studies in Modern Languages, New ser. (Cambridge, MA: Harvard University Press, 1950). For a recent example, Alison Morgan, *Dante and the Medieval Other World*, Cambridge Studies in Medieval Literature 8 (Cambridge University Press, 1990).

2 For examples of bridges in medieval descriptions of the Other World, see Patch, *The Other World*, Index, sv. *bridge*, 374; D. D. R. Owen, *The Vision of Hell: Infernal Journeys in Medieval French Literature* (Edinburgh: Scottish Academic Press, 1970), Index, s.v. *bridge*, 315; Peter Dinzelbacher, "The Way to the Other World in Medieval Literature and Art," *Folklore*, 97 (1986), 76–77; Eileen Gardner, ed., *Visions of Heaven and Hell before Dante* (New York: Italica Press, 1989), Index, s.v. *bridge*; and Morgan, *Dante*, 33–37.

3 See Gardner, *Visions*, 149–95, 219–36; Aaron J. Gurevich, "Oral and Written Culture of the Middle Ages: Two 'Peasant Visions' of the Late Twelfth–Early Thirteenth Centuries," *New Literary History*, 16 (1984), 51–66; Dinzelbacher, "Way to the Other World," 71; and Morgan, *Dante*, Index, s.v. *Godeschalc*, 251.

4 Bennett's edition of the *Lai du cort mantel*, also known as the *Mantel mautaillié* (*The Badly-Tailored Mantle*), is reprinted with the Old Norse version of the lai known as *Mottuls saga*, ed. and trans. Kalinke; the English trans. of the saga is reprinted in *The Romance of Arthur*, ed. Wilhelm, 207–23.

5 This is more clearly true of the *Lai du cor* than of the *Lai du cort mantel*. See Jeff Rider, "Courtly Marriage in Robert Biket's *Lai du cor*," *Romania*, 106 (1985), 173–97.

6 On Merlin's role, see Robert Hanning, *The Vision of History in Early Britain, from Gildas to Geoffrey of Monmouth* (New York: Columbia University Press, 1966), 154.

7 See Hugh of Saint Victor, *De tribus diebus, Patrologia Latina*, vol. 176, 811–38; and Thomas Aquinas, *Summa Contra Gentiles* 3.101, 102 (Rome: Desclée, Herder, 1934), 349–50; trans. Anton C. Pegis, Saint Thomas Aquinas, *Basic Writings*, 2 vols. (New York: Random House, 1945), vol. 2, 198–99, 199–200, and *Summa Theologica* 1ª, q. 105, a. 7, ed. and trans. Thomas Gilby *et al.*, 60 vols. (London: Blackfriars and McGraw-Hill, 1964–76), vol. 14, 84, 85.

8 "L'Autre Monde celtique et l'élément chrétien dans les lais anonymes," in *The Legend of Arthur in the Middle Ages: Studies presented to A. H. Diverres by colleagues, pupils and friends*, ed. P. B. Grout, R. A. Lodge, C. E. Pickford, and E. K. C. Varty (Cambridge: D. S. Brewer, 1983), 65.

9 See De Caluwé, "L'Autre Monde celtique," 63–65.

10 On monsters, see Christine Alfano, "The Issue of Feminine Monstrosity: A Reevaluation of Grendel's Mother," *Comitatus*, 23 (1993), 1–16; Albrecht Classen, "Monsters, Devils, Giants, and other Creatures: 'The Other' in Medieval Narratives and Epics, with Special Emphasis on Middle High German Literature," in *Canon and Canon Transgression in Medieval German Literature*, ed. Albrecht Classen, Göppinger Arbeiten zur Germanistik 573 (Göppingen: Kummerle, 1993), 83–121; Jeffrey Cohen, "The Limits of Knowing: Monsters and the Regulation of Medieval Popular Culture," *Medieval-Folklore*, 3 (1994), 1–37; *idem*, "The Use of Monsters and the Middle Ages," *Journal of the Spanish Society for Medieval English Language and Literature / Revista de la Sociedad Espanol de Legua y Literatúre Inglesa Medieval*, 2 (1992), 47–69; John Ganim, "Medieval Literature as Monster: The Grotesque before

and after Bakhtin," *Exemplaria*, 7 (1995), 27–40; and David Williams, *Deformed Discourse: The Function of the Monster in Mediaeval Thought and Literature* (Montreal: McGill-Queen's University Press, 1996).

11 There is no comprehensive work on the function of other worlds in medieval romance but their functions in single romances or relatively small corpora of romances have been studied within the framework of certain more comprehensive interpretations of those romances. See, for example, Susan Aronstein, "Chevaliers Estre Deüssiez: Power, Discourse and the Chivalric in Chrétien's *Conte du Graal*," *Assays*, 6 (1991), 3–28; Anne Berthelot, "The Other-World Incarnate: 'Chastel Mortel' and 'Chastel des Armes' in the Perlesvaus," in *Contexts: Style and Values in Medieval Art and Literature*, ed. Daniel Poirion and Nancy Freeman Regalado, *Yale French Studies* special issue (1991), 210–22; and Keith Busby, "The Characters and the Setting," in *The Legacy of Chrétien de Troyes*, ed. Norris J. Lacy, Douglas Kelly and Keith Busby, 2 vols. (Amsterdam: Rodopi, 1987), vol. 1, 57–89.

SUGGESTIONS FOR FURTHER READING

Dinzelbacher, Peter. *Vision und Visionsliteratur im Mittelalter*. Monographien zur Geschichte des Mittelalters 23. Stuttgart: Anton Hiersemann, 1981.

Easting, Robert. *Visions of the Other World in Middle English*. Annotated Bibliographies of Old and Middle English Literature 3. Rochester, NY: D. S. Brewer, 1997.

Flint, Valerie. "Monsters and the Antipodes in the Early Middle Ages and Enlightenment." *Viator*, 15 (1984), 65–80.

Friedman, John Block. *The Monstrous Races in Medieval Art and Thought*. Cambridge, MA: Harvard University Press, 1981.

Gardner, Eileen, ed. *Visions of Heaven and Hell before Dante*. New York: Italica Press, 1989.

Kendall, Calvin B., and Peter S. Wells, eds. *Voyage to the Other World: The Legacy of Sutton Hoo*. Medieval Studies at Minnesota 5. Minneapolis: University of Minnesota Press, 1992.

Owen, D. D. R. *The Vision of Hell: Infernal Journeys in Medieval French Literature*. Edinburgh: Scottish Academic Press, 1970.

Patch, Howard Rollin. *The Other World According to Descriptions in Medieval Literature*. Smith College Studies in Modern Languages, New ser. Cambridge, MA: Harvard University Press, 1950.

Rider, Jeff. "Marvels and the Marvelous." In Norris J. Lacy, ed. *The Arthurian Encyclopedia*. 2nd ed. New York: Garland, 1991. 311–13.

Thomas, J. W. "The Other Kingdom in the Arthurian Romances of Medieval Germany and the Motif of Departure and Return." *Germanic Notes and Reviews*, 25 (1994), 3–5.

Williams, David. *Deformed Discourse: The Function of the Monster in Medieval Thought and Literature*. Montreal: McGill-Queen's University Press, 1996.

8

ROBERTA L. KRUEGER

Questions of gender in Old French courtly romance

Critics and historians have long acknowledged that medieval French romances helped to promulgate ideals of chivalry and love throughout European courtly society and that those ideals held men and women to different standards of conduct. Notions of idealized "masculine" and "feminine" comportment were so forcefully articulated in medieval romances and didactic literature that their outlines survived well beyond the Victorian age: well-bred men should exercise courage and prudence in the public domains of government and war; ladies should devote themselves to the private sphere and cultivate the arts of adornment, sentimental refinement, and mothering. Scholars and critics today are quick to question such cultural constructions and to seek to discern the social realities that lie behind them, as do Richard Kaeuper and Sarah Kay in this volume, for example.

But critical reflection is not the exclusive purview of modern readers. Although many of the more than 200 extant French romances seem to uphold traditional gender roles without questioning them, others provide more complex, critical views of relations between men and women. Beginning with the earliest instances of *romans d'antiquité*, lais, and Arthurian romances, many courtly fictions opened up a discursive space where gender roles were scrutinized and where underlying social and sexual tensions were explored. After looking briefly at the historical context in which aristocratic gender roles evolved, this essay will take the intriguing thirteenth-century *Roman de Silence* as a guidepost for some of the questions of gender raised by selected earlier and contemporaneous courtly fictions.

That Old French courtly romances portray gender relations as fraught with tension is not surprising. Courtly literature flourished as emerging elites attempted to construct an ethos of moral superiority, grounded simultaneously in sanctioned violence by men against outsiders or transgressors and in sentimental refinement toward members of the group, especially women. In different and sometimes opposing ways, aristocratic families and the Church attempted to shape the practices and behavior that constituted social life. After a period of relative autonomy for religious women, controversies raged in the Church over clerical marriages, double monasteries, and the place of sexuality in men's and women's lives.[1] Noblewomen were vital to the reproduction of aristocratic heirs and their sexuality was closely guarded; despite the Church's doctrine of consensual marriage, women's desires were often secondary to political expediency.[2] The intellectual renaissance of the twelfth century, the expansion of administrative clerical culture, and the growth of universities in the thirteenth century extended the franchise of learning for many men of means, but educational opportunities were restricted for all but the most privileged women, who were themselves excluded from higher learning.[3]

There is ample evidence that elite women were literate as readers and less often as writers throughout the Middle Ages.[4] The extant record of women's correspondence, lyric and narrative poetry, and devotional writing in Latin and in French is especially strong in Anglo-Norman and French culture, where examples of female patronage abound.[5] Yet the vast majority of extant medieval texts are the products of male clerics, many of whom viewed women's social agency with caution, if not hostility.[6] Opportunities for female literacy and for women's production of culture only gradually extended to a broader population throughout the Middle Ages. The flowering of vernacular culture in courts and wealthy households occurred within the context of a dynamic social tapestry, in which women's voices were inextricably woven, sometimes as silent participants, less frequently as powerful agents, and, more rarely but significantly, as protesters. Against this evolving backdrop, Old French romances frequently portray gender relations as open to interrogation.

The *Roman de Silence*, written around the mid thirteenth century by Heldris de Cornuälle, offers a striking example of how romance presents debate about gender within a courtly frame. The romance tells how the eponymous heroine Silence, sole heir of Count Cador and Eufemie, daughter of Count Renaut, has been raised as a boy so that she may preserve her birthright in the face of King Ebains's interdiction on female inheritance. Silence learns to ride and joust better than all "his" male peers. But at the age of twelve, a biological awakening for the young woman takes the form of a spirited debate between Nature, who reproaches Silence for betraying her "natural" femininity, and Nurture and Reason, who remind Silence of the social advantages men enjoy over women (*Silence*, 2500–656). After Nature has urged Silence to go to her room to sew – "Va en la cambre a la costure" (2528) – Reason reminds the confused adolescent that a man's life is better than a woman's "miols valt li us d'om / que l'us de feme / c'est la some" (2636–37). The narrator's inclusion of a mock-philosophical debate, possibly modeled on Alain of Lille's *De Planctu Naturae*, seems to invite his audience's reflection about the nature of gender roles.

After weighing the pros and cons, Silence concludes that a man's life is easier than a woman's and continues to excel in masculine pursuits, fighting valiantly for the Kings of Cornwall and France, and attracting the attentions of the lascivious Queen Eufeme. The central episodes in this romance thus relate how a woman who represses her feminine "nature" can successfully act like a knight and enjoy all the privileges and risks of masculinity. In the end, however, Silence's secret is finally disclosed by Merlin, who can only be captured by a woman. Silence's female sex is revealed when she is forced to strip before the King's court. Evil Queen Eufeme is shown to have consorted with a man cross-dressed as priest. Having opened up a fictive space where gender roles were transgressed, the romance reimposes traditional notions of sexual identity and social roles. King Ebains marries Silence after killing his wicked, adulterous wife. In his Epilogue, the narrator apologizes to his "good" women readers for having treated Eufeme so harshly and urges them to attend to his praise of Silence, whose positive example they should strive hard to emulate:

> Se j'ai jehi blasmee Eufeme
> Ne s'en doit irier bone feme.
> Se j'ai Eufeme moult blasmee
> Jo ai Silence plus loëe.
> Ne s'en doit irier bone fame,
> Ne sor li prendre altrui blasme,
> Mais efforcier plus de bien faire. (6695–98)

[If today I have blamed Eufeme, the good woman should not be angry. If I have greatly blamed Eufeme, I have praised Silence even more. The good woman should not be angry, nor take the other's blame upon herself, but should strive all the harder to do good.]

The author/narrator of this adventurous yet solemn tale has been variously hailed by modern critics as proto-feminist, misogynist, homophobic, and even possibly female.[7] That such opposing interpretations can be offered for *Silence* suggests that the medieval narrator sought to stimulate debate and reflection in the audience.

The *Roman de Silence* comes down to us in a single manuscript; we know nothing about its author. With a plot that strikingly reverses the traditional knight-pursues-lady plot of many biographical romances, and its complex mingling of literary genres, the romance may seem an anomaly. However, the issues that *Silence* addresses so explicitly are presented openly or indirectly in French verse romance from its inception. *ubiq. or app./real.*

FEMALE READERS AND PATRONS OF ROMANCE

The "bone feme," those good women readers, whom Heldris addresses in his Epilogue are anonymous, but their appearance reflects the prominence of noblewomen and their importance as an audience in Anglo-Norman and northern French courts from the twelfth century onward. Numerous dedications to historical women and to unidentified "dames" grace the Prologues and Epilogues of romances and other vernacular texts.[8] One of the earliest and most influential of female patrons was Eleanor of Aquitaine, grand-daughter of Guillaume IX of Aquitaine, the first troubadour.[9] After producing two daughters in her marriage to Louis VII of France, Eleanor divorced Louis and married Henry II Plantagenet of England, at whose court she helped to foster the vogue for literary productions "en romanz." Both the *Roman de Brut* and the *Roman de Troie* show evidence of having been dedicated to her; some scholars associate her with the *Roman d'Eneas* and the *Tristan* of Thomas as well. Some time later in northern France, Chrétien de Troyes wrote the *Chevalier de la Charrette* at the "command" of Eleanor's daughter, Marie, Countess of Champagne. Other historical dedicatees include Marie of Ponthieu, for whom Gerbert de Montreuil wrote *Le Roman de la Violette*; Eleanor of Castile, named as the dedicatee of Girart d'Amiens's *Escanor*; Marie of Brabant, Queen of France, and Blanche of Castille, daughter of St. Louis, to whom Adenet le roi dedicated *Cleomadés*; Marie, Duchess of Bar, who was named as recipient of Jean d'Arras' *Mélusine* along with her brother, Jean, Duke of Berry. These dedications, as well as notices in library inventories and wills, prove that noblewomen in France and England prized their association with romances and that they bequeathed them to their daughters and sons.

To be sure, pious works and didactic texts comprised the greatest portion of books associated with medieval women, even in the case of women not renowned for their piety, such as the late medieval Queen Isabeau de Bavière, whose library consisted principally of devotional works.[10] But romances comprise the second largest genre owned and/or transmitted by women.[11] After her castle was sacked, Mahaut d'Artois demanded restitution from Parliament in 1316 of a list of books that included three Tristan romances and the *Roman de la Violette*, among other secular works.[12] The widespread female readership of Arthurian romance in England can be seen in records of female ownership of romances variously about Tristan, Lancelot, Arthur, and Merlin in the fourteenth and fifteenth centuries.[13] Women's possession and readership of romances extended well beyond the period of their composition. A 1507 inventory of the library at Moulins, at the end of this period, includes a great number of medieval romances which would have been enjoyed by men and women in the Bourbon court, including Anne de France, daughter of Louis XI who wrote a conduct book for her daughter.[14] Moralists may have warned against the dangers of reading books that described the delights of love, as they did repeatedly throughout the Middle Ages, but their warnings were evidently not heeded: noble and bourgeois women constituted an important audience for all forms of courtly fiction.

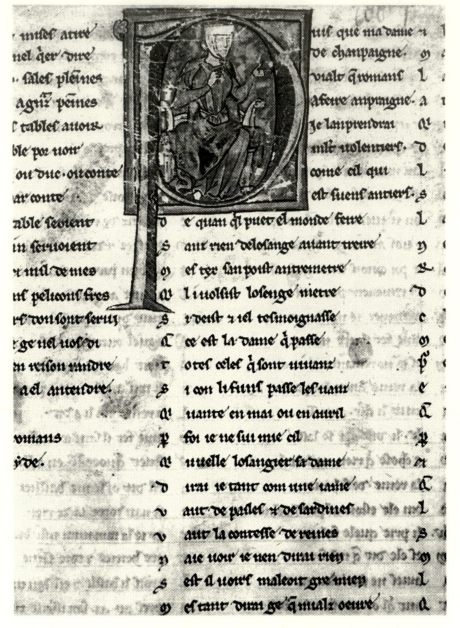

8.1 Opening initial of Chrétien de Troyes's *Le Chevalier de la Charrette (Lancelot)* depicting Countess Marie de Champagne, to whom Chrétien dedicates his romance.

THE TROUBLE WITH WOMEN: AMBIGUOUS AGENTS OF ROMANCE

The indisputable fact of female patronage, ownership, and reception tells us little about how the fictional portrayals of female characters either reflected or shaped the lives of their readers. If we turn to examine the representation of women's roles within romance, we find complex and often ambiguous portrayals of female subjectivity that seem to mirror women's paradoxical position in courtly culture, where they were both privileged centers of attention, and marginal players in a game whose rules were written by men. Although women figure more prominently in romances than in most contemporaneous *chansons de gestes*, those same romances cast women more often as desired objects rather than as active subjects in chivalric adventures or quests – a point that has been emphasized in feminist re-readings of courtly fiction. One of the most sobering reassessments is the claim that many Arthurian romances "aestheticize" or romanticize women's role as helpless victims of rape or male violence and thus make crimes against women a seemingly "normal" aspect of the fabric of chivalric life.[15]

Yet, as we have seen in *Silence*, female characters in romance often play roles that challenge social conventions or disrupt traditional codes. Many romancers portray women in a way that highlights their troublesome sexuality, their disruptive agency, or their resistant voices. In many courtly fictions, women's transgressive acts or disruptive speech make readers question chivalric ideals and courtly conventions.[16]

Evidence of women's extraordinary and problematic role is found among the earliest *romans d'antiquité*. When Lavinia writes a love-letter to Eneas and fires it with an arrow into the Trojan camp, thereby nearly rekindling the war (*Eneas*, 8775 ff.), her action combines female literacy, passion, and resourceful intrusion into a sphere usually reserved for men. This scene does not appear in Virgil's *Aeneid*; its innovative blending of Ovidian and chivalric elements, its surprising marriage of erotic and military impulses and reversal of gender roles might seem to signal the entrance of cultivated, resourceful women who wield authority in the courtly domain by their association with letters and by their clever, circuitous manipulation of culture. Yet Lavinia's gesture responds to an earlier argument with her mother, in which the latter tries to dissuade her daughter from loving a man she brandishes as a "sodomite" (8583); the future matron of Rome thus acts as a focal point for the narrator's anxiety about sexual identity within a romance that examines a range of sexual roles.[17] Even as she acts as an agent of sexual provocation, Lavinia is no less a founding mother whose reproductive sexuality is vital to imperial aims. Like Silence, Lavinia compels readers to wonder how women "fit" in courtly culture – as welcome agents of cultural change, or as troublesome forces of nature who must be domesticated as wives and mothers?

Following the lead of the *Eneas*, early French romancers take up the "question of women" and the debate about gender as one of the fundamental concerns of their narratives. All the works of Chrétien de Troyes, author of the first full-fledged Arthurian romance who set his successors' critical agenda for several generations, portray a woman or women as a catalyst for questions that profoundly trouble the courtly world. When Enide in *Erec et Enide* laments that her husband's excessive love for her has led to charges of *recreantise*, or lazy knighthood, among his peers, Erec leads her on a series of adventures where she repeatedly defies his interdiction to speak in order to ensure his safety. Her disruptive speech evokes the threat of women to undermine the chivalric enterprise, a threat enacted by Enide's cousin, who has entrapped her lover in a "courtly" garden.[18] Rather than spell out just *why* Erec set out to test his wife, the narrator tells his audience that he has already told them about the knight's motivations (*Erec*, 6420–29) – a rhetorical device that encourages readers to reflect on the romance's portrayal of gender relations.

In *Cligés*, *Yvain*, the *Chevalier de la Charrette*, and the *Conte du Graal*, Chrétien continues to represent women paradoxically both as objects of masculine exchange and as potentially troubling subjects whose desires can thwart the projects of empire, impose restrictions upon a knight's freedom or obstacles to his yearnings, or divert him from his spiritual quest, as well as engender in men a more "noble" heart. One of Chrétien's most memorable female characters, the clever servant Lunete, who resolves tensions by means of verbal tricks in *Yvain*, is a prototype of the resourceful female go-between (and ingenious narratorial agent) in later romances. Arthurian fictions and other courtly adventure stories long after Chrétien continued to cast women as alternately dependent and spellbinding figures whose elusive presence was crucial to the knight's quest for honor – yet who sometimes acted as disruptive forces or as catalysts for the author's and reader's critique.

Another strain of romances situated women closer to the heart of the story. We can trace the origins of femino-centric romance to Marie de France, who probably wrote in England in the 1170s. Marie states in the Prologue to her *Lais* that she will not translate from Latin texts, as so many of her (male) contemporaries have done; her aesthetic choices and her narrative voice establish her feminine difference within masculine courtly discourse.[19] Marie's collection of twelve lais (short tales that are not full-blown romances) feature women who speak and act according to their desires as they attempt to surmount the obstacles that limit their lives. Young and unhappily married women, or *mal mariées*, populate half the lais; the others recount stories of maidens who undergo crises of identity on the cusp of adulthood. Marie often deploys marvelous interventions or extraordinary acts or encounters that allow her heroines to explore alternate realities, to transform their lives, or to amend the moral vision of those around them. An orphaned maiden in *Fresne* generously bestows the beautiful coverlet, in which she was abandoned at birth, upon her beloved, who has just married another woman; her gesture sets off a chain of events in which she is revealed to be the bride's twin sister, the first marriage is annulled, and the eponymous heroine marries the knight she desires. After the damsel in *Milun* has a child out of wedlock with a lover whom she cannot marry, the couple arranges adoption and she submits to an arranged marriage; the lady maintains contact with her *ami* by means of an extraordinary swan for twenty years, until finally mother, father and son are united as a legitimate family. The generous wife in *Eliduc* does not react with jealousy (as does Iseut of the White Hands in the Tristan legend) when she discovers her husband's mistress in a coma; instead, Guildeluec revives the maiden, Guiliadon, with a magic herb and joins a nunnery so her husband may marry the maiden. Years later, this couple also rejects secular love and enters religious orders.

Precisely because Marie's fictions imagine unusual answers to ordinary, yet intractable problems, they highlight the constraints and tensions faced by men and women in "real" life, where no ideal solutions can be found. By assembling twelve diverse stories that fail to converge around a simple moral truth, Marie invites her audience to add their own "surplus de . . . sens" ("reservoir of meaning") and to ponder the ethical dimensions of sexual and social relations, which are inevitably thorny. Marie, like Chrétien, inaugurates debate and reflection about gender issues. She also develops the type of resourceful heroine who will flourish in later *romans réalistes*, some of which draw inspiration directly from her (such as *Galeran de Bretagne,* which derives from *Fresne*) or which emerge from independent sources, such *as Silence.*[20]

MAIDENS, WIVES, FAIRIES, QUEENS: THE PATHS OF ROMANCE WOMEN

The three principal female characters in *Silence* suggest the broad range of roles enacted by women in romance. The clever, virtuous maiden is framed by two contrasting women: her mother Eufemie, the good mother whose love for her husband provides a model of reciprocal love and consensual marriage; and Queen Eufeme the wicked queen whose arranged marriage to the King is sterile, who attempts to seduce Silence, and who carries on an adulterous affair with a knight cross-dressed as a priest. Between these two extremes of idealized female comportment, Silence evolves as a character who hides her femaleness and adopts the male roles of young man, jongleur, knight, and courtier. Other twelfth- and thirteenth-century romances present a gallery of female portraits

8.2 A crowd of ladies and noble companions observe as Lancelot and other knights fight. In this image, as in many romance tournament scenes, women figure prominently as observers. From the Old French Prose *Lancelot*.

ranging from virtuous wife to lascivious temptress and feature a number of memorable characters like Silence, who manage to preserve their integrity despite the odds.

Outstanding among these independent heroines is Jean Renart's Lïenor, in the *Roman de la Rose ou de Guillaume de Dole*, who manages to defend herself against the man who has maligned her virginity by framing him for a rape that he has not committed. After planting items of her clothing (said to be from another lady) on the unsuspecting seneschal, Lïenor cleverly backs her slanderer into the trap of having to admit that he has never seen her, much less slept with her – and undergoing trial by ordeal to prove it. Lïenor's resplendent beauty, her association with the world of women's embroidery and song, her verbal "engin" or cleverness all contribute to a remarkably dynamic portrait that contrasts with the passive roles played by her brother, Guillaume, and the Emperor Conrad, whom she eventually marries.[21] Jean Renart's *Escoufle* and Renaut's *Galeran de Bretagne* (modeled on Marie's lai, *Fresne*) each follow an unmarried heroine, Aélis and Fresne respectively, as she ventures forth from her family to quest for her chosen mate. During their period of autonomy, the heroines form close bonds with lower-class women, upon whom they depend for support and friendship; both work as seamstresses or embroiderers. By means of industry, artistry and luck each maiden arranges to be reunited with her estranged *ami* in a prosperous marriage. Although these stories end conventionally, their central episodes explore how gender roles and social identities may be shaped in new ways. The stories of these resourceful damsels, along with those of other unmarried *puceles* who proliferate in romance, suggest that the plot of singlewomen who seek autonomous adventures away from the confines of home or court may have appealed to adolescents and young women in the medieval audience.[22]

If Silence and Lïenor use their talents to safeguard virginity, other romance heroines, like Eufeme, use subterfuge to mask adultery. The two romance heroines with the most lasting influence in European literature are not virtuous maidens but adulterous queens. Iseut's and Guenevere's passionate attachments to knights who were prized vassals of their royal husbands were the subject of continual fascination for medieval authors and audiences, who may have explored, through these fictional transgressors, cultural anxieties about women's capacity to wield power and threaten legitimate succession at a time when the role of historical queens was increasingly limited.[23]

Unlike Eufeme, neither Iseut nor Guenevere is killed for her treason, and, despite the offense of adultery to religious precepts and the political order, romancers often show a surprising degree of sympathy for the adulteresses. The narrator of Béroul's "non-courtly" version of the legend often seems to side with the lovers, for example. He delights in describing how Iseut escapes from punishment by means of an ambiguous oath in which she claims to have held between her legs only her husband, King Mark, and the leper who has just carried her across a ford (and is Tristan in disguise).

In the Prose *Lancelot*, Guenevere occupies a paradoxical role both as a queen who betrays her husband and as the woman whose love has inspired the best knight in the world. It is she who knights Lancelot, whose prowess derives from his love for her. Because she dares to love in such an unconventional fashion and yet remains the highest-ranking woman at court, she at times seems to usurp the power of men at court.[24] Guenevere's elusive and ambiguous actions in the Prose *Lancelot* combine with those of the shadowy figures of Morgan, Arthur's sister, and the Lady of the Lake, who raises Lancelot, as well as with those of dozens of anonymous damsels to create a vast network of female characters who both assist the male protagonists in their quest for honor and threaten to undermine their independence or integrity.

The *Queste del Saint Graal*, written in a more austere, religious register, portrays Guenevere as an accomplice of "l'enemi," the devil, who decides that the easiest way to trap Lancelot into sin is through a woman, as the examples of Adam, Solomon and others have proved. As a hermit explains to Lancelot,

> "Quant tu veis qu'ele te resgarda, si i pensas; et maintenant te feri li anemis d'un de ses darz a descovert, si durement qu'il te fist chanceler."

> [When you saw that she was looking at you, you directed your thoughts to her, and at that moment the enemy struck you with one of his arrows so hard that he made you stagger] *(Queste*, ed. Pauphilet p. 125).

If we read back to the earlier scene in which Guenevere's glance inspires Lancelot's heroism, we see how these conjoined romances vacillate in their presentation of the queen as both dangerous and worthy of the greatest esteem. In the *Mort le Roi Artu*, Guenevere, now aged fifty-four, retains all of her beauty and her status as object of desire and honor. She is beloved by Lancelot, despite his repentance; condemned and then reconciled with Arthur; coveted by Mordred. After her liaison with Lancelot triggers events that bring about the destruction of the kingdom, Guenevere retires to an abbey where her tragic end and her "beautiful" repentance surpass all others: "mes onque haute dame plus bele fin n'ot ne plus bele repentance, ne plus doucement criast merci Nostre Seigneur qu'ele fist" (*Mort*, ed. Frappier 254). Such language confers both nobility and exemplarity upon a woman who, despite her obvious circumscription within the Arthurian realm, retains an autonomy lacking to most of the knights, who are drawn into an inexorable internecine struggle.

Even the moralistic *Queste* does not paint an unrelentingly negative image of women, however, for this same text portrays a woman who is a vehicle for the knight's redemption, a parallel to Mary, as Guenevere is to Eve. The narrator reminds us that if woman causes man's fall, she is also the agent of his salvation, "que par fame estoit vie perdue et par fame seroit restoree" (*Queste*, p. 213). Perceval's sister, daughter of King Pellehan, leads Galahad to Bors and Perceval so that they may board the ship that Solomon built, acting on the advice of his wife. Perceval's sister has cut off her hair to provide hangings for the Sword of Strange Hangings; in imitation of Christian sacrifice, she expires as her arm bleeds into an *escuele*, a bowl that recalls the Grail, thus healing a female leper and enabling her brother and his companions to complete their quest.[25] The maiden's sacrifice cleanses sin and prepares the way for spiritual redemption of the elected knights after her death. The royal virgin's sacrificial blood refigures and purifies the malevolent female body in a gesture that could be read either as a mystical celebration of the regenerative powers of women's love or as an extreme example of self-abnegation.

No characters embody the potential powers and dangers of women more poignantly than fairies and women versed in the arts of magic; these include Lanval's lady in Marie de France's *Lanval*; the Lady of the Lake and Morgan in the Prose *Lancelot* and other Arthurian fictions; and the serpentine Mélusine in Jean d'Arras's romance, which describes the marvelous fertility of the founding mother of the Lusignan line.[26] Whether these alluring women attempt to entrap the hero or carry him off to another world (in what one critic has called the "Morganian" model) or whether they deploy their special powers to found noble families (in the "Mélusinian" model),[27] these fantastic women enjoy autonomy denied to historic women in courts and households. Romance's beguiling fairies reveal much about the fears and desires of authors and audiences concerning women, sexuality, and power.

ROMANCE AND MASCULINITY: PROBLEMATIC PROPOSITIONS

If the ideal female behavior promulgated by romances might have been difficult for women to embrace, the armor of a model romance knight was no easier to don. As they celebrate male prowess, many romances reveal the burden of masculinity, the shame of dishonor, the difficulty of sacrificing one's sentimental life for the greater cause, the obligation of amorous relations, or a knight's failure to adhere to a code. In Chrétien's *Conte du Graal*, Perceval's mother tells him how to behave in the presence of women, but he misapplies her lesson by forcing a kiss on a damsel, at his peril. Gauvain, the paragon of chivalry, is presented in a series of thirteenth-century French romances as never quite living up to the reputation that has preceded him and of being either embarrassed by unwonted female attention, as in the *Vengeance Raguidel*, or shunned by women for lack of sexual prowess, as in the *Chevalier à l'épée*.[28] The failure of men to live up to the ideals of Christian knighthood is thematized starkly in the Vulgate Cycle, where only three knights emerge as capable of seeing the Grail.

Chivalry imposed constraints on both men and women who would conform to courtly ideals. The ideal of the perfect knight which dictates that the best knight wins, necessitates that many men be losers, defeated in battle and shunned by the most beautiful lady. Ladies may wait as passive objects while knights fight to take possession of them, yet the knights who fail to win their sexual prize, like Calogrenant who loses at Laudine's fountain in *Yvain*, wear an unmistakable badge of *honte*, shame. Romance misogyny sometimes scapegoats women as the arbiters of a system in which men compete for scarce sexual and material resources and private needs must be sacrificed for public obligations. For every lover who succeeds in conducting an adulterous affair with a beautiful queen or countess lurks a cuckolded husband, embarrassed before his peers like King Marc, or vengeful in his wrath like the angry husband in Marie de France's *Laüstic*, who kills the nightingale that served as pretext for his wife's chaste trysts, or the vindictive spouse of *Roman du Castelain de Couci*, who punishes his adulterous wife by serving her a dish concocted out of her lover's heart. If knights are the self-appointed protectors of women and if they often decide women's fate, only a select few are simultaneously powerful, honorable, and beloved. Violence between knights, jealousy between men over women, and verbal and physical abuse of women run as strong currents throughout romance. These destructive forces suggest that the physical superiority, sexual prowess, and moral perfection of the "ideal" romance knight were impossible to sustain in reality – and that women often bore the brunt of men's resentment.

It may be generally conceded that epics examine men's bonds with other men, whereas romances explore men's relationship to women. Yet, companionship between men is not absent from chivalric romance. Instead, as Simon Gaunt and others have shown, homosocial ties in romance are mediated in complicated ways by women.[29] The *Roman d'Eneas,* for example, marginalizes the male companionship of Nisus and Euryalis and the friendship of Eneas and Pallas, which are treated in early episodes. After exploring and rejecting the disruptive love of Dido for Eneas, the narrative arrives at the normative heterosexual love of Eneas and Lavinia – which is accompanied by harsh homophobic diatribes delivered by female characters. Yet if the romance succeeds in legitimating a patriarchal empire and in establishing heterosexual, marital love as the norm for romance, it does so by dramatizing the attractions and dangers of those relationships that it has suppressed.

Indeed, strong bonds between men continue to oppose or subtend heterosexual couples in romance, as stunningly illustrated in the love that Galehaut professes for Lancelot in the *Lancelot en prose*. The valiant, victorious Galehaut admits defeat to King Arthur in order to win the pleasure of Lancelot's company. When he realizes how hopelessly his desired knight is in love with the Queen, it is Galehaut who arranges for, and witnesses, the couple's first kiss. Galehaut dies midway through the *Lancelot* and his story is left untold by many subsequent adaptors. But his love for Lancelot is by no means incidental. Rather, the affection of Galehaut for another man invites readers of the Prose *Lancelot* to consider the transgression of gender roles in other instances throughout the romance, as E. Jane Burns has shown.[30] Galehaut's feelings for Lancelot are echoed by Gawain who, at one point, exclaims that he would "become the most beautiful damsel in the world" if only Lancelot would love him forever.[31]

Lancelot himself is often described in terms that are both masculine and femi-nine – as having " the mouth, neck, and hands of a lady" as well as "the hips and stance, the chest and shoulders of the perfect knight," as Burns observes.[32] By describing men and women in terms that intersect and overlap, by reversing con-ventional roles, many courtly texts, like *Silence*, create a space in which the adornments, gestures, discourses and desires that define courtly identities are fluid and ambiguous, rather than fixed according to binary sexual division.

ROMANCE AND THE TRANSFORMATIONS OF SOCIAL IDENTITY

Silence thus joins numerous other French romances in constructing gender rela-tions as fluid and open to question, rather than fixed and immutable. If moral-ists condemned the reading of these works, it is perhaps not only because they sometimes portrayed adultery and "amer par amours" (passionate love) as pow-erful attractions, but also because they often portrayed characters who trans-gressed the boundaries of "proper" gender roles.

Despite the many powerful queens, resourceful heroines, elusive fairies, virtu-ous wives, and transgressive men and women whose tales are told, in the final analysis, and in the last episode, the majority of romances uphold the traditional values of chivalric, Christian society – where most historical women played mar-ginal public roles. But within the fictive space of their stories, romancers could explore more fully the tensions within and resistances to gender norms in a way that escaped the grasp of moralists.

In the early fifteenth century, the historical woman writer Christine de Pizan, who composed poetry, fiction, and didactic treatises at the courts of Charles VI and the Dukes of Burgundy, seemed to recognize the promise and the limitations of romance for women. She decried the blatant antifeminism of Jean de Meun's *Roman de la Rose* and warned repeatedly against the dangers of adulterous love for women. Yet, in her own mini-romance, *Le Livre du Duc des Vrais Amants*, she both criticized the masculinist conventions of courtly fiction and demon-strated her understanding of romance's appeal for men and women.[33] Christine may have preferred that her female readers spend their time with pious works, lives of saints, and other moral tales, but her own work attests to the abiding popularity of transgressive courtly fictions. In the *Cité des dames*, she warns women not to follow the examples of the dame de Fayel (mistress of the Chatelain de Couci), the Chastelaine de Vergi, or Iseut, who loved Tristan – all women who died for love in courtly fiction.[34]Although hers is the first historical female voice to offer a full-scale rebuttal of misogyny and to call for the re-eval-uation of women's cultural roles, her role as active, public participant in the "querelle des femmes" may have been prepared and empowered, at least in part, by the tradition of debate between and about men and women within the frames of courtly romance.

French courtly romance's legacy for noblewomen and, later, for bourgeoises, is as multifaceted and ambivalent as the stories' complex representation of women and men. Some romances, such as the *Roman de la Violette*, may have praised women's virtue and have offered consolation to historical noblewomen who found themselves in difficult situations; Marie de Ponthieu, *Violette*'s dedicatee, lost her lands when her husband was punished by the king, and had them eventually restored to her.[35] Other romances, such as the story of the eaten heart in the *Castelain de Couci*, may have evoked an enticing realm of pleasure and danger. A genealogical romance like *Mélusine* explored the astounding generative powers of a female founding mother, providing an example of admirable and awesome fertility. Still other courtly fictions – from the *Lais* of Marie de France and the Arthurian adventures of Chrétien de Troyes to the romances of Jean Renart and the *Roman de Silence* – may have invited their readers to observe the ways that gender identities are constructed within language and to explore the transformative possibilities of fiction.

Medieval French romances provide evidence of elite women's continual literary activity as readers, patrons, and sometimes as creators; they also suggest that women participated along with men in an ongoing investigation of and debate about sexual and social identity. Courtly romance opened up a discursive space for male and female readers in which boundaries could be temporarily confused, subverted or resisted – at least in the space of a fiction – even as they were maintained.

NOTES

1 See Jo Ann McNamara, "*The Herrenfrage*: The Restructuring of the Gender System, 1050–1150," in *Medieval Masculinities: Regarding Men in the Middle Ages*, ed. Clare A. Lees, 3–30.

2 For an overview of constraints and opportunities for women in medieval doctrines and practices, see *A History of Women in the West: Silences of the Middle Ages*, ed. Christiane Klapisch-Zuber (Cambridge, MA: Belknap Press of Harvard University, 1992).

3 On women's education, see Charles Jourdain, "Mémoire sur l'éducation des femmes au Moyen Age," in *Mémoires de l'Institut National de France: Académie des Inscriptions et des Belles-Lettres* (Paris: Imprimerie Nationale, 1874), 79–133. A perceptive analysis of the problematization of women's education within medieval literature is offered by Solterer, *The Master and Minerva*.

4 See Joan M. Ferrante, *To the Glory of Her Sex: Women's Roles in the Composition of Medieval Texts* (Bloomington: University of Indiana Press, 1997); on female patrons, see June Hall McCash, ed. *The Cultural Patronage of Medieval Women* (Athens, GA: University of Georgia Press, 1996).

5 Reto Bezzola's account of women's literary activities at the courts of Blois, England, and Champagne offers a useful point of departure; see his *Les Origines et la formation de la littérature courtoise en occident (500–1200)*, vols. 2 and 3, (Paris: Champion, 1966–67): on Adèle of Blois, see vol. 2, 369–83; on Eleanor of Aquitaine and Marie de Champagne, see vol. 3, 247–311 and 373–85.

6 On antifeminism in courtly texts, see R. Howard Bloch, *Medieval Misogyny and the Invention of Western Romantic Love* (University of Chicago Press, 1991).

7 A spectrum of interpretative views on this romance is provided by the special issue on *Le Roman de Silence* edited by F. Regina Psaki in *Arthuriana* 7, 2 (1997).

8 See Rita Lejeune, "La femme dans les littératures française et occitane du XIe au XIIIe siècle," *Cahiers de civilisation médiévale*, 20 (1977), 201–18; a list of romances dedicated to women is provided by Krueger, *Women Readers and the Ideology of Gender*, 253–58.

9 Discussion of Eleanor's political and literary influence can be found in William Kibler, ed., *Eleanor of Aquitaine: Patron and Politician* (Austin: University of Texas Press, 1976).

10 Isabeau's library is described by Auguste Vallet de Viriville, "La bibliothèque d'Isabeau de Bavière, reine de France," *Bulletin du bibliophile et du bibliothécaire*, 36 (1858), 663–87.

11 Carol M. Meale, "'. . . alle the bokes that I haue of latyn, englisch, and frensche'. Laywomen and their Books in Late Medieval England," in Meale, ed., *Women and Literature in Britain*, 139.

12 On Mahaut's literary interests, see Jules-Marie Richard, *Une petite nièce de Saint Louis: Mahaut, Contesse d'Artois et de Bourgogne (1302–1329)* (Paris: Champion, 1887), 99–121.

13 Meale, "Laywomen," in Meale, ed., *Women and Literature in Britain*, 138–41.

14 A. M. Chazaud, ed., *Les Enseignements d'Anne de France . . . à sa fille, Susanne de Bourbon* (Moulins: C. Desrosiers, 1878; repr. Marseille: Laffittee, 1978).

15 See Kathryn Gravdal, *Ravishing Maidens*, 42–71.

16 For an investigation of this phenomenon in a variety of medieval texts, see Jane Burns, *Bodytalk*.

17 See Simon Gaunt, "From Epic to Romance: Gender and Sexuality in the *Roman d'Eneas*," *Romanic Review*, 83 (1992), 1–27, and Gaunt, *Gender and Genre*, 75–86.

18 The disruptive power of women's speech and storytelling in *Erec et Enide* is analyzed by Burns, *Bodytalk*, 151–202.

19 See Michelle A. Freeman, "Marie de France's Poetics of Silence: The Implications for a Feminine Translatio," *PMLA*, 99 (1984), 860–83.

20 See Roberta L. Krueger, "Transforming Maidens: Singlewomen's Stories in Marie de France's *Lais* and Later French Courtly Narratives," in *Singlewomen in the European Past 1250–1800*, ed. Judith M. Bennett and Amy M. Froide (Philadelphia: University of Pennsylvania Press, 1999), 146–91.

21 See Nancy A. Jones, "The Uses of Embroidery in the Romances of Jean Renart: Gender, History, Textuality," in *Jean Renart and the Art of Romance: Essays on "Guillaume de Dole"*, ed. Nancy Vine Durling (Gainesville: University Press of Florida, 1997), 3–44.

22 As I have argued in "Transforming Maidens."

23 This argument is developed by Peggy McCracken, *The Romance of Adultery*.

24 See E. Jane Burns, "Which Queen? Guinevere's Transvestism in the French Prose *Lancelot*," in Walters, ed., *Lancelot and Guinevere: A Casebook*, 247–65.

25 On the exclusion of Perceval's sister from the highest religious experience, reserved for men, see Susan Aronstein, "Rewriting Perceval's Sister: Eucharistic Vision and Typological Destiny in the *Queste del San Graal*," *Women's Studies: An Interdisciplinary Journal* 21, 2 (1922), 211–30.

26 An array of perspectives on this intriguing romance are offered in *Melusine of Lusignan: Founding Fiction in Late Medieval France*, ed. Donald Maddox and Sara Sturm-Maddox (Athens, GA: University of Georgia Press, 1996).

27 Laurence Harf-Lancner, *Les fées au Moyen Age: Morgane et Mélusine, la naissance des fées* (Paris: Champion, 1984).

28 See Keith Busby, *Gawain in Old French Literature* (Amsterdam: Rodopoi, 1980); Krueger, *Women Readers*, 83–100.

29 Gaunt, *Gender and Genre*, 75–85; see also Christopher Baswell, "Men in the *Roman d'Eneas*: The Construction of Empire," in *Medieval Masculinities: Regarding Men in the Middle Ages*, ed. Clare A. Lees, 149–68.

30 E. Jane Burns, "Refashioning Courtly Love: Lancelot as Ladies' Man or Lady/Man?" in *Constructing Medieval Sexuality*, ed. Karma Lochrie, Peggy McCracken, and James A. Schultz (Minneapolis: University of Minnesota Press, 1997), 111–34.

31 *Lancelot*, ed. Micha, 8.94, cited by Burns, "Refashioning," 119.

32 Burns, "Refashioning," 126.

33 Christine de Pizan, *Le Livre du Duc des Vrais Amants*, ed. Thelma S. Fenster (Binghamton, NY: Medieval and Renaissance Texts and Series, 1994); translated by Fenster as *The Book of the Duke of True Lovers* (New York: Persea Books, 1991).

34 Christine de Pizan, *Le livre de la Cité des Dames*, tr. Eric Hicks and Thérèse Moreau (Paris: Stock, 1986), 225.

35 See the discussion by Buffum in his edition of Gerbert de Montreuil, *Le Roman de la Violette*, lv–lviii.

SUGGESTIONS FOR FURTHER READING

Burns, E. Jane. *Bodytalk: When Women Speak in Old French Literature*. Philadelphia: University of Pennsylvania Press, 1993.

Fenster, Thelma S., ed. *Arthurian Women: A Casebook*. New York: Garland, 1996.

Ferrante, Joan. *To the Glory of Her Sex: Women's Roles in the Composition of Medieval Texts*. Bloomington, Indiana: Indiana University Press, 1997.

Gaunt, Simon. *Gender and Genre in Medieval French Literature*. Cambridge University Press, 1995.

Gravdal, Kathryn. *Ravishing Maidens: Writing Rape in Medieval French Literature and Law*. Philadelphia: University of Pennsylvania Press, 1991.

Krueger, Roberta L. *Women Readers and the Ideology of Gender in Old French Verse Romance*. Cambridge University Press, 1993.

Lees, Clare A., ed. *Medieval Masculinities: Regarding Men in the Middle Ages*. Minneapolis: University of Minnesota Press, 1994.

McCash, June Hall., ed. *The Cultural Patronage of Medieval Women*. Athens, GA: University of Georgia Press, 1996.

McCracken, Peggy. *The Romance of Adultery: Queenship and Sexual Transgression in Old French Literature*. Philadelphia: University of Pennsylvania Press, 1998.

Meale, Carol M., ed. *Women and Literature in Britain, 1150–1500*. Cambridge University Press, 1993.

Solterer, Helen. *The Master and Minerva: Disputing Women in French Medieval Culture*. Berkeley: University of California Press, 1995.

Walters, Lori., ed. *Lancelot and Guinevere: A Casebook*. New York: Garland, 1996.

9

SHEILA FISHER

Women and men in late medieval English romance

"For al so siker as *In principio*
Mulier est hominis confusio –
Madame, the sentence of this Latyn is
Womman is mannes joye and al his blis."
Chaucer, *The Nun's Priest's Tale* (VII, 3163–66)[1]

When Chauntecleer, a cocky cock, but clearly no Latinist, woos Dame Pertelote with this paltry pick-up line, the only connection he is making between women and romance involves what he hopes will happen once he gets her off her perch. The Nun's Priest, however, makes this connection explicit fifty lines later when he ironically asserts the improbable veracity of his mock heroic beast fable: "This storie is also trewe, I undertake, / As is the booke of Launcelot de Lake, / That wommen holde in greet reverence" (*CT*, VII. 3211–13). The dense irony, humor, and ambiguity of *The Nun's Priest's Tale* make it hard to tell where the narrator (let alone Chaucer) stands on women and/or romance (or on anything else, for that matter). One thing, however, is clear: women have been a confusion to men since the beginning ("In principio"), but, as Chauntecleer's mistranslation indicates, they have also been a significant source of men's joy, a confusing state of affairs, to say the least. One way to handle the *confusio*, however, is to trivialize women or to try to dismiss them.

This strategy appears in the romances of the three best-known writers in Middle English: the *Gawain*-poet, Geoffrey Chaucer, and Sir Thomas Malory. That students of medieval English literature have most likely read these authors' romances is reason enough to examine them together. What is more, their writings span the hundred or so years that ranged from the mid-fourteenth through the mid-fifteenth century: the period roughly coincident with England's Hundred Years War with France as well as with a flourishing of English literature often attributed to the rise in nationalism and the growing interest in English as an official language inspired by that war. Even if these three writers were not self-consciously constructing a distinctly English tradition of representing gender in romance, in hindsight at least, they gave a national inflection to such representations, despite their other differences.

These differences are apparent in the place of romance in their literary production, as well as in their styles and in the sources that influenced them. Among the four poems that can be attributed with certainty to the anonymous north-west Midlands author of *Sir Gawain and the Green Knight* (*fl.* second half of the fourteenth century), we find his only romance alongside three religious allegorical narratives, *Pearl*, *Patience*, and *Cleanness*. Despite his provincial dialect, the sophistication of his intricate style and his range of literary and cultural references suggest that he may have been associated with one of the country courts of Edward III or John of Gaunt. Yet *Sir Gawain*, even as it shows Celtic roots and continental as well as English influences, is provocatively *sui generis*. It is as unique as the single manuscript (London, British Library, Cotton Nero A.x) in which it has survived.

The associations Chaucer (1340?–1400) held with the courts of John of Gaunt and Richard II are well known, as is the fact that romance has a complex place within his vast and varied work.[2] *Troilus and Criseyde* (*c*. 1385), often considered Chaucer's masterpiece, is his most extended excursion into romance. Adapted and expanded from Boccaccio's *Il Filostrato*, Chaucer's five-book treatment of an episode from the Trojan War shows the same interest in Classical sources as *The Knight's Tale* of Theseus (a considerably condensed version of Boccaccio's *Il Teseida*). Yet even if the Knight's offering begins *The Canterbury Tales*, romance itself occupies a secondary place in this virtual compendium of literary genres. After *The Knight's Tale* (a courtly love piece that seems remarkably uninterested in courtly love), romance is either diffuse, rambling, and interrupted, as in *The Squire's Tale*; parodied in its popular, minstrel form (and interrupted) in the pilgrim-Chaucer's *Tale of Sir Thopas*; or told by bourgeois narrators, as are the Franklin's Breton lai and *The Wife of Bath's Tale*.

Malory (1410?–1471) wrote only romance, redacting the whole Arthurian cycle in his single known writing, the long, prose *Works* (finished 1469). The product, in large part, of his frequent imprisonments as he fell in and out of favor with Edward IV and the law, the *Works* relies heavily on French Arthurian romances, both prose and verse. Significantly, Malory shows markedly less concern for women and courtly love than do his French sources. Indeed, with the qualified exception of Chaucer, all three of these writers, for all their differences, have just this in common: they seem less interested in women than do their continental counterparts, the Nun's Priest's flagging of romance as a "female" genre notwithstanding.

All three writers can be seen to emphasize bonds between and among men, often at the cost of exploring the heterosexual love relationships for which romance as a genre is famous. In the representations and positionings of women in their romances, they register an anxiety about masculinity and masculine identity that is deeply implicated in their treatments of women.[3] Women often figure significantly not so much for their own sakes, but in order to become involved in the construction (and at times, the destruction) of men's chivalric identities. For all three, bonds among men are both affirmed and threatened (and sometimes both at once) by women. As a result, their shared uneasiness about masculinity becomes an uneasiness about women, and especially about women's potential to be *hominis confusio*.

If women are confusion in these writers' romances, confusion still has the inherent ability to raise questions and possibilities, some of which these works deliberately and self-consciously engage. These questions and possibilities have not been lost on recent readers, either, as we see in the range of critical responses to them.[4] If women in these romances are the confusion of men, who is to blame, the woman who can confuse or the man who can be confused by her? If men are anxious about their masculinity, is it because of the feminizing threat of women or because women represent a different system of values that calls into question the chivalric ethos? If men dismiss women, is it because women are inferior and trivial, or is it because women pose a fearsome threat to the masculine *status quo*? If women betray or endanger men, is it because they are as putatively fickle or evil as Eve, or is women's fickleness constructed and determined by the very circumstances of their position? Are women victims or agents, or sometimes the one when they seem most the other?

These questions (like Chauntecleer's quotation and its mistranslation) suggest two poles of interpretation for women in romance. But the representations of gender in these Middle English works are more problematic than such dualizing questions (and their answers) might suggest. These texts attempt to solve the problem of "woman" by trying, not always successfully, to marginalize women, even and perhaps especially when they have been central to the narrative and to defining masculine chivalric identities. In the process, the *Gawain*-poet, Chaucer, and Malory engage the problem of men's ability to exchange women between themselves in order to form dynastic, political, and/or affective bonds of the kind that the exchange of historical women in the dynamics of medieval marriage assured noble and aristocratic men.[5] In their works, women who try to make exchanges on their own are figured as profoundly threatening.

Sir Gawain might be read as a virtual case study of this paradigm of marginalizing women who involve themselves in exchanges with men. Readers of this short, witty, meticulously structured romance are usually even more surprised, at the end, when Morgan is revealed as responsible for the entire plot than they were by Bertilak's disclosure that Gawain's testing occurred in the bedroom, at the hands of his wife, and not at the Green Chapel, at the hands of the Green Knight (who is also Bertilak). Indeed, so surprised are readers that they tend to dismiss Morgan's relevance to the poem's themes: Gawain's chivalric identity; his worth as he enters and emerges from his testing; the reputation of Arthur's court that it is Gawain's duty to uphold. Leaving Morgan till the end might seem an effective strategy for marginalizing her and her influence. She is, however, central to this romance's designs.[6]

Structurally and thematically, women are at the center of this poem. It is in the middle that we meet the beautiful, sexy, unnamed young wife of Bertilak along with her antithesis and companion, the aged, withered Morgan, who resembles the Lady in gender and namelessness alone. By the time we encounter them, our attention has been effectively focused on the Green Knight and his beheading game, on Gawain's pending reunion with him, and on the masculine values of Christian chivalry emblematized in the pentangle on Gawain's shield and surcoat. These values stress the knight's obligations to other men. In a lighter vein, so does Bertilak when he engages Gawain in a promise to exchange winnings with him at the end of each day of his hunt. Gawain, resting in the castle before his rendez-vous at the Green Chapel, is not alone in wondering what he will be able to offer Bertilak in exchange for his kill.

The Lady gives him the answer: the incremental number of kisses she offers him on each of the three progressively seductive mornings she corners him in bed. Gawain dutifully resists the increasing pressure of the lady's advances. But the Lady here is smart and wily. She lures Gawain into the perilous exchanges of courtly dalliance by persistently calling into question his much vaunted reputation for chivalry and courtliness. In essence, she asks him to prove he is Gawain. Because the erotic courtesy she seeks is rather different from the Christian kind tied up in the pentangle's "endeles knot" (630),[7] Gawain is forced to deny his reputation in order to save it. He is not, he insists, the Gawain she has in mind: "'I be not now he that ye of speken'" (1243).

But the Lady goes one step further and shows how dangerous it is for men when women initiate exchanges with them. She says: "'And al the wele of the worlde were in myn honde, And I schulde chepen and chose to cheue me a lorde, / . . . / Ther schulde no freke vpon folde bifore yow be chosen'" (1270–75) ("'If all the wealth in the world were in my hand, / And I should bargain and choose to get me a lord, / There should no man on the earth be chosen before you"'"). She would, that is, bargain for Gawain in the same kind of exchange that aristocratic men use to acquire aristocratic women in the makings of medieval marriage. The commercialized language in which the Lady frames her desires puts Gawain on the market.[8] Nothing could be more dangerous to masculine aristocratic power, prerogative, and privilege than women buying their own men.

Trapped in bed, unarmed and disarmed, objectified, Gawain is in a tight spot, his chivalric identity and his obligations to men deeply threatened by the Lady in the bedroom. This is a private space, one that, arguably, is feminized by its association with the Lady and by its removal from scenes of masculine testing and activity: the hunt outside the castle, even the banquet hall where men make compacts with each other. But the bedroom is always an overdetermined space. Private though it may seem, it is not, in any simple sense, "the woman's sphere." The values of the outside world, of the public man, are as fully present and prevalent here as they are on the battlefield or the tournament ground. The links between the private and the public are emblematized in the green girdle that the lady prevails upon Gawain to accept and keep hidden, not only as her love token, but also because of its putative capacity to protect the wearer from harm. Gawain breaks his word to Bertilak and hides the girdle, not out of love for the lady, but in order to save his life. For this transgression, however, he receives just a nick on the neck. Did the woman's gift protect him, or is it the source of the only injury he receives?

Mulier est hominis confusio. This is, essentially, Gawain's reaction to Bertilak's multiple revelations at the end of the poem. Although Bertilak underplays Gawain's failing, Gawain reacts with considerable self-flagellation to being found out keeping the girdle: "'Corsed worth cowarddyse and couetyse bothe! / In yow is vylany and vyse that vertue disstryez'" (2374–75) ("'Cursed be cowardice and covetousness both! / In you is villainy and vice that destroys virtue'"). He is not wrong about his failings. Within the codes of chivalry, it is dangerous for a man to privilege his own private life over the bonds of knighthood. Gawain is chastened, but his chastening makes him a man (again). Two stanzas later, Gawain manages to assuage at least a little of his guilt by invoking his own brand of garden-variety medieval misogyny (2414ff.). He reasserts his bonds with men across the common experience, shared, he says, by great men since the time of Adam, of being deceived by women.

By the time Morgan's agency is revealed less than a hundred lines from the end of the poem, it has been marginalized to the point that it appears irrelevant. Her plot becomes associated with her desire not only to test the Round Table's reputation, but also "'to haf greued Gaynour and gart hir to dye'" (2460) ("'to have dismayed Guinevere and caused her to die'") with the sight of the Green Knight, standing head in hand at Christmas time in Camelot. This second motivation trivializes Morgan's power. The threat of the woman as a free agent who can construct her own exchanges with men is undermined and marginalized by being projected onto Morgan's jealousy of Arthur's wife. But given Guinevere's implication in the Round Table's collapse, even this motivation underscores the danger of women within Arthur's court.

This pattern of marginalizing women at the center appears again in Chaucer's Canterbury romances. In *The Knight's Tale*, for example, Emelye, the captured Amazon princess who becomes Duke Theseus's sister-in-law, causes the entire plot. The two Theban cousins, Palamon and Arcite, fall in love with Emelye, but unbeknownst to her, when they see her walking below the window of their tower prison. Because of her, they become enemies, pine for years, defy Theseus, return from exile, escape from jail, and hack each other to bits in a forest clearing. Because of her, Theseus commands them to assemble 200 men to fight in a tournament and spends a whole year and much money building tournament grounds and temples. Because of her, and despite her useless prayer to Diana to remain a virgin, the cousins fight; Arcite wins Emelye but loses his life; and Theseus stages an elaborate funeral. Finally, he gives Emelye to Palamon. All the while, Emelye does little and says less. Aside from her prayer to Diana, she seems to have lost all contact with her Amazonian roots. A trophy won by Theseus, she is his to exchange when and where he wills.[9]

Despite the Wife of Bath's notorious challenges to male power, her romance tale leaves men little to fear.[10] Here, an ungrateful young rapist has his life spared by (a curiously unnamed) Guinevere if he can discover what women most desire. The knight is rescued by a magical old hag, who will give him the answer if he will give her the next thing she asks. Women, she tells him, want power, a salutary lesson for the young rapist. He repays the hag by being none-too-pleased when she makes him marry her. After discovering on her wedding night that her new groom resents her for being old, ugly, and poor, the hag gives him a lecture filled with pious platitudes exalting said defects, before letting him choose whether she will be a fickle, young beauty or a faithful old hag. He gives her the choice, and she rewards him by instantly becoming beautiful, young, loving: "And she obeyed hym in every thyng / That myghte doon hym plesaunce or likyng" (1255–56). If this is women's power, one has to wonder what powerlessness would look like.

But it is Chaucer's *Troilus and Criseyde* that is his longest, most sophisticated, and most intricate romance. In his Criseyde, he has formed the most fully realized representation of a woman's consciousness and self-consciousness in the Middle English romance tradition.[11] Troilus begins the work young, virginal, and scornful of love. When he falls in love, he falls hard and fast. Criseyde, in contrast, is the experienced woman, probably older, widowed, thus sexually aware, and independently wealthy enough to keep her own household. Yet, because her father Calchas, a soothsayer, has foreseen the city's defeat and defected to the Greeks, Criseyde is a woman ambiguously situated, simultaneously self-assured and vulnerable. At the public gathering to honor Pallas Athena, "yet she stod ful lowe and stille allone, / . . . / neigh the dore, ay under shames drede, / . . . / With ful assuryed lokyng and manere"(*TC*, 1.178–82). The contradictions she embodies in our first view of her will persist almost till the end, when Troilus's final view of her attempts to resolve them, once and for all.

Criseyde is fully aware of her ambiguous position. In Book II, as her uncle Pandarus proposes the idea of loving Troilus to her, Chaucer offers us her insights and hesitations about this prospect. She considers her own position in Troy, her fears for herself, and her sense of her worth in a long internal mono-logue (*TC*, II.707–810) that seems, at times, an exercise in equivocation. (This woman is self-conscious, but she also seems a confusion even to herself.) If she rejects the king's son, perhaps she will stand "'in worse plyt'" (*TC*, II.712) in Troy, given her father's defection. She is flattered by his love and by the fact that she has his fate in her hands, but then men can be fickle and can dishonor women. Should she sacrifice her present freedom from a man's demands for the uncertain future of love? She tells herself: "'I am myn owene womman, wel at ese – / I thank it God – as after myn estat, /. . ./ . . . / Shal non housbonde seyn to me "Chekmat"'" (*TC*, II.750–54). The course of the romance, however, will demonstrate what Criseyde already knows, her assertion of independence aside. She is not entirely her own woman. As a woman, she is perilously subject to the forces of the world around her. These forces become embodied, close to home, in the person of her uncle Pandarus, her only remaining male protector in Troy. For Pandarus is also Troilus's best friend and has volunteered to become the most energetic go-between in romance.

It is Pandarus, arguably, who genders the two lovers, and not only by success-fully bringing them together. By playing upon Criseyde's sense of her own vul-nerability in Troy and on her need for Troilus's protection, he erodes her sense that she owns herself. Simultaneously, Pandarus moves Troilus toward masculin-ity and away from the hyper-emotional, hesitant, and feminized posture of the typical male courtly lover. Above all, Pandarus genders the lovers and engenders their affair specifically by becoming the consummate exchanger of the woman that his name, thanks to Chaucer, has subsequently come to imply. Pandarus knows exactly what he's doing for his friend: "'for the am I becomen / Bytwixen game and ernest swych a mene / As maken wommen unto men to comen – / Al sey I nought, thow wost wel what I mene'" (*TC*, III.253–56). Though Pandarus disclaims any "'coveytise'" (*TC*, III.261) as motivation and thus technically dis-claims pimping, it seems clear that Troilus, too, knows exactly what he means. To prove his faith that Pandarus is not engaging in "'bauderye'" (*TC*, III.397), Troilus promptly volunteers to return the favor, offering Pandarus his "'faire suster Polixene, / Cassandre, Eleyne, or ony of the frape'" (*TC*, III.410–11). No matter how naïve Troilus is at this point, he should have learned that transact-ing Helen from one man to another has already caused Trojans enough trouble.

Criseyde's status as the object of exchange is made clear in the middle of the romance, at the climax in the consummation scene. Trapped at Pandarus's house by rain and in bed by the peculiarly convenient architecture of her uncle's bedroom, Criseyde has Troilus thrust upon her. Although Troilus's masculiniza-tion suffers a temporary set-back when he faints from nervousness, he recovers within the space of a line (*TC*, III.1191–92). While Criseyde "[r]ight as an aspes

lef . . . gan to quake" (*TC*, III.1200), Troilus's first words to her make her position and his more than clear: "'Now be ye kaught, now is ther but we tweyne. /
Now yeldeth yow'" (*TC*, III.1207–08). Troilus is wrong about one thing, however:
they are not alone, just the two of them. Pandarus is still outside the bed cur-
tains, near the fire where he had previously withdrawn "to loke upon an old
romaunce" (*TC*, III.980). And the audience has also been invited into bed with
the couple. The reader, specifically marked here as a heterosexual male, is treated
to a detailed description of Criseyde's naked body and invited to identify with
the now fully masculinized Troilus as he repeatedly kisses her (*TC*, III.1247–53).
This bedroom is no private and therefore feminized space. It is fairly overpopu-
lated by men: Troilus and Pandarus; the male members of the audience who, voy-
euristically, gaze upon Criseyde (the female audience is not shown Troilus); and
the masculine values that endorse women's exchangeability and men's rights to
exchange them. Compared to Criseyde trapped in bed, Gawain cornered by the
Lady looks downright self-determining.

If Criseyde's status as the woman in the middle is underlined by the logistics
of the consummation scene, it is writ large in the politics of the romance's final
books. Although Criseyde is not literally a prisoner in her home city, she is posi-
tioned as one when the Trojan parliament decides that she will be exchanged to
the Greeks for Antenor, a Trojan prisoner-of-war, at the suggestion of her traitor
father. Troilus cannot compromise his honor or hers by resisting the exchange.
Hector is the sole voice of protest when he asserts, "'We usen here no wommen
for to selle'" (*TC*, IV.182). But the war that is the reason the exchange needs to
occur in the first place shows that, if Trojans are not accustomed to selling
women, they have some track record at stealing them.

As the tragic end of the romance unfolds, Criseyde, throughout a figure of
ambiguity, becomes fixed in and because of her very lack of fixity.[12] Fully feminized as the pawn in men's personal and political exchanges, she is represented
as the embodiment of change itself. When, in the Greek camp, she finds herself
once again in a vulnerable position, she succumbs to the aggressively amorous
advances of the Greek Diomede much more quickly than she did to Troilus's. In
the process, Criseyde, the woman exchanged twice before in this romance,
becomes a threat to Troilus and to Troy because, this time, she exchanges herself.
Is Criseyde here the victim of circumstance or a traitor?

A romance that is often as ambiguous as Criseyde herself tries to leave this
question open. While the final portrait of her in Book v may want to be even-
handed, it concludes with a phrase that is not, in the end, as ambiguous as it
might seem. Criseyde is "slydynge of corage" (*TC*, v.825), fixed in her lack of
fixity, fickle as Eve or as Fortune, the essential(ized) woman. Criseyde's fickleness
will be fixed as her reputation. So much both Chaucer and Criseyde know. The
narrator would "excuse hire yet for routhe" (*TC*, v.1099) because "[h]ire name,

allas, is punysshed so wyde / That for hire gilt it oughte ynow suffise" (*TC*, v.1095). But Criseyde, self-conscious about her compromised position till the end, knows that no good name will follow her, especially among women: "'these bokes wol me shende / . . . / And wommen most wol hate me of alle /. . . / Thei wol seyn, inasmuche as in me is, / I have hem don dishonour, weylaway!'" (*TC*, v.1060–67).

Not so for Troilus, whose devotion makes his name virtually synonymous (as well as consonant) with "trouthe." As in *Sir Gawain*, "trouthe" is the essence of chivalric virtue, the antithesis of the feminine, of the woman who is "slydynge of corage." Chaucer's romance makes Troilus's sorrow the occasion for his ennobling. Fully aware of Criseyde's defection, Troilus asserts that he could not "'unloven her a quarter of a day'" (*TC*, v.1698). His suffering because of Criseyde, first in the naïve throes of new love and finally in the mature pains of love forever lost, creates his apotheosis. He ends as the fully realized chivalric ideal, as we see when he throws himself wildly into his final battle. But Troilus's apotheosis has one more step to go if he is to conquer the confusion of Criseyde. After his death, he looks down on earth and delivers a laugh of sublime irony at the futility of "[t]he blynde lust, the which that may not laste" (*TC*, v.1824). He has attained a fully mature and philosophical transcendence of the world and of women. He has dismissed Criseyde and resolved his confusion.

Because Thomas Malory sets out to redact the entire Arthurian cycle from Arthur's conception to his death, transcendence of women, in one sense, can only come in his *Works* as late as it does in *Sir Gawain* and *Troilus and Criseyde* – on the margins, at the very end. But as Arthur is ushered to Avalon on a boat freighted with his sisters and the Lady of the Lake, it might seem that the "once and future king" never achieves such transcendence. Lancelot, however, does, if only after the collapse of the Round Table, in part because Guinevere enters a nunnery and then dies, in part because he enters the priesthood and then dies, with a smile on his lips and an entourage of angels. His final apotheosis is a match for Troilus's. In another sense, however, this transcendence of women actually begins much earlier. Indeed, it is perceptible throughout Malory's *Works*, because even the most prominent and (in)famous women of Arthurian legend are persistently dismissed, marginalized, made, at most, secondary to men's ongoing struggles to construct their knightly identities.

Certainly, given the ambitious scope of Malory's project, it is not surprising that we find a larger and more diverse cast of female characters here than we do in *Sir Gawain* and *Troilus and Criseyde*. He includes the good girls and the bad and everyone in between, from Nineva and Percival's sister, Morgan le Fay and Isolde, to Elaine and Morgause.[13] And, of course, there is Guinevere, quite naturally the most important female character. Even though Malory's representations of women are not his strong suit, Guinevere comes closest to being developed in any detail. Certainly, Guinevere is the most complex. Yet representing Guinevere poses a significant problem for Malory, given one of his primary emphases in his *Works*. As critics have long noted, this soldier-adventurer, so often out of favor that he wrote much of his work in prison, is centrally concerned with making Lancelot his hero.[14] But how can the pillar of the Round Table's strength and reputation betray his king by bedding the king's wife – and still remain the repository of chivalric virtue, escaping as relatively blameless as he can from the catastrophe of Camelot's collapse?

Malory's most effective strategy for solving this problem bears marked resemblances to those we have seen at work in *Sir Gawain* and *Troilus and Criseyde*: Malory marginalizes Guinevere and the love affair. In "The Vengeance of Sir Gawain," for example, Arthur himself voices Guinevere's marginality within his court in the same breath that he articulates the exchangeability and the interchangeability of women (even, perhaps especially, the highest). As the tensions within the Round Table are about to explode around the forced revelation of Guinevere's infidelity, Arthur laments: " 'And much more I am soryar for my good knyghtes losse than for the losse of my fayre quene; for quenys I myght have inow, but such a felyship of good knyghtes shal never be togydirs in no company' " (Bk. XX, II, p. 685).[15] Despite the fact that Malory here underlines a sad, practical truth, both in Arthurian legend and in medieval history, he and Arthur are stuck with this queen. But the least Malory can do is to minimize her presence in his text.

A striking example of the way in which Malory accomplishes this erasure of Guinevere occurs later in "The Vengeance of Gawain." At the Pope's command, Lancelot must return Guinevere to Arthur at Carlisle. In a scene fraught with high drama and emotion, Malory devotes more space to a description of Lancelot's entourage and its ceremonial array than to any reaction Guinevere might be having as she is transacted between her lover and her husband (Bk. XX, II, pp. 693–98). After long, courtly speeches to Arthur and his retinue, Lancelot delivers his parting, noble, and deliberately public address to Guinevere, kisses her farewell, and hands her over to Arthur. Through it all, Guinevere is mute. While we learn that everyone on both sides (except Gawain) weeps copiously at this tragic parting, Malory gives no indication of Guinevere's individual reaction. She is as silent at this crucial moment as she is during her one very brief appearance in *Sir Gawain*. In *Sir Gawain*, however, Guinevere is at least conspicuous in her lavish dress and beauty as a sign of Arthur's power and prestige. Here, she might as well be, indeed she is, invisible.

Malory's second strategy for representing Guinevere so as to valorize Lancelot may, at first glance, seem to defeat his purpose. At second glance, however, we see that it has some psychological, if not logical, persuasiveness. When Guinevere is not being written out of the text, she emerges, for the most part, as a fairly unattractive character. She is capricious, jealous, fickle, and manipulative. At the mere rumor of Lancelot's association with another woman, she banishes him from court. Indeed, so precarious is her reputation and so little the affection and respect Arthur's knights have for their queen that, in "The Poisoned Apple," it takes but a small leap for her chivalrous companions to assume, if a knight keels over dead at one of Guinevere's dinner parties, then Guinevere must be to blame. But Guinevere's knack for getting herself into trouble (or being suspected of it) means that she spends more than her share of time in dangerous proximity to the stake. This is a position for Guinevere that works to Malory's advantage in characterizing Lancelot, for Lancelot, banished or not, is constantly on call to rescue her. And rescue her he does. Malory can make political and ideological capital out of Guinevere's personal weaknesses because they go a distance toward constructing and reinforcing Lancelot's heroism, loyalty, and unswerving fidelity to his queen, who also happens to be his lover. It really is no paradox in Malory's configuration of chivalric masculinity that Lancelot emerges as Arthur's premier knight specifically because he is the champion of Arthur's frequently imperiled wife.

If, in this text, Guinevere is not represented as terrifically lovable (no Julie Andrews or Julie Christie or Julia Ormond, she), then why would a knight of Lancelot's stature and goodness, a knight who came as close to the Grail as any sinner could, a knight who loves his king, why would such a knight risk all to love this woman? The answer comes in Malory's third strategy for representing Guinevere: his rehabilitation of her in the final movements of *Morte Darthur*. For Malory, the ultimate destruction of Arthur's Round Table and realm derives not so much from the adulterous, treasonous affair between Lancelot and Guinevere as from the heinous ambitions of the patricidal Mordred. (Arthur's guilt for begetting Mordred in an incestuous union with his sister is here conveniently elided.) In "The Day of Destiny," Guinevere herself is rehabilitated when Mordred trains his aspirations on forcing her to marry him. But no sooner does Guinevere attract sympathy in this role as potential victim than she attracts admiration, for she turns her manipulativeness, for once, to good purpose by tricking Mordred and barricading herself, amply provisioned, in the Tower of London.

This resourcefulness becomes the hallmark of the rehabilitated Guinevere's character for the rest of her brief time in Malory's work. In what may be the only exchange that the medieval woman in these romances can safely make on her own, Guinevere gives herself to God and retires to a convent. Her action underlines not only the spiritual development of her character (and the fact that she now can neither cause nor get into trouble), but also Lancelot's recurrent and tragic belatedness in the final episodes of Malory's *Works*. He arrives too late to save Arthur from Mordred or Guinevere from the nunnery, and when he himself has taken vows at her example, too late to see her one last time. Lancelot's own dwindling and death derive from a sorrow deeply implicated in his love for Guinevere, a sorrow, like that of the mature and philosophical Troilus, which is the final stage of his apotheosis. His deathbed speech intertwines his memory of their love with his love for Arthur and a deep Christian humility and repentance for having contributed to the demise of all he valued most on earth. Little wonder, then, that Lancelot dies with the scent of sweetness around him, for Malory has completed the glorification of his hero, the generous, self-sacrificing knight who has almost had and done it all.

Here, oddly, Lancelot suggests the strange truth of Chauntecleer's inadvertent mistranslation: woman is the confusion of man, but she is also all his joy and bliss. Interestingly, given Malory's conspicuous lack of sympathy for women, it is his hero who dies in the knowledge that, if women confuse men, men are at least partly to blame. Perhaps Lancelot and Malory can afford this particular generosity because the confusion that is Guinevere has been resolved with some finality by her death. It is not so simple for the other authors and their heroes. For the *Gawain*-poet and his Gawain, women, though marginalized, still lurk and work within the court. They are still peril *in potentia* that can render impotent men's best attempts to be chivalric brothers. While Chaucer may seem to give Troilus the last laugh, Criseyde, of course, lives on.

The romances of the *Gawain*-poet, Chaucer, and Malory mark the height as well as the end of this genre in Middle English. In their works, all three writers register an anxiety about women and about the ways in which women can make and unmake men. As different as the thematic emphases of their works may be, all three engage issues surrounding women's exchangeability (and sometimes their interchangeability) at the same time that they show the dangers that arise when women attempt to make their own deals. These late Middle English writers end by marginalizing women, and especially by relegating many of the moments of their greatest activity literally to the margins of the texts. They all, in one way or another, echo Chauntecleer, who, of course, was not the first or the last to crow, "'*Mulier est hominis confusio.*'"

For these reasons, the *Gawain*-poet, Geoffrey Chaucer, and Thomas Malory share a common ground in their romances' representations of women and men that sets them apart from many of their French precursors in this genre. While we might not be able to say that they were self-consciously forming a distinctly English romance tradition, it is not too much to claim that they were self-consciously aware of themselves as English writers separate from, even as they relied on, continental sources. Moreover, in a century that saw the repercussions in England of the Hundred Years War with France and its immediate aftermath, it is not too much to claim that these men registered a nationalist self-consciousness and some measure of anxiety about English as a language appropriate for composing "high" literature. As they wrote, they might well have experienced, in addition, a national and nationalist anxiety about issues that, in their fictional forms, were the very stuff of romance: about English chivalry and knighthood and about English aristocratic masculinity in relation to the long war England was destined ultimately to lose. In their own encounters with a genre as deeply "French" as the romance, then, these late medieval English writers may have been expressing an anxiety about masculinity, marginalization, and belatedness that voiced itself in the persistent marginalization of women. But that, too, would end up being a losing battle.

NOTES

1 Quotations from Chaucer's works are taken from *The Riverside Chaucer* and cited by fragment and line number for *The Canterbury Tales* and by book and line number for *Troilus and Criseyde* within the essay.

2 A. C. Spearing, *Medieval to Renaissance in English Poetry* (Cambridge University Press, 1985) and Susan Crane, *Gender and Romance in Chaucer's* "Canterbury Tales."

3 See Elaine Tuttle Hansen, *Chaucer and the Fictions of Gender*; Carolyn Dinshaw, *Chaucer's Sexual Poetics*; and Sheila Fisher, "Taken Men and Token Women in *Sir Gawain and the Green Knight*," and "Leaving Morgan Aside: Women, History, and Revisionism in *Sir Gawain and the Green Knight*."

4 Meale, ed., *Women and Literature in Britain 1150–1500*.

5 Gayle Rubin, "The Traffic in Women: Notes on the 'Political Economy of Sex,'" in *Toward an Anthropology of Women*, ed. Rayna Reiter (New York: Monthly Review Press, 1975), 157–210; Eve Kosofsky Sedgwick, *Between Men: English Literature and Male Homosocial Desire* (New York: Columbia University Press, 1985); Shulamith Shahar, *The Fourth Estate: A History of Women in the Middle Ages*, tr. Chaya Galai (New York: Methuen, 1983); Roberta L. Krueger, "Double Jeopardy: The Appropriation of Woman in Four Old French Romances of the 'Cycle de la Gageure,'" in *Seeking the Woman in Late Medieval and Renaissance Writings: Essays in Feminist Contextual Criticism*, ed. Sheila Fisher and Janet E. Halley (Knoxville: University of Tennessee Press, 1989), 21–50.

6 See my essays on *Sir Gawain* cited in note 3. Also, Geraldine Heng, "Feminine Knots and the Other *Sir Gawain and the Green Knight*," *PMLA*, 106 (1991), 500–14, and Clare R. Kinney, "The (Dis)Embodied Hero and the Signs of Manhood in *Sir Gawain and the Green Knight*," in *Medieval Masculinities: Regarding Men in the Middle Ages*, ed. Clare A. Lees with Thelma Fenster and Jo Ann McNamara, Medieval Cultures 7 (Minneapolis: University of Minnesota Press, 1994), 47–57.

7 Quotations from *Sir Gawain and the Green Knight* are taken from the Tolkein, Gordon, and Davis edition and cited by line number within the essay. For the purpose of orthographic convenience and to aid the reader, I have transliterated the thorn as "th" and the yogh as "gh" or "y" depending on its nearest Modern English equivalent. All translations of *Sir Gawain* are my own.

8 "Taken Men and Token Women in *Sir Gawain and the Green Knight*," and R. A. Shoaf, *The Poem as Green Girdle: "Commercium" in "Sir Gawain and the Green Knight."*

9 Crane, *Gender and Romance in Chaucer's* "Canterbury Tales", esp. ch. 5, and Hansen, *Chaucer and the Fictions of Gender*, ch. 8.

10 In addition to the books of Crane, Dinshaw, and Hansen, see Peggy Knapp, *Chaucer and the Social Contest* (New York: Routledge, 1990); H. Marshall Leicester, Jr., "Of a Fire in the Dark: Public and Private Feminism in the *Wife of Bath's Tale*," *Women's Studies*, 11 (1984), 157–78; Priscilla Martin, *Chaucer's Women: Nuns, Wives, and Amazons* (Iowa City: University of Iowa Press, 1990); Ross Murfin, "Feminist Criticism and the Wife of Bath" and Elaine Tuttle Hansen, "'Of his love daungerous to me': Liberation, Subversion, and Domestic Violence in the Wife of Bath's Prologue and Tale," both in *Geoffrey Chaucer: The Wife of Bath*, ed. Peter G. Beidler (Boston: Bedford Books, 1996), 255–71 and 271–89, respectively.

11 Dinshaw, *Chaucer's Sexual Poetics*, ch. 1; Hansen, *Chaucer and the Fictions of Gender*, ch. 6; Arlyn Diamond, "*Troilus and Criseyde*: The Politics of Love," in *Chaucer in the Eighties*, ed. Julian N. Wasserman and Robert J. Blanch (Syracuse University Press, 1986), 93–104, and David Aers, *Chaucer, Langland, and the Creative Imagination* (London: Routledge & Kegan Paul, 1980) and *Community, Gender, and Individual Identity: English Writing 1360–1430* (London: Routledge, 1988).

12 See R. A. Shoaf, *Dante, Chaucer, and the Currency of the Word: Money, Images, and Reference in Late Medieval Poetry* (Norman: Pilgrim Books, 1983).

13 A good example of the ways in which Malory makes even important Arthurian women secondary is his treatment of so major a figure as Isolde. She is so scattered and fragmented across the 250-plus pages of *The Book of Sir Tristram de Lyones* that, like Humpty Dumpty, she cannot be put back together again.

14 In his compendious notes, Vinaver tracks the many changes that Malory made in his French sources in order to aggrandize Lancelot. See, for example, pp. 744, 759, and 768.

15 Quotations from Malory's *Works* are taken from the Vinaver edition and cited by book and page number in the essay. See Terence McCarthy, "*Le Morte Darthur* and Romance," *Studies in Medieval English Romances: Some New Approaches*, ed. Derek Brewer (Cambridge: Boydell & Brewer, 1988), 148–75.

SUGGESTIONS FOR FURTHER READING

Aers, David. *Community, Gender, and Individual Identity: English Writing 1360–1430.* London: Routledge, 1988.

Crane, Susan. *Gender and Romance in Chaucer's* "Canterbury Tales." Princeton University Press, 1994.

Dinshaw, Carolyn. *Chaucer's Sexual Poetics.* Madison: University of Wisconsin Press, 1989.

Fisher, Sheila. "Leaving Morgan Aside: History, Revisionism, and Women in *Sir Gawain and the Green Knight.*" *The Passing of Arthur: New Essays in Arthurian Traditions.* Ed. Christopher Baswell and William Sharpe. New York: Garland, 1988. 129–51. (Rptd. in *Medieval English Poetry.* Ed. Stephanie Trigg. London: Longman, 1993. Also rptd. in *Arthurian Women: A Casebook.* Ed. Thelma S. Fenster. New York: Garland, 1996.)

Fisher, Sheila. "Taken Men and Token Women in *Sir Gawain and the Green Knight.*" *Seeking the Woman in Late Medieval and Renaissance Writings: Essays in Feminist*

Contextual Criticism. Ed. Sheila Fisher and Janet E. Halley. Knoxville: University of Tennessee Press, 1989. 71–105.

Hansen, Elaine Tuttle. *Chaucer and the Fictions of Gender*. Berkeley: University of California Press, 1992.

Meale, Carol M., ed. *Women and Literature in Britain, 1150–1500*. Cambridge University Press, 1993.

Shoaf, R. A. *The Poem as Green Girdle: "Commercium" in* "Sir Gawain and the Green Knight." Humanities Monograph Series 55. Gainesville: University of Florida Press, 1984.

III

EUROPEAN TRANSFORMATIONS

10

NORRIS J. LACY

The evolution and legacy of French prose romance

French romances occupy a central position in the development of medieval European literature. Their most popular subject matter by far was the Arthurian legend, which, though it had its origins elsewhere, was first cast in romance form in France: the Round Table, the tragic love story of Lancelot and Guinevere, and the notion of the Grail quest were all French innovations. So too was the very genre of romance, a sophisticated and complex form that dramatized quests and tests and explored the connections – and often the conflicts – of love and adventure.

The legacy of French romance in other literatures is almost incalculable. Writers in every language of Western Europe adapted or translated French texts; and even when they were not openly reworking French sources, indeed even when they sought to assert their independence from those sources, their own romances frequently betray a decided Gallic influence in their use of the structures and conventions of romance, their borrowing of popular motifs or characters, or their rhetorical procedures.

Throughout the second half of the twelfth century, with the great masterpieces of Chrétien de Troyes, the Tristan and Iseut romances of Thomas and Béroul, and a number of other works, verse had been the preferred vehicle for the composition of romances, which were generally intended to be read aloud before groups of listeners. Prose was at that time reserved largely for history writing, for legal documents, and for sermons and other religious texts. Then, early in the thirteenth century, authors began to cast romances, apparently intended for private as well as public reading, in prose (although verse romances continued to be written as well throughout the thirteenth century). The adoption of prose for use in purely literary texts clearly was not a casual historical development, nor was prose by any means taken merely as a free alternative to verse. Instead, the change was to a good extent the inevitable consequence of the emerging view that prose was essential for the presentation of truth.

A number of medieval writers make this point explicitly; for example, an anonymous translator of the *Pseudo-Turpin* announces bluntly that *Nus contes rimé n'est verais*: "no rhymed tale is true."[1] The explanation is that, in order to accommodate the demands of metre and rhyme, an author or translator must introduce distortions, such as unnatural syntax, additional syllables, or a word chosen for rhyme rather than meaning. Since anything that takes precedence over the direct communication of meaning falsifies the text, it follows that only prose, unfettered by artifice, could convey truth. Indeed, to some commentators, verse became a virtual synonym for "falsehood."

Prose had other advantages as well. It is capable of supporting, far better than verse, the length and narrative complications (such as the prolongation of a knight's ordeals or, more particularly, the simultaneous advancement of multiple story lines) that increasingly characterize romance beyond the twelfth century. Even some of the earliest prose romances are long and complex, and we have some romances and cycles that run to many hundreds, even several thousands, of pages.

In fact, as French romance moves into the thirteenth century, it develops in two entirely distinct directions. Verse compositions, which tend to be shorter, are generally episodic texts that deal with a limited time span and concentrate on the adventures of a single knight or of two, the second one often Gawain, a popular figure who may be the hero or a foil for another character. Prose romances, on the other hand, tend to treat an extended period, often a full lifetime, multiple generations, or even, as parts of cycles, universal history. Finally, verse and prose may be distinguished, again with some exceptions, by the nature of the subject matter: in general, Grail material is reserved for treatment in prose.[2]

The categories of prose and verse, however, are neither absolute nor mutually exclusive. Many of the verse romances were eventually adapted into prose, and in rare cases prose texts were versified.

EARLY FRENCH PROSE ROMANCES

The overwhelming majority of French prose romances are Arthurian. Moreover, many deal not only with the reign of Arthur, but also with the Grail quest. The Grail, which in Chrétien de Troyes had been a mysterious dish from which light emanated, soon came to be identified with the vessel of the Last Supper. Perceval, a naïve but gifted Welsh youth who soon becomes one of the greatest figures of the Round Table, is the dominant character of several of these texts: of *Perlesvaus*, an important composition that is one of the first French prose romances; of a shorter romance known as the *Didot-Perceval* (named for the former owner of one of the manuscripts); and of the non-cyclic version of the *Lancelot-Grail*.

Dating from the first decade or two of the thirteenth century, the anonymous

Perlesvaus is in part an expansion and recasting of the Grail material drawn from *Le Roman de Perceval, ou le conte du Graal*, the last romance of Chrétien de Troyes. Although the hero is directly inspired by the protagonist of Chrétien's text, he is here named Perlesvaus rather than Perceval, and the work itself glosses his name as the equivalent of *perd-les-vaux* (meaning the one who "loses the vales" of Kamaalot [= Camelot]). The author presents Perlesvaus's failure to ask about the Grail as the source of a complex of woes afflicting the realm: Arthur's indolence, the malady of the Fisher King, and the ineffectiveness of the Round Table.

Perlesvaus presents a series of adventures by four protagonists: Arthur, Gawain, Lancelot, and Perlesvaus. Gawain and Lancelot find their way to the Grail Castle but cannot complete the quest. The former sees the Grail but, enthralled, fails to ask about it; Lancelot's adulterous relationship with the Queen renders him unworthy even of the vision. It will thus fall to Perlesvaus to make retribution for his own earlier failure and to free the realm, but this romance allies military prowess with rigorous piety, and the hero must recapture the Grail Castle before posing the question.

This romance owes a great deal to Chrétien's but also departs from it in important ways. Love – except the love of God – has little place in it, and even the relationship of Lancelot and Guenevere is passed over in almost perfunctory manner. Largely lacking the refined courtly spirit of Chrétien's compositions, *Perlesvaus* is distinguished by its spirit of militant Christianity, as well as by its length and complexity and by the profusion of adventures and episodes. It also makes prominent use of allegorical associations with objects, places, and names; Perlesvaus's mother, for example, is named Yglais, suggesting "yglise, église" ("church"). The *Perlesvaus* is an important contribution to Grail literature, but it has not received the attention and study it merits. That relative neglect is undoubtedly due to the enormous success enjoyed, almost from the beginning, by several imposing cycles of Grail romances.

THE LANCELOT-GRAIL CYCLE

With the obvious exception of Chrétien de Troyes, the most influential writer within the French romance tradition may well be Robert de Boron, who around the year 1200 composed a verse trilogy that is extant only in part but that altered the character and direction of Arthurian literature. Robert's texts were quickly expanded and prosified and were recast in two forms. One, generally called *Le Roman du Graal*, is a trilogy depicting early Grail history, Arthur's advent, and the Grail quest and decline of the Arthurian world.

The other is the great *Lancelot-Grail* Cycle of Arthurian romance, also known as the Prose *Lancelot*, the Vulgate Cycle, or the Pseudo-Map Cycle. This is one of the most extraordinary and most influential of medieval literary creations. Composed between about 1215 and 1235, the lengthy and elaborate cycle comprises five separate but closely interrelated romances. Reflecting the period's taste for encyclopedic works, the *Lancelot-Grail* offers a thorough compendium of Arthurian and Grail history and prehistory – the origin of the Grail, the story of Merlin, Arthur's birth and life, the love of Lancelot and Guinevere, the Grail quest (ultimately accomplished by the final Grail king, Galahad), and the destruction of the Round Table. It furthermore connects these themes to a schema of sacred history extending back from the Crucifixion of Christ through the stories of Solomon and King David to the Garden of Eden.

Even though the *Lancelot-Grail* in general and one of its romances, *La Queste del saint Graal*, in particular tend to explain almost everything to us, often in exhaustive detail, it nevertheless leaves us with some intriguing mysteries. While most involve interpretation or method, one of them concerns its own authorship. The text itself informs us that Walter Map was the author – or at least one of the authors – of the cycle. That the putative authorship of this fiction is itself a fiction is undeniable: Walter, a jurist and writer at the court of Henry II Plantagenet, inconveniently died in 1209, that is, some years before the earliest possible date for the romances. This false attribution of the cycle to Walter explains one of the general titles given it: the Pseudo-Map Cycle.

But if Walter is known not to have composed the cycle, scholars have not identified the actual authors. The most commonly accepted theory is Jean Frappier's notion of an "architect" of the cycle. According to Frappier's hypothesis, one or more persons planned the original cycle and may have composed the central *Lancelot* romance or another part; other writers completed the rest in accordance with a strict and detailed plan.[3]

One of the facts that sponsor this theory is the technique of interlace in the cycle. The texts repeatedly leave adventures in suspension in order to present another story, the change of subject often being indicated by a formula such as "Or dist li contes . . ." ("Now the story tells us . . ."). They also digress frequently to offer accounts of past events or to treat accessory themes. Yet, all the segments are intricately interlaced so as to lead us back eventually to the suspended sequences and advance them further. Moreover, many hundreds of references to previous and eventual developments offer additional evidence that a carefully formulated plan guided the anonymous authors of these romances.

Originally, however, the plan for the cycle appears to have accounted for only the last three of the five romances that now constitute it. Those three are the *Lancelot* (also called the *Lancelot* Proper to distinguish it from the cycle as a whole), *La Queste del saint Graal*, and *La Mort le Roi Artu*. The first of these three, a massive romance that constitutes about half of the entire cycle, presents the early life and the adventures of Lancelot, his successes as a knight, and his and Guinevere's love. In presenting that adulterous affair, it offers the cycle's principal exposition of courtly love, a literary convention in which the chivalric efforts of a knight are both motivated and validated by his love for his lady. Set in the larger context of the cycle, however, the validity of courtly love is debated and shown to be ultimately destructive.

Galahad's destiny as the chosen Grail Knight, the subject of *La Queste del saint Graal*, is repeatedly predicted and promised throughout the cycle. For example, at the end of the *Lancelot* Proper, a hermit announces to Arthur, "Rois Artus, je te di por voir an confession que au jor de Pentecoste qui vient sera noviaux chevaliers cil qui les aventures del Saint Graal metra a fin" ("King Arthur, I tell you in true confession that on the coming Pentecost there will be a new-made knight who will bring the adventures of the Holy Grail to an end").[4] This prediction is confirmed when Galahad arrives at court and demonstrates his destiny by withdrawing a sword from a block of stone (a test that reflects but surpasses Arthur's earlier demonstration of his right to be king). It is then discovered that the young knight's name has been mysteriously inscribed on a seat reserved for the Grail Knight: "CI EST LI SIEGES GALAAD": "Here is Galahad's seat."[5]

The *Queste* then traces the quest for the Grail, a challenge accepted by numerous knights and ultimately met only by Galahad. Throughout this text, the events of this world are presented as mere reflections of larger truths, and the characters' adventures, dreams, and visions are interpreted by holy men as allegorical stages in a struggle between the forces of good and evil, between God and the devil, and between the Old Law and the New.

The product, apparently, of a Cistercian author preoccupied with questions of sin and temptation, the *Queste* is uncompromising in its ideological rigor. The narrator explains that only those knights who are morally superior can have even remote hope of success, and we eventually learn that they number three: Bors, Perceval, and Galahad. Yet even the first two of them are finally disqualified, because their purity is not absolute. The text establishes two degrees of sexual propriety, known as *pucelage* and *virginité*, often translated as "maidenhood" and "virginity." The former is a matter of physical fact: it refers to a person who has never experienced sexual intercourse. But the highest state is virginity, which defines a person who has never had even the *desire* for carnal relations. As that state is attained only by Galahad, the completely pure knight, only he is privileged to witness all the Grail secrets and succeed the Grail King.

By contrast to the *Queste*, the final romance is somber, stark, pessimistic, and solidly grounded in the material reality of the Arthurian world. With the Grail adventures concluded, the knights who return to court, we are told, are those who had failed in the quest. The narrator, speaking of Arthur and his knights, immediately announces his project, naming it *La Mort le Roi Artu*: he will recount "la fin de ceus dont il avoit fet devant mention et conment cil morurent dont il avoit amenteües les proesces en son livre" ("the deaths of those he had mentioned before and the kind of end met by those whose accomplishments he had mentioned in his book").[6] The text turns almost immediately to Lancelot, who, having earlier renounced Guinevere, quickly lapses again into sin with her. This adulterous relationship is eventually identified as a principal cause of the Arthurian tragedy. A war that everyone is powerless to prevent destroys both forces and, as the cycle closes, leaves Arthur dead at the hands of Mordred.

Soon after the composition of these three texts, two other romances were added to the head of it, thus providing, as Jean Frappier noted, a "retrospective sequel" or "a portico for the edifice."[7] The first is the *Estoire del saint Graal*, concerning the source and writing of the cycle and foreshadowing (though after the fact) many of the events presented later in the cycle. The other is *Merlin*, which offers the story of the enchanter and his role in the early career of King Arthur.

Yet, the structure of the cycle is by no means as clear and unambiguous as this description may suggest. First of all, there exists a non-cyclic version of the *Lancelot* that does not prefigure the apotheosis of Galahad; in that version, the anticipated hero (as in the *Perlesvaus*) is not Galahad but Perceval. In addition, there were several different compositions (e.g., *Le Livre d'Artus*) that, in various manuscript traditions, were intended to form a bridge between the *Merlin* romance and the three original romances (*Lancelot*, *La Queste del saint Graal*, and *La Mort Artu*).

In short, the identification of five romances as constituent elements in the cycle is to a good extent a critical convenience. In fact, from manuscript to manuscript, the texts often differ in form and in their combination with other works. Yet the majority of scholars continue to conceive of the *Lancelot-Grail* as comprising five closely interrelated romances offering a full Arthurian and Grail history and prehistory. These texts place alternating emphasis on sacred and secular themes, and they also appear to constitute a debate on the efficacy of chivalry and, as noted above, on the nature and value of courtly love.

As these comments indicate, the subjects of the *Lancelot- Grail* are multiple and seem to shift with our point of view. Whatever the perspective, though, the cycle is very much about the competition between two value systems. Although we could make the case that, in the *Perlesvaus*, Arthurian chivalry and the Grail ideal were, or potentially could be, compatible and even complementary ideals, the division in the *Lancelot-Grail* is absolute. Indeed, the narrators, particularly in the *Queste del saint Graal*, establish a moral, religious, and especially sexual standard that can be met by only one human – the romance's Christ figure, Galahad.

In such an ethical climate, it is virtually inevitable that Arthurian (that is, secular) chivalry will be discredited. That traditional chivalry is incompatible with the Grail ethos is underlined by Arthur himself, who, instead of embracing and sponsoring the Grail quest, is distraught when his knights decide to undertake it. He rebukes Gawain, who first vowed to undertake the quest: "vos m'avez mort par le veu que vos avez fet, car vos m'avez ci tolue la plus bele compaignie et la plus loial que je onques trovasse, et ce est la compaignie de la Table Reonde" ("You have killed me by the vow you have made, for you have taken from me the finest and most loyal company that I have ever known, and that is the company of the Round Table").[8]

Although Arthurian chivalry is no longer efficacious in the world of the *Queste*, it is not negated or discarded as much as it is radically remade after a religious model. Not only does the author repeatedly describe priestly vestments as the "armes de Sainte Eglise" or "de Nostre Seignor" ("the armor of Holy Church; the armor of Our Lord"), but the text promulgates what he calls "chevalerie celeste" ("celestial chivalry"), which must supplant the "chevalerie terrienne," the "earthly chivalry," of Arthur's court. Celestial chivalry, the tenets of which are spiritual rather than social or even ethical, requires not only devotion, confession, and contrition, but also perfect purity.

In the *Queste*, the futile adventures of knights who are destined to fail are rendered more dramatic because they are contrasted with those of the chosen knights – Perceval, Bors, and especially Galahad. To effect such a juxtaposition, the authors had recourse, as noted, to the technique of structural or narrative interlace (described above). The method is simple in principle but difficult of execution, and it makes heavy demands on even the most careful of readers. We must keep previous sequences and motifs in mind in order to link them up with later repetitions, contrasts, and variations.

To the uninitiated reader, the effect of interlace may seem haphazard and disorienting. It is certainly true that the *Lancelot-Grail* does not exhibit the kind of unity that we might expect in later texts. Instead, the aesthetic of the period called for a method of composition predicated on ideals of expansiveness and digression. Yet, without being unified in our sense of the word, the cycle is an intricately patterned composition in which plots and episodes, some left incomplete for long periods, eventually converge to dramatize its two climactic events: Galahad's Grail triumph and the marginalization and ultimate destruction of the Round Table. The *Lancelot-Grail*, ingenious in its conception and sweeping in its scope, is also a masterpiece of compositional intricacy.

THE PROSE TRISTAN

But literary methods and tastes were evolving rapidly, and if we have come to an adequate, if not full, understanding of the compositional methods of the *Lancelot-Grail* author(s), we have not reached the same point with later prose works, which appear to have been designed in accord with a guiding principle that has to some considerable degree eluded critics. That evolution is already evident in works that follow closely upon the *Lancelot-Grail* and will become most apparent in later compilations of Arthurian material.

The first such work is another great cycle, the immense Prose *Tristan*.[9] To judge by the number of surviving manuscripts (over eighty, though a good many are fragments) this long cycle must have been one of the most popular literary compositions of the Middle Ages. The Prose *Tristan* is extant in two forms, dating from the second and third quarters of the thirteenth century. The former is attributed in the text itself to one Luces de Gat, the second to Hélie de Borron. Neither name is known from other sources, and most scholars are skeptical of both attributions.

The most striking feature of the cycle is the comparatively full integration of its hero, Tristan, into an Arthurian context. From the time of Béroul's verse *Tristan* (late twelfth century), there had been contact, albeit slight, between the legend of Arthur and that of Tristan, but only with the Prose *Tristan* does the hero become a full member of Arthur's circle. He is a knight of the Round Table, the friend of Lancelot, and a participant in the Grail quest.

That Lancelot and Tristan would be paired is entirely natural. Not only is each described frequently in medieval texts as "the best knight in the world," but, most strikingly, they occupy parallel positions in the two most famous love triangles of medieval literature: Lancelot–Guenevere–Arthur and Tristan–Iseut–Marc. The characters are partially remade, however, from their earlier incarnations in verse, and indeed Marc, a character of ambiguous morality in some very early texts, here becomes a genuine villain who kills Tristan in a jealous rage and is to a good extent responsible for the final destruction of the Round Table.

The Prose *Tristan* represents an attempt to compose a kind of Arthurian *summa*. The cycle begins with an account of Tristan's ancestry – he is descended from the brother-in-law of Joseph of Arimathea – before narrating his birth, youth, and then, as a knight-errant, his continuing quest for adventures. Especially in the early portions of the cycle, the author, in addition to composing original material, includes sequences clearly modeled on the earlier verse versions of the Tristan story. As the romance progresses, Tristan, Iseut, and Marc cease to dominate the narrative, and Arthur and his court come to the fore.

The conception and treatment of the material differ in significant ways from those of the *Lancelot-Grail*. Although the text occasionally offers what Vinaver describes as "some fine examples of tragic lyricism,"[10] the narrator is generally less intent upon analyzing a lover's emotions or duties than upon the presentation of action and adventures. Nor, for the most part, does he explore the chivalric vocation itself or the duties of a knight, and when he does so, it is often with an unexpected twist provided by one of his most delightful creations:

Dinadan, a pragmatist and a jovial cynic. Dinadan consistently questions the conventions of chivalry and condemns, for example, the folly of doing battle for no purpose other than to demonstrate valor. He is equally cynical about love, mocking lovers who are tormented by their emotion; he wants no part of a love that brings not joy but suffering. Dinadan serves as the voice of skeptical reason and practicality.

In many other parts, though, the Prose *Tristan* is likely to strike most readers as a comparatively routine though extraordinarily lengthy compilation of events. With its emphasis on action more than on emotion, the cycle presents, often in great detail, an account of numerous tourneys, battles, and chivalric adventures, whose relationship to one another or to the central development of the narrative is not always evident. In some cases, long sections of other romances, such as the thirteenth-century *Palamedes* and even the Vulgate *Queste* and *Mort Artu*, were interpolated into the cycle.

As a result, even readers who understand that architectonic precision and intricacy are compatible with a discursive method of narration, as they are in the *Lancelot-Grail*, may be disconcerted by the Prose *Tristan*. Interlace is still used, but the technique has decayed considerably in the short time since the *Lancelot-Grail*; narrative threads are introduced and then suspended, as in the earlier cycle, but in many cases they are never taken up again. Interrupted adventures may not be resumed, and quests may not be completed. For many readers, the overall effect is therefore almost an impression of formlessness, of accumulation rather than composition.

Whether or not this cycle is indeed as formless as portions of it may appear to be – and, as noted, it is possible that we have not yet understood its compositional principles – it obviously appealed to the changing tastes of medieval audiences. Both authors and readers now appear less concerned with overall structure than with the appeal of individual and more or less self-contained episodes. In this regard, the Prose *Tristan* may well stand as the most immediate precursor of a popular trend in the late Middle Ages, the Arthurian compilation (see below).

In any event, in its scope and popularity, its only near rival is the *Lancelot-Grail* Cycle, of which it serves in some ways as an extension or sequel. And in terms of literary influence, even the *Lancelot-Grail* almost pales in contrast to the Prose *Tristan*. In addition to the eighty manuscripts and fragments, the composition survives in eight early printed editions, and it inspired translations or adaptations in several languages.

THE POST-VULGATE CYCLE

Almost as soon as the *Lancelot-Grail* Cycle was formulated, it was recast in a form generally known as the Post-Vulgate or, formerly, the Pseudo-Robert de

Boron Cycle (so called because it falsely claims Robert de Boron as its author). The Post-Vulgate is extant in French only in a number of fragments; fortunately, it was adapted very early into Spanish and Portuguese, and it has been largely reconstructed from all those sources.

In the form in which we have it, the cycle represents a radical rehandling of some of the Vulgate material. Although the *Merlin* and perhaps the *Estoire* were taken over, largely intact, from the Vulgate, the rest is remade. A *Suite du Merlin* (a continuation) formed a bridge to the following texts. There is no full romance that corresponds to the Vulgate *Lancelot*, the emphasis on the adulterous love of Lancelot and Guenevere being accordingly reduced. The narrator, who comments frequently on his own method, explains that the omission of the central romance reflects a concern with length, symmetry, and narrative balance, but he is surely guided not only by aesthetic considerations. Rather, the changes he has wrought also represent an obvious attempt to deemphasize the courtly, social content in favor of spiritual concerns. To that same end, the Post-Vulgate expanded the *Queste del saint Graal*, thereafter concluding the cycle with a dramatically truncated *Mort Artu*.

The result is a cycle that is undeniably more unified, in vision and presentation, than the *Lancelot-Grail*, but it also lacks the fascinating tension that its predecessor had developed between secular and spiritual concerns, between courtly and divine love, between earthly and celestial chivalry, between the ideals of the Arthurian court and the higher religious calling answered only by a select few. The Post-Vulgate proved extremely popular and influential, especially in Spain and Portugal, where it may have been even more extensively adapted, translated, or imitated, than was the Vulgate.

LATE FRENCH ROMANCE

The later Middle Ages are a fascinating period for the development of romances, but most of the works themselves are poorly known, either because they are simply overshadowed by the major compositions of earlier centuries or because, in some cases, they are dauntingly long and complex. Some are still not edited in their entirety.

A number of late romance authors set about expanding and amplifying traditional themes. Typical of such efforts is *Perceforest*, which has been described by one of its editors as being of "heroic proportions."[11] Indeed this single romance, from the first half of the fourteenth century, is longer than any of the cycles discussed above. Its author extends not only length but, as with the Prose *Tristan*, also temporal boundaries: the hero, we are told, is established as British king by Alexander the Great, and the civilization he founds is eventually destroyed by Julius Caesar.

The temporal context is also expanded, though more modestly, in *Ysaïe le Triste*. This romance, from the late fourteenth or early fifteenth century, offers the story of Tristan's son Ysaïe and traces in great detail the painful process by which Ysaïe and his own son restore peace and order to a realm left in ruins and anarchy after Arthur's death.

The later Middle Ages have also left us a number of Arthurian "compilations," long and complicated works that often recombine material from the Vulgate, the Prose *Tristan*, and other sources. Among these compilations are the works of Jehan Vaillant, Michot Gonnot, and Rusticien de Pise (or Rusticiano da Pisa, as he was an Italian writing in French). In some cases, such as Rusticien's, the mass of assembled material might later be divided to yield separate romances. The reader impressed (or simply numbed) by the prolixity and the apparent preference for quantity rather than careful composition may well be surprised by the extraordinary popularity achieved by some of the compilations.

In curious contrast to this tendency toward dramatic amplification are occasional efforts to simplify, reduce, and compose compact romances. We have, for example, a relatively concise late Prose *Yvain*, consisting of seven episodes, only the first of which concerns the Yvain who is a character from Chrétien de Troyes. We also have, from the sixteenth century, a brief *Tristan* by Pierre Sala (who develops further the theme of Lancelot's and Tristan's friendship) and a *Nouveau Tristan*, by Jean Maugin, who recasts traditional themes such as Tristan and Iseut's love potion in an effort to accommodate the story to "modern" tastes.

In addition to these newly composed works, the late Middle Ages have also left us large numbers of prose adaptations or "modernizations" of earlier verse texts, including Chrétien's *Erec* and *Cligés*, in which the prosifier often condenses and in some cases almost summarizes the originals.

All the romances heretofore discussed are Arthurian compositions. French offers a reasonable number of non-Arthurian verse romances, but only a few in prose. Of those, the most important are doubtless the romances that belong to the Seven Sages cycle, and even one of those uses Arthurian material. The Seven Sages, known in several European literatures, is a narrative cycle that began in verse versions but achieved its broadest diffusion and popularity in prose; it offers a frame structure in which tales told in an attempt to condemn the Roman emperor's son are countered by other narratives offered in his defense. In prose, from the thirteenth century, we have *Les Sept Sages* proper, to which are loosely appended other "branches" named after their central characters: a resolutely misogynistic *Marques de Rome*, *Laurin* (whose hero is brought into contact with the Arthurian world), *Cassidorus*, *Helcanus* (or *Peliarmenus*), and *Kanor*.

Aside from these compositions, the list of French non-Arthurian romances includes, as noted, a good many late prosifications of earlier verse texts.

Otherwise, only a comparatively few non-Arthurian prose texts are indisputably romances: *La Fille du comte de Pontieu*, the early thirteenth-century story of Saladin's mother; *Le Roi Flore et la belle Jehanne* (thirteenth century), in which a man wagers that he can seduce another's wife and then falsely boasts of his success; Jean d'Arras's 1392–93 treatment of the *Mélusine* legend; and a small handful of others.

INFLUENCE OF FRENCH PROSE ROMANCES

The centrality of French romance is indisputable, and its influence, in both verse and prose, was pervasive throughout other countries and languages. Some cultures, especially in the north, drew more heavily from French verse than from prose romances; Scandinavian literature, for example, includes translations or adaptations of several of Chrétien de Troyes's romances and of Thomas's verse *Tristan*. In the south, that is, on the Iberian Peninsula and in Italy, the most influential texts proved to be the Vulgate (*Lancelot-Grail*), the Post-Vulgate, and the Prose *Tristan*. This division between north and south is however a relative matter, as the original three romances of the *Lancelot-Grail* were also translated or adapted, for example, into Middle Dutch.

As noted, medieval writers in Spain and Portugal translated or adapted portions of the Vulgate and, especially, the Post-Vulgate, the latter done by Brother Juan Vives (or Bivas) around 1313. The French *Tristan* cycle was also the source of several Spanish and Portuguese compositions, although in some cases there may have been intermediary texts (in Italian, French, or Provençal) between the source and the resulting works on the Iberian Peninsula.

The Prose *Tristan* provided the primary inspiration and a good deal of the material for a number of Italian compositions (as detailed in Regina Psaki's chapter in the present volume). For example, *La Tavola Ritonda*, the only full Tristan cycle in Italy, combines material from the Prose *Tristan*, the Vulgate *Queste*, and other sources.

English literature, too, shows the obvious influence of French sources, especially of the *Lancelot-Grail* cycle, in works such as the Middle Scots *Lancelot of the Laik*, a *Merlin*, a semi-alliterative *Joseph of Arimathie*, and Henry Lovelich's *History of the Holy Grail*. Clearly, though, the most substantial evidence of the influence of French romances is offered by Sir Thomas Malory's *Morte Darthur*.

Malory had multiple sources, including the English Alliterative *Morte Arthure* and Stanzaic *Le Morte Arthur*, but central to his composition was what his printer William Caxton called "certeyn bookes of Frensshe." Those books included large portions of the *Lancelot-Grail* Cycle, the Post-Vulgate, and the Prose *Tristan* (the last, for example, providing much of the material for Malory's Books VIII–XII[12]).

Though relying heavily on his sources, Malory does not follow them slavishly. He often works from two or more sources to construct his own account of events, and he never hesitates to alter or simply suppress material that does not accord with his vision. He thus redefines character, event, and the tone of the work as a whole. For example, working from the *Lancelot-Grail*, Malory remakes Lancelot. Terence McCarthy summarizes that transformation: the French Lancelot, he states, is "a sentimental, effeminate youth," whereas "Malory's Lancelot is a sterner, more manly figure."[13] An illustration of this transformation may be drawn from a comparison of similar passages from the two works. In the French *Lancelot*, when a young woman tries to seduce the hero, he is embarrassed and petulant, and when she kisses him, he runs away "et commence a crachier en despit de ce qu'ele l'a baisié" ("and begins to spit in distaste at her having kissed him").[14] When Malory's Lancelot faces a worse situation – forced to die or choose among four young women – his reaction is more direct: "I had rather die in this prison with worship than to have one of you as my paramour, in spite of my head. Therefore ye are answered: I will have no one of you."[15]

So it is with other characters and with Malory's themes: "what he borrows becomes, in a real sense, his own."[16] That can be taken as his strength or, depending on one's point of view, his flaw: some critics may praise him for recasting material in such a way as to deemphasize, for example, the sentimentality and self-absorption of a Lancelot, whereas others may well criticize him for his emphasis on warfare and knighthood at the expense of the courtly refinement and the concern for love that had formerly balanced and, to no small extent, sponsored chivalric endeavor. But whether we praise or condemn Malory for his treatment of the "bookes of Frensshe," his reliance on them cannot be denied: they are central to his enterprise.

Not only literary tastes, but also the principles and methods of literary composition in fifteenth-century England were very much unlike those that had prevailed on the Continent two centuries earlier. While interlace is not entirely absent from Malory's works, it is by no means the prominent structuring method it was in the French Vulgate romances or even in the Prose *Tristan*. The interlaced French texts are, as Vinaver has noted, elaborate tapestries in which many threads are interwoven; Malory provided a more rapid and direct narrative line. His basic treatment of French sources involved the extraction of a single or double narrative thread from his inherited narrative tapestry and the development of that thread until it was completed and replaced by another.

Neither method is inherently superior to the other. But the present point is less the literary value of the result than what it reveals about the continuing prestige of, and interest in, French romance. Even though the very compositional method underlying the sources may have been considered confused and unacceptable in the fifteenth century, the value of the material itself and the authority it conferred on Malory's own work give persuasive evidence that, even at the end of the Middle Ages, the French romances in prose remained, to a considerable extent, the authoritative standard for Arthurian authors.

EPILOGUE

The steady evolution in literary taste (and consequently in technique) had multiple causes, two of them being surely the troubled military, economic, and political climate that afflicted many European countries in the late Middle Ages (following the Black Death and the Hundred Years War, for example), and the expansion of literacy into populations other than the refined leisure classes of the French and other courts. As a result, new and expanded audiences, perhaps impatient with meandering romances that multiplied characters and intrigues and abandoned storylines or suspended them for hundreds of pages, came to prefer more direct, more realistic, and generally more succinct narratives.

Another fact that obviously contributed to the decline of the kind of romance that had so dominated European literature was its gradual merging with other prose forms. In fact, the definition of "romance" itself had never been unambiguous, and the genre had always shared techniques and characteristics with chronicles, for example, and with some allegorical works. But toward the end of the Middle Ages, the margins of genres became even less distinct, and romances, family chronicles and memoirs, and other forms overlapped and blended to a significant degree.

The birth and infancy of the novel were the consequence of these changes and a further contributing factor to the declining fortunes of romance. In the mid-fifteenth century (before 1456), Antoine de la Sale composed a work entitled *Le petit Jehan de Saintré*, which some scholars have taken as the first "modern" novel. Whether it is that or not – and many would dispute it – there can be no doubt that a new kind of narrative fiction is gradually emerging as the Middle Ages draw to a close.

The novel owes a good deal to the romance but is not properly speaking a continuation of it (even though the French word *roman* designates both). In contrast to the romance, the novel tends generally toward a more linear structure, with direct links between cause and effect, with character providing the main impetus for narrative developments, and with an emphasis, unknown to earlier periods, on individual psychology. Put more generally but no less accurately, the romance and the novel spring from different aesthetic roots, have different concerns, and reflect different mentalities.

Yet the romance proved resilient and retained its popularity through much of the sixteenth century. A good many prestigious writers of the French Renaissance, such as Pierre de Ronsard and Joachim du Bellay, explicitly praised

Arthurian romances, though more for their value as epic material or national history than for their literary interest. In addition, authors and compilers continued to produce romances, the majority of which were compilations, prosified expansions, or recombinations of earlier material. As noted above, however, some were newly created works, and a few others represent a conscious effort to achieve some concision, as in some late reworkings and abridgments of the *Lancelot-Grail* cycle or parts of it. It is only toward the end of the sixteenth century that we find explicit disapproval of these works, and such judgments appear to bear both on their subject matter and on their presumed lack of literary worth. Montaigne, most notably, disparages them, considering them useful only as a source of entertainment for children.

Changing literary tastes and social conditions, a wholesale rejection of things medieval, the merging of genres, and the growth of the novel all conspired to threaten the survival of romances. Some of them were indeed modernized and republished during the eighteenth and nineteenth centuries (while others received scholarly editions); they seem to have achieved modest popularity, but they were no longer vital expressions of the literary art. Even when the romantics rediscovered the Middle Ages and enthusiastically took them as a source of poetic or novelistic inspiration, these rambling tales of knights and ladies, of love and adventure, of holy quests, of magic and mystery – these stories appear to have been considered, at best, wonderful but puzzling relics of a distant, colorful past.

But that is not to say that romance was – or is – dead. More precisely, from the Renaissance on, the form itself was no longer viable, and romances were scarcely read or known for two or three centuries. Yet the spirit of romance survived. It influenced every Western literature's choice of characters and subjects, it largely formed our traditional understanding of romantic love, and in its emphasis on quests, tests, and adventures, it offered productive models of individual and collective heroism. Were concrete evidence of its survival required, the modern vogue of Arthurian literature in particular amply illustrates the legacy of romance and its ability, still today, to provide pleasure to a discerning audience. Its imprint on the character of its own age – and of our own – is indelible.

NOTES

1 Quoted by Gaston Paris in *De Pseudo-Turpino* (Paris: A. Franck, 1865), 44.
2 In French, for example, the only verse compositions to deal with Grail matter are early romances: Chrétien's *Perceval*, its Continuations, and Robert de Boron's verse trilogy.
3 See Jean Frappier's discussion in his chapter on "The Vulgate Cycle," in *Arthurian Literature in the Middle Ages: A Collaborative History*, ed. Roger Sherman Loomis (Oxford: Clarendon Press, 1959), 295–318.
4 *Lancelot: roman en prose du XIIIe siècle*, ed. Alexandre Micha (Geneva: Droz, 1978–83), vol. 6, 244.
5 *La Queste del saint Graal*, ed. Albert Pauphilet (Paris: Champion, 1921), 8.

6 *La Mort le Roi Artu*, ed. Jean Frappier (Geneva: Droz, 1936; 3rd ed. 1959), 1.
7 "The Vulgate Cycle," 313, 316 (see above, note 3).
8 *La Queste del saint Graal*, 17.
9 More precisely, it *may* be the first: the chronology of the great Arthurian cycles is not easily established. The non-cyclic *Lancelot*, the *Lancelot-Grail* cycle, the Post-Vulgate, and the first version of the Prose *Tristan* may all have been written within a period of some thirty years, and the composition of some of these, if not all, surely overlapped.
10 Eugène Vinaver, "The Prose Tristan," in Loomis, ed., *Arthurian Literature in the Middle Ages*, 339–47, here quoting 343.
11 By Jane H. M. Taylor. See *"Perceforest,"* in Lacy, *et al.*, eds., *The New Arthurian Encyclopedia*, 355.
12 I refer to the books as they are established by Malory's first printer, Caxton. The Winchester manuscript divides the work into eight books.
13 *An Introduction to Malory* (Cambridge: Brewer, 1988), 149.
14 *Lancelot*, ed. Alexandre Micha, vol. 1, 324.
15 Sir Thomas Malory, *Le Morte Darthur*, ed. R. M. Lumiansky (New York: Macmillan, 1982), 144.
16 *An Introduction to Malory*, 150.

SUGGESTIONS FOR FURTHER READING

Burns, E. Jane. *Arthurian Fictions: Re-reading the Vulgate Cycle*. Columbus: Ohio State University Press, 1985.

Kelly, Douglas. *The Art of Medieval French Romance*. Madison: University of Wisconsin Press, 1992.

Medieval French Romance. New York: Twayne, 1993.

Kennedy, Elspeth. *Lancelot do Lac: The Non-Cyclic Old French Prose Romance*. 2 vols. Oxford: Clarendon Press, 1980.

Lacy, Norris J., and Geoffrey Ashe, with Debra N. Mancoff. *The Arthurian Handbook*. 1988; New York: Garland, 1997.

Lacy, Norris J., *et al.*, eds. *The New Arthurian Encyclopedia, Updated Edition*. New York: Garland, 1996.

Loomis, Roger Sherman, ed. *Arthurian Literature in the Middle Ages: A Collaborative History*. Oxford: Clarendon Press, 1959.

Taylor, Jane H. M. "The Fourteenth Century: Context, Text and Intertext." In *The Legacy of Chrétien de Troyes*. Ed. Norris J. Lacy, Douglas Kelly, and Keith Busby, 2 vols. Amsterdam: Rodopi, 1987–88. Vol. 1, 267–332.

Vinaver, Eugène. *A la recherche d'une poétique médiévale*. Paris: Nizet, 1970.

II

ANN MARIE RASMUSSEN

Medieval German romance

THE FIRST JOURNEYS OF ROMANCE

As a literary tradition, medieval German romance arose in the middle of the twelfth century and in different literary guises retained its popularity until and beyond the fifteenth century. The German tradition is rich and diverse: it encompasses some fifty to eighty texts; it includes verse narrative and, beginning in the middle of the thirteenth century, prose translations as well; it sustains a wide variety of genres, the most important of which are Arthurian romances and love adventure stories; and it makes the transition from manuscript culture to print, that is to say, it continues beyond the Middle Ages into the Early Modern period. Nor is the northern European, Germanic-language romance tradition confined to those regions in northern and central Europe that correspond roughly to the modern nation states of Austria, Germany, and Switzerland, although these regions will be the focus of this essay. There are rich medieval romance traditions in other Germanic languages such as Dutch, Flemish, and Old Norse.[1] For our purposes, this essay embarks upon a selective overview of medieval German romance in order to provide a sense of its richness and diversity.

The story of German-language romance is a story of borrowing, adapting, and refashioning romance. One of the early medieval German verse romances tells a story about its own origins. It concerns the theft of a book and is recounted in the epilogue of the German *Eneide*, a reworking by the poet-cleric Heinrich von Veldeke (*c.* 1140–*c.* 1190) of the Old French *Roman d'Eneas*, which itself reimagines the Latin tale of adventure and conquest, the *Aeneid*, through the lens of romance. In the epilogue, a third-person narrator relates that Heinrich had finished his adaptation up to the point where Eneas reads Lavinia's letter when fate intervened to hinder completion of the project. Heinrich had lent the partially completed work to the "generous, good, and noble-spirited Countess of Cleve" (13448–50) so that she could "read and examine" it (13446). At her wedding to Landgrave Ludwig III of Thuringia (*c.* 1174), one Count Henry (probably an enemy of Ludwig III) took the book from a lady-in-waiting and "sent it back to his home in Thuringia" (13459–60).[2] This theft, which the epilogue characterizes as "an outrage" (13443), made it impossible for Heinrich to finish his work, and it may also have interrupted the economic and social relationship of patronage that sustained his work.

Yet according to the epilogue, the seductive powers of literature can transform a theft – wrongful borrowing – into grounds for the creation of more vernacular romance. After some nine years, Heinrich von Veldeke was able to follow his book to Thuringia because Count Hermann of Thuringia (d. 1217), Landgrave Ludwig III's brother, asked him to come and complete the work, which was probably finished before 1186. We are told that Hermann "found the story good and the poem masterful" (13478–79). Hermann, who became Landgrave of Thuringia in 1191 after Ludwig's death, was one of the great patrons of medieval German literature, supporting at his court not just Heinrich von Veldeke but also artists such as the poet Walther von der Vogelweide and the romance author Wolfram von Eschenbach. The *Eneide* presents this new patron as being captivated – perhaps even inspired to further deeds of literary patronage – by the artistry of the work. In the end, the epilogue's story of the stolen book is something of a romance itself. Book and author suffer nine years of separation and adversity, until fortune unites them again in a state of greater bliss than before, at the court of a great and powerful patron. And it is the allure of romance itself – the poet's narrative wizardry and the powerful beguilement of the story – that have inspired a great and wealthy lord to its defense and promotion.

The *Eneide*'s epilogue establishes a crucial fact for understanding medieval German romance: while narrative adventure stories such as the so-called *Spielmannsdichtung*, heroic epics such as the *Nibelungenlied*, and love stories were being written in German following indigenous traditions both before and during the period of courtly romance, the direct sources for courtly romances are French. Heinrich von Veldeke's source was the anonymous Old French *Roman d'Eneas*; Hartmann von Aue adapted Chrétien de Troyes's Arthurian romances; Gottfried von Strassburg reworked Thomas of England's *Tristan*. Surviving evidence suggests that Old French romance literature first met the medieval German cultural sphere in the 1170s in principalities along the lower Rhine, located in a small region around present-day Limburg and Maastricht. Straddling the present-day borders of Germany, Belgium, and The Netherlands, this region bridges, then as now, the French and German spheres politically, culturally, and linguistically. The "generous, good, and noble-spirited Countess of Cleve" mentioned in the *Eneide*'s epilogue came from this region. Perhaps the *Trierer Floyris* (late twelfth century), an anonymous adaptation of the "aristocratic" branch of the Old French *Floire et Blancheflor* (c. 1147–60), was produced for the neighboring court of Loon (present-day Looz, in modern Belgium between Liège and Hasselt). The fragmentary *Trierer Floyris* is the oldest textual witness, in any language, for the *Floire and Blancheflor* tradition.[3]

The romance texts that traveled to German-speaking courts represent but one facet of a larger social and cultural development in the European aristocracy: the fashioning of new beliefs and new practices about nobility summed up in the term "courtliness." Romance texts shape and dramatize the new notions of prowess and love that are central to courtly ideals. For example, in chivalric romances, knighthood includes ethical considerations (as opposed to mere martial heroism) and is best summed up in its key term, "honor." Chivalric love is a romantic-erotic relationship between a man and a woman based on love service, in which a knight submits his will to his lady love and performs in her name all manner of tasks. Often military tasks, in which the knight upholds justice, love service tasks can also involve general acts of strength and prowess in which the knight upholds honor and good repute, or merely seeks to comply with his lady's wishes. Chivalric romances were popular in Germany, as were love adventure romances. These tales of ancient origin celebrate the power and limitlessness of love by narrating the life-threatening adventures of young, noble lovers who become separated and endure singly all manner of hostile acts (kidnapping, enslavement, banishment) only to be happily reunited in the end.

The relationship of romance ideals to the political, social, and military practices of the nobility who commissioned and heard these fictions is anything but simple. Romance literature often imagines marriages based on love; for the medieval nobility, the norm was the arranged marriage, which was a key political strategy. Romance literature imagines knights as exemplary warriors serving virtue and justice; in reality, medieval warfare was brutal, vengeful, and often directed towards noncombatants. These contradictions remind us that medieval German romance does not reflect reality in an unmediated way; rather, the best medieval romances establish narrative ground for enacting the contradictions of noble life.

We cannot know whether noble patrons were lovers of literature, though we may wish to imagine them enjoying the works whose production they funded. The great twelfth- and thirteenth-century lords appear, however, to have fostered literary patronage at their courts as one of many ways to confirm their status as members of an aristocratic community, to enhance their prestige, and to legitimate their political aspirations. Ultimately, their cultivation of medieval German romance was linked to claims of political autonomy, territorial sovereignty, and imperial status. Great patrons such as Landgrave Hermann I of Thuringia, The Guelph Duke Henry the Lion, and Dukes Berthold IV and Berthold V of Zähringen, have close familial ties to royal dynasties such as the Staufer in Germany and the Plantagenets of the Anglo-Norman realm. During the turbulent decades around 1200, when virtually all the great German romances were being composed, they or their sons advanced claims on the imperial title in Germany held by the Staufer dynasty. In a time when imperial rights were bitterly contested, supporting the composition of romance texts may have provided the great princes with one way to culturally display their claims to imperial status.

It is reasonable to assume that the lesser free nobility also cultivated romance, but little evidence of their participation has survived. We do know that the courts of the great twelfth- and thirteenth-century lords, which formed the first audiences for vernacular German romance, were populated both by free nobles who were the great lords' vassals, and by a second group of noblemen whose social and political circumstances were unique to Germany, the noble bondsmen, from whose ranks a number of poets – Hartmann von Aue, Ulrich von Liechtenstein – were drawn. Unlike a vassal, who was a free noble, the noble bondsman (Latin: *ministerialis*; German: *dienstman*) was of servile status. This legal condition, which one inherited at birth, meant that one was bound in service to the household of another lord (who might be free or servile himself), and that there were legal restrictions on, among other things, one's choice of marriage partner and on one's right to sell inherited land. Noble bondsmen were often on balance more reliable and loyal administrators and advisors for great lords than the vassals, the free nobles (whose political aims might well diverge from their overlord's). In the twelfth and thirteenth centuries, in southwestern Germany and Austria, the ranks of the free nobles were dwindling, while the number of noble bondsmen was rising. During this same period, powerful noble bondsmen came to be indistinguishable in lifestyle and wealth from the free nobility (the great dynasties of noble bondsmen had noble bondsmen themselves!), but the stigma of their unfree birth remained.[4]

Romance and its idealizing notions of chivalry and love may have provided one answer to the ambiguities and tensions of this social and political situation. Romance's ethos of nobility could create a culturally based aristocratic identity to which impoverished free nobles, rich noble bondsmen, and great princes alike could aspire, regardless of the legal, economic, and social divisions that separated them in real life. Romance thus came to serve a local, German need by producing an idealizing notion of nobility that could mask tensions within the nobility and unify the upper class – if only in fantasy – against those who stood below them.

Finally, the *Eneide* reminds us that medieval romances often call into question our modern notion of the singular, autonomously produced text. Medieval literature celebrates some individual authors, yet medieval romances come down to us in manuscript versions that differ markedly from one another. Sometimes these differing versions of texts appear to originate from an author, or from the circles in which he worked. But the process of creating new versions of a single text also continued decades after an author's death, as compilers and scribes adapted texts to suit their audiences' needs. Only rarely can we tell from the surviving evidence who composed these parallel versions, or why, or when. Usually we cannot distinguish between parallel versions that originated with the author, and parallel versions that arose out of the early telling and retelling – or reading and rereading – of a work.[5] What we can say is that the adaptability of romance reflects in part the extraordinary popularity of the material, and in part the creative freedom with which medieval authors, scribes, and artists approached it.

Romance motifs often adorned material objects, luxury goods from the households of the rich. Sometimes a single motif recalls a whole story, such as the famous garden scene from *Tristan* in which King Mark, perched in a tree, spies on the lovers. This motif is often found on combs and small boxes. A few elaborate picture cycles illustrating famous romances have also survived, some in illuminated manuscripts, some as wall paintings, and some on luxury textiles such as tapestries, bed hangings, and coverlets. Such narrative cycles in pictures can also, as we shall see below, represent new readings of romance texts.[6]

HARTMANN VON AUE

In his German verse adaptations of Chrétien de Troyes's Arthurian romances, the poet and noble bondsman Hartmann von Aue celebrated the ideals of chivalric romance: merit and dedication to justice define knighthood and guarantee the virtuous knight's good fortune. These notions are epigrammatically expressed in the opening lines of Hartmann von Aue's *Iwein* (*c.* 1200), his adaptation of Chrétien's *Le Chevalier au Lion*:

> Swer an rehte güete
> wendet sîn gemüete
> dem volget sælde und êre.

He who aspires to virtue in spirit and deed has honor and good fortune in his company.   (1–3)

Hartmann probably composed at the court of a great lord, and his early audiences doubtless included both free nobles and noble bondsmen such as himself. The popularity of his work and the praise he garnered from fellow poets such as Gottfried von Strassburg suggest that Hartmann's artistic achievement and the ideals of romance and chivalry he advocated resonated strongly with German audiences. Hartmann's adaptation of Chrétien de Troyes's *Erec* was done in the 1180s (perhaps as late as 1190) and is the first Arthurian romance in German-speaking regions.[7]

Hartmann's adaptations of Chrétien's romances go far beyond the work of translation. His *Erec* (10,135 lines) is fifty per cent longer than his source. Hartmann expands passages and he excels in descriptions where his rhetorical skill can shine: the depiction of Enite's horse (7286–766); the tournament after Erec and Enite's wedding (2413–825; four times longer than the source); Enite's lament over Erec, whom she supposes to be dead (5774–6061; six times longer); Erec's fight with Mabinogrin (9070–315; three times longer). Hartmann makes subtle changes highlighting the structure of the story and its contrasting cycles of adventures, acts that imply careful study of his source and of the symbolism inherent in the plot structure. Only one complete manuscript of Hartmann's *Erec* survives. Fragments from an early manuscript strongly suggest that *Erec* was composed and circulated in parallel versions.

It is Hartmann's innovation to create a distinctive voice for the role of narrator. His narrator looms much larger in the story than Chrétien's, often giving descriptive reports where Chrétien uses direct speech, making more comments, judgments, and asides, and introducing elaborate rhetorical passages that highlight his skill. Hartmann also sets new accents in the characterization of the protagonists, Erec and Enite, sometimes adding, sometimes deleting material in order to change our understanding of their motivations. The net effect of Hartmann's changes is to focus the story on Erec, whose active role as a knight in pursuit of honor is underscored. Enite becomes a more passive character, who is clearly subordinated to Erec. At the same time, Hartmann's narrator actively seeks to ameliorate and reconcile the conflicts between men and women that are acted out by the characters in Chrétien's texts. For example, at the end of Enite's trials, Chrétien's Erec confirms that Enite has passed the test of her loyalty, and forgives her; in Hartmann, the narrator adds the explanation that Enite has overcome these unjustified adversities and hardships, and then relates that Erec begs Enite's forgiveness for the distress and the uncompanionable and unfriendly life he inflicted on her (6798–99). The tendency in Hartmann's *Erec* is to resolve deep conflicts, such as those based on gender dynamics, which are often left open in the Old French sources. Many later German romances also lean towards happy endings and the harmonious reconciliation of conflicts.

Hartmann's *Iwein* (c. 1200; 8165 lines) is extant in fifteen complete manuscripts and seventeen fragments, a substantial transmission for a medieval German romance. Based on Chrétien's *Le Chevalier au Lion*, the German adaptation is only twenty per cent longer than the source. Overall, the ironic and ambiguous narrative tone in *Iwein* contrasts with the straightforward tone in *Erec*, as though Hartmann were playing with the tensions and contrasts implicit in the tale's themes and structures in order to reflect critically on chivalric romance. Structural tendencies similar to those in *Erec* organize the adaptation. Hartmann expands the use of indirect narration and introduces a commenting narrator who enters the story (for example the dialogue with *Frau Minne* [Lady

Love] regarding the exchange of hearts, 2971–3024). He also reshapes and gently reorders events with an eye towards clarification and greater structural balance and he sets clear accents in the women's roles.

Hartmann's portrayal of Laudine tones down elements derived from the convention of the widow overly hasty to remarry, a negative stereotype common in medieval fiction. In the final scene of reconciliation between Laudine and Iwein, Laudine accepts the trick her lady-in-waiting, Lunette, has played on her and takes Iwein back as her husband. One version of Hartmann's text follows Chrétien closely and ends this scene with Iwein's expression of remorse and happiness. A parallel version, however, clarifies Laudine's state of mind and expands on the reciprocity of the reconciliation. This version adds a speech for Laudine in which she falls on her knees before Iwein (repeating a legal gesture of subordination that Iwein has just performed before her) and asks his forgiveness in turn:

> her îwein, lieber herre mîn,
> tuot gnædeclîche an mir.
> grôzen kumber habt ir
> von mînen schulden erliten.
> des wil ich iuch durch got biten
> daz ir ruochet mir vergebn,
> wander ich, unz ich hân daz lebn,
> von herzen iemer riuwen muoz. (8121–29)

[Lord Iwein, my dear lord, show mercy towards me. You have suffered great distress on my account. By the love of God I beg that you consider forgiving me, for I will wholeheartedly regret what happened as long as I live.]

THE IWEIN STORY IN PICTURES

Early thirteenth-century wall paintings of the *Iwein* story have survived in the castle at Rodenegg (near Brixen, South Tyrol, Italy) and in Schmaldkalden (a small city in the province of Thuringia, Germany). Both sets of paintings are examples of revisions of Hartmann's work. In particular, the paintings in the castle of Rodenegg reflect critically on chivalric romance, and provide a rare and revealing glimpse into the role romance played for noble bondsmen.

Badly faded *Iwein* wall paintings dating from *c.* 1230–1250 adorn a medieval building (perhaps once a small palace or hall) in Schmaldkalden. A small, first-floor room (*c.* 3.6 by 4.2 meters and probably unheated) contains scenes from the first two-thirds of the *Iwein* story. Most of the painted scenes are arranged on the vaulted ceiling, and depict indoor scenes or scenes from courtly life. On an end wall, a kind of "generic" courtly feast, which is not clearly linked to the *Iwein* story, suggests that the room was once used for festive gathering and dining. The entire sequence of pictures suggests that the *Iwein* story in Schmaldkalden was used to evoke an ambiance of courtliness and courtly leisure.

In 1972–73, partially preserved *Ywain* (the spelling of the hero's name in the paintings) frescoes were discovered at the castle of Rodenegg (built before 1147 by Friederich von Rodank). The frescoes, dated to the 1210s or 1230s, adorn an indoor room measuring about 7 by 4 meters. Eleven scenes from the first half of Hartmann's *Iwein* unfold on the four walls, with each vivid and dramatic painting filling up the wall space vertically.[8] The final scene in the painted sequence has puzzled scholars. It is not, as one might assume, the marriage of Iwein and Laudine with which the Hartmann text closed Iwein's first adventure series. Rather, the final picture shows the moment of grief and uncertainty immediately preceding the reconciliation and marriage. Ywain, who has killed Laudine's husband and promptly fallen in love with her, is shown humbly kneeling in submission before her, with a remorseful expression on his face. Laudine bows her head, her features contorted with grief, while Lunette, her shrewd lady-in-waiting, stands behind Ywain and gestures towards Laudine. Lunette's gesture points towards the marriage, but the main characters themselves are frozen in postures of mourning and remorse. Because there is no architectural indication that the narrative fresco cycle was continued elsewhere, one scholar has suggested that the disposition of the paintings in the room might tell us why the pictorial cycle ends on this unexpected note.[9] Upon entering the room from the east wall, the viewer first sees in the center of the opposite west wall the death of Askalon (Laudine's first husband). As the midpoint of the pictorial narrative, Askalon's death divides scenes of knightly glory on the north wall from scenes of mourning, chaos, and despair on the south wall. This spatial division of the pictures contrasts the glories of knighthood (the north wall) with the tragic price others pay for its success (the south wall), and so suggests visually that chivalric romance has two sides. Further, the *Ywain* frescoes reread and restage Hartmann's *Iwein* to underscore not only the ethical ambiguities of romance, but also its potential for gendered perspectives. On the north wall we view the male quest for knightly glory; on the south wall we see the grave and often catastrophic consequences of this quest for women.

WOLFRAM VON ESCHENBACH AND THE GRAIL ROMANCES

The most popular verse romance in Germany was Wolfram von Eschenbach's *Parzival* (*c.* 1205–1212). Wolfram based his story on the unfinished *Le Conte du Graal* by Chrétien de Troyes, but his expansions and independently invented stories go so far beyond his source that it seems inaccurate to speak of an adaptation. Arguably the greatest thirteenth-century European knightly adventure story, *Parzival* contains multiple perspectives on chivalry and romance. It ultimately critiques chivalric love service and advances its own vision of a healing and potentially spiritualized relationship between prowess and love. In *Parzival* there are two co-existing worlds – the world of the secular nobility and the semi-religious world of the Grail – which each have their own story line. The central figure, Parzival, moves between the two worlds before ultimately joining the Grail world. A second narrative strand, whose hero is Gawein, is set in the world of secular nobility and provides a counterpoint, at times comic, to Parzival's exploits. In addition to the complexity of unfolding two story lines, Wolfram invents a past for both worlds and weaves the history of his characters and their families into his story. For example, *Parzival* opens with the story of love and adventure that unites the hero's parents, Gahmuret and Herzeloyde, and also brings about their untimely deaths. The reader is thus equipped to comprehend Parzival's paternal heritage of knighthood, courage, and adventure, a heritage that the youthful Parzival fails to live up to in his very first adventures. But only slowly, in bits and pieces as the story unfolds, is the extent and meaning of Parzival's maternal heritage – the Grail lineage comes to him through Herzeloyde – made clear. Unraveling this puzzle reveals that the ties of kinship have critical consequences for Parzival. So the reader must penetrate the elaborate family trees invented by Wolfram for his characters – a narrative feature echoing the social world in which Wolfram worked, with the medieval nobility's emphasis on dynastic lineage.

It is impossible to do justice to the richness of *Parzival*'s fictional world in a few short paragraphs. Wolfram exactly calculated the chronology of events for both story lines, so that they unfold in precise temporal relationship to one another, to the seasons, and to the religious calendar. This temporal design creates another level of symbolic meaning. Wolfram weaves into his story many kinds of medieval lore – healing arts, astronomy, magic, geography, mathematics – integrating this lore both structurally and symbolically. The portrayals of female characters amend or overthrow the stereotypes of women common in medieval fiction. Wolfram's depictions explore more fully the stages of women's lives – girlhood, motherhood, wifehood, widowhood – and imagine the actions and feelings of women from unexpected angles – a battered wife, a grieving, widowed virgin, a learned sorceress. Finally, the narrator himself is a character in his own right. Created with depth and subjectivity, he jokes, puns, teases, chastises, mourns and laughs, sometimes with his readers, sometimes at them.

Wolfram's unfinished work, *Titurel*, composed in a complicated stanzaic form of his own devising, magnified his artistic impulse for weaving romance plots and motifs into gigantic tapestries of family sagas. *Titurel* tells the stories of characters from the Grail dynasty in *Parzival* by enlarging on hints and motifs *Parzival* contains. Wolfram left *Titurel* unfinished, perhaps only completing some one hundred stanzas. However, between 1260 and 1272, the poet Albrecht embedded Wolfram's stanzas in his own continuation, expanding *Titurel* into a massive family saga about the Grail dynasty known as the *Younger Titurel*. Wolfram's influence loomed large over Albrecht, who in most of the work pretends that the author really is Wolfram. This pretense doubtless contributed to the *Younger Titurel's* success with medieval audiences, who were won over by the authorial fiction and generally attributed the entire work to Wolfram.

THE TRISTAN TRADITION

The story of a tragic love that tears apart the fragile fabric of a noble court offered a different opportunity for poets and audiences to assess the ideals of romance. German audiences were early recipients of the *Tristan* stories. *Tristrant* was written by Eilhart of Oberg in the 1170s, perhaps for the court of Duke Henry the Lion. Only fragments of the twelfth-century version survive, and the later manuscripts that preserve the entire epic may well be based on a thirteenth-century revision of the original, twelfth-century epic. *Tristrant* adapts an otherwise unknown Old French *Tristan* source which must have shared features with the Old French version by Béroul.

A second German *Tristan* tale survives in Gottfried von Strassburg's *Tristan und Isolde* (*c.* 1200–1210), an adaptation of the Old French tale by Thomas. Gottfried's *Tristan* breaks off abruptly after about 19,500 lines just as the hero is contemplating marriage to Isolde of the White Hands. Later medieval continuers assert that this rupture was caused by Gottfried's death. Direct comparisons of Gottfried and his source, Thomas, are difficult because almost no overlapping segments have been preserved. Recently, however, a new Old French fragment surfaced which does overlap with Gottfried's work.[10]

Unlike the stories of Hartmann and Wolfram, which generally resolve the problems of love through happy marriages, Gottfried von Strassburg's *Tristan* argues that the conflict between passionate love and the demands of courtly life is ultimately irreconcilable. Celebrating passion, suffering, and erotic desire in the guise of adulterous love would have been familiar to noble audiences from conventions of courtly love poetry, an art form cultivated by the nobility throughout the French, Anglo-Norman, and German-speaking realms. Yet in some ways *Tristan* must have been a challenging text for its medieval audiences because its lengthy, sympathetic portrayal of adultery between a young lord and the king's wife differs markedly from what we know of noble mores. (History records noble husbands who murdered their wives on suspicion of adultery.) Instead of treating the *Tristan* story as a cautionary tale in which sinfulness leads to a wicked end, as the social context might lead some to expect, Gottfried shows empathy for Tristan and Isolde's plight and for the force and dignity of their love.

Gottfried's *Tristan* can be understood as a narrative study exploring the fundamentally contradictary relationship of worldly, noble honor and love. Using elaborate commentaries and great rhetorical artistry, the narrator deliberately sets out to engage the reader's pity. The prologue suggests that by contemplating the inextricable duality of love and sorrow embodied by Tristan and Isolde's passion, the reader will arrive at a deeper, more empathetic understanding of the nature of worldly love, and come to accept the idea that pain is not opposed to love but rather an essential element of it. The narrator claims that this reading process, whose profile is related to Christian thinking, promotes virtue and healing in the reader, healing not in the sense of "cure" but in the sense of integration and acceptance. Gottfried's *Tristan* suggests that an erotic love which challenges and negates social conventions can serve as a path to healing knowledge and as a positive and enduring example of constancy.

> al eine und sîn si (Tristan and Isolde, my note) lange tôt,
> ir süezer name der lebet noch
> und sol ir tôt der werlde noch
> ze guote lange und iemer leben,
> den triuwe gernden triuwe geben,
> den êre gernden êre:
> ir tôt muoz iemer mêre
> uns lebenden leben und niuwe wesen;
> wan swâ man noch hoeret lesen
> ir triuwe, ir triuwen reinekeit,
> ir herzeliep, ir herzeleit,
> deist aller edelen herzen brôt.
> hie mite sô lebet ir beider tôt.
> wir lesen ir leben, wir lesen ir tôt
> und ist uns daz süeze alse brôt.

[And though they (Tristan and Isolde, my note) be long dead, their sweet name lives on. May their death have in this world a good and long life, giving constancy to those who desire constancy, honor to those desiring honor. May their death always live, renewing the living. For whenever we hear told of their constancy and the purity of their constancy, their heartfelt joy and heartfelt sorrow, it is bread for all noble hearts. With this their deaths live. We read their life, we read their death, and like bread it is sweet.]

The challenges of Gottfried's *Tristan* were answered in a number of ways. At the imperial court between 1220 and 1243 at least three new *Tristan*-related works were composed and read. Around 1235, the imperial noble bondsman Conrad von Winterstetten (*d.* 1243) commissioned a continuation of Gottfried's *Tristan* from Ulrich von Türheim, a ministerial from the circles around the bishops of Augsburg. Ulrich's continuation, which is 3730 lines long, apparently uses as its source a version of Eilhart's *Tristrant* rather than Gottfried's Old

French source, Thomas. Ulrich's continuation gives a moralistic answer to the sexual dilemmas and challenges posed by Gottfried's *Tristan*. In Ulrich's text, the problem is Isolde's adultery and her compromised sexual chastity, and this problem is solved by making Isolde the villain who has seduced and corrupted a good knight. The continuation specifically warns the reader against imitation.

Ulrich's continuation can be understood as an interpretation and a critique of Gottfried's *Tristan*. (Around 1290, another continuation of Gottfried's *Tristan* was written by Ulrich von Freiburg for an important Bohemian-German noble family. It, too, is based on Eilhart's *Tristrant*.) Two more romances originating at the thirteenth-century German Staufer court also seek socially acceptable solutions to the "Isolde" problem, that it to say, the problem of having a romance heroine who not only gets away with having sex with two men (her husband and her lover) but is even excused for doing so. One of these romances is Chrétien's *Cligés*, which was rendered into German sometime after 1220, again by Ulrich von Türheim. Chrétien's *Cligés* was first translated into German after 1210 by Konrad Fleck. Because Fleck's version is lost and only 400 lines of Ulrich's version survive, the relationship between the two versions cannot be determined. It seems that neither version circulated widely in Germany. In it, the heroine finally marries her beloved as a virgin because her use of magic has allowed her to avoid sexual intercourse with the king to whom she has first been married against her will. Unlike Isolde, Cligés never has sex with any man besides the husband who is her beloved, thereby compromising neither her sexual chastity nor social conventions about noblewomen's chastity.

The second romance contesting the *Tristan* model of love is *Wilhelm von Orlens*, which was written around 1235 by Rudolf von Ems (*fl.* 1215–c. 1256). Based on an Old French source no longer extant but related to *Jehan et Blonde*, the romance opens with an account of Wilhelm's courtly education and chivalric deeds and the love he shares with the noble Amelie. The lovers remain constant despite trials and tribulations (Amelie's forced engagement to another suitor; Wilhelm's injury and banishment) and are ultimately united in marriage. *Wilhelm* is a love adventure romance placed in a chivalric setting. Its happy ending talks back to the tragic world view in Gottfried's *Tristan* by proposing a world view in which the protagonists are socially rewarded for their endurance and steadfastness. The number of surviving manuscripts and the appearance of the protagonists on material objects such as bed coverings suggest that *Wilhelm* was a popular story.

OTHER TRADITIONS OF ROMANCE[11]

When texts urging radically different views of love and chivalry are all read at one court it suggests that medieval audiences appreciated the potential for debate created by romance. Comedy, too, can be a vehicle for arguing about courtly ideals. A masterpiece of comic romance, *Frauendienst* ("Service of Ladies"), was written around 1255 by a wealthy and influential noble bondsman from Austria, Ulrich von Liechtenstein (*c.* 1200–1275). Told in the form of an autobiography, the narrator, now older and wiser, recounts his youthful misadventures while pursuing the lady of his dreams according to the "rules" of courtly love service. More than fifty of Ulrich's poems are embedded into the fabric of *Frauendienst*. The narrator's first courtship dominates the story. It is directed towards a woman of much higher rank (perhaps a free noblewoman), whose repeated rebuffs of the headstrong and deluded young knight are the source of much of the epic's drastic comedy. At one point, the young man is so eager to prove his love that he dons a marvelous white dress and two artificial, waist-length braids entwined with pearls, and so disguised as "Lady Venus" rides across the countryside, jousting and besting all of the many knights who challenge him. The aura of authenticity created by *Frauendienst*'s autobiographical stance is sustained in the descriptions of "Lady Venus's" male opponents, whose names correspond to the names of Ulrich's contemporaries. Modern readers are as entertained by youthful Ulrich's cross-dressing and the dilemmas in which it lands him as is the audience in the text. What is perhaps less obvious to us today is that *Frauendienst* also plays with role reversals between freeborn nobility and noble bondsmen. Perhaps Ulrich is humorously calling into question a social order that separated the nobles from powerful ministerials like the Liechtensteins, who were their equals in everything but the crucial accident of birth. Ulrich's text might then be promoting – in comic fashion – the integration of the great ministerial lineages with the old nobility into a new estate of lords.[12]

Love adventure romances flourished in medieval Germany.[13] Tales from the Old French *Floire et Blancheflor* tradition were especially popular in northern Germany, including Flemish/Dutch-speaking regions, as noted earlier. Though Floire and Blancheflor are born and raised at the same court, Floire is the son of the pagan king, while Blancheflor is the daughter of an enslaved, Christian noblewoman. They have loved one another since childhood. After some twelve years, Floire's parents seek to sever this unwelcome bond by secretly selling Blancheflor into slavery and telling Floire that she has died. Floire succeeds, however, in finding Blancheflor, who has been sold into a sultan's harem and yet managed to remain faithful to Floire. After more trials, the lovers are at last united in marriage, and Floire converts to Christianity.

At least five separate German versions of this story existed, but our knowledge of them is limited by the fact that two versions survive only as fragments. The fragmentary *Trierer Floyris* (1170s) has already been mentioned. Around 1200–1220 Konrad Fleck retold the story in his *Flore und Blanscheflur*. A third adaptation from the first half of the thirteenth century, *Flors inde Blanzeflors*, is anonymous. Made in the region of the cities Aachen and Cologne, it is represented, like the *Trierer Floyris*, by a single fragment. These three versions appear to have been written independently of one another. A 4000-line medieval Dutch adaptation, *Floris*, was made by the Fleming Diederic van Assende around 1260. A fifth version, *Flos unde Blankeflos*, was anonymously composed in medieval Low German, probably at the beginning of the fourteenth century. (Now considered a dialect, Low German was then the standard language of the thriving merchant cities of northern Germany.) *Flos unde Blankeflos* drastically shortens its source (probably *Flors inde Blanzeflors*), in part by eliminating courtly elements, so that the noble setting becomes a generic backdrop that creates a kind of fairy-tale atmosphere. Notions of exchange function as a leitmotif. Blankeflos is not sold into slavery but rather "exchanged for treasure"; Flos buys with gold the loyalty of friends and foe alike. Finally, dramatic speeches and dialogues focus the story on the protagonists' emotions. Perhaps such transformations accommodated the tastes of the northern German urban merchant households which probably comprised its audience.

One of the last great love adventure romances was finished in 1314 by Johann von Würzburg. *Wilhelm von Österreich* tells of the noble lovers Wilhelm and Aglye, who have been devoted to one another since their childhood. Surprisingly, the romance concludes with an unhappy ending based on the love–death motif, in which a lover's unparalleled devotion makes life without his or her beloved unsustainable. (*Tristan* ends in this fashion.) After enduring many trials and, at last, marrying, Wilhelm is murdered by his enemies while hunting. Aglye rushes to his side, and, upon seeing his corpse, also dies. Her death enacts the depth of her love for Wilhelm.

LATE MEDIEVAL TRANSFORMATIONS OF ROMANCE

Kinig artus hauf (King Arthur's court; also known as *Widwilt*) is an anonymous, late medieval, Old Yiddish romance. (Old Yiddish, a medieval German dialect written in Hebrew script with many loan words from Hebrew and Slavic languages, was spoken by Jews throughout Europe.) Perhaps written sometime in the fourteenth century, *Widwilt* adapts a very popular Arthurian romance, *Wigalois*, which was written by Wirnt von Gravenberg around 1210 and in turn based on stories related to Old French tales (the twelfth-century *Bel Inconnu* of Renaud de Beaujeu).[14] Both stories recount the adventures of the knight Wigalois, the son of Gawain and Flories. *Widwilt* dechristianizes the story and alters the character of the festival and marriage scenes to reflect Jewish customs. That an Arthurian romance found its way into an urban, late medieval Jewish milieu demonstrates the literary appeal of romance texts. It also suggests that medieval Jewish culture was less isolated than is sometimes imagined.

The prestige of courtly themes in medieval literary culture remained high in fifteenth-century Germany. Wall paintings at the castle of Runkelstein (South Tyrol, Italy) employed romance motifs to legitimize the castleowners' claims to wealth, power, and cultural sophistication. Runkelstein was extensively remodeled around 1400 by new owners, Niklaus and Franz Vintler from the city of Bozen (now South Tyrol, Italy), wealthy commoners who as financiers loaned money to nobles and who had purchased the castle around 1375. These paintings, which appear to have adorned almost every room in the living quarters on the site, gesture fixedly towards a glamorous chivalric past. There are scenes of courtly pursuits (jousting, dancing, games, conversation), pictures grouping the three best Arthurian knights (Parzival, Gawein, and Iwein) and the three most loving couples (Wilhelm von Österreich and Aglye, Tristan and Isolde, and Wilhelm von Orlens and Amelie), and even "epic rooms" in which the paintings faithfully render celebrated chivalric romances in pictorial form.

The most striking feature of the epic rooms at Runkelstein is how carefully they strive to reproduce exactly the events of literary texts in pictoral form. The Rodenegg *Ywain* frescoes, mentioned earlier, painted at the most a few decades after Hartmann composed his work, advanced a new reading of the literary text. In contrast, the Runkelstein frescoes carefully illustrate in pictures venerable literary texts – the romances depicted in the epic rooms were between 100- and 200-years old in 1400. Rather than creating new stories or new interpretations, the Runkelstein program conserves images of knighthood and romance that now glowed with the idealizing patina of time past. Festive splendor suffuses the entire ensemble of images. Perhaps when the Vintlers gathered with guests in these rooms, they imagined themselves as participants in the scenes. And perhaps, too, the Runkelstein paintings signal the Vintlers' claim to a conservative, noble identity whose venerable prestige is created and commemorated in these pictures.

The chivalric nostalgia at work in the Runkelstein paintings was shared by the late fifteenth-century medieval German aristocracy. When the Habsburg emperor Maximilian I (a passionate lover of knighthood as it appeared in the old romances) took possession of castle Runkelstein at the beginning of the sixteenth century, he had the wall paintings renovated. Only a few decades earlier, the Munich painter Ulrich Füetrer (d. 1496) produced a series of monumental anthologies about romance heroes for the court of Duke Albrecht IV of Bavaria and his wife Kunigunde, Emperor Maximilian's sister. For these works Füetrer adapted earlier romances. Both his prose *Lanzelot* and his verse *Lannzilet*, which was written in the *Titurel*-stanza, are based on the thirteenth-century *Prose Lancelot*. Füetrer's *Buch der Liebe* ("Book of Love", 1480) is an enormous anthology, also written in *Titurel*-stanzas, that adapts earlier romances to tell the life stories of exemplary knights such as Parzival and Wigalois.

While Füetrer was composing works for aristocratic circles, the first printers were at work in the thriving urban centers of Germany producing prose books based on medieval romances, which were presumably marketed to both commoners and nobles. In Augsburg, Anton Sorg produced in 1484 an illustrated prose version of Eilhart's *Tristrant*, and in 1493, Hans Schönperger published *Wigoleiss*, a prose version of Wirnt's *Wigalois*.

No new long, verse romances were composed in German after *c.* 1350. Instead, newer genres such as short, rhymed couplet poems (the *Märe* and the *Minnerede*) took up notions of romance, chivalry, and love service. For example, Konrad von Würzburg's thirteenth-century tragic verse short story, *Das Herzmäre* ("The Story of the Heart", adapted from the Old French *Roman du castelain de Couci*) was often recopied in the later Middle Ages. It uses the love–death motif to tell about steadfast lovers whose deaths seal their love. In an entirely different vein, an anonymous, fifteenth-century *Minnerede* entitled *Die Beichte einer Frau* ("A Woman's Confession") features an adulteress whose detailed description of the virtues of chivalric love service convinces a priest that her love affair is not sinful.

Single, rhymed couplet texts were almost always compiled into long, anthology-like manuscripts, which circulated among the nobility and among the urban elite – wealthy merchants, patricians, and educated professionals such as lawyers and doctors. The mostly anonymous manuscript compilers, who were careful about how they selected and arranged the texts, sometimes artfully grouped serious and comic tales on the subject of love. In this way, the individual stories could represent different positions in a larger debate about the meaning of love and romance. Although a single rhymed couplet text is only 500 to 700 lines long, such a group of four- to six-rhymed couplet texts, called a minne constellation, might approach the length of a romance.[15] One Low German manuscript, compiled in 1431 (Berlin, Staatsbibliothek zu Berlin Preußischer Kulturbesitz, mgo 186) has a minne constellation of six texts which fills about sixty folios (or about 120 pages). The texts are: *Schule der Minne* ("School of Love"), an allegory of the virtues of love; *Streitgespräch zweier Frauen über die Minne* ("Debate Between Two Women about Love"), in which two women argue about whether happiness derives from the presence or absence of love; *Frauentreue* ("The Fidelity of Women"), a tale of genuine female fidelity; *Die treue Magd* ("The Faithful Maid"), a comic tale that confirms women's mastery of erotic situations; and *Des Minners Anklagen* ("The Lover's Lament"), a disputation between love and beauty that yields to a trial scene in which the Virtues pass judgment on the narrator's beloved. The stories in this minne constellation converse with one another about romance, about its virtues and ideals, about its limits and possibilities, about its ambiguities and ironies. They are particularly interested in exploring women's perspectives on love (can romance make women happy?) and in contrasting romance's sometimes contradictory perspectives on women – are women capable of fidelity? Can women be trusted? Do virtuous, loving women exist? The theme of romance is continued in the long tale chosen to follow the minne constellation in the manuscript Berlin mgo 186. This is the Low German *Flos unde Blankeflos*, mentioned earlier, the charming love adventure romance in which the unselfish devotion of steadfast child lovers convinces even their worst enemy to overturn their death sentences and release them so that they may marry one another. This romance suggests a fantasy that answers back to the troubled queries of the preceeding minne constellation, for it imagines an erotic love so pure, so powerful, and so unswervingly true that it can overcome every obstacle and yet still be its own reward.

Medieval German romance was created by and for a specific group of people at a unique moment in time – the medieval aristocracy of the late twelfth and early thirteenth centuries. The ideals of love and honor that are made meaningful in these works from long ago took hold not just of the medieval imagination, or of the early modern imagination, but also of our own. The extraordinary staying power of the ideal of romance testifies to its imaginative force, and to the continuity across time of our shared human desire to profoundly connect with one another.

NOTES

1 For introductory information on Dutch, Flemish, and Old Norse romance, the reader is referred to the following works: Erik Kooper, ed., *Medieval Dutch Literature in its European Context*, Cambridge Studies in Medieval Literature 21 (Cambridge University Press, 1994), which includes maps, chronological tables, and a bibliography of translations; Margaret Schlauch, *Romance in Iceland* (New York: Russell and Russell; Princeton University Press, 1934); Marianne Kalinke, "Norse Romance (*Riddarasögur*)," in *Old Norse-Icelandic Literature: A Critical Guide*, ed. by Carol J. Clover and John Lindow (Ithaca, NY: Cornell University Press, 1985).

2 See Bernd Bastert, "'*Dô si der lantgrâve nam*': Zur 'Klever Hochzeit' und der Genese des Eneas-Romans," *Zeitschrift für deutsches Altertum*, 123 (1994), 253–73. The most important work on patrons and patronage in medieval German literature is Joachim Bumke, *Mäzene im Mittelalter: Die Gönner und Auftraggeber der höfischen Literatur in Deutschland 1150–1300* (Munich: Beck, 1979).

3 The *Trierer Floyris* (so called because it is now housed in the German city of Trier) is a fragment; 368 lines out of an estimated 3700 lines survive. See Hartmut Beckers, "Literatur am klevischen Hof vom 1174 bis 1542: Zeugnisse, Spuren, Mutmassungen," *Zeitschrift für deutsche Philologie*, 112 (1993), 426–34.

4 See John B. Freed, *Noble Bondsmen: Ministerial Marriages in the Archdiocese of Salzburg, 1100–1343* (Ithaca, NY: Cornell University Press, 1995).

5 See Joachim Bumke, "Der unfeste Text," in *Aufführung und Schrift in Mittelalter und Früher Neuzeit*, ed. Jan-Dirk Müller, Germanistische Symposien-Berichtsbände vol. 17 (Stuttgart: Metzler, 1996), 118–29.

6 See Norbert H. Ott, "Epische Stoffe in mittelalterlichen Bildzeugnissen," in *Epische*

Stoffe des Mittelalters, ed. Volker Mertens and Ulrich Müller (Stuttgart: Kröner, 1984), 449–74. In addition to the article by Norbert H. Ott, see also Stephanie Cain Van D'Elden, "Reading Illustrations of *Tristan*," in *Literary Aspects of Courtly Culture*, ed. Donald Maddox and Sara Sturm-Maddox (Rochester, NY: Boydel and Brewer, 1994), 343–51, and *eadem*, "Discursive Illustrations in Three *Tristan* Manuscripts," in *Word and Image in Arthurian Literature*, ed. Keith Busby (New York: Garland, 1996), 284–319.

7 *Lanzelet*, a German romance in the *Lancelot* tradition, was translated from an Old French source around 1194/95 by a cleric, Ulrich of Zatzikhoven. Ulrich's text is something of a puzzle. In some details it bears a strong resemblance to Chrétien's text, *Le chevalier de la Charette*, yet it is more marvelous and less courtly. About his source, Ulrich says only that it was a "French book" (*welsche buoch*) furnished by Huc de Morville, an Anglo-Norman nobleman who in 1194 was at the court of the Staufer emperor Henry VI (d. 1198) as a hostage for the released Plantagenet King, Richard Lionheart.

The Lancelot material received another treatment in German: the *Prosa-Lancelot* (c. 1250 for parts I and II; c.1300 for part III), the oldest prose novel in German, which is a lengthy and anonymous translation of the Old French *Lancelot en prose*. In contrast to other German adaptations of Old French romances, the *Prosa-Lancelot* is a remarkably faithful translation of its source. Only a sixteenth-century fragment survives from another thirteenth-century Lancelot story, *Der Mantel*, which is attributed to Heinrich von dem Türlin and was freely adapted from the Old French *Du mantel mautaillié*.

8 Beginning with the scene to the immediate right of the door in the middle of the east wall and progressing around the room, these scenes are: Ywain's departure; Ywain with the wild man; Ywain at the magic fountain; Ywain's battle with Ascalon, lance phase; Ywain's battle with Ascalon, sword phase; Ywain trapped by the falling gate; Death of Ascalon; Lunette giving Ywain the ring; Ascalon on his bier; Search for the invisible Ywain; Ywain kneeling before a sorrowful and despairing Laudine.

9 For a fine new study of these wall paintings see James A. Rushing, Jr., *Images of Adventure: Ywain in the Visual Arts* (Philadelphia: University of Pennsylvania Press, 1995). The information and arguments in this essay on Iwein in wall paintings derive from Rushing's book.

10 See Michael Benskin, Tony Hunt and Ian Short, "Un nouveau fragment du Tristan de Thomas," *Romania*, 113 (1992), 3–4, 289–319, and Ulrike Jantzen and Niels Kröner, "Zum neugefundenen *Tristan*-Fragment des Thomas d'Angleterre. Editionskritik und Vergleich mit Gottfrieds Bearbeitung," *Euphorion*, 91 (1997), 291–309.

11 Of the many medieval German romances that cannot be discussed in this essay, I here mention three for which English translations exist. *Diu Crône* ["The Crown"] (c. 1250) by Heinrich von dem Türlin, is a Gawein story; *Daniel von dem blühenden Tal* ["Daniel from the Flowering Valley"] (c. 1230–1250), by der Stricker, is a magical-fantastic Arthurian tale that also represents the first independent German Arthurian romance; and *Garel von dem blühenden Tal* ["Garel from the Flowering Valley"] (c. 1250–1280) by der Pleier, is an Arthurian romance that sets out to correct der Stricker's work by returning to the more traditional repertoire of Arthurian motifs.

12 See Freed, *Noble Bondsmen*, 224–49.

13 Love adventure romances flourished in the second half of the thirteenth century for

reasons that have yet to be investigated by literary scholars. Available in English translation are two romances written in the 1270s or 1280s by der Pleier: *Meleranz*, which combines Arthurian and love adventure material, and *Tandareis und Flordibel*.

14 On the Old Yiddish *Widwilt* see Robert G. Warnock, "The Arthurian Tradition in Hebrew and Yiddish," in *King Arthur through the Ages*, 1, ed. Valerie M. Lagorio and Mildred Leake Day (New York: Garland, 1990), 189–208.

15 For a definition and discussion of the term "minne constellation," see Sarah Westphal, *Textual Poetics of German Manuscripts 1300–1500* (Columbia, SC: Camden House, 1993). On the minne constellation from Berlin, Staatsbibliothek zu Berlin Preußischer Kulturbesitz, mgo 186, which is discussed below, see especially pages 120–25.

SUGGESTIONS FOR FURTHER READING

Arthurian Women: A Casebook, ed. with intro. Thelma S. Fenster. New York: Garland, 1996.

Bumke, Joachim. *Courtly Culture: Literature and Society in the High Middle Ages.* Berkeley: University of California Press, 1991. Translation of *Höfische Kultur: Literatur und Gesellschaft im hohen Mittelalter.* Munich: Deutscher Taschenbuchverlag, 1986. This surveys all aspects of aristocratic society and culture from the eleventh to the fourteenth century, focusing particularly on medieval documents and sources from continental Europe. Topics discussed include meaning of courtliness; court administration; position of women; courtly education; courtly ethics; ideology of knighthood; church and court; orality and literacy; language of gesture. An invaluable resource.

Bumke, Joachim. *Mäzene im Mittelalter: Die Gönner und Auftraggeber der höfischen Literatur in Deutschland 1150–1300.* Munich: Beck, 1979 [Patrons in the Middle Ages: the benefactors and sponsors of courtly literature in Germany, 1150–1300]. First, and to date only, study that surveys everything scholars know and surmise about the patrons of medieval German literature. Though dated in some of its details, provides both a fascinating glimpse of the medieval courts in which romance literature was cultivated, and a careful and well-reasoned account of the historical evidence and the scholarly misunderstandings and wishful thinking to which its huge gaps have sometimes given rise. Also reprints in a lengthy appendix all of the important literary passages referring to patrons in late twelfth- and early thirteenth-century German literature.

Chrétien de Troyes and the German Middle Ages: Papers from an International Symposium, ed. with intro. Martin H. Jones and Roy Wisbey. Arthurian Series 26; Publications of the Institute of Germanic Studies 53. Cambridge: D. S. Brewer; London: Institute of Germanic Studies, 1993. Comparative articles by eminent American, British, French, and German scholars on crucial questions of the German Arthurian tradition, such as Hartmann's and Wolfram's adaptions of Chrétien, *Cligés* and the Lancelot material in Germany, and the wall paintings at Rodenegg. Includes two articles on Hartmann's *Erec* that are concerned with gender dynamics.

Epische Stoffe des Mittelalters, ed. Volker Mertens and Ulrich Müller. Stuttgart: Kröner, 1984. For those who read German, a superb general reference work that comprehensively surveys popular medieval legends and stories in the European vernaculars. Organized thematically in individually authored chapters on, for example,

Arthurian material, antique epics, grail epics, Tristan material, hellenistic love adventure romances, epic material in visual representations. Includes excellent bibliographies of primary sources.

Gottfried von Strassburg and the Medieval Tristan Legend: Papers from an Anglo-North American Symposium, ed. with intro. Adrian Stevens and Roy Wisbey. Arthurian Series 23. Cambridge: D. S. Brewer; Rochester, NY: Boydell & Brewer, 1990.

Grieve, Patricia E. *"Floire and Blancheflor" and the European Romance*. Cambridge University Press, 1997. Although this study does not deal extensively with the German versions, its scope and excellent bibliographies make it an indispensable starting point for any work on the tradition. Includes discussions of the Scandinavian material.

Groos, Arthur. *Romancing the Grail: Genre, Science, and Quest in Wolfram's Parzival*. Ithaca: Cornell University Press, 1995.

Jackson, W. H. *Chivalry in Twelfth-century Germany: The Works of Hartmann von Aue*. Arthurian Series 34. Cambridge: D. S. Brewer, 1994.

Rasmussen, Ann Marie. *Mothers and Daughters in Medieval German Literature*. Syracuse University Press, 1997. Includes chapters on Heinrich's *Eneide* and on Gottfried's *Tristan* that argue for gendered readings of romance motifs.

Rushing, James A. Jr. *Images of Adventure: Ywain in the Visual Arts*. Philadelphia: University of Pennsylvania, 1995.

Schultz, James A. *The Shape of the Round Table: Structures of Middle High German Arthurian Romance*. University of Toronto Press, 1983.

12

F. REGINA PSAKI

Chivalry and medieval Italian romance

Medieval vernacular romance is assumed to bear the stamp of the class to which it was first directed, namely the French feudal aristocracy of the twelfth century. Typically, in fact, the romances of other times, places, and socio-political contexts are compared to the first generation of French romance, and judged inadequate. The Old Italian *romanzi* rarely win praise from romance scholars, who tend to assume that their authors and audiences did not really understand what chivalry and chivalric literature originally meant. This assumption deserves scrutiny in light of the unusual, even unique, example of the Italian peninsula in the Middle Ages.

The Italian peninsula featured a variety of political systems quite unusual for medieval Europe. The south, including Sicily, was dominated by a monarchical model; after the death of Frederick II in 1250, though, the southern kingdom split into two hostile kingdoms, Angevin in Naples and Aragonese in Sicily. In the center and north, on the other hand, there was a myriad of smaller political organizations: semi-independent city-states called communes; the republic of Venice; the Papal State, including the territory around and north of Rome; the towns and lands governed by one noble family; and other intermediate forms of government. This political heterogeneity was not peaceful. Indeed, alliances and allegiances were unstable and violent, organized around the two poles of papacy and empire, which competed for hegemony even more violently in Italy than elsewhere. Italy represents an unusually dynamic variety of political forms in close proximity, with a correspondingly dynamic variety of powerful socio-economic classes.

The audience for romance narratives was thus also quite varied: nobles, wealthy bourgeois, petty bourgeois, artisans, an urban underclass, and clerics, to name only a few classes, constituted a notably heterogeneous market for romance in many forms. Chronologically first among these forms are French texts in their original language. There was a considerable French influence and presence in Italian territory, both in the northern courts and in the south (and particularly after the Angevin conquest of Naples). Even without a French

203

political presence, though, the different Romance languages were transparent enough to educated speakers for texts to circulate without translation. The Tuscan Brunetto Latini called French "the most universal and delightful of all languages," and composed his encyclopedic *Li livres dou Tresor* (1266) in it. There was thus an audience for the French prose romances written in France and sent to Italy, and in the second half of the thirteenth century romances in French were both copied (in the Visconti and Anjou courts) and composed on the Italian peninsula. Rustichello (or Rusticiano) da Pisa, to whom Marco Polo would later dictate his memoirs, also composed the long French romance *Meliadus* based on the Tristan and Lancelot material (*c*. 1270).

The French Prose *Lancelot* figures in Dante's most famous reference to romance, *Inferno* v.127–38. Dante makes his character Francesca, damned for lust to the second circle of hell, blame her sinful love for her husband's brother on the seductive influence of the *Lancelot* romance. The historical Francesca was murdered by her husband in the early 1280s; Dante wrote his version before 1310, and it tells us that the Prose *Lancelot* was very familiar to northern Italian readers at this time. *Inferno* v criticizes Francesca's self-justification more pointedly than it does the love portrayed in chivalric romance, and elsewhere Dante tends to praise rather than condemn chivalric ideals. In any case, although the French prose romances reach Italian territory from the 1220s on, and circulate in French, authors soon began to translate them into Italian, and to compose new romance texts in Italian.

Among these Italian compositions are the *cantari*, verse narratives composed in eight-line stanzas and sung in public places such as piazzas and taverns. The *cantari*, which date from the mid-thirteenth to the late fifteenth centuries, tend to be short, about fifty stanzas each, or divided into fifty-stanza sections. There are *cantari* on Carolingian, Trojan, Arthurian, Ovidian, courtly, and purely fantastic subjects, and their lively and enjoyable style won them lasting popularity. Arthurian and courtly *cantari* typically narrate either single episodes from a familiar romance (such as a combat between Lancelot and Tristan) or a short romance (such as *Fiorio e Biancifiore*, condensed from *Floire et Blancheflor*, which exists in many medieval languages). These pieces are typically thought to have been written for more popular audiences, and consequently to be less sophisticated versions of the romances that were produced for an educated or aristocratic elite.

The Italian prose romances, on the other hand, were composed for a broad, though clearly literate and urban, audience of Italian readers. There is no evidence that they were performed publicly in any way other than perhaps reading aloud; the earliest manuscript which preserves romance material in an Italian dialect, the *Tristano Riccardiano*, dates from near the end of the thirteenth century, and is so unadorned and utilitarian a copy that it was probably produced for private reading. It is just such a scene of private reading that Francesca describes, for example. The prose romances, like their French originals, tend to be long and convoluted, and feature multiple protagonists whose adventures are interwoven in the interlace style typical of French prose romance. The Italian corpus includes five major Tristan romances, all of which derive ultimately from the French *Tristan en prose*; two Lancelot romances; and romances on the Merlin material, such as the *Storia di Merlino* (early fourteenth century). The production and circulation of these texts continued until the late sixteenth century, with variations tailored to their contexts and purpose.

Boccaccio wrote another adaptation of the French *Floire et Blancheflor*, the *Filocolo* (1336–38); it is much more elaborate than the *cantare*, though written in the same form. Produced for the court at Naples, the love story of a Christian princess and a pagan prince features the wanderings and vicissitudes typical of both courtly romance and the Italian versions of the Carolingian material. Boccaccio was nothing if not an experimental author, and his foray into chivalric romance was not typical of the genre, but it is in some way typical of the heterogeneous nature of the material in Italy.

The form of medieval romance would enjoy a new life in the Italian Renaissance epic, Pulci's *Morgante* (1473), Boiardo's *Orlando Innamorato* (1476–94), and Ariosto's *Orlando Furioso* (1516–32). These verse epics, also written in eight-line stanzas, feature the cast of characters of the Carolingian material (Charlemagne, Roland, Oliver, and many others), but they combine these epic figures with the interlaced plots and chivalric value system of the Arthurian romance material. Massively influential particularly in English literature, these works do not simply restate the value system of the romance material, which was complex and subtle in itself. Rather the two Orlando epics attempt to link a time-honored tradition of nobility and chivalry, by then perceived as irrevocably in decline, to the origin of the Este family and its rule. They propose a renewed and restored version of the knightly virtues for a modern world, through the uniquely legitimate rule of the Este. The last of the major epics, Tasso's *Gerusalemme Liberata* (1560–75), was written in a different cultural environment, namely the Counter-Reformation. It subordinates the style and substance of the romance material and the epic world to a central Christian subject, the Crusades, much as the Vulgate Cycle had recast Arthurian romance in the thirteenth century.

Their variety of context, audience, and literary form gives Italian romances a unique historical and sociological value for the study of romance in general. The Carolingian material, written in French and Italian, was more popular in Italy; but the Italian refashionings of courtly and Arthurian romance, the so-called matter of Britain, allow us to focus on the question of chivalry in the Italian context. The versions created for the Tuscan communes, for the Angevin court of Naples, for the *signorie* of the Po Valley, for the Venetian republic, all foreground elements which suit these new environments. A new study needs to be written on the entire corpus of Italian romance, including the fourteenth- and fifteenth-century *cantari*; the prose romances; Boccaccio's self-consciously literary reworkings for the court of Naples; the Renaissance epics by Boiardo and Ariosto; and the sixteenth-century poems and prose works, among others. The last such survey, Edmund Gardner's 1930 work *The Arthurian Tradition in Italian Literature*, urgently needs updating.[1]

Also in need of an update is the tendency to privilege as the pinnacle of the genre French twelfth-century verse romance, with its symbolic landscape of adventure, itinerary of maturation, and inner conflicts of chivalry between individual and society. Later romance is often slighted for not adhering to this model, yet even in France these categories are already problematized by the early thirteenth-century prose compilation romance. Whereas the "biographical" Arthurian romance in verse focuses clearly on a single male hero and his ethical maturation and integration into his society, the cyclical or compilation romance follows the adventures of many knights, all of whom interest us less for themselves than because they serve an ideal court. The compilation romances tend to tell of the decline and fall of Arthurian society, rather than of a single knight's successful adventures in love and war. They exalt the collectivity of the Round Table as the provisional "guarantor of stability and order, political and military control,"[2] rather than one particular knight. Although we inevitably witness the failure of the earthly chivalric ideal, that ideal, while it does last, resides in the Arthurian court. The compilation model does not betray or fail the ideological agenda of biographical romance; rather, both models are themselves a simplification of complex tendencies present in the whole romance corpus, as we shall see in examining the Italian Tristan romances.

Identifying the ideal of knightly behavior and ethics which informs medieval European chivalric romance is a problematic task, particularly once we remove that literary ideal from its matrix in feudal France. The south of Italy and Sicily were conquered by Norman knights, who imported their literature, values, and tastes;[3] the communes in the north, on the other hand, have been seen as less culturally colonized. The common interpretation of chivalric literature in Italy is that the original values of French romance degenerated as the material traveled into new countries, languages, forms, and socio-economic and class strata.[4] This assumes that the new bourgeois and lower-class audiences for romance in northern Italy understood little of the ethical intent of the French originals, and took over only their external forms.[5] If twelfth-century romance was created to entertain and socialize a refined northern European court audience, the Italian derivations were meant to offer bourgeois audiences "a kind of collective escapism" and "improvised patents of nobility."[6] This account dismisses the new consumers of romance as limited and literal-minded poseurs. In this model of romance entropy, the chivalric ideal declines once its literature moves into Italy, away from its original context, producers, and audience; it is so context-specific that it risks complete degeneration when transplanted.

To dismiss Italian romance as derivative and its version of chivalry as artificial is not necessarily accurate, however. John Larner, a historian of medieval Italy, attributes the widespread conviction that chivalry was a construct out of place in Italy to a common misconception about early capitalism, namely that it emerged from the middle class. But Larner claims that it was actually the ideology of chivalry – "reckless courage balanced by intelligence, a contempt for wealth" – that enabled great risk and consequently great profit, giving rise to capitalism and eventually to a middle class.[7] Moreover, Aldo Scaglione reminds us that whatever political, economic, social, and intellectual conditions – in Italy or elsewhere – might diverge from a feudal model, mentalities outlive the material conditions that generated them.[8] Indeed, in our own time we can see that certain cultural models persist although their experiential bases have all but vanished; these models continue to serve as sources of inspiration (or frustration) as we measure ourselves against them.

The Italian romances, influenced by the compilation model but not adhering to it exclusively, are a goldmine of information about what values, and particularly what version of chivalry, romance offered its audience. Geography, language, audience, period, political organization, and literary horizon all prompted Italian authors (and translators) to include specific textual emphases which colored the ideal of chivalry, defined by Scaglione as "the ethico-ideological frame of mind that extended from knights to other classes and that informed patterns of behavior regarded as 'noble.'"[9] We have difficulty identifying the precise notion of chivalry prevailing in any one time or place, for several reasons: we cannot safely extrapolate real-world beliefs or behavior from fiction, especially highly conventional fiction; and literary works are inconsistent on what constitutes chivalry in the first place. But ultimately what underlies our difficulty in fixing chivalry as a set of mores for imaginary (and in some fashion for real) characters, is the fact that chivalry is itself constantly under scrutiny in the romances. The romances are fundamentally a search for a working definition of chivalric virtue, and each offers different answers.

The ethos of chivalry as it is described and portrayed in three northern Italian prose Tristan romances, between about 1280 and 1340, reflects both the French source texts and the specific context in which they were translated and adapted. The relevant feature of that context is primarily civic strife, the political instability and savagery which Dante's *Commedia* describes with such rancor and regret. The three versions of the Tristan story accessible in modern editions each portray an ideology of knighthood specific to its time and place. The plot points

I wish to display as examples are themselves frequently dictated by the source material; I will show however that the realization of certain aspects of plot is inflected by the specific goals of the single texts, all of which include imagining a resolution of power struggle and bloody discord. By restricting our attention to a single form, from a specific period and territory, we can see how chivalry is understood and appropriated by its various northern Italian audiences.

The *Tristano Riccardiano* is an incomplete late thirteenth-century Tuscan translation of the French prose *Tristan*.[10] The *Tristano Veneto* is a late thirteenth- or early fourteenth- century adaptation, in the Veneto dialect, of two French works: the prose *Tristan* and Rustichello's *Meliadus*.[11] The *Tavola Ritonda* is an early to mid-fourteenth-century Tuscan (perhaps Pisan) romance whose first half depends heavily on the *Tristano Riccardiano*, and its second on the prose *Tristan*.[12] In other words, the *Tristano Riccardiano* and the first sections of the *Tristano Veneto* and the *Tavola Ritonda* contain virtually the same material; in all these works Tristano is the first and best of a large cast of characters. All three thus have the multiple focus of the compilation model, but the exclusive exaltation of Tristano and structural focus on him more reminiscent of the biographical pole of romance.

As I read them, the Italian Tristan romances heighten the tensions between individualism and the collectivity that are latent in all romances and in the Tristan story in particular (a move that occurs already in the French prose *Tristan*, when Tristan is absorbed into the Arthurian world). In its own way, each romance scrutinizes the chivalric ethos as an ideal that attempts to reconcile private desires and collective needs; and each does so in a way that responds to the particular social climate of thirteenth- and fourteenth-century Italy – even as the ideals of chivalry themselves seem to survive intact.

The criteria for literary chivalry are those that adorn the knights held up to us as models in the romances; the *Tavola Ritonda*, for example, justifies its claim that Tristano is the finest knight in the world by listing his qualities:

> Imperò il nostro libro pone e dà sentenzia, che messer Tristano fu lo piú pro' cavaliere mondano e 'l piú ardito che mai natura formasse . . . egli fu pro' e savio combattente, e fu il piú vigoroso e 'l piú ardito e lo piú cortese e 'l piú bello e 'l piú leale cavaliere che mai cignesse spada . . . (503)

> [Therefore our book does set down the decision that Sir Tristano was the best secular knight and the boldest that nature ever formed . . . he was a brave and wise fighter, the most vigorous, bravest, noblest, most courteous, handsome, and loyal knight who ever belted on a sword.] (320–21)

Instructional figures and scenes function to articulate these values within the narration; Gornemant in the Perceval romances, and Governale in the Tristano romances, are the teachers and guardians of knightly honor.[13] The knight whom everyone in the romance calls perfect (Lancelot in the French material, Tristan in the Italian) has them all; the promising knight has most of them, with perhaps a flaw or two. But as the works foreground both the individual quest for identity and social integration, and the collective quest for social and political equilibrium, they present as chivalrous various and even conflicting characteristics and behaviors.

It is not always clear which of the two quests is ultimately more important in the romance.[14] In fact, these three prose romances combine the biographical (individual, episodic, single-protagonist) and compilation (cyclical, interlaced, multi-protagonist) models so pointedly as to deliberately problematize them. In the case of the Tristan plot in particular, founded as it is on the conflict between illicit love and society, between private desires and public roles, the chivalric narrative is an explicit meditation on the nature of love and honor in such a setting.[15] Italian romances have been characterized by their "bourgeois" inclusion of slices of everyday life, realistic scenes and figures, or alternately by their frequent implication that merit, not birth, determines nobility. Their true specificity, however, lies in a detectably urban anxiety about order, harmony, fairness, and peace, and their placing of knight-errantry at their service of these concerns.[16] All three romances emphasize the importance of chivalry for the social collectivity, or rather the social and collective orientation and nature of chivalry, subordinating both love *and* prowess to the common good.

THE *TRISTANO RICCARDIANO*

The *Tristano Riccardiano*, the earliest prose romance in Italian, is conserved in its entirety in only one manuscript, at the Riccardiana Library in Florence. The codex contains only this romance, and toward the end a spreading stain makes the last several folios unreadable. It is in any case incomplete, moving from before Tristan's birth, to his marriage with the second Isotta. With its cramped cursive script and absence of decoration this was no deluxe or presentation copy, and its plainness and portability suggest that it might have been made for a mercantile or bourgeois buyer rather than a noble one. Linguistic forms and spelling make it possible that a Florentine copyist might have copied it from a western Tuscan original. The *Tristano Riccardiano* features a rather bland narrative voice who rarely intervenes to comment on the narrative in any detail, and who lets the protagonists' actions and appearance communicate their emotional state rather than glossing their feelings explicitly. Generic formulae, such as "now the story says that . . ." and "but if anyone were to ask me, I should say that . . .", abound, giving the romance an apparently simple verbal surface. The fact that descriptions and commentary are so very condensed from its French source marks it as not for consumption by an elite audience alone.

The very first chapter of the *Tristano Riccardiano* sets out to reveal King Marco, Tristano's uncle, as the antithesis of chivalry, an anti-Tristan. Marco's younger brother Pernam tries to inspire and then shame Marco into fighting for Cornwall's honor and independence; Marco, resentful, later murders him even as Pernam cries out for mercy. This shocking violation immediately brands Marco and indeed all of Cornwall as innately unchivalrous. That Marco would rather murder his brother than fight to save his people establishes his utter baseness. Regardless of his lineage or title, he can claim no meaningful nobility if he lacks the will and courage to fight for the commonality.

By contrast, the innate chivalric perfections of the young Tristan are established from the outset; from an absurdly young age he understands the dictates of honor and loyalty. When the daughter of the King of Gaules approaches him through his tutor Governale, Tristano refuses her love because of the loyalty he owes her father. Governale had relayed the maiden's message as a kind of test for his ward; since his task is to rear an honorable knight, he is pleased with Tristano's scruples, and the girl's subsequent suicide does not make either of them reconsider Tristano's rejection of her.

I noted earlier that the chivalric romance is articulated as a search for chivalry itself; this is certainly evident in the *Tristano Riccardiano*, structured as a systematic search for the "pro cavaliere" ("valiant knight") in oneself and in others. Every real knight seems absorbed by an undisguised search for valor in himself, as in the identity-quest and maturation-tale of verse romance. Tristano, eager to fight L'Amoroldo, tells his tutor,

> s'io vegno a la battaglia kollui ed io lo vinco, sie acquisteroe io grande pregio e a questa battaglia konosceroe io sed io debbo esser prod'uomo d'arme. Esse io prodd'uomo non debbo essere, meglio èe k'io muoia in questa battaglia a onore ke vivere servo ko li malvagi cavalieri di Cornovaglia. (70)

> [if I go into battle against him and win, then I will gain great renown and by this battle I will know if I am to be a valiant man at arms. And if I am not to be a valiant man, it is better for me to die in this battle honorably than live enslaved with the craven knights of Cornwall.]

Similarly, the heroes pursue other knights famed for prowess, such as Lancillotto, in order to identify and isolate, even appropriate, the essence of chivalry. Being a knight is thus not a stable identity to acquire and keep; it is the object of a vexed pursuit, of constant reevaluation and comparison; it is vulnerable to loss or devaluation; it must be re-won in every encounter.

The narrative interrogation and pursuit of knighthood is not the concern of the characters alone, however. The narrator and the romance plot itself constantly measure competing definitions of chivalry against each other, enacting an examination of the term so marked as to be almost explicit. Only Tristano is by definition never unchivalrous, even when his behavior seems incongruous with his oft-noted perfection. His occasional dalliances, for example, or his hundred-page (two-week) detour adventuring in the forest of Nerlantes while Isotta desperately waits for him in prison, do not diminish his chivalry, but paradoxically confirm it. The Cornish knights and King Marco, by contrast, are never chivalrous even when they behave well. The tension between the chivalry which one has or lacks *a priori* (e.g., Tristano's and Marco's) and the chivalry which one can win or lose by one's behavior (e.g., Palamidesso's) reveals a vital dimension of chivalric perfection. That perfection is a combination of behavior and being parallel to merit and grace in Christian salvation, and can be neither willed, nor replicated, nor maintained. It is a balance so delicate that it can only be imagined, and never reached.

The manuscript of the *Tristano Riccardiano* breaks off during a battle between Tristano and Prezzivale, and no other manuscript contains the conclusion either. But a look at the romance's structure makes it clear that Tristano and Lancialotto, after seeking each other throughout the text, will ultimately converge. Lancialotto, declared an ideal knight, is the ultimate foil who will definitively establish Tristano's superior chivalry. Tristano defeats a series of increasingly valiant opponents, from L'Amoroldo to Brunoro, Galeotto, L'Amoratto, Chieso, Arturo and Prezzivale. Even without any consideration of the source material, or of other Italian versions, a meeting with Lancialotto to confirm Tristano's superiority is a virtual certainty, given this intensifying series of contests and the fact that the two heroes are closing in on each other. The plot itself, without any of the abundant narratorial commentary of the *Tristano Veneto* and the *Tavola Ritonda*, declares that Tristano will prevail.

THE *TRISTANO VENETO*

Translated and adapted from French into an Italian strongly marked with the Veneto dialect, the *Tristano Veneto* contains the entire story of Tristano from before his birth to after his death. The codex which preserves this romance is a paper manuscript dated 10 March 1487, but it is clearly a copy of an earlier (lost) version dating from 1300 or even earlier.[17] Again, the author/translator is anonymous, and much information that an earlier manuscript could have given us about the text's original audience and milieu has been lost. But the *Tristano Veneto*'s richer lexicon and copious narrative embellishment make it likely to have been aimed at a literate and privileged audience.

Slight differences between the *Tristano Riccardiano*, the *Tristano Veneto* and the *Tavola Ritonda* thematize the competing claims of individualism and collectivism on many occasions, and privilege one or the other in subtle shifts of emphasis. One particularly revealing episode is that of the Island of the Giants, in which the knights must compete in prowess and their ladies in beauty. The losers, of course, die: the knights die in battle, and their ladies are decapitated by the winning knight. In the *Tristano Riccardiano* the custom is portrayed as merely regrettable, but Tristano abides by it. The *Tristano Veneto* augments Tristano's revulsion at the evil custom (*malvasie costume*, 193), his shame and fury at having to behead his defeated opponent's wife, and his wish that Arthur would do something to change it. The court and its representatives are understood as having a civilizing mission, and it offends Tristano's sense of that mission to comply with the custom. Once the "base deed" (*vil chossa*, 192) is done, however, Tristano and Isotta are ecstatic to stay on the island:

> elli non domandava cià mai eser liberadi . . . ella non domandava altro de soa vita ni altro solaço ni altro paradiso noma' lui . . . ello non domandava plui altro al nondo. Elo non priegava Dio ni richiriva altro forssi qu'ello li mantegna in queste çogie et in questa bona ventura, et cià mai altra bona aventura non li mandasse lo Nostro Signor. (200)

> [he never wished to be freed . . . she asked nothing else of her life, no other pleasure or paradise, than him alone . . . he asked nothing else but her in the world . . . he prayed God for nothing else but to keep him in these joys and this good fortune, and never to send him any other.]

The *Tristano Veneto* intensifies both the hero's social responsibility and his erotic amnesia, highlighting much more than the *Tristano Riccardiano* had done the conflict between chivalry's private and public obligations.

The *Tristano Veneto* turns at midpoint from a Tristano-centered plot to an interlace structure of multiple protagonists, quests and adventures, based on Rustichello's *Meliadus*. When Tristano renounces adventuring to return to Cornwall, however, the romance returns to showing its hero as the solitary, impassioned lover, singing and harping his love-laments, and no longer a knight of Arturo's court.[18] Wounded by Marco's poisoned lance, Tristano dies, reconciled to Marco and embracing Isotta. Tristano's long and poignant laments for his own impending death soon spread to include the entire court at Tintagel and then Arturo's kingdom as well. Tristano and Isotta lament his perfection as a lover; Tristano, Marco, and the Cornish court lament his great deeds of chivalry and his protection of that land. Arturo's court receives the news of his death as the worst of many defeats to the Round Table, decimated by the Grail quest. A year later Lancillotto takes a hundred knights to Cornwall to avenge Tristano, and destroys Tintagel and King Marco.

This romance's editor points out the "coexistence of the protagonist's private, individual dimension and his historical, political one."[19] In fact however the two dimensions are kept forcibly apart in the romance's two-part structure: the first section follows Tristano the lone knight-errant, and the second integrates him into the whole cast of Arthurian knights. Only in the general grief at his death do they come together. Clearly both dimensions are required for Tristano's exemplary chivalry, but the narrator does not explicitly resolve the question of their incompatibility; indeed, it is this very unsustainability that makes Tristano exemplary. The collapse of the Round Table is assured from the moment Tristano exists, and the prevailing tone of this romance is elegiac: perfection is inevitably a part of the past, not the present or future.[20]

THE *TAVOLA RITONDA*

The *Tavola Ritonda* is the latest of the three romances, composed in Tuscany around 1330 or 1340. Eight manuscripts are known to survive, and this text is acknowledged to contain the most original material of the three Italian Tristano romances. Again, we have no information about its author but what the text itself and its language can tell us. The narrative voice is much more partisan and high-profile than in the other two romances, more given to overt evaluative asides. Despite an increased emphasis on what chivalry owes to society, the text showcases Tristano on every occasion, and thus integrates the biographical and compilation models more thoroughly than the other two.

We have seen that the plot these three romances share requires the young Tristano to show his chivalrous nature by rejecting a "dishonorable" love. But in all three romances his noble response is subject to revision not long afterwards, and individual gratification easily takes precedence over social equilibrium or loyalty to his lord. Before Tristano and Isotta ever fall in love, Tristano flirts with a lady at Marco's court. Although this lady is both newly married and the object of Marco's affections, Tristano does not hesitate to go to her bed, where they have an uninhibited frolic. While both the *Tristano Riccardiano* and the *Tristano Veneto* record the matter factually and without condemnation, the *Tavola Ritonda* interpolates the following solemn caveat:

> Vero è che la donzella avea preso marito di sedici giorni dinanzi, non che ancora si fossono congiunti insieme: imperò ch'egli era usanza a quel tempo, che quando gli cavalieri prendeano dama, egli stavano trenta giorni innanzi ch'eglino si congiug-nessono insieme; e ciascuno giorno insieme udivano messa, acciò che Iddio perdo-nasse loro l'offense, e anche perchè perdeano la loro verginitade e venivano al conoscimento carnale; e pregavano Iddio che di lor uscisse frutto che fosse pro al mondo e grazioso alla gente e degno a Dio, e che portassono loro matrimonio con leanza. (93)

> [It is true that the damsel had taken a husband just sixteen days before, but they had not yet consummated their marriage. It was the custom of that time that when a knight took a wife they waited thirty days before consummation, hearing mass together each day so that God might pardon their sins and forgive them the loss of

their virginity and their coming to carnal knowledge. And they prayed that their children might be noble in the world, gracious to all people, and blessed by God, and that they themselves would be faithful in marriage.]   (62)

This text alone takes care, if not to condemn Tristano, at least to contrast his erotic frolic to the social and sacramental weight of marriage. Individual gratification prevails in this case of mutual desire, but the collective and spiritual dimension of the infraction is foregrounded for the audience as it is not in the other two, or for that matter in the French original. Tristano, always the *Tavola*'s ideal hero, is never criticized; but his lust is juxtaposed with more serious matters, and thus tacitly trivialized.

Tristano's true love of course is to be Isotta. When Marco sends Tristano to win Isotta for him, actually meaning for him to die there, Tristano accepts the commission in good faith and fulfills it honorably. Isotta's father asks Tristano to marry her himself; only in the *Tavola Ritonda* does he decline the offer on the grounds that if he were to take a wife he could no longer be a knight-errant. But on their way to Cornwall, of course, they fall in love because of a magic potion, and Tristano will never again be able to relinquish Isotta on the grounds of honor or obligation. Isotta's father had called Tristano the epitome of chivalry because of his nobility, courtesy, prowess, and beauty, but these are not enough for chivalric perfection; Tristano must also love beyond his own control, and until that happens he is merely a superhero. The knight is not ideal until he is also irresistibly in love, completing the full range of chivalric perfections – perfections which yet cannot coexist, which must contest and erode each other, as individual desire and social obligation collide.

In a single passage the *Tavola Ritonda* claims explicitly that chivalry is both derived from love and subordinate to society. The Round Table carries this inscription:

> A tutti gli cavlieri erranti gli quali disiano onore di cavalleria. Io vi foe manifesto che lo amore si è una cosa e una via la quale mena altrui a prodezza e a cortesia . . . E imperò voi che disiate onore e nominanza di prodezza, servite bene e lealmente l'amore, e abbiate innamorato lo vostro cuore.   (230)

> [To all the knights-errant who desire the honor of chivalry, I reveal unto you that love is a condition and a way that leads to all prowess and courtesy . . . As you desire honor and a name for prowess, serve love loyally and well, and hold love in your heart.]   (149)

The narrator then specifies the terms of a chivalrous life; the chivalrous, in this definition, are not part of society, nor are they allowed to be. They are a virtuous elite guard for the collectivity, and must not be distracted from their lofty purpose by sharing the comfortable pleasures of those whom they protect.

S'egli aveva cura di reame o di città o di castello, non poteva ancora essere ligittima
mente, acciò che la sollecitudine della avarizia nollo traesse della prodezza. E anche
cavaliere errante non poteva essere s'egli aveva mogliera, acciò che la cura e la pigri-
zia nollo traesse della prodezza. E da sè egli doveva cessare ogni altro pensiere, di
non avere cura nè a rendite nè a ricchezze nè a tesoro nè a cosa che 'n sua cavalleria lo potesse impedimentire.   (231)

[If [a knight] had the care of a kingdom or city or castle, he could not then be sworn
[to the Round Table], because the cares of avarice do not accord with prowess. Also
a knight-errant could not be married, because the responsibilities and the laziness
of that do not encourage chivalry. He should give up all thoughts of himself, and
have no concern for income, riches, treasure, or anything that could impede his
deeds of chivalry.]   (149)

This ethos applies to Tristano as well as his peers. It is precisely the incompatibility of private desires and public roles that generates chivalry; it is in the
conflict, not in any possible resolution, that the text locates the ethical value of
chivalry.

For Daniela Delcorno Branca, "the *Tavola Ritonda* is actually *The Story of
Tristano*";[21] at the same time, she explains, the romance's paramount value is not
the knight as individual, but rather as the representative of order, the guarantor
of peace and justice.[22] Tristano's chivalry is not an end in itself, but a mechanism
to stabilize and better society; the motif of chivalric excellence as a function of
love for a lady

> is always animated by a different vision, more directly moral and social, of the
> ideals and function of chivalry. Perhaps the author discerns in chivalry the best
> guarantee of that justice which communal ordinances of his time were not always
> capable of realizing.[23]

The violent civil strife that ravaged the Italian peninsula, perpetuated by the very
papal and imperial forces and followers whose moral duty it was to promote
peace, is a constant, disquieting presence in the literatures of that territory. It is
in this collective imperative – that some noble service should gain stability for the
commonality – that the specifically Italian and communal dimension to chivalry
may be located.

NOTES

1 Edmund G. Gardner, *The Arthurian Legend in Italian Literature* (London: Dent,
  1930).
2 Aulo Donaldello, "Introduzione," in *Il libro di messer Tristano ("Tristano Veneto")*,
  ed. A. Donaldello (Venice: Marsilio, 1994), 11–30.
3 Maurice Keen, *Chivalry* (New Haven: Yale University Press, 1984), 33.
4 See, for example, Michelangelo Picone, "La 'matière de Bretagne,'" in *I cantari:
  Struttura e tradizione*, Atti del Convegno Internazionale di Montréal, 1981 (Florence:
  Olschki, 1984), 87–102.

5 *Ibid.*, 93–94.

6 *Ibid.*, 90–91.

7 John Larner, "Chivalric Culture in the Age of Dante," *Renaissance Studies*, 2/2 (1988), 115–30, here p. 129.

8 Aldo Scaglione, *Knights at Court: Courtliness, Chivalry, and Courtesy from Ottonian Germany to the Italian Renaissance* (Berkeley: University of California Press, 1991), 28.

9 *Ibid.*, 8.

10 *Il Romanzo di Tristano ("Tristano Riccardiano")*, ed. Antonio Scolari (Genoa: Costa and Nolan, 1990). References are to the page numbers of this edition.

11 References are to the page numbers of the Donaldello edition (see note 2).

12 *La Tavola Ritonda*, ed. F. L. Polidori (Bologna: Romagnoli, 1864–65). I refer to the page numbers of this edition, and quote (with occasional adaptation) the translation by Anne Shaver, *Tristan and the Round Table* (Binghamton, NY: Medieval and Renaissance Texts and Studies, 1983).

13 On knightly perfection, see also Scaglione, *Knights at Court*, 50, 65–66, 347; and C. Stephen Jaeger, *The Origins of Courtliness: Civilizing Trends and the Formation of Courtly Ideals 939–1210* (Philadelphia: University of Pennsylvania Press, 1985), 30–48.

14 While Branca, Ferrante and Shaver maintain that the *Tavola Ritonda* shows a marked concern for the social dimensions of chivalry, Hoffman argues instead that it returns to a focus on the individual and on love. Daniela Delcorno Branca, *I romanzi italiani di Tristano* (Florence: Olschki, 1968), 184–95; Joan Ferrante, *The Conflict of Love and Honor: The Medieval Tristan Legend* (The Hague and Paris: Mouton, 1973); Shaver, "Introduction," *Tristan and the Round Table*; and Donald L. Hoffman, "Radix Amoris: The *Tavola Ritonda* and its Response to Dante's Paolo and Francesca," in *Tristan and Isolde: A Casebook*, ed. Joan Tasker Grimbert (New York: Garland, 1995), 207–22.

15 Ferrante, *The Conflict of Love and Honor*, 100–13.

16 Ferrante, *The Conflict of Love and Honor*; Delcorno Branca, *I romanzi*; Scaglione, *Knights at Court*, 187; and Franco Cardini, "Concetto di cavalleria e mentalità cavalleresca nei romanzi e nei cantari fiorentini," in *I ceti dirigenti nella Toscana tardo comunale*, Comitato di studi sulla storia dei ceti dirigenti in Toscana, Proceedings of the Third Congress: Florence, 5–7 December 1980 (Florence: Papafava Editore, 1980), 157–92 (esp. 182–90).

17 Donaldello (see note 2), Introduzione, 18–19.

18 *Ibid.*, 25–26.

19 *Ibid.*, 24.

20 *Ibid.*, 26.

21 Delcorno Branca, *I romanzi*, 95.

22 *Ibid.*, 185–96.

23 *Ibid.*, 195.

SUGGESTIONS FOR FURTHER READING

Allaire, Gloria. *Andrea da Barberino and the Language of Chivalry*. Gainesville, FL: University Press of Florida, 1997.

Brand, Peter and Lino Pertile, eds. *The Cambridge History of Italian Literature.* Cambridge University Press, 1996.

Duggan, Christopher. *A Concise History of Italy.* Cambridge University Press, 1994.

Ferrante, Joan. *The Conflict of Love and Honor: The Medieval Tristan Legend.* The Hague and Paris: Mouton, 1973.

Gardner, Edmund. *The Arthurian Legend in Italy.* London: Dent, 1930.

Grimbert, Joan Tasker. *Tristan and Isolde: A Casebook.* New York: Garland, 1995.

Jaeger, C. Stephen. *The Origins of Courtliness: Civilizing Trends and the Formation of Courtly Ideals 939–1210.* Philadelphia: University of Pennsylvania Press, 1985.

Keen, Maurice. *Chivalry.* New Haven: Yale University Press, 1984.

Larner, John. "Chivalric Culture in the Age of Dante," Renaissance Studies, 2/2 (1988), 115–30.

Larner, John. *Italy in the Age of Dante and Petrarch, 1216–1380.* London and New York: Longman, 1980.

Scaglione, Aldo. *Knights at Court: Courtliness, Chivalry and Courtesy from Ottonian Germany to the Italian Renaissance.* Berkeley: University of California Press, 1991.

13

THOMAS HAHN

Gawain and popular chivalric romance in Britain

The earliest texts that preserve stories of Gawain present him not as a popular hero, but as a traditional champion. Tales in the Welsh *Mabinogion*, and scattered allusions from other Celtic works, suggest that Gawain was well-established in oral narratives as the nephew, companion, and defender of the great king. Welsh translations of Geoffrey of Monmouth's Latin *History of the Kings of Britain* confirm this match of Walwanus (Gawain) and Gwalchmai mab Gwyar, a man of action around whom adventures swirled, a renowned figure about whom audiences wished to hear more.[1] Behind these earliest surviving stories there may lurk traces of divinity or superhuman stature, linking Gawain to solar heroes whose strength surges before noon, and wanes with the setting sun. Despite his stature and centrality in Celtic tradition, Gawain was scarcely "popular" in the sense of being available to diverse constituencies or multiple genres. Nonetheless, by the early twelfth century his fame seems to have spread far beyond the audiences for traditional oral narratives, making him a familiar figure in European ecclesiastical and learned culture. The cosmopolitan appeal of Arthurian story emerges early in a sculpture (dated before 1109) at the Cathedral in Modena, Italy; this depicts Gawain undertaking a siege, together with Arthur and two other knights. The Anglo-Norman historian William of Malmesbury, in his *History of the English Kings* (c. 1125), inserts an allusion to Gawain as a warrior renowned in his own right and as Arthur's sister's son; through his casualness, William implies a thorough acquaintance with Gawain among his Latin readers. Glancing allusions to Gawain and his companions in other high literate writers of the twelfth century, such as Peter of Blois and Gerald of Wales, suggest the familiarity of Arthurian story as a traditional or mythic component of British identity, but, for these very reasons, a matter on which no "serious" writer would lavish detailed attention.

Geoffrey of Monmouth's *History of the Kings of Britain* notably breaks precedent, then, in retelling traditional, vernacular stories in a medium – as defined by genre, subject, style, audience, and Latinity itself – targeted for a tiny, learned elite. Among the most stirring exploits portrayed in Geoffrey's book are the spirited, headstrong, valorous actions of Gawain. Described several times as Arthur's sister's son (and once as Arthur's maternal first cousin), Gawain leads the delegation that defies the Roman Emperor Lucius, and during negotiations he decapitates the Emperor's nephew. In the pitched battle against the Romans, he leads one of Arthur's divisions and rallies the Britons against their enemy. During Arthur's last campaign, Gawain leads the forces against his brother Mordred, by whom he is killed at Richborough. In Geoffrey's narrative, which some have called the most influential book written in the Western Middle Ages, Gawain plays a preeminent role; many of the other renowned knights of Arthurian romance (Lancelot, Galahad, Percival, Tristan) are, by contrast, not named, alluded to solely by their functions (Kay the Seneschal, Bedevere the cup-bearer), or barely mentioned in passing (Yvain). The astounding impact of Geoffrey's *History* on vernacular writing may have enhanced the fame Gawain enjoyed among Latin scholars. Within a generation or two after Geoffrey's book, a learned pedigree (*Gawain: The Early Years*) appeared; this charted the private life and pre-adolescent adventures of the hero with a lumbering monotony that highlights Geoffrey's narrative talents. In the thirteenth century, an anti-matrimonial satire frequently reproduced in university circles (*On Not Taking a Wife*) attached itself to Gawain's name in more than a dozen of the surviving copies, suggesting that his status as chivalric hero – in particular, as a knight whose dedication to fighting left little time for a settled union – had become so familiar that it was available for playful appropriation in an academic milieu.

Gawain's increasing celebrity as a literary hero coincides with the unprecedented outpouring of romance in French and Anglo-Norman, from about 1155 to 1225.[2] His role in *Yvain* (*c.* 1180) by Chrétien de Troyes establishes his preeminence as the Arthurian knight most dedicated to masculine adventure and competition. In Chrétien's *Lancelot* and *Perceval*, and especially in *Yvain*, Gawain stands as a foil to heroes motivated by consuming erotic or religious drives. In contrast to these title characters, whose unique identities emerge from the defining plots and particularities of their stories, Gawain persists as the prototypical knight, bodying forth the chivalric and Arthurian ambiance as he pursues, from one romance to the next, the attractions of open-ended, opportunistic errancy. In *Yvain*, Gawain expressly intervenes to disengage the hero from the household and the love of Laudine, and to draw him into the exclusively masculine and mobile world of tournaments. While Yvain obviously enjoys the adventures that he shares with Gawain, Chrétien tells us virtually nothing of these stock chivalric exploits; instead, he focuses the narrative upon the way in which these all-male adventures nearly undo the union with Laudine, and upon the trials that ultimately enable heterosexual love to triumph. Gawain's prominence in Chrétien's works, and in the various Continuations of the *Perceval*, helped establish him as the chief knight of Arthur's affinity and the supreme

exemplar of "secular" knighthood. In a series of some ten French romances, produced from the time of Chrétien through about 1250, Gawain habitually exemplifies a distinctive model of masculinity, founded on an unstinting appetite for
energetic encounters; these matches stage a narcissistic rivalry that allows
Gawain's prowess to outshine that of all other men, and they render him a
magnet for the desire of a long sequence of women.

Gawain's centrality to Arthurian story, and his standard role as the Young
Man, available for both adventure and love, mean that active, competitive masculinity – as opposed, for example, to the socially integrated masculinity of
Cliges or Eric, the illicit attachments of Lancelot or Tristan, or the spiritual drive
of Perceval or Galahad – is both defined and tested through his exploits. This
unconstrained ubiquity within early Arthurian romance elevated Gawain to
chevalier exemplaire, the paragon against which manhood is measured, but also,
and inevitably, the chief instance by which the human impossibility of ideal chivalry is illustrated. Gawain's charismatic openness to serial exploits perhaps made
him the natural target for attacks on the volatility and solipsism of knighthood:
in the *Queste del Saint Graal* (before 1230), Gawain figures once again as the outstanding instance of relentless devotion to physical exertion and worldly honor,
although the fervently ascetic underpinnings of the *Queste* represent such activity as debased and iniquitous. Gawain is made to reject any hardship associated
with piety, and consequently to suffer disappointment when he seeks adventure.
A nameless, holy hermit eventually banishes him from the narrative, pronounc-
ing that this great champion, like all who live their lives "astride the powerful
war-horse . . . will always live in mortal sin, a prey to pride and envy and many
other vices" (*Queste*, trans. Matarasso, 173–75). In singling out Gawain, the
Queste pays tribute to his unique stature and broad celebrity as *the* knight of
adventure; moreover, by expressly calling into question the motives, traits, and
expectations that made such chivalric heroes admirable, this "anti-romance"
helps pinpoint the crucial components of his popularity.

The massive and intense enthusiasm that greeted French and Anglo-Norman
Arthurian romances produced immediate responses – including translations,
imitations, and reworkings – in other European languages. Hartmann von Aue's
Iwein (c. 1200) reworks Chrétien's *Yvain* in the resonant idioms of Old High
German, though it follows the French romance in making Gawain's devotion to
manly prowess the ground against which the perplexities of the hero are defined.
Wolfram von Eschenbach's *Parzival* (c. 1210), one of the most wondrously enigmatic of Arthurian poems, presents a Gawain who, while provocatively inscru-
table at times, remains the emblem of an earthly chivalry that sets off the
contradictory workings of worldly and spiritual, comic and serious instincts that
define Parzival's character. Gawain's minor role in a number of other romances
(Hartmann's *Erek* [before 1190], *Wigalois* [c. 1210], *Wigamur* [c. 1250]) operates

typically as an anchor securing sundry heroes and adventures to Arthurian contexts. Gawain takes a leading part in the Austrian *Diu Krône* (*c.* 1220) and in the
Dutch *Walewein* (early fourteenth century); the miscellaneous adventures fused
in these works highlight his courtesy and his derring-do, though their content
and narrative structure underscore Gawain's nature as a knight for all occasions
rather than a hero shaped by distinctive drives or a particular destiny. Gawain
appears in later Latin and French narratives, in other German and Dutch texts,
and in Iberian, Italian, Hebrew, and Scandinavian romances. Survival across this
expanse of time, space, and narrative profusion required of Gawain not only a
dominant persona and extraordinary name recognition within Arthurian tradition, but also an elastic versatility, exemplified above all in a continuous hunger
for man-to-man, and man-to-woman, encounters.

Though narratives of knightly prowess and wonder circulated in Britain from
the mid-twelfth century, most surviving texts, such as Wace's *Brut* (1155, translated from Geoffrey's Latin *History*), were written not in English but in Anglo-
Norman, the prestige, literary vernacular. Layamon's *Brut* (*c.* 1200–25), an
Englishing of Wace, initiates the "chronicle" tradition of Arthurian narrative,
though it seems to have had a sparse readership and limited influence. A number
of "sequels" centering on heroes of the Round Table – for example, *Arthur and
Merlin* (later thirteenth century), and *Sir Perceval of Galles* (early fourteenth
century) – recount minor deeds of Gawain, but when he finally enters the literary scene in *Ywain and Gawain* and *Libeaus Desconus* (both before 1350), he
establishes himself as the unblemished paragon of chivalric virtue.[3] *Ywain*, for
example, empties out much of the ambiguity that Chrétien interjects through the
conflict of masculine adventure and heterosexual love; though Ywain and
Alundyne do ultimately reconcile, the heart of the narrative consists in the
exploits that Gawain initiates through his bald declaration that "a knyght es [is]
chevalrousse" only when he chooses "To haunt armes" and "wende infere
[wander together]" with other males. Two well-known poems from the chronicle tradition provide Gawain a featured role: in the stanzaic *Morte Arthur* (before
1400), Gawain plays out his role from the *Mort Artu*. The alliterative *Morte
Arthure* (*c.* 1360), rivaled in vigor only by the late *Gologras and Gawain*, represents Gawain as the supreme exemplar of valiant manliness. His slayer and half-
brother Mordred offers a eulogy of Gawain, unparalleled in any other version;
it describes him as "makles one molde," "the graciouseste gome . . . man har-
dyeste of hande . . . the hendeste in hawle . . . the lordelieste of ledynge"
(3875–3880; "matchless on earth, the most courteous knight, hardiest in
strength, most affable in hall, most gentle in conduct"). When King Arthur hears
the news of his nephew's death, he cries, "thou was worthy to be kynge, thofe
[though] I the corowne bare [bore] . . . I am uttirly undone" (3962, 3966). Sir
Thomas Malory knew both these poems, and the portrayal of Gawain in the

Morte Darthur (completed 1469, published 1485), as a figure whose sublime nobility and insatiable desire for revenge help precipitate the downfall of the Round Table, represents the culmination of his character in the chronicle tradition.

Beginning in the thirteenth century, English writers and performers seem to have invented numerous popular vehicles to accommodate Gawain's celebrity, though most survive only in the later versions discussed below. Gawain's high visibility as the pattern of chivalry caught even the elite imagination: Chaucer's Squire, that most sentimentally chivalric of narrators, associates the "reverence and obeisaunce / As wel in speche as in counptenaunce" of ideal knighthood with the figure of "Gawayn, with his olde curteisye . . . comen ayeyn [again] out of Fairye" (*Squire's Tale*, 89 ff.). In *The Awntyrs of Arthur* (c. 1375), a high literate author (probably a cleric) chose Gawain as the cement for a remarkable literary structure, combining popular story, academic learning, and extravagant alliterative stylistics. For the last century and more, the hero's reputation has been chiefly bolstered by *Sir Gawain and the Green Knight* (c. 1375), an alliterative poem whose simultaneous freshness and intricacy place it among the most sophisticated narratives of the Middle Ages. The poet, who aimed for a readership that could (and would) savor every word and image, casts Gawain as the convergence point of self-examination and self-promotion, of niggling conscience and unflinching violence. In its unique appropriation of an all-purpose champion, *Sir Gawain and the Green Knight* reprocesses popular culture to interrogate the ethos of knighthood and to transmute the genre of romance, rendering it a splendid anomaly among English Gawain stories.

The peculiar appeal of *Sir Gawain and the Green Knight* rests largely on Gawain's profound familiarity among audiences in medieval Britain, and this renown in turn derived its source and substance from a cluster of popular English Gawain romances.[4] About a dozen of these narratives survive; they almost certainly circulated from the thirteenth century on, but extant manuscripts (all of which show signs of modest origins and constant use) date from the fifteenth to the mid-seventeenth centuries. Each retells one or more self-contained episodes, and often these anecdotes bear stronger affinities to international tales, traditional stories, and folklore than to established literary sources. In *The Greene Knight*, *The Turke and Sir Gawain*, *Sir Gawain and the Carle of Carlisle*, and *The Wedding of Sir Gawain and Dame Ragnelle* (as well as in the ballad retellings of the latter two, *The Carle of Carlisle* and *The Marriage of Sir Gawain*), the hero faces off against otherworldly giants, whom he overcomes or transforms through his courtesy and prowess. In *The Greene Knight*, *Ragnelle*, *Marriage*, *The Awntyrs of Arthur*, and *King Arthur and King Cornwall*, Gawain encounters ghosts, sprites, and shape-shifting Loathly Ladies, whom he conquers outright or reconciles to the court of Arthur. In *The Avowyng of Arthur*, Gawain *and Gologras*, *The Jeaste of Sir Gawain*, and *Awntyrs*, the champion of the Round Table meets more conventionally chivalric opponents; through his valor, Gawain defeats each of these, and through his charisma he succeeds in attracting them as allies to his king.

What unifies this group of a dozen or so popular Middle English romances is, above all, the figure of Gawain. The consolidating pressure that emanates from Gawain arises not, however, through some novelistic sense of "character," dependent upon a unique and consistent personality with individualized traits, complexly drawn motives, or psychologized feelings. Instead, Gawain plays a *role*; he routinely facilitates the extravagant adventures that happen around him, and does so to such an extent that one might even think of him almost as a narrative function. The romances emphatically mark out, in social as well as narrative terms, just what this role encompasses: Gawain is a generation removed from the father-figure of the king, to whom he stands in the crucial relation of mother's brother-sister's son. Gawain shares this slot in the social order with his brothers, Aggravayne and the illegitimate Mordred, but he is clearly the good "son"; despite his exuberance and superior physical prowess, he is unwilling to challenge the fatherly authority of the king. Gawain's courtesy, in both martial and domestic situations, in this way makes him the chief mediator of the Father's Law, the Young Man who, in demonstrating the suppleness and strength of the rules governing the social order, offers the ultimate reassurance about the status quo.

As the exemplary Young Man in these romances, Gawain remains unfettered by trammels of authority, the need to think hard about the future or make decisions of political consequence; he is on the loose, constantly ready for adventure. Over and over, Gawain proves the worth of familiar values by facing the marvelous or unknown, and rendering it manageable for the rest of his society. But his preeminence does not simply consist in unhesitating courage or unparalleled ability. Again it is Gawain's *courtesy* – perfect composure in moments of crisis – that endows him with heroic stature. Repeatedly, Gawain exhibits a willing restraint of available force or a refusal of the authority of position, which separates him from non-chivalrous opponents and also from the arbitrary bullying or domineering impertinence of a Sir Kay. Each courteous conquest stages the general triumph of civility, insuring that the rituals that organize social meaning prevail in spite of confusion or even threat to life. Gawain's exceptional performance of the precepts that bind everyday social existence thus conveys a stirring endorsement of the rightness of things as they are. Moreover, his courtesy makes his conquests all the more complete, for they entail not annihilation or brute suppression, but the ungrudging concession of Gawain's superiority by some previously hostile or unknown Other. Gawain's role in the romances works therefore to effect the reconciliation or reappropriation, rather than the destruction, of the strange or alien, and this happy resolution in turn secures the audience's identifi-cation with the hero, and with the naturalness of the social order he represents.

The predictable roles played by Gawain and his fellow knights, and the name recognition of these characters, serve as powerful, stabilizing links that join rapid-fire episodes of marvels, violence, and mysterious confrontation, or extended and detailed description. The headlong sequencing of events, often apparently unmotivated or non-causal, and the lavish attention to surface real-ities equip these popular romances with a kinetic quality that perhaps left a deeper impression on audiences than the characters themselves. This irruption of unforeseen wonders and threats is not, however, without pattern: these provide Gawain with the indispensable opportunity for heroic triumph, but they also illustrate recurrent settings, themes, and processes crucial to the social meaning of the romances. The unity that the poems attain is consequently often more the outcome of structural repetition and thematic variation than of char-acter or event.

These romances deploy a number of conventional settings for their action, including encounters in the forest and on the battlefield. Less predictable, perhaps, are the pivotal or climactic scenes staged in the intimate, domestic space of the bedroom. *Avowyng, Jeaste, Ragnelle,* and *Carlisle* (together with the ballad versions of the latter two, *Marriage* and *Carle*) all include episodes that take place in women's beds, yet none of these have to do primarily with hetero-sexual passion; instead, these private spaces take on a theatrical ambiance, making a trial of social ties – in the marriage contract between a woman and her husband, and even more in the ties between men within a fictionalized chivalric code. Courtesy's definition depends upon Gawain's response to the Carl of Carlisle's manly claims over his wife's and daughter's sexual availability, or upon Baldwin's response to Arthur's bed trick in *Avowyng*, and the resolution of soci-etal disruption comes about through the courteous and rule-bound exchange of women among men. In *Ragnelle*, Gawain's bedroom scene enacts this process of reconciliation – between female and male, private and public, old and young, wretched and handsome, peasant and noble – through the outright physical transformation of the loathly lady into a beautiful young woman. Sympathetic audiences, medieval and modern, surely find pleasure in the singular improbabil-ity and the poetic justice of this spectacular turn of events (as they likewise do in the ethnic or estate-based magical transformations within *Carle, Turke,* and *Greene Knight*). Audiences recognize as well, if only subliminally, that such satis-fying endings depend on listeners' anticipation and endorsement of the norma-tive integration that these marvelous transformations symbolize; the reiteration of such motifs in story after story is irrefutable evidence that they arise from the desire of listeners and readers, even as they assist in producing this desire. In *Ragnelle* and *Carlisle*, the threatening figures of hag and churl – rough, ugly, ignoble, menacing – are literally transformed by Gawain's *gentilesse* into refined, handsome figures who "naturally" take their place among the ruling elite. This pattern recurs, with only slight structural variations, in *Marriage* and *Carle*, as well as in *Greene Knight* and *Turke*, which introduce elements of the exotic to the characterization of the outsider. In *Gologras* (and to a lesser extent in *Avowyng*, *Cornwall*, and *Jeaste*), the happy ending is achieved not through shape-shifting but through the transformative submission of enemies to the chivalric ethos.

These happy endings produce a "magical resolution" typical of romance: in this world of unmotivated marvels and wishes fulfilled, social interests quite opposed in the "real world" move into alignment. The stirring portrayals of triumphant courtesy and justice vindicated that mark the conclusions of romances potentially work to hold their diverse audiences together, to reproduce in them the feeling of integration that the narrated transformations dramatize, and to effect a *sense* of social cohesion (not at all dependent on social reality) that enables the established order to prevail.[5] In its crudest formulation, such a view of the romances would give them a crucial function in the conspiratorial imposition of dominant values upon a docile and homogeneous public; their reading would dull perceptions of social inequities and diminish the potential for political change. Yet spectacularly decisive resolutions, like those of the Gawain romances, do not inevitably or uniformly support the ruling order. As the magical realism of Latin American writers like Borges, Garcia Marquez, or Esquivel has recently demonstrated, fantastic narratives can open a space for political critique; contradictions and absurdities, rather than being swallowed whole, constitute a basis from which audiences – starting from quite different social positions – may formulate alternative or subversive understandings. Moreover, the magical transformations that proliferate in these romances mirror the poems' protean appeal to quite mixed social groupings. These hybrid compositions – narratives about the nobility that circulate and are profoundly modified in popular milieux – trace out a storytelling transmigration across elite, bourgeois, and laboring audiences, reproducing the plotlines that allow characters to cross the boundaries of otherwise circumscribed groups.

Just how audiences received these romances – the precise nature and extent of their popularity within specific social contexts – has remained vague. Two pieces of evidence may help illustrate the environment in which such popular chivalric romances flourished – how, when, and by whom they were composed, performed, listened to, read, and copied. In the later 1470s Sir John Paston commissioned an "Inventory off Englysshe bokis" from his own library.[6] These included religious and devotional works, "a boke off nyw statutys from [King] Edward the iiii," Christine de Pizan's *Epistle of Othea*, some treatises by Cicero, an impressive collection of Chaucer's writings, and various romances; among the latter were *Guy of Warwick, Kyng Richard Cure de lyon* (the Lionheart), and *Guy and Colbronde* (perhaps in Lydgate's version). A series of volumes reveal Paston's dedication to heraldry and chivalry: "myn olde boke off blasonyngys," "the newe boke portrayed and blasonyd," "a copy off blasonyngys off armys," "a boke wyth armys portrayed in paper." The list records as well "my boke off knyththod and therin . . . off making off knyghtys, off justys, off torn[aments, off] fyghtyng in lystys . . . and chalengys, statutys off weer [war] . . ." Paston assembled a home encyclopedia of coats of arms, and a reference library of descriptive and how-to books on chivalry – a collection that must have held urgent interest for the first member of a socially mobile family elevated to a knighthood.[7]

The crowning items (for the purposes of the present essay) in this collection are two romances: the very first title, "A boke . . . off the Dethe off Arthur," and, in a later group, "the Greene Knyght." The appearance of a narrative on the "Dethe off Arthur" in Paston's library is especially arresting since Malory composed his *Morte Darthur* less than a decade earlier (1469), and Caxton published "thys noble and Ioyous book entytled le morte Darthur" only a few years later, in 1485. The pride of place awarded this volume within the inventory perhaps implies the special value or interest that Arthurian romance held for Sir John. The "Greene Knyght" which Paston had collected is almost certainly a retelling of the greatest of all English Arthurian poems. Nonetheless, the romance mentioned here as a single, anthologized item in "a blak boke" was probably neither *Sir Gawain and the Green Knight* nor the *Greene Knight*, but another, intermediary version of this Gawain story. Its place within Paston's library shows that this story circulated more widely than scholars have usually allowed, and that it was preserved through the interests of readers whose disparate tastes might range from folk narratives to translations of Cicero.

As a reader, an owner, and thereby even a sponsor of popular Arthurian romance, Sir John Paston represents a telling segment of the audience for such stories. Paston was a member of an influential and wealthy family. Though perhaps less dedicated to the acquisition of property than his father, his possession of statute books and albums of armorial bearings reveals that his interest in knighthood was by no means anchored in fanciful romance. His careful attention to the law and his jealous regard for his family arms (and for those of others in power or on the move) show his energetic engagement with the harshly competitive life of the courts, both legal and royal. At the same time, life as a courtier made him an active devotee of chivalry: in 1473 he had himself fitted for a complete suit of armor by the outfitter of that colorfully named *chevalier*, the Bastard of Burgundy. Earlier, in 1467, he took part in a tournament at Eltham on the King's side (slightly injuring his hand), and later that year he made his own account of the jousting between Lord Scales and the Bastard of Burgundy. Paston's enthusiasm for popular chivalric romance seems then not to have been divorced from, but to have complemented, his personal, familial, and public ambitions. In glorifying a fabulous Arthurian past, tales like Paston's "Greene Knyght" glorified the present as well, and their stylized, even fantasized ideals of knighthood simply reinforced his own sense of knightly identity and social order.

A second private document, this one a description written some hundred years after Paston's inventory, supplies still more striking clues about the social processes that sustained the preservation and enjoyment of popular chivalric romances. Robert Laneham published *A Letter* describing "the entertainment" presented before Queen Elizabeth at Kenilworth Castle in 1575.[8] Among the festivities arranged by the Earl of Leicester – the central theme of which was King Arthur and the Table Round – was an "olld storiall sheaw . . . expressed in actions and rymes," an historical and carnivalesque pageant which ends with English women taking the invading Danes captive. This was performed by players from neighboring Coventry, led by Captain Cox, a mason by day who seems also to have been a performance artist of sorts – "an od man I promis yoo . . . very cunning in sens, and hardy as Gawin," blustering about with his sword, acting, impersonating, singing, reciting, with "great oversight . . . in matters of storie." Laneham's unthinking comparison of the Captain to Gawain attests that his popularity as the proverbial epitome of noble English manhood continued from Chaucer's time through Shakespeare's.

So impressed was Laneham that he devoted several pages of his letter to the Captain's repertoire. These included an enormous "bunch of ballets [ballads] and songs all auncient," which Laneham records by their familiar first lines; "a hundred more [which] he hath fair wrapt up in Parchment and bound with a whipcord"; traditional tales like "Robin Hood," "Adam Bel," "Clim of the Clough," "The King and the Tanner," "The Seargeaunt that became a Fryar," "Skogan," and "The Nutbrooun Maid"; more current stories such as "Gargantua," "Collyn Cloout," "The Sheperds Kalender," and "The Ship of Fools"; and matters of "Philosophy both morall and naturall." The Captain could also draw upon a huge store of medieval chivalric romances – "Bevys of Hampton," "The Squyre of Lo Degree," "Syr Eglamoour," "Sir Tryamoour," "Syr Isenbras" – and he seems to have had particular knowledge of Arthurian narratives, namely "King Arthurs book" and "Syr Gawyn." Although J. C. Holt has assumed that the last named romance was *Sir Gawain and the Green Knight*, it seems quite unlikely that a performance artist like Captain Cox would have access to, or any interest in, so highly literate a text. On the other hand, the skills and repertoire of the Captain and the mixed character of his audience – aristocratic, urban, and rural, consisting of women and men from the queen to commoners – might well be taken as a heightened rendition of the diverse social environment in which Gawain romances continuously thrived.

Laneham presents the Captain as capable of reciting not only romances like "Syr Gawyn," but "many moe [tales] then I rehears heere: I beleeve hee have them all at his fingers ends." Laneham refers to the bundle of written ballads that Cox carries, to the "omberty [abundance] of his books," and to his having "as fair a library for . . . sciences" as foreign competitors like "Nostradam of Frauns." On their face, these remarks seem to imply that Cox's romance performances were scripted and textual (though in the latter comments Laneham may have meant the abundance of titles in the "library" that Cox could reproduce memorially, "at his fingers ends"). Nonetheless, it is clear that what most impressed Laneham was the Captain's resources as an oral performer who could spontaneously produce "many goodly monuments both in prose and poetry and at afternoons can talk as much without book, as ony Inholder [inn keeper] betwixt Brainford and Bagshot, what degree soever he be."[9] In general, the surviving Gawain romances reflect just such a combined oral-literate context of performance. The missing lines, gaps in the narratives, and the well-used (not to say dilapidated) quality of the manuscripts suggest that reciters must have carried them about – perhaps "bound with a whipcord" – and worked from them, beginning at the time of their composition and circulation in the fourteenth century, through the time of Captain Cox, and at least until the compiling of the Percy Folio Manuscript in the mid-seventeenth century. And Laneham's elaborate tribute makes clear that for the occasional literate listener like himself, as well as for large audiences from all ranks and areas, their appeal remained undiminished into the lifetime of Shakespeare.

The pervasive presence and broad appeal of popular chivalric romances raises a further question, however: can they ever be taken as in any sense "the literature of the people"? Must we regard the celebration of knighthood as an imposition of the dominant culture, by which those largely outside political power are brought to celebrate secular society's most potent institution, and its symbol of the unequal division of estates or classes? When Captain Cox (or any one of his nameless predecessors) performed his "Sir Gawyn" before the queen, a great lord, or even the Lord Mayor of Coventry, was he reinforcing the position of an elite class over him, or was he giving shape to an identity he as a stone mason shared with other workers, who must have constituted his chief audience? Such questions point to the elusive character of "popular" culture, and the difficulties that stand in the way of defining it in terms of the historical interests or lived experience of any distinct or exclusive social group or class. The censure of chivalric romance in high literary writing, in popular burlesque (*The Tournament of Tottenham*, for example), or in ecclesiastical chastisements presents an emphatically negative view of popular culture; these imply that only the most simple and undemanding audience could sit through the exaggerations, absurdities, and contradictions of these tales, thereby making "popular" equivalent to ignorant or just plain bad.

Yet the persistence of hostility towards chivalric romances from various quarters in itself proves that popular culture did not simply and irresistibly reproduce the values of a dominant order for mindless reception by a passive audience. Some medieval people – especially those in official positions, and those committed to refined or elite literacy – regarded these tales as potentially subversive, and this rejection marks out one space for resistant or alternative readings and responses. Modern readers have often followed this negative assessment of popular culture in their own reaction to the romances. A recent translator of the Gawain stories, for example, remarks that they are "primitive," "rustic," and "crude," though at times "charming" or "touching."[10] This critical perspective, in seeking to mitigate the deficiency of these romances as failed attempts at psychological realism, too easily dismisses the potential in these narratives for laughter and disruption. The mixed character of the romances, their open disavowal of literary credibility in favor of the fantastic, their frequent comic tone and resort to extravagance and hyperbole, all have the effect of highlighting the absurdities, inequalities, and contradictions of feudal order or chivalric ideals, even as they are idealized or celebrated. These seemingly naïve and artless Arthurian stories, in giving pleasure and simple assurance to listeners at diverse social levels, openly exploit the paradoxical impulses that motivate the adventures of a bourgeois knight, and in doing so they foreshadow the ultimate satire of this typically medieval hybrid, Cervantes's *Don Quixote*.

A fuller appreciation of the Gawain romances' popularity requires, then, a more vivid sense of the pleasure they gave to their sponsoring audiences. Though they may have appeared lacking in sophistication to committed readers of Chaucer's *Knight's Tale* or *Sir Gawain and the Green Knight*, the broad support for these stories among late medieval people reflects a deep enjoyment in listening or reading as a social (rather than solitary) event. The circumstances of public performance make "audience" itself perhaps too confining a term, since listeners must have taken some active part in such readings (as implied by the frequent injunctions that the audience behave), or become storytellers in their own right on other occasions. Performance artists must have given boisterous and flamboyantly histrionic recitals, impersonating roles through change of voice and gesture, playing the melodramatic sentimentality and violence to the utmost, priming and inciting their listeners' responses to the wondrous (and perhaps even more, to the incredible) elements in their plots. Chivalric romances must often have achieved popularity by combining the narrative obviousness of a television sit-com with the ambiance of a professional wrestling match. Having to read these romances, rather than hear and watch them performed, makes their participatory spontaneity difficult for modern audiences to relish, all the more so because they are in Middle English. Yet it was clearly as popular performance art, with strong elements of mimicry and burlesque, that they initially brought pleasure to the majority of their earliest listeners.

The performance-oriented character of these romances emerges also in their narrative technique and narrative content. Self-conscious writers considered the apparently simple meter of popular stories to be chief among their literary offenses; Chaucer has his Host declare the romance of *Thopas* "rym dogerel" and "drasty rymyng . . . nat worth a toord," and his Parson refuses to "geeste 'rum, ram, ruf' by lettre" – that is, to use the linking rhymes and alliterative formulas associated with many chivalric romances and tales. But partisans of popular romance did not seek the novelty of plot, individualized character, verbal ambiguities, subtle allusion, or variation in theme and image so dear to Chaucer. Like those who attend live musical concerts, they expected to hear lyrics they already knew, performed to a memorable beat that allowed them to vocalize along with the performer. Anyone who has attended a modern sporting event easily understands the power of rhythmic clapping, whether initiated by the crowd, the scoreboard, or the piped-in music of the rock group Queen ("We will, we will, rock you"). It was just this kind of participatory and moving experience that made the reading event so enjoyable for the audiences of chivalric romances, and made the romances so disreputable with the keepers of high culture.

The stylistic gestures and storylines that defined popular romance appear in almost exemplary form in the story of the Loathly Lady's transformation, as retold in *The Wedding of Sir Gawain and Dame Ragnelle*. In outline, the romance plot resembles a number of early Irish tales; the first version to appear in England seems to have been a masque of sorts, organized by King Edward I for performance by and for his knights in the late thirteenth century. The staging of this masque before the most elite audience in the realm suggests that Edward presumed that all his knights, and perhaps all his contemporaries, would recognize the story. Though *The Wedding of Sir Gawain and Dame Ragnelle* survives in only one manuscript (so thoroughly read that it is missing a leaf) which dates from the sixteenth century, versions of the tale that circulated from the thirteenth century or before must have resembled the extant romance in their structure and details. At the heart of the romance lies the question of how the unknown, the marvelous, or the demonized are brought into line with normative, idealized chivalric values. Dame Ragnelle, in her poverty, unkemptness, and outlandish ugliness, symbolizes everything that is not courtly, and the poem takes special pleasure in embellishing her appearance:

Her face was red, her nose snotyd withalle,
Here mowithe wyde, her tethe yalowe overe alle,
With bleryd eyen gretter then a balle . . .
Her tethe hyng overe her lyppes,
Her chekys syde as wemens hippes . . .   *wide as*
Her nek long and therto greatt;
Her here cloteryd on an hepe . . .   *piled in a heap*
Hangyng pappys to be an hors lode,   *breasts, heavy as a horse-load*
And lyke a barelle she was made.   (231–42)

The terrifying quest that the romance imposes on a hapless Arthur and courteous Gawain entails not strenuous combat or risk, but the decipherment of an
impossible enigma: "what [do] wemen desyren most" (406). The inherent gal-
lantry that Gawain possesses in all these tales stirs him to allow the Lady to
decide her final challenge, whether she will be fair by day or by night, for herself;
this show of deference and civility transforms hag from the "foulyst wyghte" and
"fowlyst wyfe," completely beyond her husband's control, to "the fayrest creature / That evere he sawe, withoute mesure" (641–62). Moreover, once Gawain
has given his new wife "sovereynté / Of alle his body and goodes," she promises

"Shalle I nevere wrathe the serteyn . . .   *anger*
Whilles that I lyve I shal be obaysaunt;   *compliant*
To God above I shalle it warraunt,
And nevere with you to debate."   (782–86)

Ragnelle's transformation from Beast to Beauty, from frog to princess, neatly
solves Gawain's domestic predicament, and simultaneously produces a magical
resolution for all the tensions of the romance. Indeed, the lady unfailingly holds
the plot together, passing as she does among all the male characters, and thereby
making the fraternal and hierarchic bonds of an idealized chivalry seem entirely
viable. Through Ragnelle's mediation, everyone (including the heroine) is established at the conclusion in her or his proper place, and the romance thereby
ratifies the power of custom and civility in maintaining traditional order.

The elements that generically mark *Ragnelle* as a popular romance – marvelous landscapes, semi-monstrous characters, preposterous metamorphoses,
unmotivated but delightful twists in plot, absolute closure, all sustained by spectacular detail and boisterous narrative style – continued to captivate audiences
through the mid-seventeenth century, as reworkings in performative modes such
as the ballad illustrate. These elements, however, also strongly put off late medieval English writers with high literary aspirations, such as Chaucer and Gower:
Sir Thopas (the tale told by Chaucer the pilgrim) combines so many of these
conventions and improbabilities that the story self-destructs. Yet the energies
and attractions of popular romance were so compelling that even those who

professed disdain could not resist. In the *Confessio Amantis*, Gower rewrites the story of the Loathly Lady as "The Tale of Florent," intended to impress upon his readers the virtue of obedience exemplified by a knightly hero. Though the earliest version of the *Confessio* dubs the story a "tale," Gower later revised his alleged source to a "gret ensample" from a "Chronique," in this way manufacturing a literate pedigree for the Loathly Lady. Though Gower retains the kernel story of marvelous transformation through "trowth" and mutuality, he streamlines the storyline, making Florent a lone figure rather than a participant in a network of alliances, and stripping away much of the outrageous detail from the hag's appearance. Gower's artful rewriting makes a notable contribution to the ambitious educational scheme of the *Confessio*, engaging a literate audience in the contemplation of its purposeful construction; in endowing the story with a categorical and exemplary meaning, Gower recapitulates the process at the heart of the tale, that of imposing a singular meaning on an unruly subject. The participatory responses roused by the spectacular, excessive textures of *Ragnelle* have all but disappeared from the writerly text.

Chaucer's *Wife of Bath's Tale* is by far the best-known version of the Loathly Lady story, and the one that best illustrates the process by which romance pared away connections to oral and performative forms, and by the sixteenth century transformed itself to a prestige literary genre that foreshadowed realistic narratives. Whether Chaucer knew Gower's "Tale of Florent" remains unclear, but he seems certainly to have read or heard a romance that closely resembled *Ragnelle*. His opening episode – the rape of the nameless maiden by the nameless knight – may reflect the influence of even earlier traditional stories, but it also makes clear the decision to detach the entire story from association with the popular hero Gawain as a way of creating a new, autonomous Arthurian romance. Like Gower, Chaucer preserves the story of the Loathly Lady, the enigma of women's desire, and the transformation, and he also downplays the ornamental descriptions. In plot, the *Tale* proceeds thematically from coercion to consent, that is, from sexual assault to consensual sex between the rehabilitated knight-rapist and the transformed Lady. Chaucer alters the story, however, so that in place of a series of marvelous shape-shiftings leading to magical resolutions we have a series of edifying dialogues that effect an inner conversion in the protagonists. These consist in the Lady's refusal of "gentillesse" and "wilful poverte" as social or economic realities, and her insistence instead that they are ethical choices and personal qualities. She squarely bases her claims on *auctours*, citing Dante, Valerius, and Juvenal, and enjoining the knight, "Redeth Senek, and redeth eek Boece." When, at the conclusion of all these footnotes, the Lady does finally transform into a beautiful and submissive young woman, the change is less a stunning surprise than a charged symbol, accompanied as it is by the taming of the knight into a proper, caring spouse.

Chaucer's appropriation of popular chivalric romance has the result (according to this bald summary) of transmuting a performative text into a reading experience, and this applies not only to the protagonists (who spend so much of their bedroom time with books), but to the *Tale*'s audience as well. Any reader who can respond to the strenuous demands of these embedded *auctours* will already be aligned with the *Tale*'s implicit endorsement of literary engagement *as* self-refinement or rehabilitation. By contending that nothing "strange . . . to thy person" truly affects one's identity, the *Tale* leaves the impression that desire originates not in formative experiences or material circumstances – for example, in a taste for powerful, novel forms of love stories – but in what is natural and essential to the heart. The *Tale*'s trajectory, from sexual coercion (rape) to consensual sex (love), moves readers to feel that self-knowledge and free choice lead, ultimately and inevitably, to passionate love between women and men. The level of imaginative absorption that Chaucer embedded in his rewriting of popular stories makes the *Wife of Bath's Tale* an intense and exhilarating *read*, a literary experience that virtually collapses personal fulfillment and "compulsory heterosexuality."[11] Although these elements in the *Wife of Bath's Tale* anticipate the patterns and psychology of Renaissance romances and of the modern novel, they also potentially obscure how drastic was its departure, in form and content, from the stories most widely known in late medieval England. Re-reading these popular chivalric tales featuring Sir Gawain, and attempting to understand them on their own terms, makes clear that this was by no means the natural or exclusive tendency for the genre, and it helps to flesh out the pleasures that diverse audiences might take from romance, performed in public or in private, and presented in song, speech, or written word.

NOTES

1 This account of Sir Gawain's literary reputation rests upon the Introduction to *Sir Gawain: Eleven Romances and Tales* (Kalamazoo, MI: The Medieval Institute, 1995), 1–7. Full references to sources and scholarship are provided there.

2 Keith Busby, *Gauvain in Old French Literature* (Amsterdam: Rodopi, 1980) offers a thorough account of Gawain, with full references to all romances in which he plays a role.

3 For information on the romances mentioned here, see Helaine Newstead, "Arthurian Legends," in *A Manual of the Writings in Middle English: 1050–1500. Fascicle I: Romances*, ed. J. Burke Severs (New Haven: Connecticut Academy of Arts and Sciences, 1967), 224–56.

4 For texts of the romances discussed here, see *Sir Gawain* (note 1, above).

5 See Raymond Williams, *The Long Revolution* (New York: Columbia University Press, 1961), 65–71, who discusses such effects in more recent literature.

6 Sir John Paston of Norfolk (1442–79) is best known through the numerous letters he and other members of his family wrote. For the inventory of books discussed here, see

Paston Letters and Papers of the Fifteenth Century, ed. Norman Davis, Part I (Oxford University Press, 1971), 516–18.

7 See G. A. Lester, *Sir John Paston's "Grete Boke": A Descriptive Catalogue, with an Introduction, of British Library MS Lansdowne 285* (Cambridge: D. S. Brewer, 1984). It contains, among many other items, a formulary (pp. 80–83) for creating Knights of the Bath (a ritual mentioned at the end of *Greene Knight*), descriptions of armor, accounts of particular battles (historical and fictional), passages from Geoffrey of Monmouth's *History*, proclamations for tournaments, and so on.

8 Robert Laneham, *A Letter: Whearin part of the entertainment untoo the Queens Maiesty* . . . [1575], ed. R. C. Alston (Menston: Scolar Press, 1968), 34–36 . I have modernized the spelling in the descriptions of the festivities and of Captain Cox which occur in this facsimile edition. The Captain's reputation as a performer was sufficiently extensive for Ben Jonson to mention him and "his Hobbyhorse" in his *Masque of Owls* (1624); in his novel *Kenilworth* (1821), Sir Walter Scott gives an account of the festivities.

9 Laneham's *Letter* (pp. 46–56) gives an account of the "sollem song" of an "auncient minstrell" of Islington, who performed alongside Captain Cox at Kenilworth in 1575; for further information on the nature of this improvised performance, and its possible relationship to oral traditions and written texts, see *Sir Gawain* (note 1), 10–18.

10 See Valerie Krishna, *Five Middle English Arthurian Romances* (New York: Garland, 1991), 24–26 (on *Carlisle*). These remarks are on the whole representative of critiques found in standard literary histories.

11 See Adrienne Rich, "Compulsory Heterosexuality and Lesbian Existence," in *Powers of Desire: The Politics of Sexuality*, ed. Ann Snitow, Christine Stansell, and Sharon Thompson (New York: Monthly Review, 1983), 177–205.

SUGGESTIONS FOR FURTHER READING

The last decade or so has been a golden age for the study of medieval English romance. In particular, many poems that had previously been available only in hard to find and hard to use scholarly editions have now been printed in reliable and accessible format by the Middle English Texts Series, sponsored by the Consortium for the Teaching of the Middle Ages at the Medieval Institute in Kalamazoo, Michigan. (Bibliographical and ordering information are at www.wmich.edu/medieval/mip/mipubshome/html.) Other basic works include:

Barron, W. R. J. *English Medieval Romance*. London and New York: Longman, 1987.

Brewer, Derek, ed. *Studies in Medieval English Romances*. Cambridge: D. S. Brewer, 1988.

Crane, Susan. *Insular Romance*. Berkeley and Los Angeles: University of California Press, 1986.

Mills, Maldwyn, Jennifer Fellows, and Carol Meale, eds. *Romance in Medieval England*. Cambridge: D. S. Brewer, 1991.

Ramsey, Lee C. *Chivalric Romances*. Bloomington, IN: University of Indiana Press, 1983.

Severs, J. Burke, ed. *The Manual of Writings in Middle English,* fascicle I: *Romances*. New Haven: Connecticut Academy of Arts and Sciences, 1967.

14

FELICITY RIDDY

Middle English romance: family, marriage, intimacy

The purpose of this essay is to look at Middle English romances from the perspective of private life. It sets them in the context of late medieval patterns of family and marriage, and presents them as part of a literate but unlearned lay culture centered on the home, where many of them seem to belong. It does not provide a survey, because that has already been done several times,[1] but rather, by looking at around half-a-dozen, suggests a new approach.

The late medieval family can be thought of in two ways. First, as a group of people living together in the "nuclear family household" formation consisting of wife, husband and dependent children, whose home would also include servants and apprentices. The nuclear family, then as now, is always in process, because it comes into being with a marriage and is reshaped by the children's departure. Another way of thinking about the family, though, is as a lineage that is the route for the transmission of property and privilege. In late medieval England wealth and ownership of land provided access to social prestige and political power; the family, especially the male line, was the means whereby these were passed on from one generation to the next. From the point of view of the lineage the son's role was crucial because his marriage ensured its continuity; the marriage of the daughter who inherited took the property to another family. All this is the stuff of Middle English romance; many of its plots are derived from the crises and hiatuses of the nuclear family and the lineage, as I shall show.

What follows is divided into four sections. The first section is concerned with the household context for romance in the fourteenth and fifteenth centuries, which I define socially as "bourgeois-gentry", and with ideas of intimacy and privacy. Then I consider some implications of the fact that the heroes of romances are mostly male, relating this to the ideology of the late medieval nuclear family, to the role of sons, and to the public–private divide. This leads to an argument that the romances are the site of a reconfiguration of the love relationship under the influence of companionate marriage. The last section shifts to the family as lineage, and suggests that the demographic crisis which produced the marriageable heiresses who figure so frequently in romances of love and marriage, also generated narratives of despair at the failure of the male line.

I

One reason for treating Middle English romances as domestic is that they were read at home. "Home" does not necessarily mean a manor-house in the country: the evidence of the surviving manuscripts is that romance was also an urban phenomenon in England. One of the earliest of the major romance collections, the Auchinleck Manuscript, was compiled in London in the 1330s for a wealthy buyer.[2] In the next generation, we know from his expert parody, "The Tale of Sir Thopas," that Chaucer, a London merchant's son, must have been a romance reader. Moreover his *Troilus and Criseyde* is set in the dying city of Troy, in roomy urban "palaces" like John of Gaunt's Savoy, with parlors, chambers, stairs, gardens, and windows that overlook the street.[3] The poem is the scene of intimate activity, but there is also a sense of spaciousness about it, of the elegant living available to the rich in late fourteenth-century London. Several fifteenth-century manuscripts containing romances were owned by merchants who must have known this city ambiance well.[4] In the 1420s the London skinner, Henry Lovelich, translated *The History of the Holy Grail* and *Merlin* for his friend Henry Barton, twice Lord Mayor of London, and in the era of print many romances were published for the urban market. The urban aspect of romance production and readership is unsurprising, since towns were centers of literacy and wealth. It was in towns that the professional manuscript producers were located, and towns were also culturally heterogeneous, which may account to some extent for the diversity of the genre. Nevertheless, Harriet Hudson is not wholly wrong in arguing that romance readers were members of the gentry,[5] since this is clearly also an identifiable group: *Sir Gawain and the Green Knight* was composed for an aristocratic household in the late fourteenth century, while in the mid-fifteenth the Yorkshire landowner Robert Thornton copied out romances in his own hand, including *Sir Percyvell of Gales* and the alliterative *Morte Arthure*.[6] Sir John Paston's list of books contains several romances, as Thomas Hahn has shown in the previous chapter, and Sir Thomas Malory was also a knightly romance reader. Nevertheless, Caxton's preface to his edition of Malory's *Le Morte Darthur* aims at an audience (whom he may be flattering, of course) of "gentlemen and gentlewomen," who were no doubt as much metropolitan as rural. Urban and rural audiences converge because these were not wholly separate realms, though they can be seen separately as undergoing different kinds of change.

Late medieval towns maintained their population levels by the constant recruitment of incomers. The Black Death of the mid-fourteenth century was cataclysmic, of course, but, like all disasters, only for some. For the survivors it created new opportunities to acquire jobs, property and land, and for the young, the ambitious and the active, in particular, to leave home and try their luck. Although there was economic contraction in the fifteenth century, nevertheless general standards of living rose.[7] The Dick Whittington legend does not appear until the late sixteenth century, and yet Sir Richard Whittington and many other men like him in the fourteenth and fifteenth centuries who made their fortunes as London merchants did start out as boys from the provinces.[8] Their lives, like romances, are narratives of ambition, risk, and success.[9]

During this period the gentry as a class also underwent transformation.[10] Between the late twelfth and late thirteenth centuries, knighthood became increasingly exclusive and expensive to maintain. The effect of this exclusiveness was that many of the kinds of men who had earlier been knights were by the fourteenth century relegated to the lesser ranks of esquire and gentleman. Together these three groups formed the gentry. Nevertheless, while the knights consolidated at the top of the gentry, the gentry itself was increasingly distinguished from the nobility – dukes, earls and barons – as the thirteenth-century baronage transformed into the fifteenth-century peerage, now defined as "those who received a personal summons to attend the house of lords in parliament."[11] Gentry and nobility seem to have shared an outlook that derived in part from the fact that they lived off other people's labor and did not do manual work themselves. Nevertheless it also is true that gentry and urban elites, the groups that seem to have been readers of romances, also converged, though differently, and especially in their private identities. This convergence took place during the period in which romances were being composed and read: romances are thus one source of evidence for what I call a new "bourgeois-gentry" cultural formation.

The romances mostly survive in manuscript anthologies, many of which look broadly similar, containing miscellaneous vernacular texts in verse and prose.[12] The diversity of their contents seems to cater to the reading needs of a range of household members, including children and servants in both gentry and mercantile households, and apprentices in the latter as well.[13] Romances are not only read within the family, but also frequently take the family as their subject. They explore courtship and marriage, as in *King Horn, Horn Child and the Maiden Rymnild* and *King Ponthus and Fair Sidone*; married love, as in *Sir Orfeo* and *Sir Amadace*; childbirth, infants and children, as in *Floris and Blancheflor, William of Palerne* and *Chevelere Assigne*; separated and reunited families, as in *Octavian, Torrent of Portyngale* and *Sir Isumbras*; sons and foster-sons, as in *Sir Percyvell of Gales, Sir Degaré* and *Havelok*; brotherhood or sworn brotherhood, as in *Gamelyn, Amis and Amiloun* and *Athelston*; sisterhood, as in *Lai le Freine*, and motherhood, as in *Emaré*. These stories all have happy endings and are sometimes differentiated by historians of romance from others which end in disaster.[14] Nevertheless the disasters are still frequently familial, as I have already suggested: the Alliterative *Morte Arthure* and Malory's *Le Morte Darthur* are, in the end, tragedies of fathers, brothers, and sons.

The domestic nature of romance reading in England does not mean that it is a genre only for women and children. For men as well as women, the domestic sphere in the pre-modern household, in which elementary family relationships were paramount and private identities were formed, was one of intimacy and feeling. Romances were one of the vehicles of its differentiation. The domestic sphere generated plots of individual progression or self-fulfillment, in which marriage was frequently seen as the goal. The public sphere was, by contrast, the political realm of formal and impersonal relationships in which the knight or the civic official acted, not as father or son or lover, but as upholder of the law. These male public identities had no female equivalents, and the public sphere in this sense seems to have been structured on the exclusion of women. The private sphere required women's inclusion, because the family had as its heart the married couple. And yet public and private were mobile categories: the same men could speak both as fathers or husbands, and as aldermen or M.P.s.

II

Middle English romances almost always have knightly male protagonists, and this is one of their most striking differences from modern popular romance. This is not to underestimate the active if subsidiary roles played by women in many narratives, or to discount the possibility of reading the texts from other points of view than that of the hero. Nevertheless, fewer than a handful of romances take women's lives as their subject. Although romances are about knights, however, this does not necessarily mean that they are written, as the aptly named Stephen Knight argues, from "the viewpoint of a landowning armed class."[15] Once established in the course of the thirteenth century as a social identity, the knight became available – like the cowboy in our own day – for myth. As myth, he is a ubiquitous signifier of male autonomy and power, a focus for the fantasies of people who are not themselves members of the knightly class, just as cowboys are part of the imaginative lives of people who have never ridden a horse. From the mid-thirteenth century on, there are increasing numbers of representations of individual knights in armor, apparently detached from any social context: in stained glass, on tombs, in manuscripts, on monumental brasses, on floor tiles, in statuary and carvings.[16] The knight, like the cowboy, is instantly recognizable by his accouterments: his sword and shield, his armor and his great horse. Separated from the mundane business of landholding, office, or even army, he floats glamorously and alluringly free, always at the ready – there is a tomb-type in which he lies with his arm reaching across his body to his sword hilt – and restless for action even at prayer. The knight's horse and his social status are emblematic of mobility and freedom. Although he looks archaic, he is in many ways a new man in fourteenth-century England: an adventure-seeker and risk-taker, a uniquely accessible and adaptable locus of fantasy and desire. In late medieval English romances the knight can be seen as a "bourgeois-gentry" myth of young manhood.

The knight as myth in this sense is used explicitly in the fourteenth-century *Sir Percyvell de Gales*,[17] which does not bear much resemblance to Chrétien's *Perceval*, its point of origin. Percyvell's mother takes the boy into the woods in order to keep him in ignorance of the deeds of arms that have caused his father's death in a tournament and to save him from the same fate. Nevertheless if the romance is to go anywhere, knighthood is inevitable: romance is not a genre about boys who stay with their mothers. As young Percyvell emerges into adult life, he meets members of Arthur's court who tell him they are knights. There is a good deal of comedy in the way he has to learn to his surprise that knights are not gods; that they do not fight with darts, or ride mares; and that the best way to get a man out of his armor is not by setting him on fire. The point of the joke about Percyvell is not so much that he does not know what a knight is, as that he does not know what a knight means. He is ignorant of the cultural codes by which young men are supposed to position themselves in the world of adult male knowingness, like the uncool kid who does not recognize the brand-names or the nerd who lets his mother buy his trainers. Once he has assumed the glamorous adult identity that knighthood offers, Percyvell can get on with his role in what is essentially a family story in which he rescues his mother from a monstrous suitor and brings her home. *Sir Percyvell of Gales* raises the question, what is a knight? and then supplies the answer given by many romances: he is his father's son.

The use of the mythical figure of the knight in the domestic context of romance-reading reveals much about the role of young men in the ideology of the family and household. It both endorses the independence of the son on whom the family's hopes for the future rest, allowing him to be a risk-taker, and yet in the end makes him follow the same course as his father. The nuclear family is, after all, precisely the family formation in which the son does not necessarily move into his father's place, especially in a period of opportunity. We know that the late medieval practices of service and apprenticeship sent many, perhaps most, boys into other men's homes, to follow other men's callings. As for marriage, we probably know even less about whether it was possible for men to remain single in late medieval England than we do about women. Yet urban and county government increasingly required male-headed households and male household heads, and so one of the tasks of household ideology was to control boys' dreams of alternative futures in a changing environment. It is not surprising that romances that seem to be fantasies of freedom should turn out to endorse, again and again, the view that the supreme goal for boys and men of the propertied classes is to marry and settle down.

The thirteenth-century *King Horn* is paradigmatic in this respect. Possibly composed in London towards the end of the thirteenth century, and certainly owned by a London merchant in the fifteenth,[18] it is the story of the dispossessed prince Horn, who is loved by a princess, Rymenhild, and who, after banishment by her father, returns twice in disguise to beat off other suitors, regains his kingdom, and takes her home as his queen. *King Horn* is also paradigmatic in that its plot rests on a differentiation of private and public spheres which might be said to set Middle English romance along the course towards interiority which produced *Sir Gawain and the Green Knight* and *Troilus and Criseyde* in the late fourteenth century. Horn and Rymenhild meet in her "bur" (bower) or her bed, while public life goes on in the "hall"; he moves more easily than she does between the two locations. The "bur" is not only a place, but a state of feeling: it is where the emotional dynamism of the plot is generated. The public/private binary – like the gender binary – is not simply a modern way of thinking about the Middle Ages; it is one of the ways in which the Middle Ages thought about itself. The "bur" is not literally private – on one occasion the couple meet in the presence of sixteen maids – but it is a feminine place of intimacy, love and a different kind of speech. Rymenhild, who falls in love with Horn at first sight, invites him there because "heo ne mighte at borde / With him speke no worde, / Ne noght in the halle / Among the knightes all" (She could not speak a word with him at table, nor in the hall among all the knights; 253–56).[19] The private language of the "bur" is an enigmatic lovers' talk of dreams and objects – the ring, the horn – which only they can interpret. Rymenhild's passion for Horn is described as "wild" (252, 296, 950), and "out of witte" (652), but its wildness is not anti-social – what she wants from the very first is marriage, after all – although it might be called "pre-social," like Percyvell in the forest. Rymenhild does not envisage a world outside the "bur," or recognize that there are things Horn has to achieve in the public world, such as status, esteem and a source of livelihood, before he can take a wife.

In this narrative, as in many others, the woman has no life outside the home, but simply moves, plotlessly, from daughterhood to wifehood. Rymenhild's wildness suggests that she does not belong in the "rational" realm of the exercise of law and justice, but in the realm of fantasy and feeling. This is the location of the clandestine marriage – the unwitnessed vow made in the bedroom rather than publicly solemnized at the church door – which, precisely because of its uncontrollability, was a source of anxiety to parents and churchmen alike.[20] As I have already said, Rymenhild wants to marry Horn, and at their third secret meeting

Horn agrees, with the words: "I shal me mak thin owe / To holden and to knowe / For euerech other wighte: / And tharto my treuthe I thee plighte." (I shall make myself yours to keep and to acknowledge before all others, and thereto I give you my promise; 669–72). This sounds remarkably like the promise of future consent which, if followed by intercourse, constituted a legal marriage according to medieval canon law.[21] The question of whether it is a marriage or a betrothal, though, depends on whether the couple subsequently have intercourse and this is left, it seems, deliberately opaque.

What is clear, though, is that marriage is a process in this poem rather than an event, just as it was in contemporary English society.[22] It begins in private, and then is publicly solemnized after Horn has routed the treacherous Fikenhild, but the couple do not take up residence together until the end of the poem. The male role may be to integrate the woman's single-minded passion into the more complex trajectory formed by the man's public identity, but he does not revalue it. He learns the primacy of feeling in the course of socializing the intimate sphere.

In the two most ambitious romances of the late fourteenth century, Chaucer's *Troilus and Criseyde* and *Sir Gawain and the Green Knight*, the shift from the hall to the bower – by then called a chamber – is almost complete. It is a commonplace about both these poems that the action has been displaced from the usual sites of male heroism into domestic settings. In both poems, unlike *King Horn*, what goes on between the couple in the privacy of the bedroom is made explicit: in the one case they have intercourse and the other they do not. But both romances create a new opaque interiority in the scrutiny of conscience in *Sir Gawain* and of intention in *Troilus and Criseyde*. Both construct the mental life as a zone even more private than the "bur," and one which in the end remains secret. Whether the Green Knight is hostile or friendly, why his wife behaves as she does, whether Gawain makes a bad confession, are questions which the romance generates but refuses to answer. And in *Troilus and Criseyde* the opacity of the heroine's motivation in betraying Troilus is a byword.

III

In late medieval England, so demographers tell us, the "companionate" model of marriage dominated. This is a model in which husband and wife are close in age and marry in their twenties, after a period of independence.[23] Marriages are entered into by choice, rather than being simply arranged. Many family historians regard the "sentimental" family as a post-medieval development, and treat medieval marital relations as distant and patriarchal. Romances suggest otherwise, however. Throughout the medieval period and beyond, marriages among the nobility in England were undeniably arranged for dynastic reasons, with the couple sometimes betrothed as children. Some gentry marriages were of this sort, but recent work has emphasized the extent to which love between the couple, even at this level of society, was felt to be a prerequisite.[24] In the fifteenth century there seems to be some divergence between the nobility and gentry in this area, and it is likely that the source of the "romantic" view of marriage was urban, since we know that marriages among urban immigrants, away from family pressure, were entered into by choice.[25] They were supported by a theology of marriage that from the twelfth century had emphasized the primacy of mutual consent. The romances can be seen in this context. They provide evidence of a "bourgeois-gentry" family ideology in which private relations were governed by feeling and marriages were made for love. This ideology includes an idea of romantic love that associates the freedom of choice exercised by the landless and unpropertied with higher-status ideals of gentility and worth. This is no doubt why some family romances seem to be a form of courtesy text.

The sociologist Anthony Giddens has suggested that romantic love "provides for a long-term life trajectory, oriented to an anticipated yet malleable future; and it creates a 'shared history' that helps separate out the marital relationship from other aspects of family organisation and give it a special primacy."[26] Although Giddens believes romantic love is modern, nevertheless this seems apposite to many medieval romances in which the hero shapes the "anticipated yet malleable future," which is a future as a couple. The optimism of romance derives from a largely secular view of the world, which assumes that the goal of life is to be happy and that happiness is to be found in the marriage made for love, as in the early fifteenth-century *King Ponthus and the Fair Sidone*. This is a prose translation of the near-contemporary French *Ponthus et Sidoine*, which derives in turn from the Anglo-Norman *Roman de Horn*, as *King Horn* does. An almost complete text of *King Ponthus* survives in a manuscript made for a Yorkshire gentry family in the third quarter of the fifteenth century,[27] and another version was printed in London in 1511. It is partly a courtesy text and partly – though these are not separable – a story of romantic love. Towards the end, Ponthus takes his cousin Pollides aside and gives him this advice on how to treat his new wife:

> And also it is to vndrestonde that ye shuld be curtes and gentle vnto your wyf afor any othre, for dyuers resons; for by worshipp and by curtesie beryng vnto hir, ye shall hold the love of hir bonde vnto you; and forto be dyvers and roode vnto hir, she myght happenly chaunge, and the love of hir, so shuld ye wors reioys . . . And also be war that ye kepe selvyn true vnto hir, for it be said in Gospell that ye shuld chaunge hir for noon othre. And if ye doo thus as I say, God shall encrese you in all goode welthe and worship.[28]

Romantic love constructs gender relations within marriage as more egalitarian than the patriarchal systems of the public sphere: this courteous and faithful husband is not an authority figure, and the ideal married relationship is envisaged as a loving and mutual end in itself.

In the narrative of intimacy which romantic love furnishes, Giddens argues that "the element of sublime love tends to predominate over that of sexual ardour . . . Love breaks with sexuality while embracing it; 'virtue' begins to take on a new sense for both sexes, no longer meaning only innocence but qualities of character which pick out the other person as 'special'".[29] This helps to clarify what is going on in the course of the fourteenth and fifteenth centuries as an ideology of romantic love evolved, in which romances must have played a crucial part. We might compare *King Horn* with *King Ponthus and the Fair Sidone* in these terms. In *King Ponthus* all possibility of a clandestine marriage between the hero and heroine has been removed, and it is made elaborately plain that Sidone's desire for Ponthus is throughout not merely chaste but lady-like. For example, when she invites him to her chamber and makes her declaration of love to him, she says: "'I shall say you,' said she, 'that I wolle loue you as my knyght, and [= if] that ye be of suche maner that I may perceyve that ye thinke noon othre wyse bot forto kepe the state and the worshipp of me; and if ye thinke any velanye, I shall neuer loue you.'"[30] "Velanye" conflates class and moral terms, and means both "sexual impurity" and "ungentlemanliness." Sidone's qualified declaration to Ponthus is a long way from the anguished urgency of Rymenhild's plea: "Horn, have of me rewthe, / And plist me thi trewthe!"(Have pity on me and give me your promise; 409–10). One way of describing the difference would be to say, with Giddens, that in *King Ponthus* "sublime love triumphs over sexual ardour." The explicit emphasis on the propriety of their relationship – even in thought – is maintained throughout, while simultaneously the text stresses the power of Sidone's feelings for Ponthus, and the intensity of the bond between them. Ponthus's attractions – his piety, his humility, his gentleness, his courtesy – may be traditional knightly virtues, but seen from Sidone's perspective, as they frequently are, they are husbandly. They are what marks Ponthus out for Sidone, in what might be called an erotics of virtue, as marriageable. In Hoccleve's near-contemporary *Regement of Princes*[31] there is an attack on the marriage customs of the propertied classes, who are said to marry "for muk & good / Only, & noght for loue of þe persone" (1632–3) and thus bring only "stryf" (1635) and "heuynesse" (1637) upon themselves. *King Ponthus* does not share this preacherly premise, that money is "muk" – filth or shit. It is the product of quite a different set of attitudes to wealth, exemplified in a gift Ponthus gives to Sidone: "itt was mervell to see the riches that ther wer, for they wer prased to more value then x thovsand besantes of golde."[32] Nevertheless the discourses of luxury and of asceticism in these very different texts converge on the value they place on "loue of þe persone" as the basis for marriage.

Romantic love, then, places a particular value on the "person," and on marital personableness.[33] In *Havelok the Dane*,[34] which has an unusually wide social scope, there is a terrible moment for the heroine Goldeboru, an English princess, when she is forced to marry Havelok, believing him to be "sum cherles sone" (1092) instead of the dispossessed prince he really is. Although he is "fair," "stronge," "meke" and a virgin, she is outraged at this disparagement of her rank, complaining that no one should marry her unless he is "king or kinges eir" (1115). Luckily, about 250 lines later, lying awake in bed grieving over the fact that she has been "yeven un-kundelike" (given in marriage unnaturally, or in a way that does not conform with her descent; 1250), she realizes from a light coming out of his mouth while he sleeps that Havelok is, after all, a nobleman. This makes all the difference: "She was so fele sithes blithe / That she ne mighte hire joye mithe; / But Havelok sone anon she kiste, / And he slep and nought ne wiste" (She was so very happy that she could not restrain her joy, but immediately kissed Havelok, and he slept and knew nothing; 1277–80). Personableness in *Havelok* is more inclusive than in most romances, but it retains a sense that is found throughout them, that like should marry like. The limits of marital personableness are not only social, however. In *Le Bone Florence of Rome*,[35] Sir Garcy's plan to marry Florence is regarded by her and everyone else as disgusting because he is so old and thus inconceivable as an object of her love, while in *King Ponthus*, Sidone refuses to marry the king of Burgone because he is "evill condicioned, fatt, olde, scabbyd, and frentyke."[36]

The constraints placed upon romance by its ideological function within the "bourgeois-gentry" household prevented it from developing a radical critique in relation to what constituted marital personableness, however. Marriages made for money were condemned by sermon-writers, who fulminated at the way in which virtuous poor girls were rejected in favor of horrible rich old widows.[37] Sermons, though, are written out of a value-system that stresses the spiritual superiority of the poor over the rich, which is hardly the "bourgeois-gentry" outlook. Virtuous poor girls in romances always turn out to be princesses, like Emaré, who is an exemplary product of that outlook. *Emaré* occurs in a household anthology of the early fifteenth century and is one of the few romances with a female protagonist.[38] Emaré is a princess who is cast out from her widowed father's palace in a boat because she rejects his incestuous advances. She is rescued by a king's steward, who takes her into service in his household where she teaches embroidery and etiquette, both of which she is wonderfully skilled in. She attracts the attention of the king, who marries and has a son by her, and then is tricked into repudiating her. A complex family story of jealousy and rec-

onciliation is thus set in train. Emaré's skill as an embroiderer is a female equivalent to the knightly skill at arms: it is a status attribute. Embroidery in late medieval England was not only a lady-like pastime but a household craft in which
women of good family could serve apprenticeships. It mediated the worlds of the
urban elites and the gentry, as is shown in the words of a petition to parliament
from the silkwomen's gild in 1459: they claimed that it was "convenient, wur-
shipfull and accordaunt for gentilwymmen and oþer wymmen of wurship," and
a "vertueux occupation and labour . . . to the norishing of vertue, and eschew-
ing of vices and ydelnes."[39] This eliding of moral and social categories on the one
hand, and of bourgeois and gentle categories on the other, is precisely reproduced in this romance's handling of the erotics of virtue. In her second exile,
Emaré and her little son are taken into the household of a rich merchant where
she embroiders "yn bour" (731) as she had done at court and teaches the boy
manners. In *Havelok*, the exiled hero – a Danish prince – has to earn a living as
a kitchen porter. Emaré, by contrast, moves from the court to the city without
ever being required to transgress the boundaries of gentility, and is never perceived as anything other than a lady.

IV

Many Middle English romances are, like *Emaré*, about the marriages of heiresses, but they are usually told from the perspective of the hero's lineage and not
hers: the failure of the male line in her family is not seen as a disaster but as an
opportunity. Failure of the male line in the hero's family is a different matter
entirely and produces a different kind of story: the tragedies of descent are presented as catastrophes of sonlessness. Many romances were composed in a
period which has been described as one of a "crisis in male succession" for land-
owners, lasting from the Black Death until around 1450. In the late 1370s and
early 1380s, the worst decade of all, fewer than half of landowning families produced sons.[40] In 1419 Sir Thomas Erpingham, who had no male heir, felt the end
of his line sufficiently keenly to have a window built in the church of the Austin
friars in Norwich bearing the coats of arms of all the eighty-seven noble and
gentle families of Norfolk and Suffolk which had died out without male issue
since 1327. According to K. B. McFarlane, the antiquary William Worcestre,
describing the window, "added another 29 knights and 25 esquires to bring the
list down to 1461."[41] Sonlessness did not only afflict the aristocracy: London
mercantile dynasties were the exception rather than the rule.[42]

The Alliterative *Morte Arthure*, which survives in the same gentry household
manuscript as *Sir Percyvell of Gales*, is, by comparison with *Emaré*, public and
male. It rests on a sense of the family as a blood-line and not as a domestic group.

In *Emaré*, her son is the hope for the future; in the Alliterative *Morte Arthure* the lineage has no future because it has no sons. Probably composed in the late fourteenth century, it tells the story of King Arthur's death in the version, ultimately derived from Geoffrey of Monmouth's *History of the Kings of Britain*, which omits the adultery of Lancelot and Guinevere. As a "historical" narrative of states and nations, it looks like a product of the public sphere: chronicles were, after all, consulted by kings in the formulation of government policy. Nevertheless here, too, the poem's focus also turns out to be an intimate one, giving primacy to feeling. The personal relationships that lie at the heart of the Arthurian story mean that the public and patriarchal narrative of national aggrandizement constantly threatens to – and in the end does – collapse into the private zone of family loves and hatreds.

The Alliterative *Morte Arthure* starts with the visit to Arthur's court of envoys from the Roman emperor, demanding feudal homage which Arthur refuses to pay. It is quite different in its initial focus from the Stanzaic *Le Morte Arthur*, which belonged to a London mercer, John Colyns:[43] that poem opens on a scene of marital intimacy, with the king and queen lying in bed. The Alliterative *Morte Arthure*, by contrast, is mostly concerned with military action in the course of which Arthur conquers half Europe until news reaches him that his nephew, Mordred, has usurped his throne and seized his wife, Guenevere. Then the narrative of public history becomes a family tragedy: Arthur returns to England, and Gawain, his nephew and Mordred's brother, is killed on the English shore. Mordred is asked by one of his allies who the dead man is, and as he identifies the body he weeps "for the sake of his sib-blood [kinsman]" (3891).[44] Arthur's grief when he learns of Gawain's death is that of a father deprived of a future:

> Dere cosin of kind in care am I leved,
> For now my worship is went and my war ended!
> Here is the hope of my hele, my happing in armes,
> My herte and my hardiness holly on him lenged! (3956–59)

[Dear kinsman of my lineage, I am left in care, for now my worship has gone and my war ended! Here is my hope of comfort, my success in arms, my heart and my courage depended entirely on him.]

Patriarchal power is not vulnerable to male aggression or female treachery: what it yields to in the end is the death of promise, of "the hope of my hele" which the next generation embodies. Arthur's followers are shocked by his distress, and tell him that this is unkingly conduct:

> It is no worship, iwis, to wring thine handes:
> To weep als a woman, it is no wit holden!
> Be knightly of countenance, als a king sholde,
> And leve such clamour, for Cristes love of heven! (3977–80)

[There is certainly no honor in wringing your hands; to weep like a woman is not accounted wise! Be knightly in your bearing, as a king should, and leave such clamor, for the love of Christ in heaven.]

Kings and knights, participants in the great deeds of history, do not cry. In that impersonal public world from which women are excluded, weeping, clamoring and wringing the hands are seen as women's work. In the unhistorical sphere of the family, though, fathers do cry; Middle English romances have plenty of fathers distraught at the loss of their sons.

A little scene between Arthur and the young Idrous in the ensuing battle shifts to the son's perspective, making him the mouthpiece of the patriarchal ideology of the public sphere. Idrous's father, Sir Ewain, is surrounded and Arthur tells Idrous, who is fighting at Arthur's side, to go and rescue him, but Idrous refuses. "He is my fader, in faith, forsake shall I never– / He has me fostered and fed and my fair brethern– / But I forsake this gate, so me God help." (He is my father, truly, I shall never desert him – he has raised and fed me and my fair brothers – but I refuse this course, so God help me; 4142–44). This clean-cut youth says he has never disobeyed his father in his life and now he will be no different. His father has told him to stay with Arthur and stay he will, even though he knows that this will mean his father's death and his own: "He is elder than I, and end shall we bothen; / He shal ferk before, and I shall come after" (He is older than I, and we shall both end; he shall go before and I shall come after; 4151–52).

The good son is the spokesman for the "natural" order of things, an order in which paternal authority is the highest there is (Idrous does not give a thought for his mother), and in which sons die after, and not before, their fathers. But the death of Gawain has already shown that such an order cannot be assumed, and the horror of Arthur's last hours lies in the catastrophe of sonlessness. Confronted by the corpses of all his knights on the battlefield, half-crazed, Arthur buckles at the knees ("stotays for mad" [4271]) and collapses. He is given a speech which summons up God, king, lord, master, might and man in an over-determination of masculine public power:

> King, comly with crown, in care am I leved!
> All my lordship low in land is laid under,
> That me has given guerdones, by grace of Himselven,
> Maintained my manhed by might of their handes,
> Made me manly on molde and master in erthe . . .   (4275–79)

[O fair crowned king, I am left in sorrow! Laid low under the earth are all my lords who have given me rewards, through His grace, maintained my authority through the strength of their hands, made me powerful in the world and master on earth . . .]

Without sons, all this patriarchal authority is utterly ineffectual and Arthur is a figure of destitute and feminine abjection: "I may helpless on hethe house by mine owne, / Als a wofull widow that wantes her berne!" (I may take shelter all alone on the heath, helpless, like a grieving widow whose child is gone; 4284–85). Here, momentarily, Arthur merges with Idrous's mother, and all the women's work that has been rigorously excluded in the name of history, as history turns into a family affair.

Malory's *Le Morte Darthur*, completed by the end of the 1460s, makes the Arthurian story of dynastic failure into a wider crisis of masculinity. *Le Morte Darthur*, very unusually, tells the whole life of Arthur, from his conception to his death, as a self-contained story. Many English chronicles include accounts of Arthur's reign but they embed it in the continuing line of English kings, so that it is part of a larger genealogical narrative. Removing the life of Arthur from royal genealogy disengages it from notions of lineage and descent, and yet does not reconfigure it in terms of the nuclear family either, though we might see the adulterous wife and the misbegotten son as the idealized nuclear family's deformed shadow. The structure of the life is inception, apogee, crisis, downfall – without aftermath. It is the story of a last generation, of the impossibility of imagining a future, the very negative of the plot engendered by the ideology of romantic love. By the end all the central figures are old or at least middle-aged. Almost all the young people are dead: the Maid of Astolat was only the first in this final phase. The fathers have outlived their sons. Arthur has killed Mordred and received his death's wound in the process. Guinevere, who in the Alliterative *Morte Arthure* has children by Mordred, remains childless until she goes into the nunnery and cuts herself off for ever from all sexual contact. She rejects Lancelot's offer of marriage and will not even kiss him. Thereafter the wholesale retreat of the survivors into the religious life, which is much more complete than in any of Malory's sources, seems to have to do with celibacy rather than other religious values. It is a repudiation of lineage, a refusal or an inability to project forward to future generations. I suggested earlier that *Sir Percyvell de Gales* poses the question, what is a knight? and answers: he is his father's son. Malory's *Le Morte Darthur* could be said to ask the same question, but here the answer is tragic: he is his dead son's father.

The way of reading romances that I have proposed in this essay pays particular attention to the roles of sons, fathers and husbands in the late medieval "bourgeois-gentry" family and the ways in which the knight's story constitutes its aspirations and fantasies. By contrast, the heroines' lives are, as I have already said, plotless. Girls of all classes in late medieval England did not move directly from their fathers' homes to their husbands', as in southern Europe, but spent their teenage years in service in other people's households. This phase is largely effaced in the romances, with their primarily male focus. It is apparently not until the scene of reading – the home itself – becomes the scene of adventure, rather than the place that action starts out from and returns to, that women's lives can be retrieved from silence. That, it seems, is the task of the novel, not the romance.

NOTES

1 See Dorothy Everett, "A Characterisation of the English Medieval Romances," in Dorothy Everett, *Essays on Middle English*, ed. P. Kean (Oxford University Press, 1955), 1–22; Derek Pearsall, "The Development of Middle English Romance," *Medieval Studies*, 27 (1965), 91–116, and "English Romance in the Fifteenth Century," *Essays and Studies*, n.s. 29 (1976), 56–83; Dieter Mehl, *The Middle English Romances of the Thirteenth and Fourteenth Centuries* (London: Routledge and Kegan Paul, 1968); Susan Wittig, *Stylistic and Narrative Structures in the Middle English Romances* (Austin, TX and London: University of Texas Press, 1978); J. A. W. Bennett, *Middle English Literature*, ed. Douglas Gray (Oxford University Press, 1986), 121–201; Susan Crane, *Insular Romance: Politics, Faith and Culture in Anglo-Norman and Middle English Romance* (Berkeley, Los Angeles and London: University of California Press, 1986); Stephen Knight, "The Social Function of the Middle English Romances," in *Medieval Literature: Criticism, Ideology and History*, ed. David Aers (Brighton: Harvester Press, 1986), 99–122; W. R. J. Barron, *English Medieval Romance* (London: Longman, 1987).

2 National Library of Scotland, Advocates 19. 2. 1, containing fifteen romances.

3 See John Schofield, *Medieval London Houses* (New Haven and London: Yale University Press, 1994), 34–51.

4 Examples are Manchester, Chetham's Library, 8009; London, British Library, Harley 2252, London, Lambeth Palace Library, 306; Oxford, Bodleian Library, Rawlinson C 86.

5 Harriet Hudson, "Middle English Popular Romances: The Manuscript Evidence," *Manuscripta*, 28 (1984), 67–78.

6 Cambridge, University Library Ff. II.38.

7 See Richard Britnell, *The Commercialisation of English Society, 1000–1500* (Cambridge University Press, 1993).

8 See Caroline Barron, "Richard Whittington: The Man behind the Myth," in *Studies in London History Presented to Philip Edmund Jones*, ed. A. E. J. Hollaender and William Kellaway (London: Hodder and Stoughton, 1969), 197–250.

9 See Sylvia Thrupp, *The Merchant Class of Medieval London* (Ann Arbor: University of Chicago Press, 1962), Appendix A, "Aldermanic Families," 321–77.

10 See David Crouch, *The Image of Aristocracy in Britain, 1000–1300* (London and New York: Routledge, 1992), 132–38, Peter Coss, *The Knight in Medieval England 1000–1400* (Stroud: Sutton, 1993), 30–71, and Christopher Dyer, *Standards of Living in the Later Middle Ages: Social Change in England c. 1200–1520* (Cambridge University Press, 1989), 13.

11 Dyer, *Standards of Living*, 12–13.

12 See Gisela Guddat-Figge, *Catalogue of Manuscripts Containing Middle English Romances* (Munich: W. Fink, 1976).

13 See Malcolm Parkes, "The Literacy of the Laity," in *The Medieval World*, ed. David Daiches and Anthony Thorlby (London: Aldus, 1973), 565–66.

14 See Helen Cooper, "Counter-Romance: Civil Strife and Father-Killing in the Prose Romances," in *The Long Fifteenth Century: Essays for Douglas Gray*, ed. Helen Cooper and Sally Mapstone (Oxford University Press, 1997), 141–62.

15 Knight, "The Social Function of the Middle English Romances," 102.

16 See Coss, *The Knight in Medieval England*, 72–99. For floor-tiles, see Schofield, *Medieval London Houses*, 112.

17 In Maldwyn Mills, ed., *Ywain and Gawain, Sir Percyvell of Gales, The Anturs of Arthur* (London: Dent, 1992).

18 See Rosamund Allen, "The Date and Provenance of *King Horn*: Some Interim Assessments," in *Medieval Studies Presented to George Kane*, ed. E. D. Kennedy, R. Waldron and J. S. Wittig (Woodbridge: D.S. Brewer, 1988), 99–125, at p. 121; G. V. Smithers, *Havelok* (Oxford University Press, 1987), xiii–xiv.

19 Quotations from "King Horn," in Jennifer Fellows, ed., *Of Love and Chivalry: An Anthology of Middle English Romance* (London: Dent, 1993).

20 See R. H. Helmholz, *Marriage Litigation in Medieval England* (Cambridge University Press, 1974), 27–31.

21 See James A. Brundage, *Law, Sex and Christian Society in Medieval Europe* (Chicago and London: University of Chicago Press, 1987), 189–90, 277, 441–43; Neil Cartlidge, *Medieval Marriage: Literary Approaches 1100–1300* (Woodbridge: Boydell and Brewer, 1997).

22 See R. M. Smith, "Marriage Processes in the English Past," in *The World We Have Gained: Histories of Population and Social Structure*, ed. L. Bonfield, R. M. Smith and K. Wrightson (Oxford: Blackwell, 1986), 43–99.

23 See J. Hajnal, "European Marriage Patterns in Perspective," in *Population in History*, ed. D. V. Glass and D. E. C. Eversley (London: Edward Arnold, 1965), 101–43; R. M. Smith, "Geographical Diversity in the Resort to Marriage in Late Medieval Females: Work, Reputation and Unmarried Females in the Household Formation Systems of Northern and Southern Europe," in *Women is a Worthy Wight: Women in English Society c. 1200–1500*, ed. P. J. P. Goldberg (Stroud: Sutton, 1992), 16–59.

24 See A. S. Haskell, "The Paston Women on Marriage in Fifteenth-century England," *Viator*, 4 (1973), 459–71; C. F. Richmond, "The Pastons Revisited: Marriage and Family," *Bulletin of the Institute of Historical Research*, 58 (1985), 24–36, and Keith Dockray, "Why Did Fifteenth-Century English Gentry Marry?" in *Gentry and Lesser Nobility in Later Medieval England*, ed. Michael Jones (Gloucester and New York: Sutton, 1986), 61–80.

25 See *Love and Marriage in Late Medieval London*, intro. and trans. Shannon McSheffrey (Kalamazoo, MI: Medieval Institute Publications, 1995).

26 Anthony Giddens, *The Transformation of Intimacy: Sexuality, Love and Eroticism in Modern Societies* (Cambridge: Polity, 1992), 44–5.

27 Oxford, Bodleian Library, Digby 185. A fragment of another late fifteenth-century copy is in Bodleian Library, Douce 384. For Digby 185, see the study by Carol Meale in Felicity Riddy, ed., *Prestige, Authority and Power in Late-Medieval Manuscripts and Texts* (Woodbridge: Boydell and Brewer, forthcoming).

28 F. J. Mather, ed., *King Ponthus and the Fair Sidone*, PMLA, 12 (1897), 1–150, at p. 146.

29 Giddens, *Transformation of Intimacy*, 40.

30 King Ponthus, 17.

31 Thomas Hoccleve, *Hoccleve's Works: The Regement of Princes and Fourteen Minor Poems*, ed. F. J. Furnivall, EETS. es. 72 (Oxford, 1897). A text of this poem is in Oxford Bodleian Library, Digby 185, which also contains *King Ponthus*.

32 *King Ponthus*, 108.

33 See Marie Collins, "Feminine Response to Masculine Attractiveness in Middle English Literature," *Essays and Studies*, 38 (1985), 12–28.

34 Quotations from "Havelok the Dane" in Donald B. Sands, ed., *Middle English Verse Romances* (New York and London: Holt, Rinehart, 1966).

35 See C. F. Heffernan, ed., *Le Bone Florence of Rome* (Manchester University Press, 1976).

36 *King Ponthus*, 90.

37 See G. R. Owst, *Literature and Pulpit in Medieval England*, rev. ed. (Oxford: Blackwell, 1966), p. 381.

38 British Library, Cotton Caligula A. ii. Quotations from "Emaré" in Maldwyn Mills, ed., *Six Middle English Romances* (London: Dent, 1973).

39 J. Strachey *et al.*, eds., *Rotuli Parliamentorum*, 6 vols. (London, n.d. [1767–77]), vol. 5, 325.

40 See S. J. Payling, "Social Mobility, Demographic Change, and Landed Society in Late Medieval England," *Economic History Review*, 45 (1992), 51–73, at pp. 54–55 and 61.

41 See K. B. McFarlane, *The Nobility of Later Medieval England* (Oxford University Press, 1973), 145–46.

42 See *ibid*, 166.

43 It is included in his commonplace book: London, British Library, Harley 2252.

44 Quotations are from "Morte Arthure" in Larry D. Benson, ed., *King Arthur's Death* (Exeter University Press, 1986).

SUGGESTIONS FOR FURTHER READING

Reference works

Bordman, Gerald. *Motif Index of the English Metrical Romances*. Helsinki, 1963.

Guddat-Figge, Gisela. *Catalogue of Manuscripts Containing Middle English Romances*. Munich: W. Fink, 1976.

Severs, J. B. *A Manual of the Writings in Middle English 1050–1500, 1, Romances*. Connecticut: Connecticut Academy of Arts and Sciences, 1967.

Social history

Dyer, Christopher. *Standards of Living in the Later Middle Ages: Social Change in England c. 1200–1520*. Cambridge University Press, 1989.

Rigby, S. H. *English Society in the Later Middle Ages: Class, Status and Gender*. Manchester University Press, 1995.

Critical studies

Aertsen, Henk, and Alasdair A. MacDonald, eds. *Companion to Middle English Romance*. Amsterdam: VU University Press, 1990.

Barnes, Geraldine. *Counsel and Strategy in Middle English Romance*. Cambridge: D. S. Brewer, 1993.

Barron, W. R. J. *English Medieval Romance*. London: Longman, 1987.

Bennett, J. A. W. *Middle English Literature*, ed. Douglas Gray. Oxford University Press, 1986. Pp. 121–201, 180–82.

Brewer, Derek, ed. *Studies in Medieval English Romances: Some New Approaches*. Cambridge, 1988.

Ciccone, Nancy. "Practical Reason and Medieval Romance." *Comitatus*, 25 (1994), 43–58.

Everett, Dorothy. "A Characterisation of the English Medieval Romances." In Dorothy

Everett, *Essays on Middle English*, ed. P. Kean. Oxford University Press, 1955. Pp. 1–22.

Fellows, Jennifer, Rosamund Field, and Judith Weiss, eds. *Romance Reading on the Book*. Cardiff, 1996.

Fewster, Carol. *Traditionality and Genre in Middle English Romance*. Cambridge, 1987.

Heng, Geraldine. "A Map of Her Desire: Reading the Feminine in Arthurian Romance." In Edwin Thumboo, ed., *Perceiving Other Worlds*. Singapore: Times Academic for UNIPRESS, 1991. Pp. 250–60.

Hopkins, Andrea. *The Sinful Knights: A Study of the Middle English Penitential Romance*. Oxford, 1990.

Hudson, Harriet E. "Toward a Theory of Popular Literature: The Case of the Middle English Romances." *Journal of Popular Culture*, 23/3 (1989), 31–50.

"Middle English Popular Romances: The Manuscript Evidence." *Manuscripta*, 28/2 (1984), 67–78.

Knight, Stephen. "The Social Function of the Middle English Romances." In David Aers, ed., *Medieval Literature: Criticism, Ideology and History*. Brighton: Harvester Press, 1986. Pp. 99–122.

Meale, Carol M., ed. *Readings in Medieval English Romance*. Cambridge, 1994.

Mehl, Dieter. *The Middle English Romances of the Thirteenth and Fourteenth Centuries*. London: Routledge and Kegan Paul, 1968.

Mills, Maldwyn, Jennifer Fellows, and Carol M. Meale, eds. *Medieval Romance in England*. Cambridge: D. S. Brewer, 1991.

Pearsall, Derek. "English Romance in the Fifteenth Century." *Essays and Studies*, n.s. 29 (1976), 56–83.

"The Development of Middle English Romance." *Medieval Studies*, 27 (1965), 91–116.

Stevens, John. *Medieval Romance: Themes and Approaches*. London: Hutchinson, 1976.

Wittig, Susan. *Stylistic and Narrative Structures in the Middle English Romances*. Austin, TX, and London: University of Texas Press, 1978.

15

MARINA S. BROWNLEE

Romance at the crossroads: medieval Spanish paradigms and Cervantine revisions

Regardless of national or temporal factors – romance is the most enduring of literary forms. From the paradigmatic Garden of Eden to contemporary or even futuristic – often highly technological – expressions, this "secular scripture," as Northrop Frye terms it, continues to flourish.[1] Its origins in the folktale, the optimism projected by its representation of human heroism are clearly compelling. Yet, far from merely entailing the naïve appeal of a prelapsarian order for the individual reader, romance, as Fredric Jameson explains, involves a continuous and sophisticated reinvention of itself as a response to an ever-changing historico-political environment.[2] Indeed, we see that history frequently appropriates romance paradigms in order to legitimate itself as when, for example, Bernal Díaz clearly presents Spain's New World conquest and colonization as a continuation of the exploits of Amadís.[3] Whatever form it takes, romance is committed to the celebration of a coherent system of socio-political values. This extra-textual frame of reference can take a variety of forms – from political propaganda that offers a self-aggrandizing depiction of the nobility or equivalent patron for whom the text is being produced, to the articulation of escapist fantasy – futuristic or archaizing. It is, for example, nostalgia for the lost world of chivalric romance which Cervantes embodies in the figure of Don Quijote, a foolish old man driven insane by his obsession with this perennial literary form.

In spite of any individual differences, however, all romance texts share the same attitude toward language – that is, a belief in its transparency, its performative efficacy. The value or truth-content of words themselves is not an issue, only the hero's ability to live up to the values they represent. As such, the view of language projected by romance tends to function in a markedly different way from the novel. Mikhail Bakhtin posits a useful distinction between romance discourse (an idealizing discourse which values clarity) and the novel, which is anything but transparent: "The novel and [romance are] two genres that . . . constitute the opposite poles of the intertextual continuum. [Romance discourse] implies a transparency of language, a coincidence of works and things;

the novel starts out with a plurality of languages, discourses, and voices, and the inevitable awareness of language as such."[4]

The need to distinguish romance from novel is essential, given the notorious terminological imprecision of the word *novela* in the Spanish lexicon, its usage to designate both novel and romance. *Novela* participates in the same kind of generic ambiguity as *roman* in French and German, a term frequently used to designate all long narratives, either novelistic or romance in nature. With a similar lack of precision, English, meanwhile, employs "novel" to indicate any long prose fiction. Yet the difference between these two genres is qualitative rather than quantitative, and it has a decisive effect on our understanding of romance – its evolution – from its initial medieval Spanish manifestations to its Cervantine rethinking. And it is not simply the linguistic ambiguity implied by the word *novela* (and *libro*, an equally ambiguous designation, used particularly in medieval texts) that accounts for the confusion. Adding to the problem in Spain is the impact exerted by the Generation of 1898, an intellectual movement with a commitment to "realism" as an expression of the Spanish national character. The unreality of the chivalric romance world and the terminological imprecision of *novela* have led to the relative scholarly neglect of this genre by comparison with other European traditions.[5]

In Spain, as elsewhere in Europe, the first instance of romance to appear in the vernacular was the so-called "romance of Antiquity" of the thirteenth century. The transition from the prestige of the Latin language to the emerging vernaculars necessitated a measure of self-authentification whereby the writer could legitimate and dignify the empowering myths projected by his society, as well as his own creative literary endeavor by referring to venerable models. This self-legitimation expressed itself by the well-known *topos* of the *translatio studii et imperii*, the myth of the transference of learning and empire from Antiquity to the Middle Ages – a rhetorical tool which endowed the writer and his society with the prestige of antique examples, both intellectual and political, of which he and his society are presented as being an integral part.

If we consider the first two of more than fifty extant romances in Spain, the *Libro de Apolonio* and the *Libro de Alexandre* (both composed between 1220 and 1240), we find the accustomed adventure of personal exploits normally associated with romance as it pertains to two of the most celebrated figures of the ancient world – Apollonius of Tyre (a Greek king from the second to third century A.D.) and Alexander the Great (King of Macedonia in the fifth century B.C.). While the conventions of romance and the positivistic values that underlie the genre are very visible in both of these texts, the presentation of each hero is a hybrid one, offering a juxtaposition of the romance focus on earthly, secular personal achievement with the sacred, extra-textual considerations of eternity. We find Apolonio offering a positive model of the Christian Everyman, while

Alexander's *soberbia* leads to his demise in ethical terms, despite his exemplary military prowess.

This generic hybridization, whereby the texts consistently project considerations that exceed the space and time of the storyline itself are characteristic of Spanish romance. In fact, in Spain the impact of the long-term struggle to achieve the Reconquist of Spain from the Moors (711–1492) would not result in the development of courtly romance that celebrated the self-reflexive "vanity" of its subjects; an extra-textual dimension is always present in the Iberian texts. As Marc Bloch explains, the socio-economic realities of the Reconquest and its protracted nature precluded the growth of a feudal system of the sort that flourished in the rest of Europe.[6]

A reading of these two foundational Spanish texts also reveals their dramatic differences in both their plot structure (the *Apolonio* being short and linear, the *Alexandre* long and digressive), and in the amount of erudition they display; the *Alexandre* offering a wealth of information on such diverse topics as the lore of the Phoenix, a lengthy account of the Trojan war, Alexander's studies under the tutelage of Aristotle, even the behavior of the submarine world. It is, by far, the most erudite of all the European Alexander texts.

Both texts are products of the literary environment identified as the *mester de clerecía* (the art of clerkliness), the learned poetry of thirteenth- and fourteenth-century Spain that relied on biblical and Classical sources.[7] The *mester de clerecía* employed the meter of the *cuaderna vía* ("fourfold way"), consisting of a stanzaic structure of four fourteen-syllable lines divided by "caesura" into equal hemistichs of seven syllables each. These *clerecía* texts self-consciously contrast themselves with the *mester de juglaría* (the art of the *jongleur*/minstrel), its unlearned discourse, while very obviously utilizing it constructively. Indeed, the *Apolonio* poet celebrates *juglaría*, and by extension himself, by means of Apolonio's storytelling and his beloved daughter's (Tarsiana's) riddles and explicit identification as a *juglaresa*. Were it not for Apolonio's repeated recitation of his own life story, and she of hers, their mutual recognition of one another and their reunion with the wife/mother Luciana would literally never have occurred.

Much can be learned about the procedures and parameters of romance composition from these and other romances of Antiquity, which include the accounts of the wars at Troy and Thebes and their prosification. As was the case with the initial appearance of verse romances in the 1220s to 1240s, the first prose texts were also renderings (translations and adaptations) of antique matter. The prosification process was initiated in France as a result of the so-called "poetic crisis" of the thirteenth century, an intellectual movement that involved the reaction of Scholastics and Cistercians to twelfth-century French romance, claiming that prose is more truthful than verse (which they construed as a mendacious form based on metrical and stanzaic artifice). As a consequence of this perception many important works written originally in verse were prosified – "derhymed" – for the sake of "scientific objectivity." In spite of the importance accorded to prose, however, the derhyming project resulted at times in some very unexpected formal juxtapositions. The *Historia troyana polimetrica* (*c.* 1270) is one such case, offering a particularly intriguing example of this derhyming activity, for while it turns the verse into prose, it also contains embedded lyrics that offer a range of metrical and stanzaic virtuosity that is unequaled by any other text.[8]

Also in this connection, we recall the prosified Spanish epics and romances which King Alfonso X, the Wise (1221–84), presents as prose history. What makes prose more "scientific" in the mind of the prosifier is its effacement of the author figure. Prose, quite simply, approximates more closely the verbal structures of spontaneous oral discourse. Hence it is more faithful (thus readily believable) than the artificial (necessarily less truthful) form of poetry. Indeed, as Alfonso X's vast historiographic enterprise reveals, the advent of prose in Spain signaled nothing less than a new attitude toward the written word.

At the close of the thirteenth century and in the fourteenth, this "prosa científica" of the scholar-king gives way to the "prosa novelesca."[9] And principal among its first expressions is the *Libro del Caballero Zifar* (*c.* 1310). This text is the first original full-length romance written in Spanish, or at least the earliest surviving text of its kind. Because of its focus on the adventures of the Knight Zifar, the work tends to be labeled as Spain's first autochthonous romance of chivalry. It should be pointed out, however, that although it provides a model for subsequent chivalric romances that would be written in the style of *Amadís*, it relies heavily on the Alfonsine enterprise and the didactic mentality that underpins it. By contrast to the archetypal *libro de caballerías* which tends to privilege physical action and amorous intrigue over intellectual and ethical concerns, we encounter an obsessive concern for the exercise of one's "buen seso natural" (good judgment) including a lengthy portion of the work devoted to *castigos* – advice that Zifar offers his sons, replete with illustrative *exempla* – which find their origin in the philosophical compendium entitled *Flores de filosofía*.[10] It is important to note in this context that in Spain the term *libro de caballerías* has been used somewhat loosely as a tag to label many works which have little or nothing to do with chivalry. *El conde Partinuples*, *Flores y Blancaflor*, *Paris y Viana* and the Spanish *Guillaume d'Angleterre* texts, detailing the trials and tribulations of couples or families, are some examples of such texts for which a chivalric dimension is minimal at best.

While the didactic perspective of the *Zifar* is irrefutable, and medievalizing, it also projects a strikingly modern novelistic dimension that has led several critics to wonder whether Cervantes may have been familiar with it.[11] The dialogic structure of the Knight Zifar and his squire (the appropriately named ribald

Ribaldo) results in countless situations in which, as in the *Quijote*, the idealizing romance discourse of the master is repeatedly interrogated by the cunning squire. Indeed, the *Zifar*, like the *Quijote* after it, offers a programmatically playful mirroring of the world of romance and its flawless presentation of life that is immune to the impoverishing contingencies of daily life. One example of this procedure is the unfortunate fact that Zifar's steeds drop dead after he has ridden them for only ten days – a tremendous liability for any knight, and a grotesquely comic detail as well.

Also like the *Quijote*, the *Zifar* is identified by its anonymous prologuist as a translation. And while this type of self-presentation is so widely used as to be a time-worn authorial *topos*, both the *Zifar*-author and Cervantes employ it very pointedly in order to signal the authenticity of their respective texts. The *Zifar* presents itself as a translation from Arabic to Latin to Romance in order to endow the book with an impressive textual genealogy, thereby legitimating the writing of Spain's first prose fiction. This represents an authorial pose which Cervantes will himself adopt 300 years later both to recall for his readers the popular romance device, and to poke fun at the hide-bound literary theoreticians who were consumed by issues of historicity and verisimilitude during the Neoaristotelian controversies of his day. For both authors the identification of their works as translations is calculated to dignify their enterprise with authority. For Cervantes, of course, the legitimating gesture – claiming that the *Quijote* is a translation of a (worthless) Arabic manuscript by an obscure Cide Hamete Berengeli – is decidedly tongue-in-cheek.

The *Zifar* is also noteworthy for its Arthurian reminiscences as well (the magic boat – which Cervantes will also exploit – the Fortunate Isles, the sovereign who refuses to laugh, the battle between Arthur and the Cat of Languedoc). In spite of these references, however, the *Zifar* diverges from the Arthurian atmosphere in that it does not celebrate the heroic feats normally associated with chivalric honor, it being firmly rooted in the daily, largely unheroic, and decidedly unmystical world of Christian *humilitas* – stemming in part from its indebtedness to the *Life of St. Eustache*. Likewise, there is no courtly love celebrated; love must exist within the confines of holy matrimony or else it is inadmissible. Beyond its clearly moral valence, this is a text that valorizes the possibility of social mobility – that of Zifar himself, his wife and sons, and of Ribaldo as well.

The earliest recorded allusions to the Matter of Britain are found in Catalan poetry of the 1170s and 1190s, as well as being present in Alfonso's *General Historia* (Parts II–IV) which includes a translation of Geoffrey of Monmouth's *Historia* (Book I, 3–III, 8). In similar fashion, the *Gran conquista de Ultramar* (early fourteenth century) also alludes to the Round Table (ch. 44). In 1313 a Portuguese version of *Joseph of Arimathea* appears, and a Castillian *Tristan*, which may predate it slightly. But it is at the time during which the *Zifar* was produced that the Arthurian legends begin to exert serious influence in Iberia, for it is in fourteenth-century Spain that the greatest number of French Arthurian romances were translated, narratives devoted to Merlin and Grail texts, those concerning Lancelot, and those involving Tristan and his pursuits.[12]

As with the prosification of verse romances, here too, interesting literary experiments abound in the realm of translation. One of the most striking examples of recast Arthurian material is *La Faula (The Tale)* written *c*. 1370 by the Majorcan author Guillem Toroella. It is a long poem composed in Provençalized Catalan containing intercalated French poetic fragments, detailing the miraculous survival of King Arthur himself who had been cured by his sister Morgan and preserved in a youthful condition as a result of the yearly visit of the Grail, and who, since the time of his extraordinary convalescence, resides on a Mediterranean island.

The romance fantasy of *La Faula* is not, however, a function of its Catalan roots. That is, the realism for which the *Zifar* is frequently credited – including proof of the need for knowing how to lie convincingly and the importance of knowing how to think on one's feet – is a striking feature of two important Catalan romances which also rely to some degree on Arthurian material. The first is *Curial e Güelfa* (1443–60), a text which reveals an acquaintance with the Catalan Lancelot and Tristan texts. French heroes depicted in this text are judged rather harshly – credited as having won their reputations for bravery somewhat misleadingly since they never had occasion to fight against the (obviously superior) knights of Aragon. The axis of love and adventure that pervades the Arthurian literature is not prevalent in *Curial*, where realism abounds and the author favors the literary traditions of Classical Antiquity and Italy over the Matter of Britain.[13]

Though *Curial* displays an undeniable sense of superiority over the French heroes, this should not be construed as a consistent expression of regional sentiment characteristic of the Catalan literature being produced at the time. The better-known *Tirant lo Blanc* authored by Joannot Martorell (*c*. 1460) allies itself very centrally with Arthur's court. The eponymous hero himself claims descent from a captain of Uther Pendragon – a frequent aspiration of noblemen of the time. Even more dramatic than such genealogical claims or the iconographic depictions of Arthurian lovers and episodes of the Grail quest that decorate the walls of the Emperor of Constantinople's palace, is the depiction of Arthur himself being liberated from a trance by his sister Morgan la Fée. The liberated monarch greets the Emperor and those present all join in a celebratory dance. Beyond this celebration of Arthur, the attitudes toward sexuality are more in keeping with the French romance tradition that eschews puritanical behavior.

Yet, despite the unqualified admiration for Arthurian legend in this text, here too the idealizing world of romance is seriously interrogated as artifice. Indeed, we find grotesque elements in such details as the realistic, wholly unheroic, descriptions of warfare, the desperate, besieged citizens of Rhodes eating rats, and knights who complete their apprenticeship with an obligatory year of service in the slaughterhouses.

Such juxtaposition of romance with realism, with its attention to quotidian detail, is the feature that wins special praise from Cervantes for *Tirant*. And the praise is lavish indeed, as the priest exclaims to the barber while they carry out an inquisition of Don Quijote's personal library: "'God help me!' shouted the priest. 'Here's Tirant lo Blanc! . . . I swear to you, my friend, that it's the best book of its kind in the world. The knights in it eat, sleep, die in their beds, dictate wills before they go and many other things you cannot find in other works of this sort.'"[14] The appeal of *Tirant* for Cervantes is clear since such programmatic clashing of real and ideal worlds forms the very basis of his novelistic innovation.

At the same time as these Catalan texts, that both celebrate and interrogate the world of chivalric heroic and amorous ideals, are being written, a related but different novelizing form is developed in Castilian. This latter type of literature, the *novela sentimental* of the fifteenth century, also merits serious consideration given that it is a Spanish invention which would have considerable impact on the rest of Europe, thus reversing the earlier direction of adaptations and translations from the Continent to the Iberian peninsula. The form is often referred to as "sentimental romance," yet, here too, the term is misleading. These putative romances reveal a performative failure where not only realism intrudes upon the milieu of courtly love in order to expose its artifice, but where the breakdown in linguistic communication – verbal violence, so to speak – leads to physical violence with dire, life-threatening consequences. Juan Rodríguez del Padrón's provocatively entitled *Siervo libre de amor* (*The Free Servant of Love* or its opposite, *The Servant Freed of Love*), dating from 1440, is acknowledged as the first of this corpus of texts. This work, like the rest that pertain to this sentimental tradition, is inscribed within letters written by the author to his patron; all these romances, moreover, include exchanges of letters on the diegetic level, and all of these texts figure the author-figure himself as character, go-between and mail-carrier for the invariably doomed pair of lovers.

The *Siervo* and its fifteenth-century successors were described by Menéndez Pelayo, who first identified this literary corpus, also coining the term *novela sentimental* to characterize it. According to his definition, this literary environment is composed of a generic hybrid, a mixture of chivalric and [Italian] erotic literature, a combination of the *Amadís* and the *Elegia di madonna Fiammetta*.[15] The insufficiency of this definition arises from the fact that chivalric literature is decidedly erotic – more erotic, in fact, than the retrospective diary account of solipsistic unrequited passion that leaves Boccaccio's unfortunate heroine in a demented state. There is always an amorous motivation behind the deeds of knightly prowess, not to mention intimate encounters both verbal and physical.

Yet a more serious reservation to Menéndez Pelayo's classic formulation stems from the fact that the *Amadís* and the *Elegia* exhibit two radically different discursive environments – namely, romance and novel respectively. His definition ignores the fact that the form and meaning of a text must each be scrutinized before their combined effect and its generic expression can be fully determined. Cautioning the reader against an analogous form of discursive oversimplification, Hans-Robert Jauss remarks: "One puts a princess in a fairy tale next to a princess in a novella, and one notices the difference."[16] In other words, it is not only the subject matter itself, but, of equal importance, the discursive environment constructed by the author that is crucially important. The verbal system implied by the novel is as alien to romance as the novella is to the fairy tale. And it is precisely this type of critical differentiation of discourses – based on linguistic referentiality – that reveals the *novela sentimental* to be a subversion of romance.

The competing discourses that characterize the *novela sentimental*, the potential chasm separating word and deed these texts dramatize, culminates with *La Celestina*, which has been interpreted alternately as the culmination of the form or as a parodic response to it.[17] These texts, moreover, were best-sellers not only in Spain, but were soon translated and disseminated into a variety of European languages, whereupon they attained tremendous popularity and prestige as well. Maurice Scève's *La Deplourable fin de Flamete* is, perhaps, the most famous of these rewritings.

Nonetheless, the nominalistic skepticism reflected by the fifteenth-century *novela sentimental* would soon give way to a new attitude toward language viewed as an unproblematic communicative system, one that found its expression in the production of a great number of chivalric romances. With this dramatic renewal of interest in romance composition in the sixteenth century, the inherent power of words – their transparency – is never questioned, only the protagonist's personal fortitude in terms of such stable verbal structures and the ideological systems they represent.

The *Amadís de Gaula* is, as the priest tells us in the inquisition of Don Quijote's library, a "thing of mystery" ("cosa de misterio"), a revision and continuation which has survived in a 1508 version by Garci Rodríguez de Montalvo of a three-book version known in the mid-fourteenth century, and alluded to even in López de Ayala's fourteenth-century *Rimado de Palacio*. Although the primitive text has not survived, the hero projects values similar to the Arthurian knights; for example, he like Lancelot arrives unknown at the king's court where he falls in love with a lady close to the monarch. Likewise he has a protector possessing magical powers, and magical foes, as well as winning an enchanted residence, and having a son who will outdo his own exploits.

The extent of Montalvo's reworking, as well as Cervantes's claim that *Amadís* is "el primero de caballerías que se imprimió en España, y todos los demás han tomado principio y origen déste" ("the first chivalric romance printed in Spain, it being the origin of all the rest"; i.vi, 67) are unresolved issues. The nature of Montalvo's contribution to the earlier version cannot be precisely determined, while Cervantes's claim to its uniqueness clearly refers to the originary status of this text as the catalyst that resulted in a veritable avalanche of chivalric production in sixteenth-century Spain. Not only was Montalvo's four-book *Amadís* reprinted fifty times between 1511 and 1586, his (wholly original) fifth book of the cycle, *Las sergas de Esplandián*, which narrates the adventures of Amadis's son, also enjoyed tremendous popularity, as did the exploits of his grandson, *Lisuarte de Grecia*. Henry Thomas conveys the staggering popularity of the chivalric romance during this century when he writes: "During the hundred years that followed the publication of the *Amadís of Gaul*, fifty romances of chivalry appeared in Spain and Portugal. They were published at the rate of almost one per year between 1508 and 1550; to these were added nine more between 1550 and . . . [1588]; and three more appeared before the publication of *Don Quijote*."[18] The great number of sequels and continuations that were generated from the initial *Amadís* makes it clear that this literary form had become a veritable industry. Further proof of its ability to capture the imagination of its readers is preserved in modern geography, for example, the names California and Patagonia find their origin in episodes of *Esplandián* and *Primaleón*, the continuations of the *Amadís* and *Palmerín* texts respectively.[19]

Montalvo's *Amadís* narrates the exploits of its eponymous hero, who is the illegitimate son of King Perión of Gaul and Princess Elisena of England. The infant is set adrift in a box by his mother and raised by Gandales of Scotland. He falls in love with the Princess Oriana, but their relationship is threatened as Oriana falls prey to false accusations which lead her to reject Amadís as a result. This rejection devastates the hero, who comes close to losing his mind until the deception is disclosed and the lovers are reunited. He is recognized by his parents, and subsequently enchanted in the palace of the evil magician Arcalaus, from whom he is liberated by two wise maidens. He does battle with the monster Endriago on Devil's Island, finally managing to marry Oriana, thereupon returning to his kingdom, the Insola Firme, where a great festival takes place.

This seems to be a logical stopping point for the text. Yet, wanting to leave open the possibility for sequels and continuations, Montalvo extends the fourth book beyond these festivities in order to pave the way for Esplandián's prominence in book 5. In fact, Urganda, the enchantress, foretells an illustrious future for Amadís's son, one which will outdo his father's deeds.

Montalvo's text offers a synthesis of the most salient features of a typical Arthurian text – offering a model that resulted in an unprecedented production of texts in Spain. And it, along with Ariosto's *Orlando furioso* (1516–32), had tremendous appeal for Cervantes in the forging of the *Quijote*.

Cervantes's monumental text, published in two parts (1605, 1615), claims to be written for the sole purpose of discrediting the implausibility and excess exhibited by chivalric romance, and yet it exhibits both an admiration for and a scathing critique of the compositional features of chivalric romance. Parody need not signal disapproval. From the very beginning, with the first of the prefatory verses in praise of Don Quijote, we feel Montalvo's presence, given that the poem which initiates the Cervantine enterprise is written by none other than Urganda, the powerful enchantress of the *Amadís*.

Cervantes's cagey response to romance, a simultaneous acceptance and rejection of it, is evident from his ingeniously conceived prologue to Part I. In it we see the author recounting to an anonymous friend his lamentable inability to write a prologue because of all the obligatory pedantry this genre entails. When the author finds himself in a state of despair because he is incapable of producing the laudatory sonnets, literary allusions, and high-flown quotations from Latin and the vernacular that prologues are accustomed to having, the friend tells him simply to plagiarize from others. It is the friend, not the prologuist, who repeatedly identifies the text as one long invective against the books of chivalry, aimed at "destroying the authority and influence that books of chivalry have in the world" (30). The prologuist simply concludes the prefatory remarks, saying that he accepts the friend's suggestions as to how he might proceed, whereupon he ends the prologue without having written one.

This prologue provides an early glimpse at Cervantes's consistently slippery self-presentation. He is a discursive rather than linear thinker, one who offers mutually conflicting perspectives which readers must sort out on an individual basis. Claiming, in 1605, that he writes in order to discredit the influential chivalric form is clearly anachronistic since it had already become unfashionable reading material decades earlier. Paradoxically, as Peter Russell has remarked, the *Quijote* did much to perpetuate the earlier texts – not simply by referring to the titles or heroes themselves, but through allusion to or even the reenactment of prior episodes and key scenes (e.g., the lover's penitence, the battle with monsters, the enchanted boat), for an audience which might otherwise be unfamiliar with the chivalric romance models.

The ambivalence Cervantes projects toward the *Amadís* is aptly conveyed by the judgment of his personal library of 300 texts that the priest, barber, housekeeper and niece enact in 1.6. The mere fact of having these intellectually undistinguished figures serve as literary censors alerts us to the unconventional nature of the episode. But the mixed signals conveyed by these critics leave no doubt as to Cervantes's problematic presentation of their criteria, and perhaps, more broadly, of the activity of censorship *per se*.

In considering the romances of chivalry in Don Quijote's possession, the priest and barber decide to consign them to the flames (in a parodically conceived inquisitorial *auto da fe*). Paradoxically, however, the prime offender, the text which inspired the writing of so many offensive romances, the *Amadís* itself, is saved because the barber has heard it said that this originary text is "the best of all the books of this kind that have been written" (57). Yet the unqualified praise offered here is qualified by the fact that it is reported as hearsay rather than the product of well-considered evaluation on the part of the barber. To make matters worse, or more equivocal, the remaining contents of the library are disposed of without being granted even such questionable scrutiny because the censors are too tired to proceed any further with their task. What had been initially presented as an objective *auto de fe* concludes by being labeled as a (clearly unobjective) "massacre of innocents." Here as elsewhere in his text, Cervantes defers to the reader's judgment – on the validity of the *Amadís*, of its progeny, and of literary censorship itself – leaving us unsure as to his final word on the matter. It is the process itself, the act of reading in all its potential for complexity, which Cervantes seeks to stage rather than offering *ex cathedra* pronouncements about interpretation or the place of literature in society.

Don Quijote's decision to emulate Amadís's self-imposed exile as a rejected lover, rather than assuming the active role of Orlando, who wrought havoc, uprooting trees in his demented state, is indicative of the extent to which he has become obsessed by romance paradigms. The fact that Dulcinea is not analogous to Amadís's Oriana or to Orlando's Angelica (she has never even noticed his desperate infatuation) makes Don Quijote's behavior parodic indeed. Yet, while his behavior may be construed as disapproval of the excess and unreality that pervade the world of chivalric romance, Cervantes writes in the other extreme – that of constructive approval – in the figure of the Canon of Toledo (1.47), the most extensive literary-theoretical spokesman of the entire text. For having criticized the defects of the form in its exaggerated sixteenth-century expression, we learn that he himself has authored more than one hundred folios of a chivalric romance. Some readers interpret this as an autobiographical reference to Cervantes's composition of his own impressive romance, *Los trabajos de Persiles y Sigismunda*, a posthumously published text which he esteemed so highly that, as the prologue to the *Novelas ejemplares* explains, it "dares to compete with Heliodorus."[20]

By way of conclusion, what can be said with certainty is that Cervantes's exploration of romance – its interrogation not only of literary taste and reader-response, but of the parameters of human subjectivity – evolves into a critique of reality itself. This relentlessly skeptical, perspectival presentation not only of romance, but of reality at its most basic level, resulted not only in an incisive critical commentary on that genre, but in the forging of the modern European novel.[21]

NOTES

1 Northrup Frye, *The Secular Scripture: A Study of the Structure of Romance* (Cambridge, MA: Harvard University Press, 1976).

2 Fredric Jameson, *The Political Unconscious: Narrative as a Socially Symbolic Act* (Ithaca: Cornell University Press, 1981).

3 Stephen Gilman, "Bernal Díaz del Castillo and Amadís de Gaula," in *Studia Philologica: Homenaje ofrecido a Damaso Alonso*, 3 vols. (Madrid: Gredos, 1961), vol. 2, 99–114.

4 Mikhail Bakhtin, *The Dialogic Principle*, ed. Tzvetan Todorov (Minneapolis: University of Minnesota Press, 1984), 66.

5 Alan D. Deyermond, "The Lost Genre of Medieval Spanish Literature," *Hispanic Review*, 43 (1975), 231–59.

6 See Hans Ulrich Gumbrecht, "Literary Translation and Its Social Conditioning in the Middle Ages: Four Spanish Romance Texts of the Thirteenth Century," *Yale French Studies*, 51 (1974), 205–22.

7 See Alan D. Deyermond, "'Mester es sen pecado,'" *Romanische Forschungen*, 77 (1965), 111–16; Ian Michael, *The Treatment of Classical Material in the "Libro de Alexandre"* (Manchester University Press, 1970); Marina S. Brownlee, "Writing and Scripture in the *Libro de Apolonio*: The Conflation of Hagiography and Romance," *Hispanic Review*, 51 (1983), 159–74; and Ronald Surtz, "El héroe intelectual en el 'mester de clerecía,'" *La Torre*, 1 (1987), 265–74.

8 See Marina S. Brownlee, "Narrative Structure and the Rhetoric of Negation in the *Historia troyana polimétrica*," *Romania*, 106 (1985), 439–55, and Louise Haywood, *The Lyrics of the "Historia troyana polimétrica"* (London: Deptartment of Hispanic Studies, Queen Mary and Westfield College, 1996).

9 Diego Catalán, "Poesía y novela en la historiografía castellana de los siglos XIII y XIV," in *Mélanges offerts à Rita Lejeune*, ed. Fred Dethier, 2 vols. (Gembloux: Duclot, 1969), vol. 1, pp. 423–41.

10 See James F. Burke, *History and Vision: The Figural Structure of the "Libro del Caballero Zifar"* (London: Tamesis, 1972); Roger M. Walker, *Tradition and Technique in "El Libro del Caballero Zifar"* (London: Tamesis, 1974); and Michael Harney, "The *Libro del Caballero Zifar* as a 'Refraction' of the Life of St. Eustache," in *Saints and Their Authors: Studies in Medieval Hispanic Hagiography in Honor of John K. Walsh*, ed. Jane E. Connolly, Alan Deyermond and Brian Dutton (Madison: Medieval Hispanic Seminary, 1990), 71–82.

11 Roger M. Walker, "Did Cervantes Know the *Cavallero Zifar*?" *Bulletin of Hispanic Studies*, 49 (1972), 120–27.

12 See María Rosa Lida's concise treatment of the subject in "Arthurian Literature in Spain and Portugal," in *Arthurian Literature in the Middle Ages*, ed. Roger Sherman Loomis (Oxford: Clarendon Press, 1959), 406–18, and Harvey Sharrer, *A Critical Bibliography of Hispanic Arthurian Material* (London: Grant and Cutler, 1978).

13 For a recent overview of scholarship on the subject see Montserrat Piera, "Critical Approaches to *Curial y Guelfa*," in *Volume in Memory of Pauli Bellet*, ed. Ellen Ginsberg (New York: Peter Lang, 1992), 83–93.

14 On this topic see Lola Badia, "El *Tirant* en la tardor medieval catalana," in *Actes del Symposium "Tirant lo Blanc"* (Barcelona: Quaderns Crema, 1993), 35–99; and Antonio Torres, *El realismo del "Tirant lo Blanch" y su influencia en el "Quijote"* (Barcelona: Puvill, 1979).

15 Marcelino Menéndez Pelayo, *Orígenes de la novela*, 4 vols. (Madrid: Bally-Ballière, 1905), vol. 1, 299.

16 Hans-Robert Jauss, *Toward an Aesthetic of Reception* (Minneapolis: University of Minnesota Press, 1982), 82.

17 In this context see María Eugenia Lacarra, "La parodia de la ficción sentimental en la *Celestina*," *Celestinesca*, 13 (1989), 11–29, Marina S. Brownlee, *The Severed Word: Ovid's "Heroides" and the "Novela Sentimental"* (Princeton University Press, 1990), and E. Michael Gerli and Joseph J. Gwara, eds., *Studies in the Sentimental Romance: Redefining a Genre* (London: Tamesis, 1997).

18 Henry Thomas, *Las novelas de caballerías españolas y portuguesas*, trans. Esteban Pujols (Madrid: Centro de Investigaciones Científicas, 1952), 113–14. For a recent treatment of essays on the chivalric romance see María Eugenia Lacarra, ed., *Evolución narrativa e ideológica de la literatura caballeresca* (Bilbao: Universidad del Pais Vasco, 1991). On the proliferation of these texts see also Daniel Eisenberg, *Romances of Chivalry in the Spanish Golden Age* (Newark, DE: Juan de la Cuesta, 1982), and Harry Sieber, "The Romance of Chivalry in Spain," in *Romance: Generic Transformation from Chrétien de Troyes to Cervantes*, ed. Kevin Brownlee and Marina S. Brownlee (Hanover, NH: University Press of New England, 1985), 203–19.

  The number cited by Thomas for the flourishing Castilian romance industry does not include the Morisco tradition (romances written by Moors converted to Christianity). Among the surviving works are an *Historia de los amores de Paris y Viana* as well as a few *aljamiado* texts, that is, works written in Spanish with Arabic characters. Extant texts of this type are from the sixteenth century and include an *aljamiado* Alexander, as well as a collection of narratives centering around important Islamic battles recast as romances. In this regard see Alvaro Galmés de Fuentes, *El libro de las batallas (narraciones caballerescas aljamiado-moriscas)* (University of Oviedo Press, 1967).

19 R. Putnam and H. I. Priestly, "California: The Name," in *University of California Publications in History*, 4 (1917), 293–365, and María Rosa Lida, "Para la toponimia argentina: Patagonia," *Hispanic Review*, 20 (1952), 321–23.

20 See Alban K. Forcione, *Cervantes, Aristotle, and the "Persiles"* (Princeton University Press, 1970), and Amy R. Williamsen, *Co(s)mic Chaos: Exploring "Los trabajos de Persiles y Sigismunda"* (Newark, DE: Juan de la Cuesta, 1994).

21 For an insightful study of romance and its Cervantine refashioning see Edwin Williamson, *The Half-Way House of Fiction: Don Quijote and Arthurian Romance* (Oxford: Clarendon Press, 1984).

SUGGESTIONS FOR FURTHER READING

Bloch, R. Howard. *Etymologies and Genealogies: A Literary Anthropology of the French Middle Ages*. University of Chicago Press, 1983.

Boase, Roger. *The Troubadour Revival: A Study of Social Change and Traditionalism in Late Medieval Spain*. London: Routledge and Kegan Paul, 1978.

Brownlee, Marina S. and Hans Ulrich Gumbrecht, eds., *Cultural Authority in Golden Age Spain*. Baltimore: Johns Hopkins University Press, 1995.

Brownlee, Marina S., Kevin Brownlee and Stephen G. Nichols, eds. *The New Medievalism*. Baltimore: Johns Hopkins University Press, 1991.

Grieve, Patricia E. *Floire and Blancheflor and the European Romance*. Cambridge University Press, 1997.

Hilgarth, J. N. *The Spanish Kingdoms, 1250–1516*. 2 vols. Oxford: Clarendon Press, 1976–78.

Lees, Clare, ed. *Medieval Masculinities: Regarding Men in the Middle Ages*. Minneapolis: University of Minnesota Press, 1994.

Linehan, Peter. *History and the Historians of Medieval Spain*. Oxford: Clarendon Press, 1993.

Mirrer, Louise. *Women, Jews and Muslims in the Texts of Reconquest Castile*. Ann Arbor: University of Michigan Press, 1996.

Netanyahu, Benzion. *The Origins of the Inquisition in Fifteenth-Century Spain*. New York: Random House, 1995.

Smith, Paul Julian. *Writing in the Margin: Spanish Literature of the Golden Age*. Oxford: Clarendon Press, 1988.

EDITIONS AND TRANSLATIONS

This bibliography provides editions of romances cited. For some works, we have listed several editions, which are based on different manuscripts or editorial policies, or which offer additional critical apparati. Selected translations in English or a modern language are noted. ** indicates an edition with the original text and facing-page translation; * indicates that the romance appears only in modern translation.

ATB = Altdeutsche Textbibliothek
CFMA = Classiques français du moyen âge
DTM = Deutsche Texte des Mittelalters
EETS = Early English Text Society
GAG = Göppinger Arbeiten zur Germanistik
SATF = Société des Anciens Textes Français
TEAMS = Consortium for the Teaching of the Middle Ages
TLF = Textes Littéraires Français

MEDIEVAL FRENCH ROMANCES (INCLUDING ANGLO-NORMAN AND OCCITAN)

Adenet le Roi. *Cleomadés*. In *Les Œuvres d'Adenet le Roi*. Ed. Albert Henry. Vol. 5. Brussels: Editions de l'Université de Bruxelles, 1971.

Aimon de Varennes. *Florimont*. Ed. Alfons Hilka. GRL 48. Göttingen: Niemeyer, 1932.

** Alexandre de Paris. *Le Roman d'Alexandre*. Ed. and trans. Laurence Harf-Lancner. Lettres gothiques. Paris: Livre de Poche, 1994.

Benoît de Sainte-Maure. *Le Roman de Troie*. Ed. Léopold Constans. SATF. 6 vols. Paris: Firmin-Didot, 1904–12; *Le Roman de Troie*. Trans. Emmanuèle Baumgartner. Paris: Union Générale d'Editions, 1987.

Béroul. *Le Roman de Tristan: poème du XIIe siècle*. Ed. Ernest Muret (4th ed. L. M. Defourques). CFMA. Paris: Champion, 1970; ** In *Tristan et Iseut. Les poèmes français, la saga norroise*. Ed. and trans. Daniel Lacroix and Philippe Walter. Lettres gothiques. Paris: Livre de Poche, 1989. Pp. 24–227. ** In *Early French Tristan Poems*. Ed. and trans. Norris J. Lacy. 2 vols. Cambridge: Brower, 1998. I, 3–216.

Le Chevalier aux deux epées. Ed. Wendelin Förster. Halle: Niemeyer, 1877; reprinted, Amsterdam: Rodopoi, 1966; * *The Knight of the Two Swords: A Thirteenth-Century Arthurian Romance*. Trans. Ross G. Arthur and Noel L. Corbett. Gainesville: University of Florida Press, 1996.

Chrétien de Troyes. ** *Œuvres complètes*. Ed. Daniel Poirion. Bibliothèque de la Pléiade. Paris: Gallimard, 1994; ** *Romans*. Ed. Michel Zink. La Pochothèque Classiques Modernes. Paris: Livre de Poche, 1994; * *The Complete Romances of Chrétien de Troyes*. Trans. David Staines. Bloomington: Indiana University Press, 1990; * *Chrétien de Troyes. Arthurian Romances*. Trans. D. D. R. Owen. London: Dent, 1987; * *Arthurian Romances*. Trans. William W. Kibler. (*Erec and Enide* trans. Carleton Carroll.) New York: Penguin, 1991.

Le Chevalier de la Charrete. Ed. Mario Roques. CFMA. Paris: Champion, 1963; ***Le Chevalier de la Charrette, ou, Le Roman de Lancelot*. Ed. and trans. Charles Méla. Lettres gothiques. Paris: Livre de Poche, 1992; * *Lancelot or the Knight of the Cart*. Ed. and trans. William W. Kibler. New York: Garland, 1984. *Le Chevalier de la Charrette, Lancelot*. Ed. Alfred Foulet and Karl D. Uitti. Paris: Bordas, 1989.

Cligés, Ed. Alexandre Micha. CFMA. Paris: Champion, 1957; ** *Cligés*. Ed. and trans. Charles Méla, Olivier Collet and Marie-Claire Gérard-Zai. Lettres gothiques. Paris: Livre de Poche, 1994.

Erec et Enide. Ed. Mario Roques. CFMA. Paris: Champion, 1952;** *Erec et Enide*. Ed. and trans. Jean-Marie Fritz. Lettres gothiques. Paris: Livre de Poche, 1992; * *Erec et Enide*. Ed. and trans. Carleton W. Carroll. New York: Garland, 1987; * *Erec and Enide*. Trans. Burton Raffel. New Haven: Yale University Press, 1997.

Le Roman de Perceval ou le Conte du Graal. Ed. William Roach. TLF. Geneva: Droz, 1959; *Le roman de Perceval, ou, Le conte du Graal*. Ed. Keith Busby. Tübingen: M. Niemeyer, 1993; ** *Le Conte du Graal ou le Roman de Perceval*. Ed. and trans. Charles Méla. Lettres gothiques. Paris: Livre de Poche, 1990; ** *The Story of the Grail (Li Contes del Graal) or Perceval*. Ed. Rupert Pickens and trans. William Kibler. New York: Garland, 1990.

Yvain. Ed. Mario Roques. CFMA. Paris: Champion, 1960. *Yvain*. Ed. T. B. W. Reid and Wendelin Foerster. Manchester University Press, 1942; ** *Le Chevalier au lion, ou, Le Roman d'Yvain*. Ed. and trans. David F. Hult. Lettres gothiques. Paris: Livre de Poche, 1994.

Chrétien de Troyes (?). *Guillaume d'Angleterre*. Ed. A. J. Holden. Textes littéraires français, 360. Geneva: Droz, 1988; * *Guillaume d'Angleterre*. Trad. Jean Trotin. Paris: Champion, 1974.

Le Conte de Floire et Blancheflor. Ed. Jean Luc Leclanche. Paris: Champion, 1983. * *Le Conte de Floire et Blancheflour: roman pré-courtois du milieu du XIIᵉ siècle*. Trans. Jean-Luc Leclanche. Paris: Champion, 1986

The Continuations of the Old French "Perceval" of Chrétien de Troyes. Ed. William Roach. 5 vols. Philadelphia: University of Pennsylvania Press, 1949–83.

Eneas: roman du XIIe siècle. Ed. J.-J. Salverda de Grave. 2 vols. CFMA 44, 62. Paris: Champion, 1964, 1968 (1929, rept. 1973); * *Eneas: A Twelfth-Century French Romance*. Trans. John A. Yunck. New York: Columbia University Press, 1974.

Les enfances Gauvain. Ed. P. Meyer. *Romania*, 39 (1910), 1–32.

** *Flamenca: Roman occitan du XIIIᵉ siècle*. Ed. Jean-Charles Huchet. Paris: Union générale d'éditions, 1988.

Floire et Blancheflor. Ed. Margaret M. Pelan. Publications de la Faculté des lettres de l'Université de Strasbourg, Textes d'étude 7. Paris: Les Belles Lettres, 1956.

Galeran de Bretagne. (attrib. Jean Renart?) Ed. Lucien Foulet. Paris: Champion, 1975; * *Galeran de Bretagne*. (attrib. Renaut ?). Trans. Jean Dufournet. Paris: Champion, 1996.

Gautier d'Arras. *Eracle*. Ed. Guy Raymaud de Lage. CFMA. Paris: Champion, 1976.
  Ille et Galeron. Ed. Frederick A. G. Cowper. SATF. Paris: A. & J. Picard, 1956.
Gerbert de Montreuil. *La Continuation de Perceval*. Ed. Mary R. Williams. Volumes 1
  and 2. Paris: Champion, 1922, 1925. Ed. Marguerite Oswald. Vol. 3. Paris:
  Champion, 1975.
  Le Roman de la violette ou de Gerart de Nevers. Ed. Douglas Labaree Buffum. SATF.
  Paris: Champion, 1928.
Girart d'Amiens. *Der Roman von "Escanor" von Gerard von Amiens*. Ed. H. Michelant.
  Tübingen: H. Laupp, 1886.
Gliglois, A French Arthurian Romance of the Thirteenth Century. Ed. Charles H.
  Livingston and Wendelin Foerster. Cambridge, MA: Harvard University Press, 1932.
Guillaume de Lorris and Jean de Meun. *Roman de la rose*. Ed. Félix Lecoy. 3 vols. CFMA
  92, 95, 98. Paris: Champion, 1968, 1966, 1970; ** *Le Roman de la Rose*. Ed. and trans.
  Michel Zink. Lettres gothiques. Paris: Livre do poche, 1992. * *The Romance of
  the Rose*. Ed. Charles W. Dunn and trans. Harry W. Robbins. New York: Dutton,
  1962.
Le Haut Livre du Graal: Perlesvaus. Ed. William A. Nitze and Thomas A. Jenkins. 2 vols.
  University of Chicago Press, 1932–37; * *The High Book of the Grail. A Translation
  of the Thirteenth-Century Romance of Perlesvaus*. Trans. Nigel Bryant. Cambridge:
  Brewer, 1978.
Heldris de Cornuälle. *Le Roman de Silence: A Thirteenth-Century Arthurian Verse-
  Romance*. Ed. Lewis Thorpe. Cambridge: Heffer, 1972; ** *Silence: A Thirteenth-
  century French Romance*. Ed. and trans. Sarah Roche-Mahdi. East Lansing:
  Colleagues Press, 1992; * *Le Roman de Silence*. Trans. Regina Psaki. New York:
  Garland, 1991.
Hue de Rotelande. *Ipomedon: poème de Hue de Rotelande (fin du XIIᵉ siècle)*. Ed. A. J.
  Holden. Paris: Klincksieck, 1979.
  Protheselaus. Ed. A. J. Holden. 2 vols. London: Anglo-Norman Text Society, 1991.
Jakemés. *Le Roman du castelain de Couci et de la dame de Fayel*. Ed. Maurice Delbouille
  and John E. Matzke. SATF. Paris: Firmin Didot, 1936; * *Le livre des amours du chas-
  tellain de Coucy et de la dame de Fayel*. Trans. Aimé Petit and François Suard. Lille:
  Presses de l'Université de Lille, 1994.
Jean d'Arras. *Mélusine, roman du XIVe siècle*. Ed. Louis Stouff. Dijon: Bernigaud et
  Privat, 1932. Rpt. 1968; * *Le Roman de Mélusine, ou l'histoire des Lusignan*. Trans.
  Michèle Perret. Paris: Stock, 1979.
Jean Renart. *L'Escoufle: Roman d'aventure*. Ed. Franklin P. Sweetser. Geneva: Droz, 1974;
  * *L'Escoufle: roman d'aventures*. Trans. Alexandre Micha. Paris: Champion, 1992.
  Le Roman de la rose ou de Guillaume de Dole. Ed. Félix Lecoy. CFMA 91. Paris:
  Champion, 1979; * *The Romance of the Rose, or, Guillaume de Dole*. Trans. Patricia
  Terry and Nancy Vine Durling. Philadelphia: University of Pennsylvania Press, 1993.
Joufroi de Poitiers. Roman d'aventures du XIIIe siècle. Ed. Percival B. Fay and John L.
  Grigsby. TLF. Geneva: Droz, 1972.
Lancelot: Roman en prose du XIIIe siècle. Ed. Alexandre Micha. 9 vols. Geneva: Droz,
  1978–83; * *Lancelot-Grail: The Old French Arthurian Vulgate and Post-Vulgate in
  Translation*. Ed. Norris J. Lacy. 5 vols. New York: Garland, 1993–96.
Lancelot do Lac: The Non-Cyclic Old French Prose Romance. Ed. Elspeth Kennedy. 2
  vols. Oxford: Clarendon Press, 1980; * *Lancelot of the Lake*. Trans. Corin F. W.
  Corley. Oxford University Press, 1989.

"Mantel" et "Cor": deux lais du XIIe siècle. Ed. Philip E. Bennett. University of Exeter Press, 1975.

Marie de France. *Les Lais de Marie de France.* Ed. Jean Rychner. CFMA 93. Paris: Champion, 1969; ** *Lais de Marie de France.* Ed. Karl Warnke. Trans. Laurence Harf-Lancner. Lettres gothiques. Paris: Livre de Poche, 1990; *Le Lai de Lanval.* Ed. Jean Rychner. Textes littéraires français, 77. Geneva: Droz, 1958; * *The Lais of Marie de France.* Trans. Glyn S. Burgess and Keith Busby. Harmondsworth: Penguin Books, 1986; * *The Lais of Marie de France.* Trans. Robert Hanning and Joan Ferrante. New York: Dutton, 1978.

Merlin: Roman en prose du XIIIe siècle. Ed. Gaston Paris and Jacob Ulrich. 2 vols. Paris: Firmin Didot, 1886.

La Mort le Roi Artu: roman du XIIIe siècle. Ed. Jean Frappier. Paris: Droz, 1936; 3rd ed. 1959; * *The Death of King Arthur.* Trans. James Cable. New York: Penguin, 1971.

La Mule sans Frein. In *Two Old French Gauvain Romances.* Ed. R. C. Johnston and D. D. R. Owen. Edinburgh and London: Scottish Academic Press, 1972.

Partonopeu de Blois: A French Romance of the Twelfth Century. Ed. Joseph Gildea, O.S.A. 2 vols. Villanova University Press, 1967–70.

La Queste del Saint Graal: roman du XIIIe siècle. Ed. Albert Pauphilet. Paris: Champion, 1923; *The Quest of the Holy Grail.* Trans. Pauline Matarasso. Harmondsworth: Penguin, 1969. * *The Quest for the Holy Grail.* Trans. E. Jane Burns. In *Lancelot-Grail. The Old French Arthurian Vulgate and Post-Vulgate in Translation.* Ed. Norris J. Lacy. 5 vols. Vol. 4 New York: Garland, 1995.

Robert Biket. *The Anglo-Norman Text of "Le Lai du Cor".* Ed. C. T. Erickson. Anglo-Norman Text Society 24. Oxford: Basil Blackwell for the Anglo-Norman Text Society, 1973; * *The Lay of the Horn.* In *Tales from the Old French.* Trans. Isabel Butler. Boston and New York: Houghton Mifflin, 1910. Pp. 92–107. Rpt. in *Arthur, King of Britain: History, Chronicle, Romance, and Criticism.* Ed. Richard L. Brengle. New York: Appleton-Century-Crofts, 1964. Pp. 103–9.

Raoul de Houdenc. *Meraugis de Portlesguez.* In *Raoul de Houdenc: Sämtliche Werke,* I. Ed. Mathias Friedwagner. Halle: Niemeyer, 1897.

   La Vengeance Raguidel. Sämtliche Werke, II. Halle: Max Niemeyer, 1909.

Renaud de Beaujeu. *Le Bel Inconnu: roman d'aventures.* Ed. G. Perrie Williams. CFMA 38. Paris: Champion, 1967; * *Le Bel inconnu: roman d'aventures du XIIIe siècle.* Trans. Michèle Perret and Isabelle Weil. Paris: Champion, 1991.

Le roman de Perceforest. Ed. Gilles Roussineau and Jane Taylor. TLF. Geneva: Droz, 1979, 1987–88, 1991, 1993.

Le Roman des sept sages de Rome: A Critical Edition of Two Verse Redactions of a Twelfth-century Romance. Ed. Mary B. Speer. Lexington, KY: French Forum, 1989.

Le Roman de Thèbes. Ed. Guy Raynaud de Lage. 2 vols. Paris: Champion, 1966, 1968; ** *Le Roman de Thèbes.* Ed. and trans. Francine Mora-Lebrun. Lettres gothiques. Paris: Livre de Poche, 1995; *Le Roman de Thèbes (The Story of Thebes).* Trans. John Smartt Coley. New York: Garland, 1986.

Le Roman de Tristan en prose. Ed. Philippe Ménard, *et al.* 8 vols. to date. Geneva: Droz, 1987– . * *The Romance of Tristan: The Thirteenth-Century Old French "Prose Tristan".* Trans. Renée Curtis. Oxford University Press, 1994.

The Romance of Hunbaut: An Arthurian poem of the thirteenth century. Ed. Margaret Winters. Leiden: E. J. Brill, 1984.

Thomas d'Angleterre. *Les Fragments du roman de Tristan: poème du XIIe siècle*. Ed. Bartina H. Wind. Textes Littéraires Français 92. Geneva: Droz, 1960; ** In *Tristan et Iseut. Les poèmes français, la saga norroise*. Ed. Daniel Lacroix and Philippe Walter. Lettres gothiques 452. Paris: Livre de Poche, 1989. Pp. 330–481. * *Thomas's Tristran*. Ed. and trans. Stewart Gregory. In *Early French Tristan Poems*. Ed. Norris J. Lacy. 2 vols. Cambridge: D. S. Brewer, 1988. II, 1–172.

Thomas of Kent. *The Anglo-Norman Alexander (Le Roman de toute chevalerie)*. Ed. Brian Foster and Ian Short. 2 vols. London: Anglo-Norman Text Society, 1976–77.

** *Les Troubadours: Jaufre, Flamenca, Barlaam et Josaphat*. Ed. and trans. René Lavaud and René Nelli. Bibliothèque Européenne. Paris: Desclée de Brouwer, 1960.

Two Old French Gauvain Romances: "Le Chevalier à l'epée" and "La Mule sans frein". Ed. R. C. Johnston and D. D. R. Owen. Edinburgh and London: Scottish Academic Press, 1972.

La Version post-Vulgate de la Queste del Saint Graal et de la mort Artu: troisième partie du Roman du Graal. Ed. Fanni Bogdanow. 4 vols. Paris: SATF, 1991. * *The Post-Vulgate, parts I–III*. Trans. Martha Asher. In *The Old French Arthurian Vulgate and Post-Vulgate in Translation*. Ed. Norris J. Lacy. 5 vols. Vol. 5 New York: Garland, 1996.

The Vulgate Version of the Arthurian Romances. Ed. H. Oskar Sommer. 7 vols. Washington: Carnegie Institution of Washington. 1909–16.

Wace. *Le Roman de Brut*. Ed. I. Arnold. 2 vols. Paris: SATF, 1938–40; *La Partie arthurienne du roman de Brut*. Ed. I. Arnold and M. M. Pelan. Bibliothèque française et romane. Série B: Textes et documents, I. Paris: C. Klincksieck, 1962.

MIDDLE ENGLISH ROMANCES

Amis and Amiloun. Ed. M. Leach, EETS os 203. London: H. Milford, 1937; In *Of Love and Chivalry*; Ed. Françoise Le Saux. Exeter: University of Exeter Press, 1993; In *Amis and Amiloun, Robert of Cisyle and Sir Amadace*. Ed. Edward E. Foster. TEAMS Middle English Texts. Kalamazoo, MI: Medieval Institute Publications, 1997.

Of Arthour and of Merlin. Ed. O. D. Macrae-Gibson. EETS 268, 279. Oxford University Press, 1973, 1979.

Athelston. In *Middle English Metrical Romances*; Ed. A. McI. Trounce, EETS os 224 Oxford University Press, 1951; In *Medieval English Romances*, eds. Schmidt and Jacobs; In *Four Romances of England*.

The Avowyng of Arthur. In *Sir Gawain: Eleven Romances and Tales*.

The Awntyrs of Arthur. In *Sir Gawain: Eleven Romances and Tales*.

The Breton Lays in Middle English. Ed. T. C. Rumble. Detroit: Wayne State University Press, 1965.

The Carle of Carlisle. In *Sir Gawain: Eleven Romances and Tales*.

Chaucer, Geoffrey. *The Riverside Chaucer*. Ed. Larry D. Benson. Boston: Houghton Mifflin, 1987.

The Canterbury Tales. In *The Works of Geoffrey Chaucer*. Ed. F. N. Robinson. 2nd ed. Boston: Houghton Mifflin, 1957; * *The Canterbury Tales*. Trans. Nevill Coghill. London: Penguin Books, 1975.

Troilus and Criseyde. Ed. B. A. Windeatt. London: Longman, 1984.

Chevelere Assigne, Ed. Henry H. Gibbs EETS es 6. London: N. Trübner, 1868; In *Medieval English Romances*, ed. Speed.

Emaré. Ed. Edith Rickert. EETS es 99. Oxford University Press, 1908; In *Middle English Metrical Romances*; In *Six Middle English Romances*.

Floris and Blancheflour: A Middle English Romance. Ed. Albert B. Taylor. Oxford: Clarendon Press, 1927; In *Of Love and Chivalry*.

Four Middle English Romances. Ed. Harriet Hudson. TEAMS Middle English Texts. Kalamazoo, MI: Medieval Institute Publications, 1996.

Four Romances of England: King Horn, Havelock the Dane, Bevis of Hampton, Athelston. Ed. Ronald B. Herzman, Graham Drake, and Eve Salisbury. TEAMS Middle English Texts. Kalamazoo, MI: Medieval Institute Publications, 1999.

Gamelyn. The Tale of Gamelyn. Ed. W. W. Skeat. Oxford: Clarendon Press, 1884; In *Middle English Metrical Romances*; In *Middle English Verse Romances*.

Gologras and Gawain. In *Sir Gawain: Eleven Romances and Tales*.

The Green Knight. In *Sir Gawain: Eleven Romances and Tales*.

Guy of Warwick. Ed. Julius Zupitza, EETS es 42, 49, 59. London: N. Trübner, 1883, 1887, 1891; *The Romance of Guy of Warwick, the second, or fifteenth-century version*, ed. Julius Zupitza, EETS es 25–26. London: N. Trübner, 1875–76; Ed. William Burton Todd. Austin: University of Texas Press, 1968.

Havelok. Ed. W. W. Skeat. 2nd ed. Oxford: Clarendon Press, 1915; rev. K. Sisam. Oxford, 1956; In *Middle English Metrical Romances*; In *Middle English Verse Romances*; Ed. G. V. Smithers. Oxford: Clarendon Press, 1987; In *Medieval English Romances*, ed. Speed; In *Four Romances of England*.

Horn Child and the Maiden Rymnild. In *King Horn: A Middle-English Romance*. Ed. J. Hall Oxford: Clarendon Press, 1901.

The Jeaste of Sir Gawain. In *Sir Gawain: Eleven Romances and Tales*.

King Arthur and King Cornwall. In *Sir Gawain: Eleven Romances and Tales*.

King Arthur's Death: The Middle English Stanzaic "Morte Arthur" and the Alliterative "Morte Arthure." Ed. Larry D. Benson, revised by Edward E. Foster. TEAMS Middle English Texts. Kalamazoo, MI: Medieval Institute Publications, 1994.

King Horn. In *Middle English Verse Romances*; In *Of Love and Chivalry*; In *Four Middle English Romances*; In *Four Romances of England*.

King Ponthus and the Fair Sidone. Ed. F. J. Mather. *PMLA*, 12 (1897), 1–150.

Lai le Freine. The Middle English Lai le Freine. Ed. Margaret Wattie. Smith College Studies in Modern Languages 10.3. Northampton, MA: n.p., 1929; In *The Breton Lays in Middle English*; In *Middle English Verse Romances*; In *The Middle English Breton Lays*.

Layamon. *Brut*. Ed. G. L. Brook and R. F. Leslie. EETS 250, 277. Oxford University Press, 1963, 1978; ** *Brut, or, Hystoria Brutonum*. Ed. and trans. W. R. J. Barron and S. C. Weinberg. Harlow: Longman, 1995.

Le Bone Florence of Rome. Ed. C. F. Heffernan. Manchester University Press, 1976.

Lybeaus Desconus. Ed. M. Mills. EETS 261. Oxford University Press, 1969.

Malory, Sir Thomas. *Morte Darthur*. In *The Works of Sir Thomas Malory*, Ed. Eugene Vinaver. 3rd ed. revised by P. J. C. Field. 3 vols. Oxford University Press, 1990; *Le Morte dArthur*. Ed. R. M. Lumiansky. New York: Macmillan, 1982.

The Marriage of Sir Gawain. In *Sir Gawain: Eleven Romance and Tales*.

Medieval English Romances. Ed. A. V. C. Schmidt and N. Jacobs. 2 vols. Oxford University Press, 1980.

Medieval English Romances. Ed. Diane Speed. Durham Medieval Texts 8. 2 vols. New Elvet: Durham, Medieval Texts, 1993.

The Middle English Breton Lays. Ed. Anne Laskaya and Eve Salisbury. TEAMS Middle English Texts. Kalamazoo, MI: Medieval Institute Publications, 1995.

Middle English Metrical Romances. Ed. W. H. French and C. B. Hale. New York: Prentice Hall, 1930.

Middle English Verse Romances. Ed. Donald B. Sands. New York and London: Holt, Rhinehart, and Winston, 1966.

Morte Arthur [stanzaic]. In *King Arthur's Death*; Ed. J. D. Bruce, EETS es 88. London: Kegan Paul, Trench, Trübner and Co., 1903; *Le Morte Arthur: A Critical Edition*. Ed. P. F. Hissiger. The Hague: Mouton, 1975.

Morte Arthure [alliterative]. In *King Arthur's Death;* Ed. George G. Perry, EETS es 8. London: Trübner, 1871; rpt. 1904 Ed. Edmund Brock; Ed. E. Björkman. Heidelberg: C. Winter, 1915; Ed. Mary Hamel. New York: Garland, 1984.

Octavian. Ed. Frances McSparran. Middle English Texts 11. Heidelberg: C. Winter, 1979; *Six Middle English Romances*; In *Four Middle English Romances*.

Of Love and Chivalry. An Anthology of Middle English Romance. Ed. Jennifer Fellows. London and Rutland, VT: Dent; Charles E. Tuttle, 1993.

** *On Not Taking a Wife. Gawain on Marriage*. Ed. and trans. A. G. Rigg. Toronto: Pontifical Institute of Medieval Studies, 1986.

** *The Rise of Gawain, Nephew of Arthur: De ortu Waluuanii nepotis Arthuri*. Ed. and trans. Mildred Leake Day. New York: Garland, 1984.

Sir Amadace. In *Six Middle English Romances*; In *Amis and Amiloun, Robert of Cisyle and Sir Amadace*, ed. Foster.

Sir Degaré. Sire Degarre. Ed. Gustav Schleich. Heidleberg: C. Winter, 1929; In *Middle English Metrical Romances*; In *Medieval English Romances*, ed. Schmidt and Jacobs; in *The Middle English Breton Lays*.

Sir Gawain: Eleven Romances and Tales. Ed. Thomas Hahn. TEAMS Middle English Texts. Kalamazoo, MI: Medieval Institute Publications, Western Michigan University, 1995.

Sir Gawain and the Green Knight. Ed. J. R. R. Tolkien and E. V. Gordon. 2nd ed., ed. Norman Davis. Oxford: Clarendon Press, 1967; *"Sir Gawain and the Green Knight," "Pearl," and "Sir Orfeo"*. Trans. J. R. R. Tolkien. 1975; rpt. New York: Ballantine, 1980; *Sir Gawain and the Green Knight*. Trans. Marie Borroff. New York: Norton, 1967.

Sir Gawain and the Carle of Carlisle. In *Sir Gawain: Eleven Romances and Tales*.

Sir Isumbras. In *Six Middle English Romances*. In *Four Middle English Romances*.

Sir Orfeo. Ed. A. J. Bliss. 2nd ed. Oxford: Clarendon Press, 1966; In *Middle English Metrical Romances*; In *Middle English Verse Romances*; In *Medieval English Romances*, ed. Schmidt and Jacobs; In *Medieval English Romances*, ed. Speed; in *The Middle English Breton Lays*. * *"Sir Gawain and the Green Knight," "Pearl," and "Sir Orfeo"*. Trans J. R. R. Tolkien. 1975; rpt. New York: Ballantine, 1980.

Sir Percyvell of Gales. In *Middle English Metrical Romances*; In *Ywain and Gawain, Sir Percyvell of Gales, The Anturs of Arthur*. Ed. Maldwyn Mills. London: J. M. Dent, 1992; In *Sir Perceval of Galles and Ywain and Gawain*. Ed. Mary Flowers Braswell. TEAMS Middle English Texts. Kalamazoo, MI: Medieval Institute Publications, 1995.

Sir Tristrem. Ed. George P. McNeill. Scottish Text Society 8. Edinburgh: W. Blackwood,

1886; In *Lancelot of the Laik and Sir Tristrem*. Ed. Alan Lupack. TEAMS Middle English Texts. Kalamazoo, MI: Medieval Institute Publications, 1994.

Six Middle English Romances. Ed. Maldwyn Mills. London: Dent, 1973.

Torrent of Portyngale. Ed. Erich Adam. EETS es 51. London: N. Trübner, 1887. Rpt. Millwood, NY: Kraus Reprint, 1981.

The Turke and Sir Gawain. In *Sir Gawain: Eleven Romances and Tales*.

The Wedding of Sir Gawain and Dame Ragnelle. In *Sir Gawain: Eleven Romances and Tales*.

William of Palerne. *The Romance of William of Palerne (otherwise known as the romance of "William and the Werewolf")*. Ed. Walter W. Skeat, EETS es 1. London: N. Trübner, 1867; *William of Palerne: A New Edition*. Ed. Norman Toby Simms Philadelphia: R. West, 1976; *William of Palerne: An Alliterative Romance*. Ed. G. H. V. Bunt. Mediaevalia Groningana 6. Groningen: Bouma's Boekhuis, 1985.

Ywain and Gawain. Ed. Albert B. Friedman and Norman T. Harrington. EETS 254. Oxford University Press, 1964.

MEDIEVAL GERMAN ROMANCES

Albrecht von Scharfenberg. *Albrechts von Schafenberg Jüngerer Titurel*. Ed. Werner Wolf and Kurt Nyholm. 6 vols. DTM 45, 55, 61, 73, 77, and 79. Berlin: Akademie Verlag, 1955–95.

Arthurian Legends or the Hebrew-German Rhymed Version of the Legend of King Arthur. Ed. Leo Landau. Teutonia 21. Leipzig: E. Avenarius, 1912.

Die Beichte einer Frau. In *Liederbuch der Clara Hätzlerin*. Ed. Karl Haltaus. Leipzig: G. Basse, 1840. Rpt. Berlin: de Gruyter, 1966. 115–22; In *Mittelhochdeutsche Minnereden*, DTM 24, 41. Berlin: Weidmann, 1913 and 1938. Rpt. as 2 vols. in 1. Dublin: Weidmann, 1967. Vol. 2, 33–42.

Eilhart von Oberg. *Tristrant und Isalde*. Ed. Danielle Buschinger and Wolfgang Spiewok. GAG 436. Göppingen: Kümmerle, 1986; *Tristrant: Synoptischer Druck der ergänzten Fragmente mit der gesamten Parallelüberlieferung*. Ed. Hadumod Bussmann. ATB 70. Tübingen: Niemeyer, 1969; * *Tristrant*. Trans. J. W. Thomas. Lincoln, NB: University of Nebraska Press, 1978.

Gottfried von Strassburg. *Tristan und Isold*. Ed. Friedrich Ranke. 11th ed. Dublin: Weidmann, 1967; *Tristan*. Ed. Karl Marold. Part One: Text. Teutonia 6. Leipzig: E. Avenarius, 1912; ** *Tristan*. Ed. and trans. Friedrich Ranke and Rüdiger Krohn. 3 vols. Stuttgart: Reclam., 1984–85; ** *Tristan*. Ed. Gottfried Weber. Darmstadt: Wissenschaftliche Buchgesellschaft, 1983; * *Tristan*. Trans. A. T. Hatto. Harmondsworth: Penguin Books, 1960; Trans. A. T. Hatto. Ed. and rev. Francis G. Gentry. The German Library Continuum, New York: 1988.

Hartmann von Aue. *Erec*. Ed. Albert Leitzmann. 6th ed. Ed. Christoph Cormeau and Kurt Gärtner. ATB 39. Tübingen: Niemeyer, 1985; * *Erec*. Trans. Michael Resler. Philadelphia: University of Pennsylvania Press, 1987.

Gregorius. Ed. Hermann Paul. 14th ed. Burghart Wachinger. ATB 2. Tübingen: Niemeyer, 1992; * *Gregorius: The Good Sinner*. Trans. Sheema Zeben Buehne. New York: F. Ungar, 1966.

Der arme Heinrich. Ed. Hermann Paul. 16th ed. Kurt Gärtner. ATB 3. Tübingen: Niemeyer, 1996; * *The Unfortunate Lord Henry*. Trans. Frank Tobin. In *German*

Medieval Tales. Ed. Francis G. Gentry. The German Library 4. New York: Continuum, 1983. Pp. 1–21.

Iwein. Ed. Karl Lachmann and Georg F. Benecke. 7th ed. Ed. Ludwig Wolff. 2 vols. Berlin: de Gruyter, 1968; ** *Iwein*. Ed. and trans. Patrick M. McConeghy. New York: Garland, 1984; * *Iwein*. Trans. J. W. Thomas. Lincoln, NB: University of Nebraska Press, 1979.

Heinrich von dem Türlin. *Das Ambraser Mantel-Fragment*. Ed. Werner Schröder. Sitzungsberichte der Wissenschaftlichen Gesellschaft an der Johann Wolfgang Goethe Universität Frankfurt am Main 33, nr. 5. Stuttgart: F. Steiner, 1995.

Diu Crône von Heinrich von dem Türlin zum ersten male. Ed. Gottlob Heinrich Friedrich Scholl. Bibliothek des Litterarischen Vereins in Stuttgart 27. Stuttgart: Litterarischer Verein, 1852. Rpt. Amsterdam: Rodopi, 1966; * *The Crown: A Tale of Sir Gawein and King Arthur's Court*. Trans. J. W. Thomas. Lincoln, NB: University of Nebraska Press, 1989; ** *Herstellungsversuche an dem Text der Crône Heinrichs von dem Türlin*. 2 vols. Ed. and trans. Werner Schröder. Akademie der Wisserschaften und der Literatur. Abhandlungen der Geistes- und Sozialwissenschaftlichen Klasse, Jahrgang 1996, 2 vols. 2, 4. Stuttgart: Steiner, 1996.

Heinrich von Freiberg. *Tristan*. Ed. Danielle Buschinger. Göppinger Arbeiten zur Germanistik 270. Göppingen: Kümmerle Verlag, 1982.

Heinrich von Veldeke. *Henric van Veldeken. Eneide*. Ed. Gabriele Schieb and Theodor Frings. 3 vols. DTM 58, 59, 62. Berlin: Akademie Verlag, 1964; ** *Eneasroman*. Ed. and trans. Dieter Kartschoke. Stuttgart: Reclam, 1986; * *Eneide*. Trans. J. W. Thomas. New York: Garland, 1985.

Johann von Würzburg. *Wilhelm von Österreich*. Ed. Ernst Regel and Karl Regel. DTM 3. Berlin: Weidmann, 1906. Rpt. Dublin: Weidmann, 1970.

Konrad Fleck. *Flore und Blanscheflur*. Ed. Emil Sommer. Bibliothek der gesammten deutschen National-Literatur 12. Leipzig: G. Basse, 1846.

Konrad von Würzburg. *Das Herzmaere*. In Konrad von Würzburg. *Kleinere Dichtungen*. Ed. Edward Schröder. 3rd ed. Vol. 1 of 3. Berlin: Weidmann, 1959; * *The Tale of the Heart*. Trans. Ernst R. Wintz. In *German Medieval Tales*. Ed. Francis G. Gentry. New York: Continuum, 1983. Pp. 118–24.

Konrads von Würzburg Partonopier und Meliur. Ed. Karl Bartsch. Vienna: W. Braumüller, 1871. Rpt. Berlin: de Gruyter, 1970.

Lancelot. Ed. Reinhold Kluge. 3 vols. DTM 42, 47, 63. Berlin: Akademie Verlag, 1948–74; ** *Prosa Lancelot*. Ed. and trans. Hans-Hugo Steinhoff and Reinhold Kluge. Frankfurt am Main: Deutscher Klassiker Verlag, 1995.

** Penninc. *Roman van Walewein*. Ed. and trans. David F. Johnson and Pieter Vostaert. New York: Garland, 1992.

Rudolf von Ems. *Willehalm von Orlens*. Ed. Viktor Junk. DTM 2. Berlin: Weidmann, 1905. Rpt. Dublin: Weidmann, 1967.

Der Stricker. *Daniel von dem blühenden Tal*. Ed. Michael Resler. 2nd ed. ATB 92. Tübingen: Niemeyer, 1995.

** *Tristan als Mönch*. Ed. Albrecht Classen. Greifswald: Reinecke Verlag, 1994.

Tristrant und Isalde. Prosaroman des fünfzehnten Jahrhunderts. Ed. Fridrich Pfaff. Bibliothek des Litterarischen Vereins in Stuttgart 152. Tübingen: Litterarischer Verein in Stuttgart, 1881; *Tristrant und Isalde: Prosaroman, Faksimileausgabe des ältesten Druckes von Augsburg aus dem Jahre 1484*. Greifswald: Reineke Verlag,

1993; *Tristan und Isold (Augsburg bei Anton Sorg, 1484)*. Ed. Helga Elsner. Deutsche Volksbücher in Faksimiledrucken, Reihe A, Bd. 16. Hildesheim: G. Olms, 1989.

Ulrich Füetrer. *Die Gralsepen in Ulrich Füetrers Bearbeitung (Buch der Abenteuer)*. Ed. Kurt Nyholm. DTM 57. Berlin: Akademie-Verlag, 1964.

Lannzilet: aus dem "Buch der Abenteuer", Str. 1–1122. Ed. Karl-Eckhard Lenk. ATB 102. Tübingen: Niemeyer, 1989; *Lannzilet: aus dem "Buch der Abenteuer", Str. 1123–6009*. Ed. Rudolf Voss. Paderborn: Schöningh, 1996.

Ulrich von Lichtenstein. *Frauendienst*. Ed. Reinhold Bechstein. Leipzig: F. A. Brockhaus, 1888; *Frauendienst*. Ed. Franz Viktor Spechtler. GAG 485. Göppingen: Kümmerle, 1987; * *Service of Ladies*. Trans. J. W. Thomas. University of North Carolina Studies in the Germanic Languages and Literatures 63. Chapel Hill, NC: University of North Carolina Press, 1969.

Ulrich von Türheim. *Cliges: Ausgabe der bisher bekannten Fragmente vermehrt um den Neufund aus St. Paul im Lavanttal*. Ed. Hans Gröchenig and Hans-Peter Pascher. Klagenfurt: Verlag Armarium, 1984.

Tristan. Ed. Thomas Kerth. ATB 89. Tübingen: Niemeyer, 1979.

Ulrich von Zatzikhoven. *Lanzelet*. Ed. Karl August Hahn. Frankfurt am Main: H. L. Brönner, 1845. Rpt. Berlin: de Gruyter, 1965; ** *Lanzelet*. Ed. Wolfgang Spiewok. Greifswald: Reineke-Verlag, 1997; * *Lanzelet: A Romance of Lancelot*. Trans. Kenneth G. T. Webster and Roger Sherman Lomis. Records of Civilization: Sources and Studies 47. New York: Columbia University Press, 1951.

Widwilt. See *Arthurian Legends or the Hebrew-German Rhymed Version of the Legend of King Arthur*.

Wirnt von Grafenberg. *Wigalois, der ritter mit dem rade*. Ed. Johannes Marie Neele Kapteyn. Bonn: F. Klopp, 1926; *Wigalois*. Greifswald: Reineke-Verlag, 1996; * *Wigalois, The Knight of Fortune's Wheel*. Trans. J. W. Thomas. Lincoln, NB: University of Nebraska Press, 1977.

Wigamur. Ed. Danielle Buschinger. GAG 320. Göppingen: Kümmerle Verlag, 1987.

Wolfram von Eschenbach. *Parzival und Titurel*. Ed. Ernst Martin. 2 vols. Halle: Verlag der Buchhandlung des Waisenhauses, 1900 and 1903. Rpt. Darmstadt: Wissenschaftliche Buchgesellschaft, 1976; *Parzival*. Ed. Karl Lachmann. 6th ed. Berlin: de Gruyter, 1926. Rpt. as *Parzival. Studienausgabe*. Berlin: de Gruyter, 1965; ** *Parzival*. Ed. Eberhard Nellmann and trans. Dieter Kühn. Frankfurt am Main: Deutscher Klassiker Verlag, 1994; ** *Parzival*. Trans. Wolfgang Spiewok. 2 vols. Stuttgart: Philipp Reclam, 1994; * *Parzival: A Knightly Epic*. Trans. Jessie L. Weston. London: D. Nutt, 1894; * *Parzival*. Trans. Helen M. Mustard and Charles E. Passage. New York: Vintage Books, 1961; * *Parzival*. Trans. André Lefevere. The German Library 2. New York: Continuum, 1991.

** *Titurel*. Ed. Wolfgang Mohr. GAG 250. Göppingen: Kümmerle Verlag, 1978; * *Titurel*. Trans. Charles E. Passage. New York: F. Ungar Pub. Co., 1984; * *Titurel and Songs*. Trans. Marion E. Gibbs and Sidney M. Johnson. New York: Garland, 1988.

MEDIEVAL ITALIAN ROMANCES

Il Bel Gherardino. In *Cantari del Trecento*. Ed. Armando Balduino. Milan: Marzorati, 1970.

Cantare di Madonna Elena. Ed. Giovanni Fontana. Florence: Accademia della Crusca, 1992.

* *Cantare on the Death of Tristan*. Trans. James J. Wilhelm. In *The Romance of Arthur: An Anthology of Medieval Texts in Translation*. Ed. James J. Wilhelm. New York: Garland, 1994.

I cantari di Carduino giuntovi quello di Tristano e Lancielotto quando combattettero al petrone di Merlino. Ed. Pio Rajna. Bologna: Commissione per i Testi di Lingua, 1968.

Cantari di Tristano. Ed. Giulio Bertoni. Modena: Società Tipografica Modenese, 1937.

Li Chantari di Lancellotto. Ed. E. T. Griffiths. Oxford: The Clarendon Press, 1924.

Il libro di messer Tristan: Tristano Veneto. Ed. Aulo Donadello. Venice: Marsilio, 1994.

La Tavola Ritonda, L'istoria di Tristano. Ed. F. L. Polidori. 2 vols. Bologna: Romagnoli, 1864–5.

Il Romanzo arturiano di Rustichello da Pisa. Ed. and trans. Fabrizio Cigni. Pisa: Cassa di Risparmio di Pisa, Pacini, 1994.

Il Romanzo di Tristano. Ed. Antonio Scolari. Genova: Costa & Nolan, 1990.

* *Tristan and the Round Table: A Translation of "La Tavola ritonda"*. Trans. Anne Shaver. Binghamton, NY: Medieval and Renaissance Texts and Studies, 1983.

* *The Tristano Panciatichiano*. Ed. and trans. Gloria Allaire. New York: Garland. Forthcoming.

Tristano Riccardiano; testo critico. Ed. E. G. Parodi, rpt. by M.-J. Heijkant. Parma: Pratiche, 1991. * *The Tristano Riccardiano*. Trans. F. Regina Psaki. New York: Garland. Forthcoming.

MEDIEVAL SPANISH ROMANCES

Alfonso X. *General estoria*. Ed. Antonio G. Solalinde. Vol. 1 of 2. Madrid: Centro de Estudios Históricos, 1930. Vol. 2 of 2. Ed. Antonio G. Solalinde, Lloyd A. Kastan and Victor R. B. Oelschläger. Madrid: CSIC, 1957.

Cervants Saavedra, Miguel de. *Don Quijote de la Mancha*. 2 vols. Ed. Martín de Riquer. New York: Las Américas, Spanish Book Center, L.A. Publishing Company, 1974. * *Don Quixote of la Mancha*. Trans. J. M. Cohen. Hammondsworth: Penguin Books, 1950.

Los trabajos de Persiles y Sigismunda. Ed. Juan Bautista Avalle-Arce. Madrid: Castalia, 1969.

El Cuento de Tristán de Leonís. Ed. George T. Northrup. The University of Chicago Press, 1928.

Curial y Guelfa. Ed. Pere Gimferrer. Madrid: Alfaguara, 1982. * *Curial and Guelfa*. Trans. Pamela Waley. London: Allen & Unwin, 1982.

Díaz de Gámez, Gutierre. *The Unconquered Knight. A Chronicle of the Deeds of Don Pero Niño, Count of Buelna*. Trans. Joan Evans. London: G. Routledge, 1928.

La gran conquista de Ultramar. Ed. Louis Cooper. 4 vols. Bogotá: Instituto Caro y Cuervo, 1979.

Guillem de Toroella. *La Faula*. Mallorca: Moll, 1995.

Historia del notable y esforzado caballero, el conde Partinuples, emperador de Constantinopla. Ed. A. Bonilla y San Martín. Nueva Biblioteca de Autores Españoles 11 (1908).

Historia de los amores de París y Viana. Ed. Alvaro Galmés de Fuentes. Madrid: Gredos, 1970.

Historia de los dos enamorados Flores y Blancaflor. Ed. A. Bonilla y San Martín. Madrid: Ruiz Hermanos, 1916.

Historia troyana en prosa y verso, texto de hacia 1270. Ed. R. Menéndez Pidal and E. Varón Vallejo. Revista de Filología Española, Anejo XVIII. Madrid: S. Aguirre, 1934.

Libro de Alexandre. Ed. Jesús M. Cañas. Madrid: Cátedra, 1988.

Libro de Apolonio. Ed. Manuel Alvar. 3 vols. Madrid: Fundación Juan March, 1976.

Libro del caballero Zifar. Ed. Joaquín González Muela. Madrid: Castalia, 1982.

Libros de caballerias, con un discurso preliminar y un catalogo razonado. Ed. Pascual Gayangos. Biblioteca de Autores Españoles 40. Madrid: M. Rivadeneyra, 1974.

Martorell, Joanot. *Tirant lo Blanc: I altres escrit.* Ed. Martín de Riquer. Barcelona: Ariel, 1969. * *Tirant lo Blanc.* Trans. David Rosenthal. New York: Schocken Books, 1984.

Palmerín de Inglaterra. Ed. Adolfo Bonilla y San Martín. Madrid: Nueva Biblioteca de Autores Españoles 11 (1908).

Primaleón los tres libros del muy esforçado cauallero Primaleón et Polentos su hermano, hójos del Emperador Pallmerin de Oliua. Venecia, 1534. [Alt. title: Primaleon].

El Rrey Guillelme. Ed. John R. Maier. University of Exeter Press, 1984.

Rodríguez de la Camara, Juan. *Siervo libre de amor.* Ed. Antonio Prieto. Madrid: Castalia, 1976.

Rodríguez de Montalvo, Garci. *Amadís de Gaula.* 2 vols. Ed. Juan Manuel Cacho Blecua. Madrid: Cátedra, 1987. * *Amadís de Gaula: A Novel of Chivalry of the 14th Century Presumably First Written in Spanish.* 2 vols. Trans. Edwin B. Place and Herbert C. Behm. Lexington: University of Kentucky Press, 1974.

Rojas, Fernando de. *La Celestina; tragicomedia de Calisto y Melibea.* Ed. Dorothy Sherman Severin. Madrid: Alianza Editorial, 1969.

OTHER PRIMARY SOURCES

Ambroise. *L'Estoire de la guerre sainte, histoire en vers de la troisième croisade (1190–1192) par Ambroise.* Ed. Gaston Paris. Paris: Imprimerie National, 1897. * *The Crusade of Richard Lion-Heart.* Trans. Merton J. Hubert and John L. La Monte. New York: Columbia University Press, 1941.

Bertran de Born. *The Poems of the Troubadour Bertran de Born.* Ed. and trans. William D. Paden, Jr., Tilde Sankovitch and Patricia H. Stäblein. Berkeley: University of California Press, 1986.

** Chandos Herald. *Life of the Black Prince.* Ed. and trans. Mildred Pope and Eleanor C. Lodge. Oxford: Clarendon Press, 1910.

Christine de Pisan. *Le Livre des fais et bonnes meurs du sage roy Charles V.* Ed. S. Solente. 2 vols. Paris: Champion, 1936.

Le livre du duc des vrais amants. Ed. Thelma S. Fenster. Binghamton, NY: Medieval and Renaissance Texts and Studies, 1995; * *The Book of the Duke of True Lovers.* Trans. Thelma S. Fenster and Nadia Margolis. New York: Persea Books, 1991.

Ecclesiastical History of Orderic Vitalis. Ed. and trans. Marjorie Chibnall. 6 vols. Oxford: Clarendon Press, 1969–80.

Froissart, Jean. *Chroniques de J. Froissart.* Ed. Siméon Luce, Gaston Raynard and Léon Mirot. 12 vols. Paris: Librarie Champion, 1869.

* Geoffroy de Charny. *The Book of Chivalry of Geoffroi de Charny: Text, Context and Translation.* Ed. and trans. Richard W. Kaeuper and Elspeth Kennedy. Middle Age Series. Philadelphia: University of Pennsylvania Press, 1996.

Geoffrey of Monmouth. *The Historia regum Britanniae.* Ed. Acton Griscom. Trans. Robert E. Jones. London: Longmans, Green and Co., 1929; *The Historia Regum*

Britannie of Geoffrey of Monmouth: I, Bern, Bugerbibliothek, MS. 586. Ed. Neil Wright. Cambridge: D. S. Brewer, 1984. * *The History of the Kings of Britain*. Trans. Lewis Thorpe. Harmondsworth: Penguin, 1966.

Gerald of Wales. *The Historical Works of Giraldus Cambrensis*. Ed. Thomas Wright. London: Bell, 1887.

Gray, Sir Thomas. *Scalacronica. The Reigns of Edward I, Edward II and Edward III* . Trans. Sir Herbert Maxwell. Glasgow: Maclehose & Sons, 1907.

L'Histoire de Guillaume le Maréchal. Ed. Paul Meyer. 3 vols. Paris: Librarie Renouard, 1891.

Jordan Fantosme. *Chronicle of the War Between the English and the Scots in 1173 and 1174*. Ed. and trans. Francisque Michel. London: J. B. Nichols, 1840.

* *The Mabinogi and Other Medieval Welsh Tales*. Trans. Patrick K. Ford. Berkeley: University of California Press, 1977.

* *Mottuls saga*. Ed. and trans. Marianne E. Kalinke. Editiones Arnamagnaeani, series B, vol. 30. Copenhagen: C. A. Reitzels, 1987. Trans. rpt. in *The Romance of Arthur: An Anthology of Medieval Texts in Translation*. Ed. James J. Wilhelm. New York: Garland, 1994. Pp. 207–23.

Ramon Llull. *Selected Works of Ramon Llull (1232–1316)*. Ed. Anthony Bonner. 2 vols. Princeton University Press, 1985.

* *The Book of the Ordre of Chyvalry [of Ramon Llull]*. Trans. Alfred T. P. Byles. Amsterdam: J. Benjamins, 1983.

Raoul de Hodenc. *Le Roman des eles. The Anonymous Ordene de chevalerie*. Ed. and trans. Keith Busby. Amsterdam: J. Benjamins, 1983.

La Vie de Louis VI le Gros. Ed. Henri Waquet. Paris: Société d'Edition "Les Belles Lettres", 1929.

INDEX

NOTE: Page numbers in italics refer to illustrations, in bold to main sections. The initial article is ignored in alphabetical sequence of titles, e.g. *Le Bel Inconnu* appears under B.